A Kodansha Comics Trade Paperback Original.

Fire Force volume 10 copyright © 2017 Atsushi Ohkubo
English translation copyright © 2018 Atsushi Ohkubo

Published in the United States by Kodansha Comics, an imprint of Kodansha USA Publishing, LLC, New York.

Publication rights for this English edition arranged through Kodansha Ltd., Tokyo.

First published in Japan in 2017 by Kodansha Ltd., Tokyo.

ISBN 978-1-63236-621-4

Printed in Italy by Grafica Veneta S.p.A.

www.kodanshacomics.com

9 8 7 6 5 4

Translation: Alethea Nibley & Athena Nibley
Lettering: AndWorld Design
Editing: Lauren Scanlan
Kodansha Comics edition cover design: Phil Balsman

FIRE FORCE

10

ATSUSHI
OHKUBO

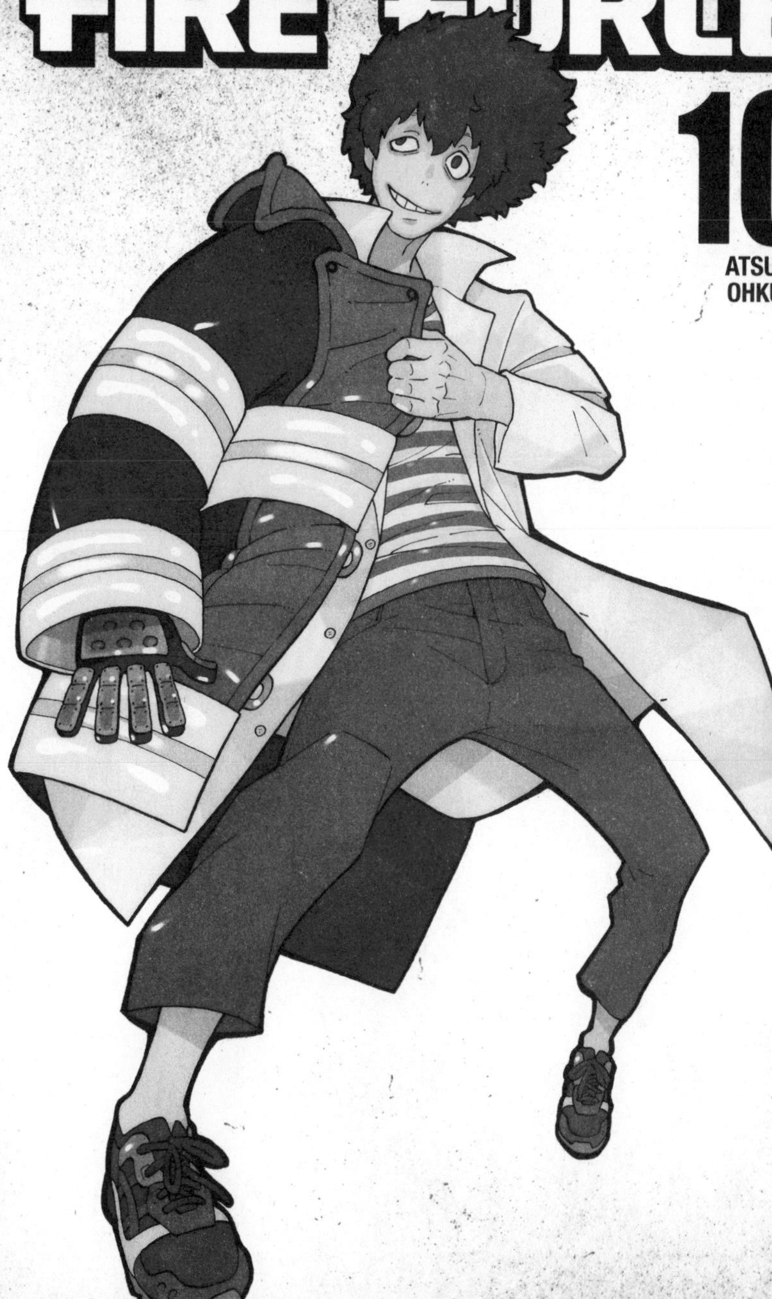

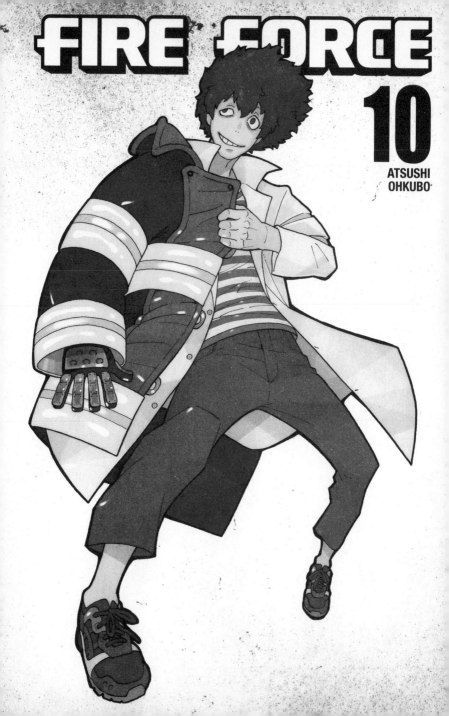

two, or...?

divine can shed the truth.

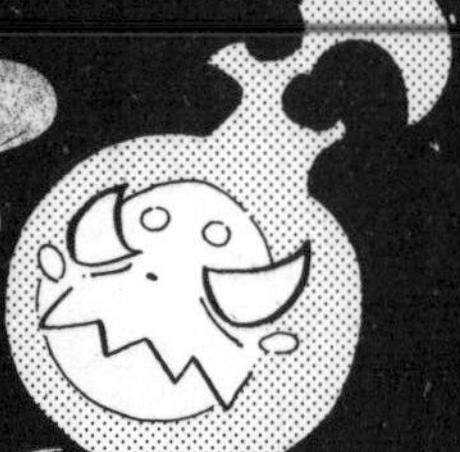

VOL. 10

ATSUSHI OHKUBO

Is it time that separates the

Only the flame

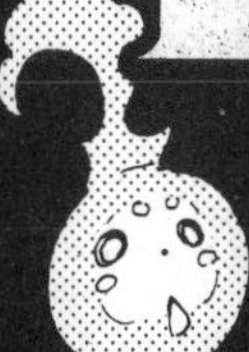

light on

FIRE FORCE

FIRE FORCE: SPECIAL FIRE FORCE ROSTER OF FIRE SOLDIERS

SPECIAL FIRE FORCE COMPANY 8

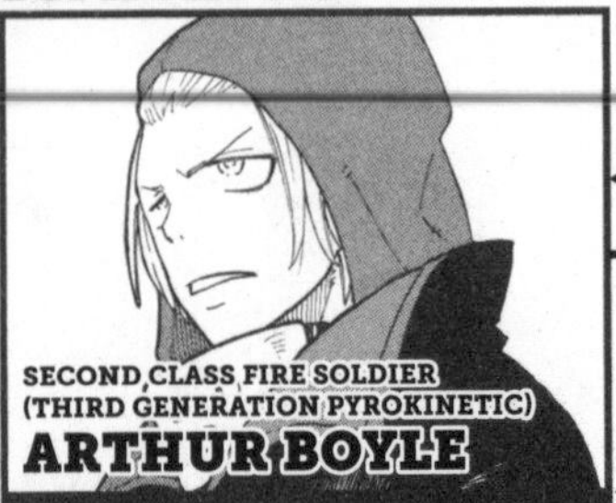

SECOND CLASS FIRE SOLDIER
(THIRD GENERATION PYROKINETIC)

ARTHUR BOYLE

Trained at the academy with Shinra. He follows his own personal code of chivalry as the self-proclaimed Knight King. He's a blockhead who is so bad at mental exercise that if he does it for too long, he starts to die. But girls love him. He creates a fire sword with a blade that can cut through most anything.

WATCHES OUT FOR

TRUSTS

CAPTAIN
(NON-POWERED)

AKITARU ŌBI

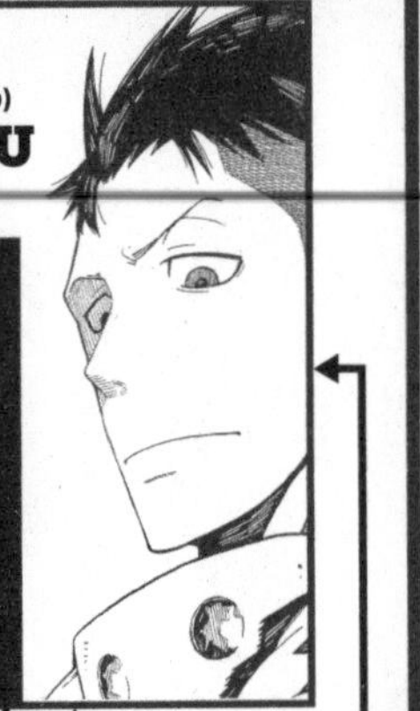

The caring leader of the newly established Company 8. His goal is to investigate the other companies and uncover the truth about spontaneous human combustion. He has no powers, but uses his finely honed muscles as a weapon in a battle style that makes him worthy of the Captain title. Has an excessive love of bodybuilding.

IDIOT!!

WATCHES OUT FOR

TRUSTS

STRONG BOND

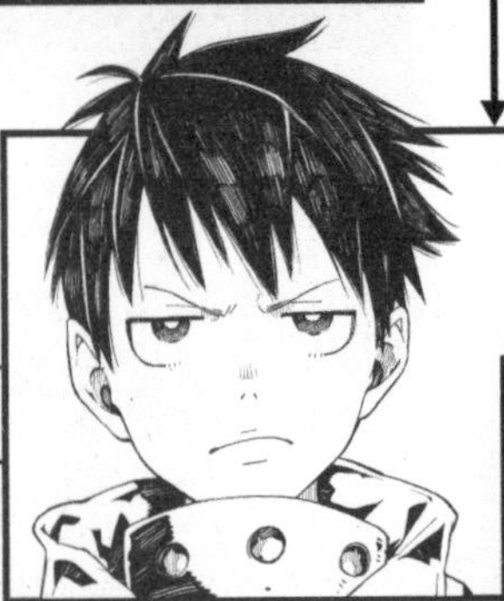

SECOND CLASS FIRE SOLDIER
(THIRD GENERATION PYROKINETIC)

SHINRA KUSAKABE

The bizarre smile that shows on his face when he gets nervous has earned him the derisive nickname of "devil." As he searches for his long-lost brother, he aims to be a hero who saves humanity from spontaneous combustion! In addition to his fiery kick, he appears to have a special flame known as the Adolla Burst....

BROTHERS

A NICE GIRL

LOOKS AWESOME ON THE JOB

A TOUGH BUT WEIRD LADY

HANG IN THERE, ROOKIE!

TERRIFIED

STRICT DISCIPLINARIAN

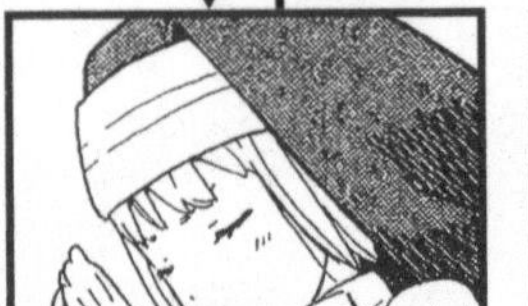

NUN
(NON-POWERED)

IRIS

A sister of the Holy Sol Temple, her prayers are an indispensable part of extinguishing Infernals. Personality-wise, she is no less than an angel. Her boobs are big. Very big. Since reconciling with Captain Hibana from Company 5, they have been as close as real sisters.

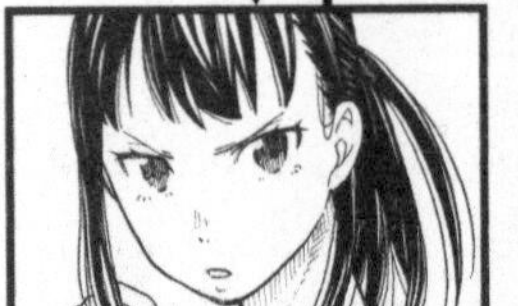

FIRST CLASS FIRE SOLDIER
(SECOND GENERATION PYROKINETIC)

MAKI OZE

A former member of the military, she is an excellent fighter who controls fire. She's a cool lady, but is mad about love stories, and her beauty is overshadowed by her "head full of flowers and wedding bells." She's friendly, but goes berserk when anyone comments on her muscles. Apparently she used to be slender.

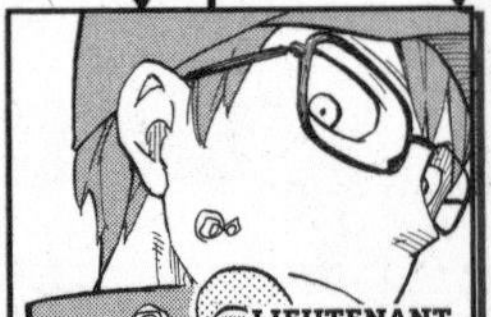

LIEUTENANT
(SECOND GENERATION PYROKINETIC)

TAKEHISA HINAWA

A dry, unemotional ex-military man, whose stern discipline is feared among the new recruits. He helped Ōbi to found Company 8. He never allows the soldiers to play with fire. The gun he uses is a cherished memento from his friend who became an Infernal.

THE GIRLS' CLUB

RESPECTS

FOLLOWERS OF THE EVANGELIST

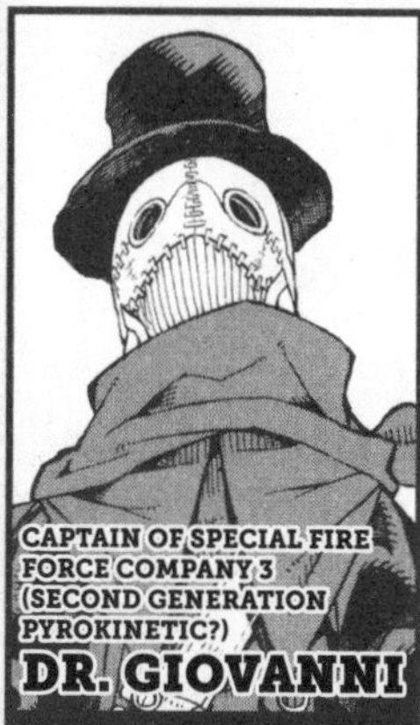

CAPTION OF SPECIAL FIRE FORCE COMPANY 3 (SECOND GENERATION PYROKINETIC?)

DR. GIOVANNI

A traitor who started working for the Evangelist despite being a captain in the Special Fire Force. He fights by using fire to control mechanical limbs. It is his policy to knock on a stone bridge multiple times before crossing it.

SUB-ORDINATE

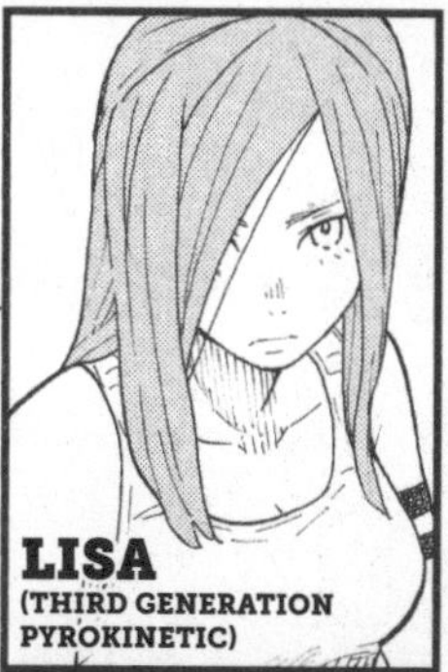

LISA

(THIRD GENERATION PYROKINETIC)

Had been living in Vulcan's home after he took her in, but was actually a spy sent by Dr. Giovanni. Controls tentacles of flame.

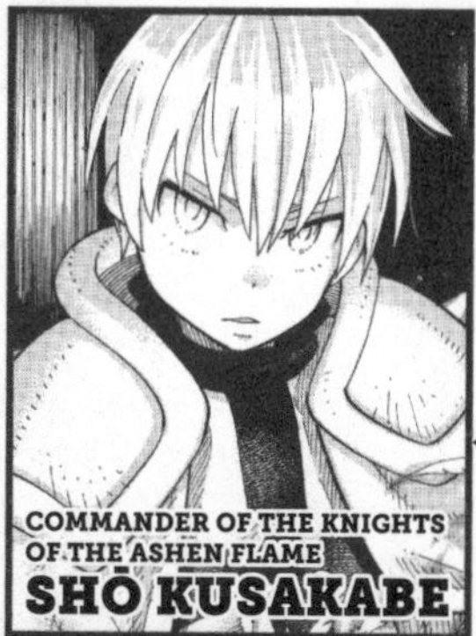

COMMANDER OF THE KNIGHTS OF THE ASHEN FLAME

SHŌ KUSAKABE

Shinra's long-lost brother, the commander of an order of knights that works for the Evangelist. His powers are still shrouded in mystery, but anyway, he's ridiculously strong!!

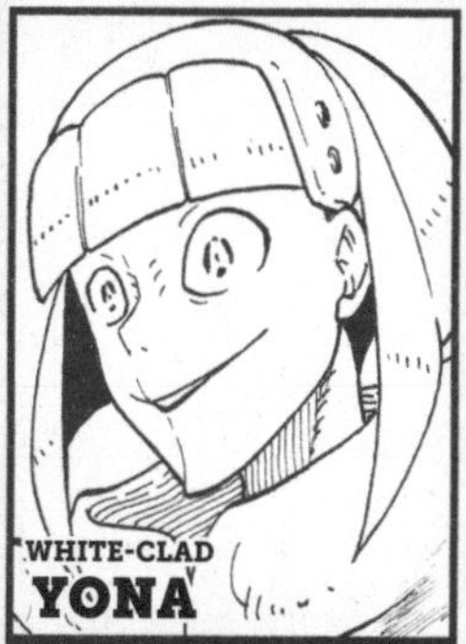

WHITE-CLAD

YONA

A white-clad soldier of the Evangelist with inhuman features. Has the power to mold and reshape others' faces.

WE'RE FAMILY!

YOU GULLIBLE BLEEDING HEART!

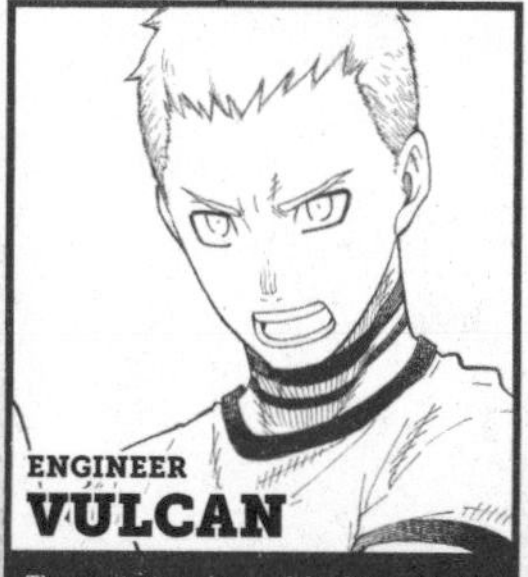

ENGINEER

VULCAN

The greatest engineer of the day, renowned as the God of Fire and the Forge. He originally hated the Fire Force, but he sympathized with Ōbi's and Shinra's ideals and agreed to join Company 8 as their engineer. His dream is to revive the world's extinct animals!

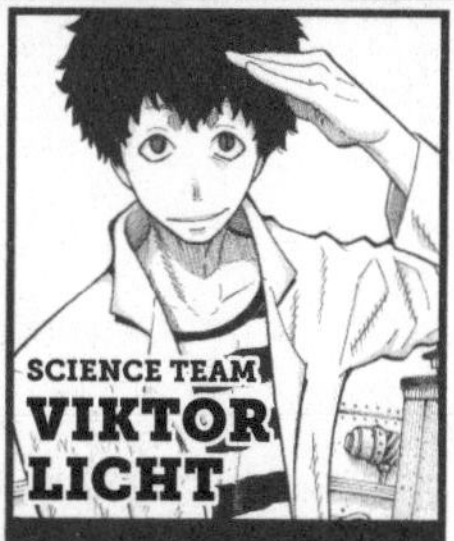

SCIENCE TEAM

VIKTOR LICHT

A morally ambiguous man deployed from Haijima Industries to fill the vacancy in Company 8's science department. Apparently a genius.

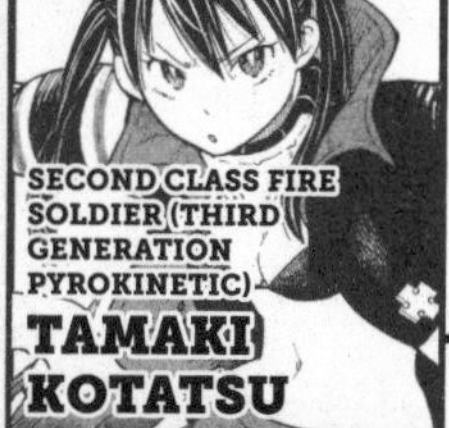

SECOND CLASS FIRE SOLDIER (THIRD GENERATION PYROKINETIC)

TAMAKI KOTATSU

Originally a rookie member of Company 1, she was caught up in the treasonous plot of her superior officer Hoshimiya, and is currently being disciplined under Company 8's watch. A tough girl with an unfortunate "lucky lecher lure" condition, she nevertheless has a pure heart.

HAS HIM ON HER MIND

SUMMARY...

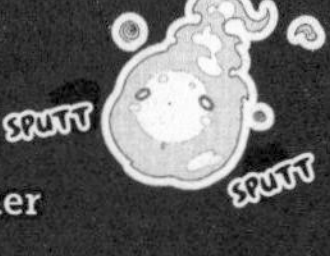
SPUTT
SPUTT

After venturing into the Nether, Company 8 is split apart by the Evangelist's soldiers' divide-and-conquer tactics. Led by an Adolla Link, Shinra finally finds his brother, but Shō's blind faith in the Evangelist deafens him to Shinra's words. Now Shinra's only option is to beat the snot out of Shō and drag him back home!! After 12 years apart, a battle breaks out between the long-lost brothers!!

FIRE FORCE 10
CONTENTS

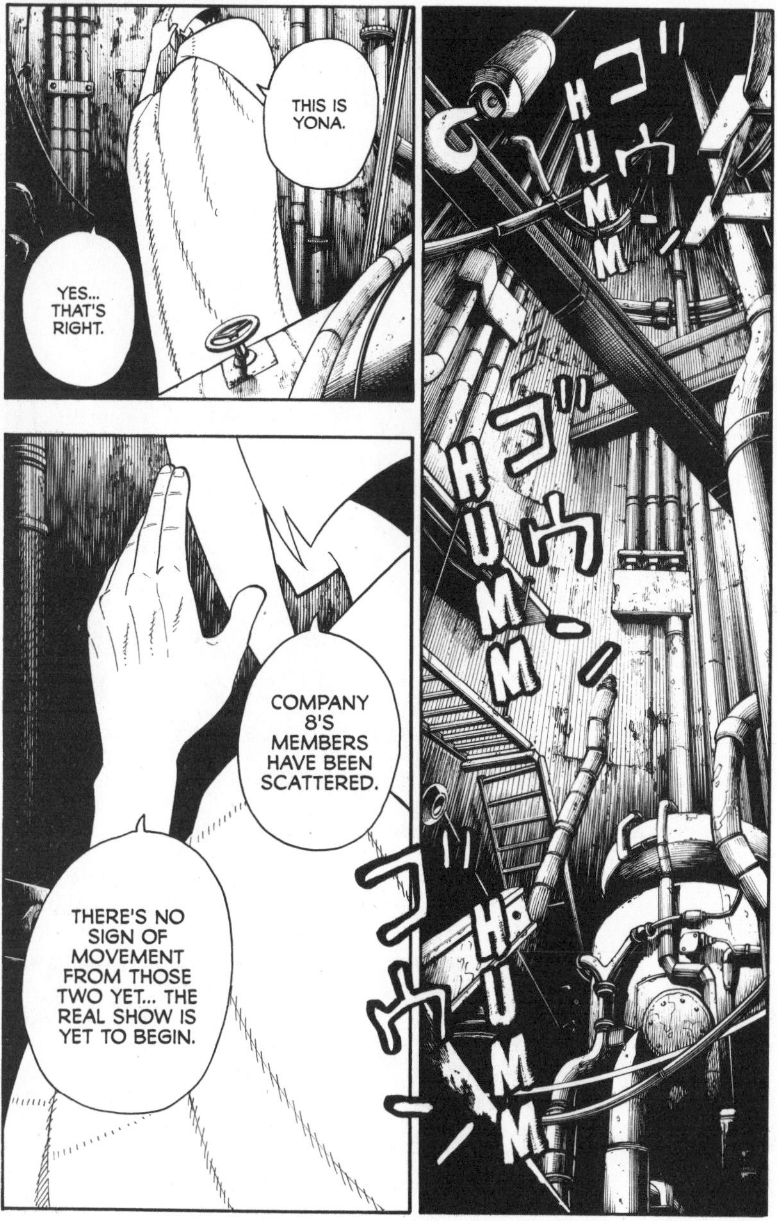
ゴウー
HUMM
ゴウー
HUMM
ゴウー
HUMM
THIS IS YONA.
YES... THAT'S RIGHT.
COMPANY 8'S MEMBERS HAVE BEEN SCATTERED.
THERE'S NO SIGN OF MOVEMENT FROM THOSE TWO YET... THE REAL SHOW IS YET TO BEGIN.

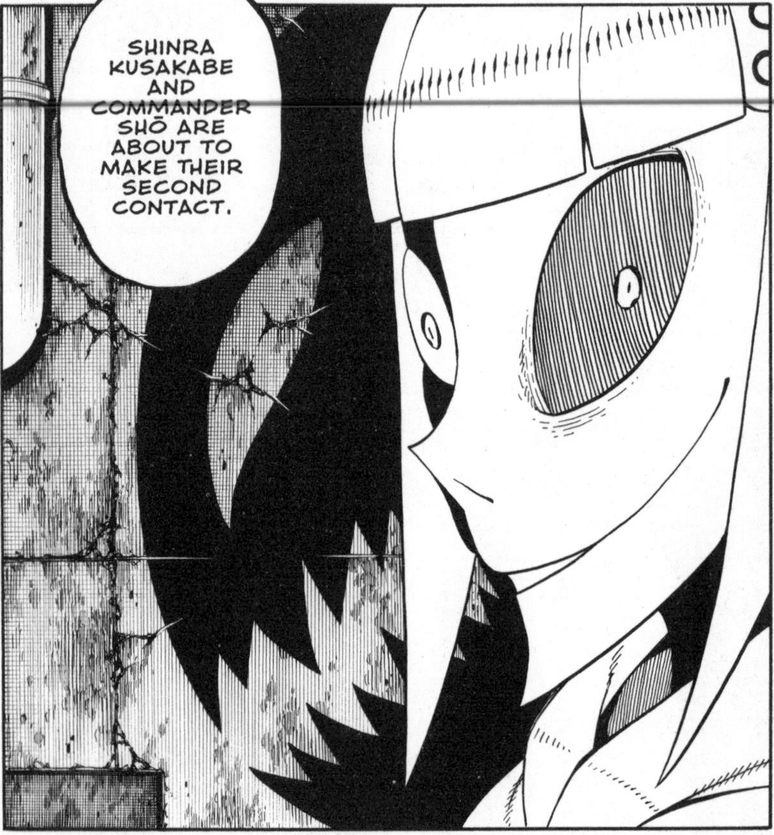
SHINRA KUSAKABE AND COMMANDER SHŌ ARE ABOUT TO MAKE THEIR SECOND CONTACT.

CHAPTER LXXIX: BEYOND THE DEATHMATCH

ALL IS AS YOU HAVE WILLED.

LÁTOM.

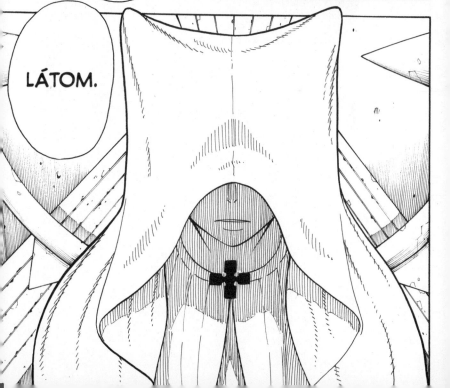

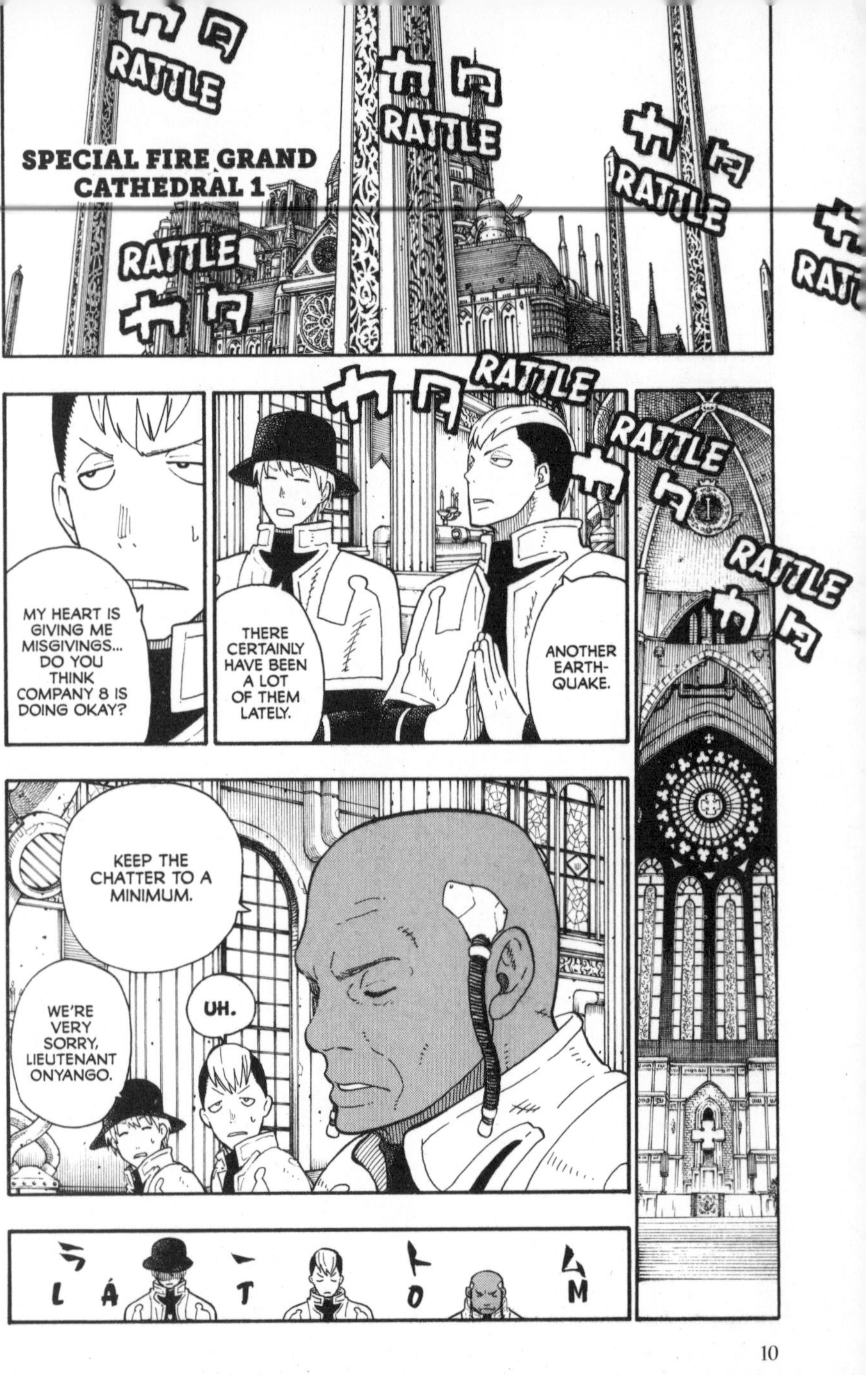
RATTLE
RATTLE
RATTLE
RATTLE
RATTLE
SPECIAL FIRE GRAND CATHEDRAL 1
RATTLE
RATTLE
RATTLE
ANOTHER EARTHQUAKE.
THERE CERTAINLY HAVE BEEN A LOT OF THEM LATELY.
MY HEART IS GIVING ME MISGIVINGS... DO YOU THINK COMPANY 8 IS DOING OKAY?
KEEP THE CHATTER TO A MINIMUM.
UH.
WE'RE VERY SORRY, LIEUTENANT ONYANGO.
LÁTOM

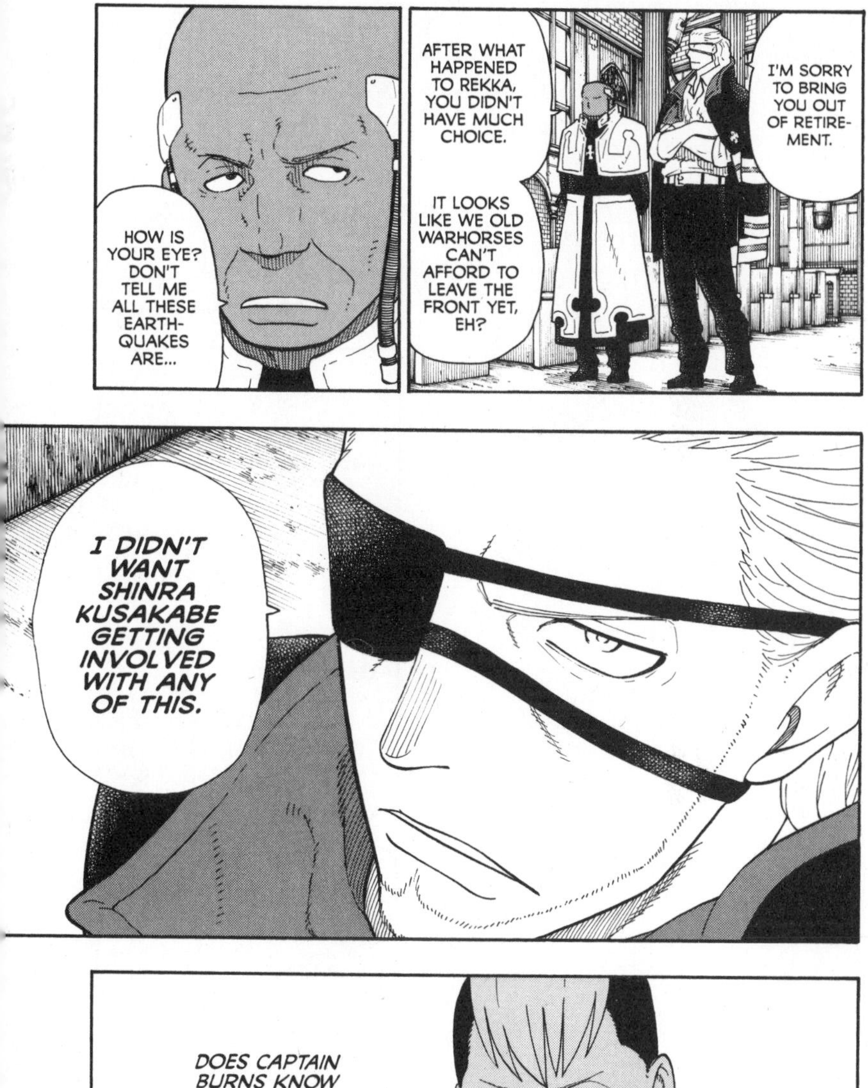
I'M SORRY TO BRING YOU OUT OF RETIRE-MENT.
AFTER WHAT HAPPENED TO REKKA, YOU DIDN'T HAVE MUCH CHOICE.
IT LOOKS LIKE WE OLD WARHORSES CAN'T AFFORD TO LEAVE THE FRONT YET, EH?
HOW IS YOUR EYE? DON'T TELL ME ALL THESE EARTH-QUAKES ARE...
I DIDN'T WANT SHINRA KUSAKABE GETTING INVOLVED WITH ANY OF THIS.
DOES CAPTAIN BURNS KNOW SOMETHING?

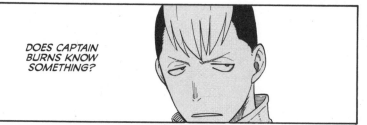

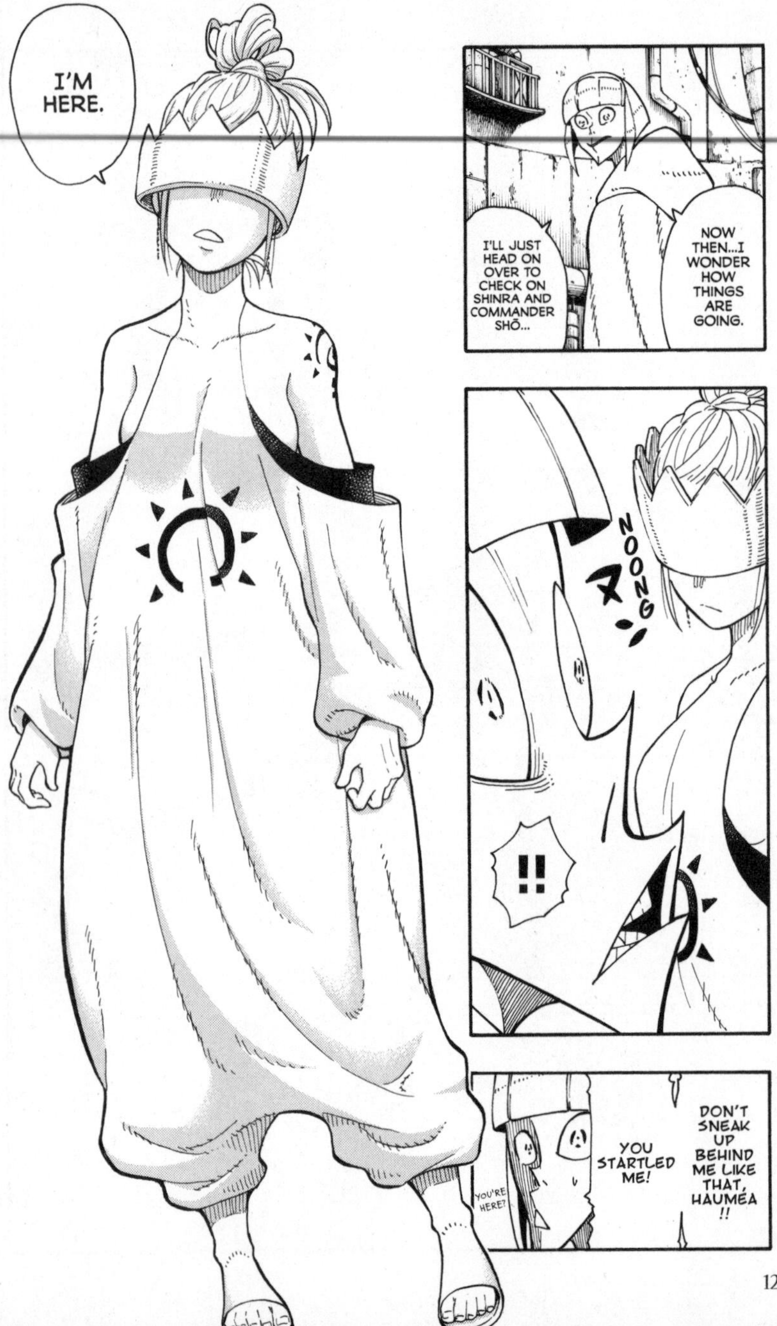
NOW THEN...I WONDER HOW THINGS ARE GOING.
I'LL JUST HEAD ON OVER TO CHECK ON SHINRA AND COMMANDER SHŌ...
NOONG
!!
DON'T SNEAK UP BEHIND ME LIKE THAT, HAUMEA !!
YOU STARTLED ME!
YOU'RE HERE?
I'M HERE.

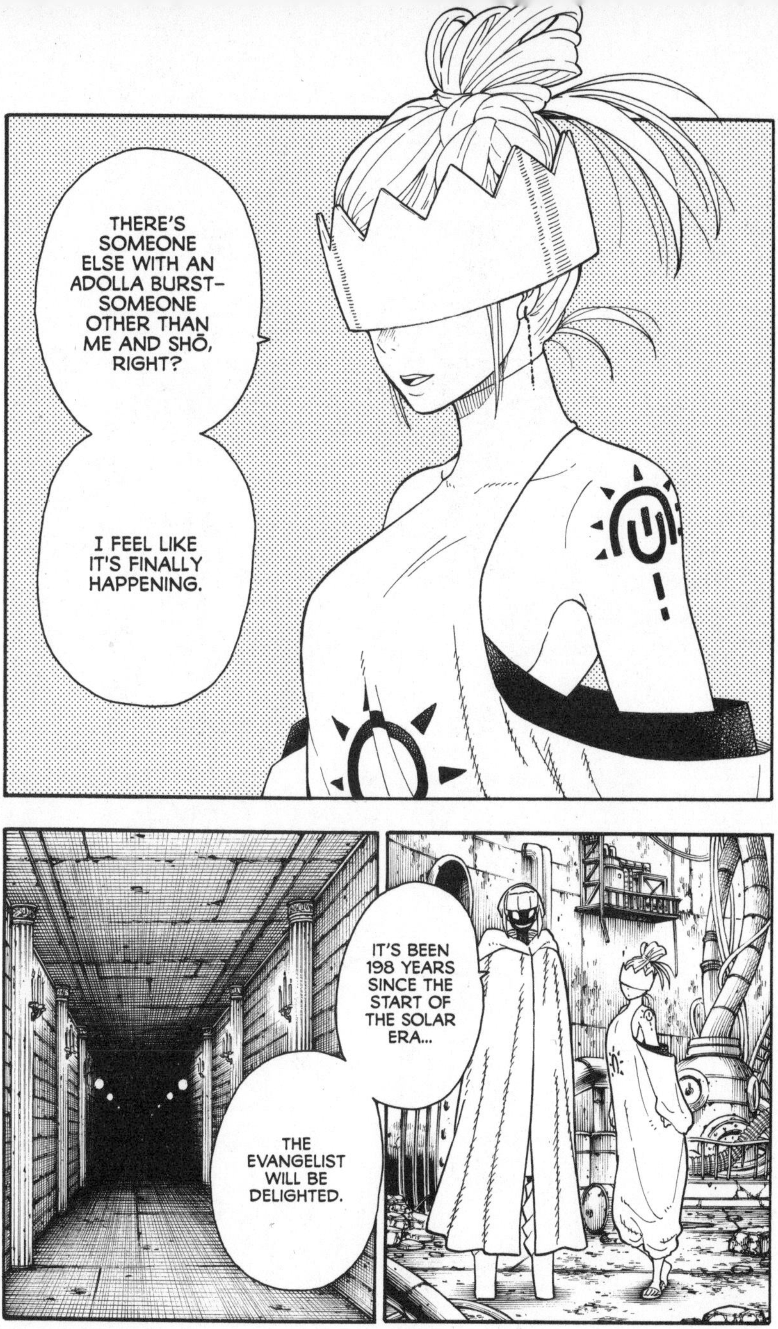
THERE'S SOMEONE ELSE WITH AN ADOLLA BURST– SOMEONE OTHER THAN ME AND SHŌ, RIGHT?
I FEEL LIKE IT'S FINALLY HAPPENING.
IT'S BEEN 198 YEARS SINCE THE START OF THE SOLAR ERA...
THE EVANGELIST WILL BE DELIGHTED.

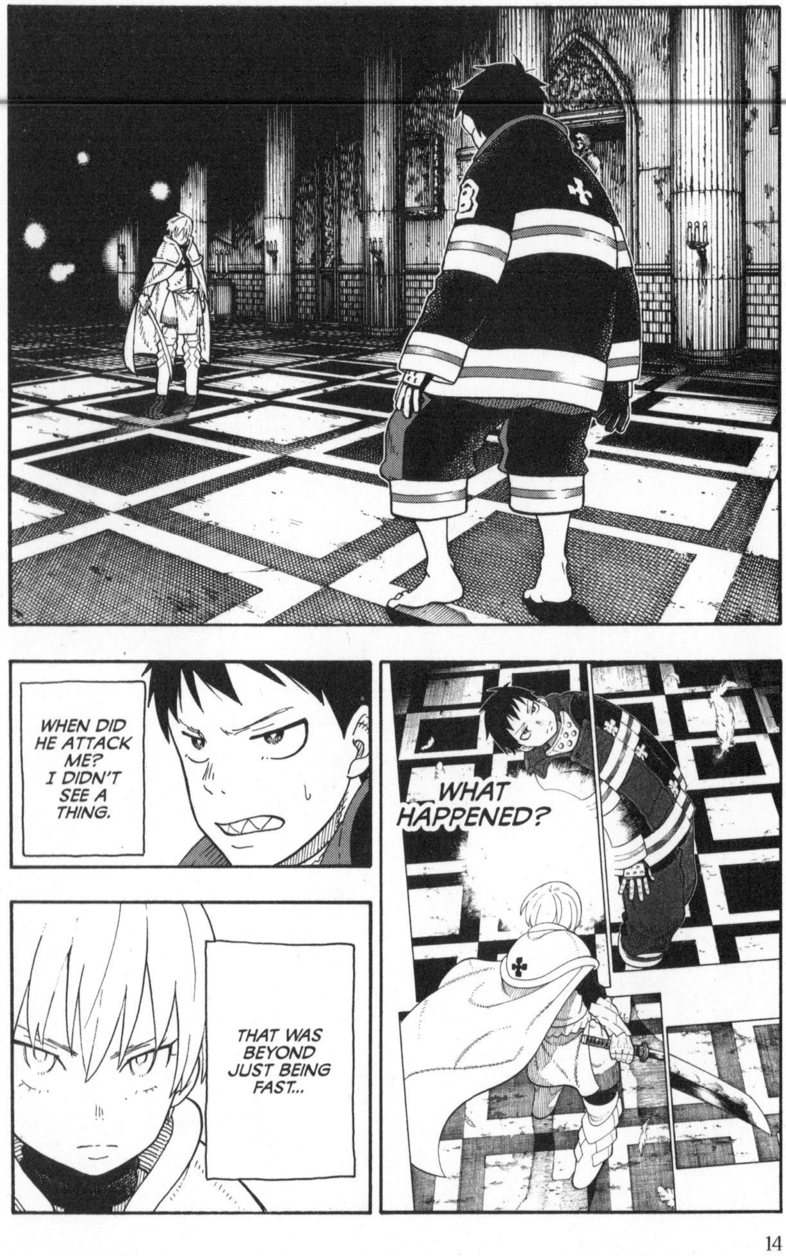
WHAT HAPPENED?
WHEN DID HE ATTACK ME? I DIDN'T SEE A THING.
THAT WAS BEYOND JUST BEING FAST...

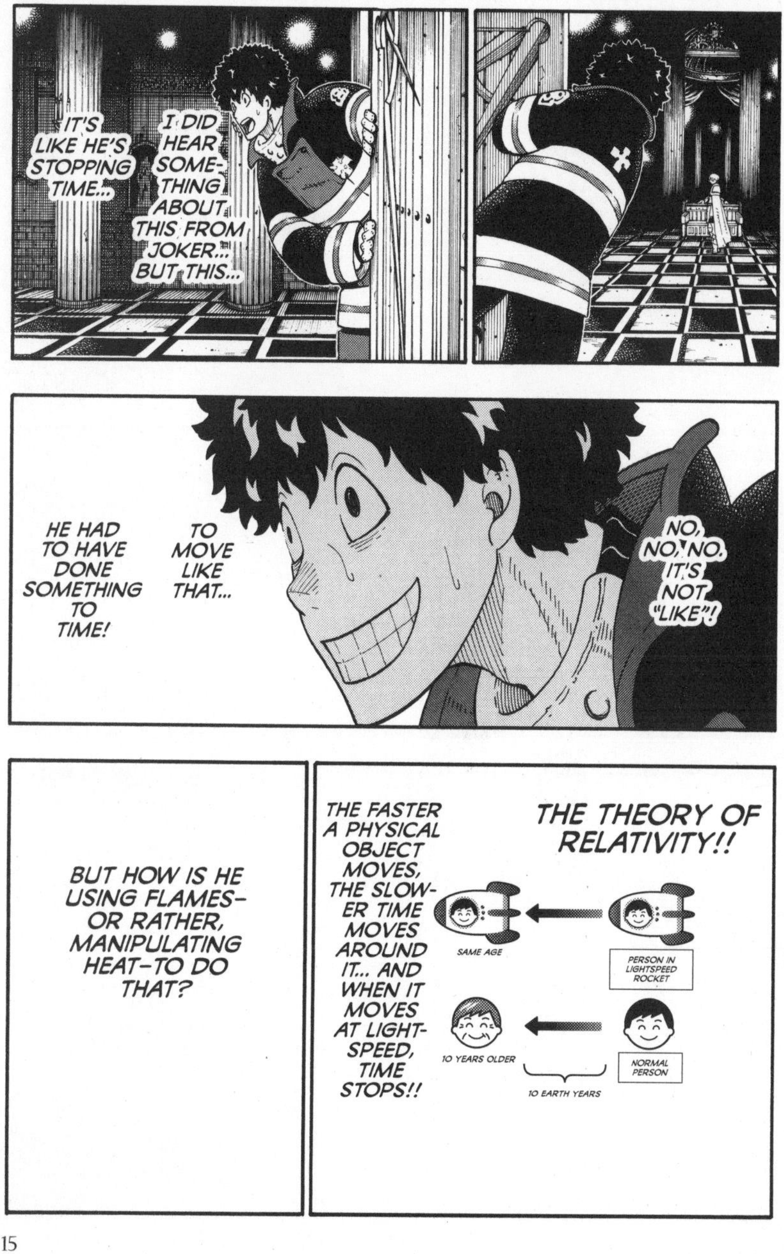
I DID HEAR SOMETHING ABOUT THIS FROM JOKER... BUT THIS...
IT'S LIKE HE'S STOPPING TIME...
NO, NO, NO. IT'S NOT "LIKE"!
TO MOVE LIKE THAT...
HE HAD TO HAVE DONE SOMETHING TO TIME!
THE THEORY OF RELATIVITY!!
THE FASTER A PHYSICAL OBJECT MOVES, THE SLOWER TIME MOVES AROUND IT... AND WHEN IT MOVES AT LIGHTSPEED, TIME STOPS!!
PERSON IN LIGHTSPEED ROCKET
SAME AGE
NORMAL PERSON
10 YEARS OLDER
10 EARTH YEARS
BUT HOW IS HE USING FLAMES—OR RATHER, MANIPULATING HEAT—TO DO THAT?

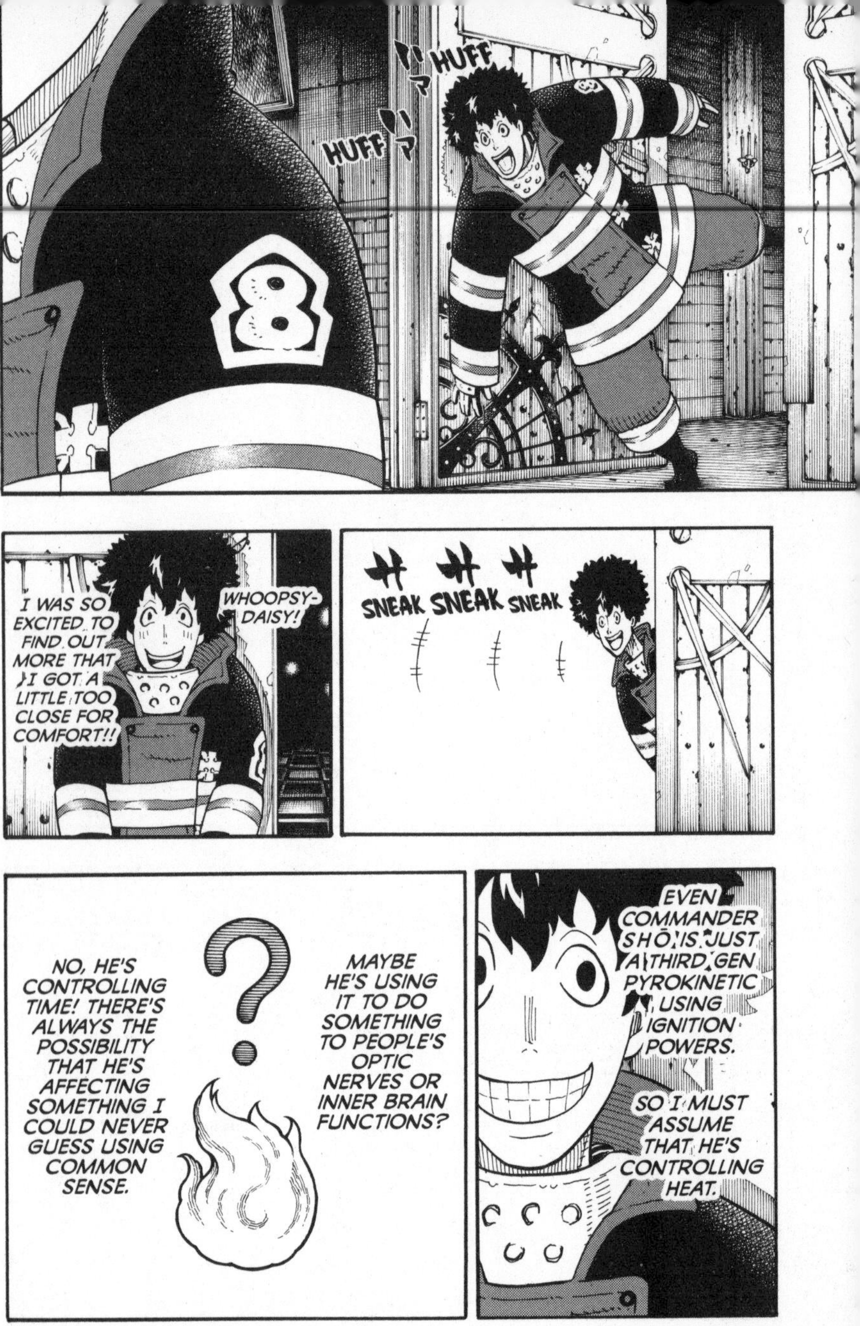
HUFF
HUFF
SNEAK SNEAK SNEAK
WHOOPSY-DAISY!
I WAS SO EXCITED TO FIND OUT MORE THAT I GOT A LITTLE TOO CLOSE FOR COMFORT!!
EVEN COMMANDER SHŌ IS JUST A THIRD GEN PYROKINETIC USING IGNITION POWERS.
SO I MUST ASSUME THAT HE'S CONTROLLING HEAT.
MAYBE HE'S USING IT TO DO SOMETHING TO PEOPLE'S OPTIC NERVES OR INNER BRAIN FUNCTIONS?
NO, HE'S CONTROLLING TIME! THERE'S ALWAYS THE POSSIBILITY THAT HE'S AFFECTING SOMETHING I COULD NEVER GUESS USING COMMON SENSE.

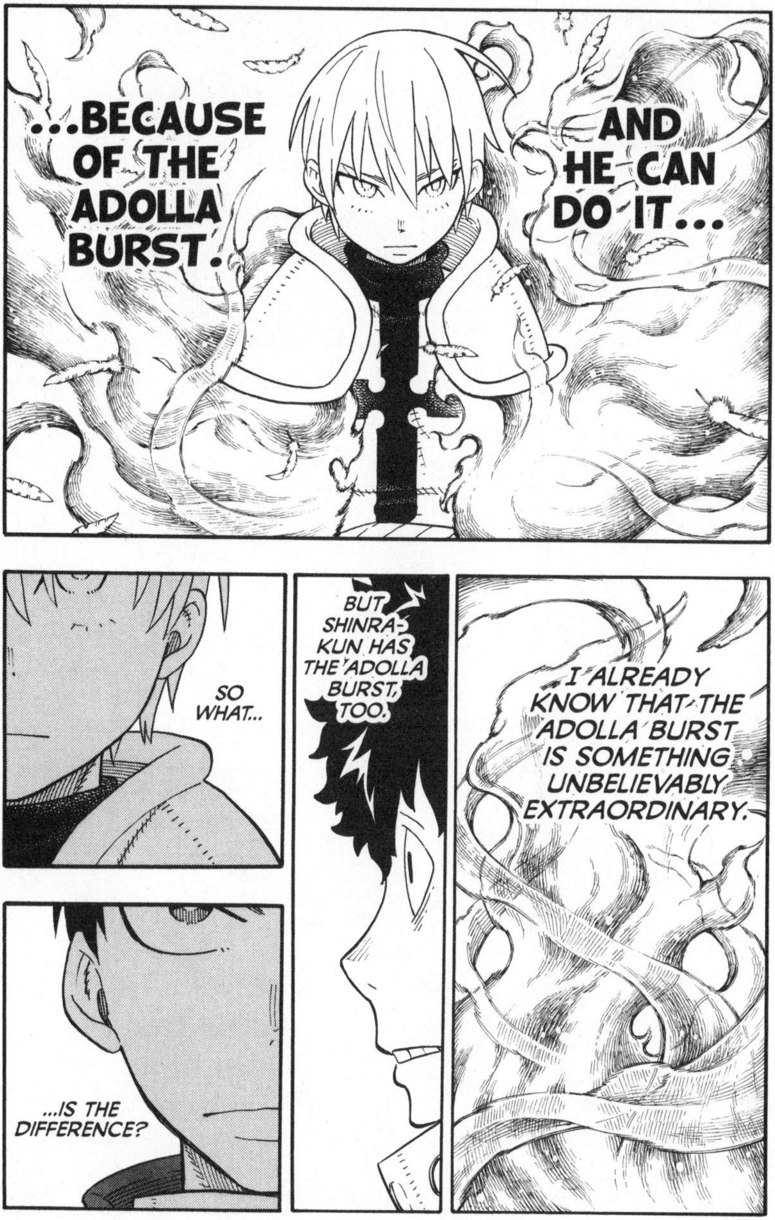
AND HE CAN DO IT...
...BECAUSE OF THE ADOLLA BURST.
I ALREADY KNOW THAT THE ADOLLA BURST IS SOMETHING UNBELIEVABLY EXTRAORDINARY.
BUT SHINRA-KUN HAS THE ADOLLA BURST, TOO.
SO WHAT...
...IS THE DIFFERENCE?

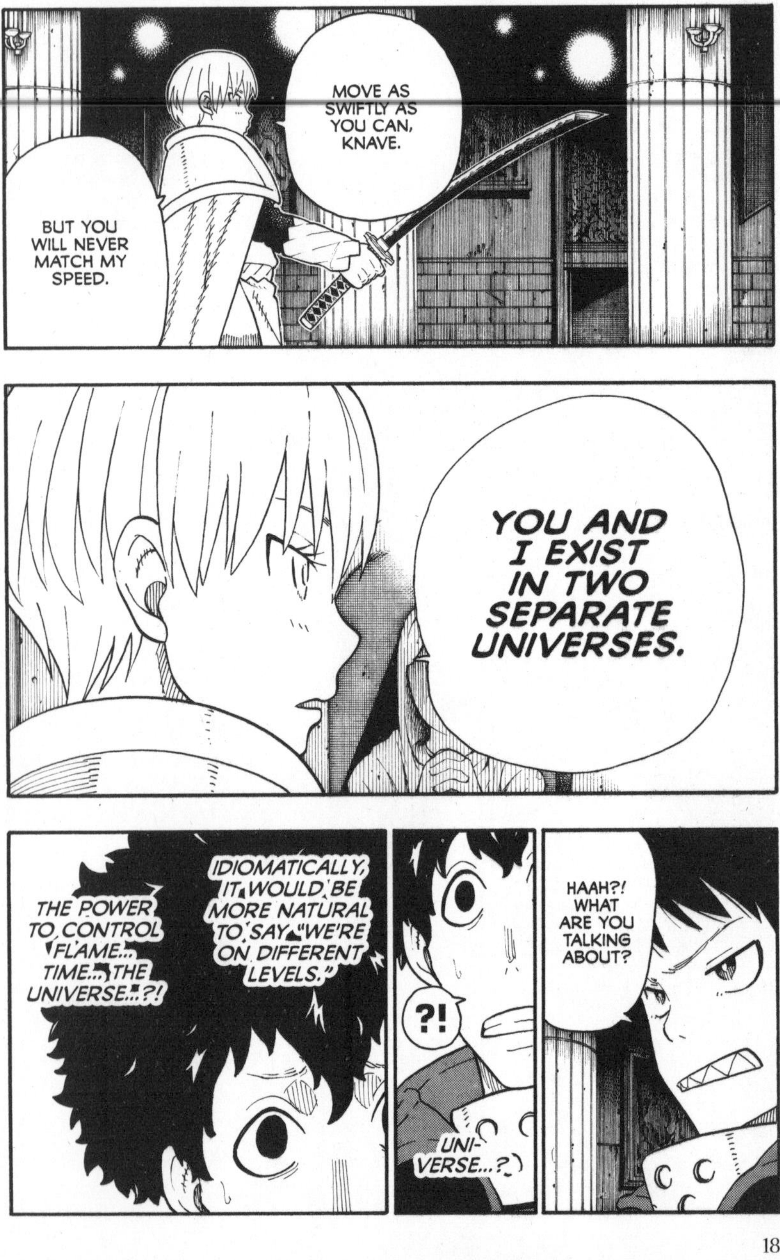
MOVE AS SWIFTLY AS YOU CAN, KNAVE.
BUT YOU WILL NEVER MATCH MY SPEED.
YOU AND I EXIST IN TWO SEPARATE UNIVERSES.
HAAH?! WHAT ARE YOU TALKING ABOUT?
?!
UNI-VERSE...?
IDIOMATICALLY, IT WOULD BE MORE NATURAL TO SAY "WE'RE ON DIFFERENT LEVELS."
THE POWER TO CONTROL FLAME... TIME... THE UNIVERSE...?!

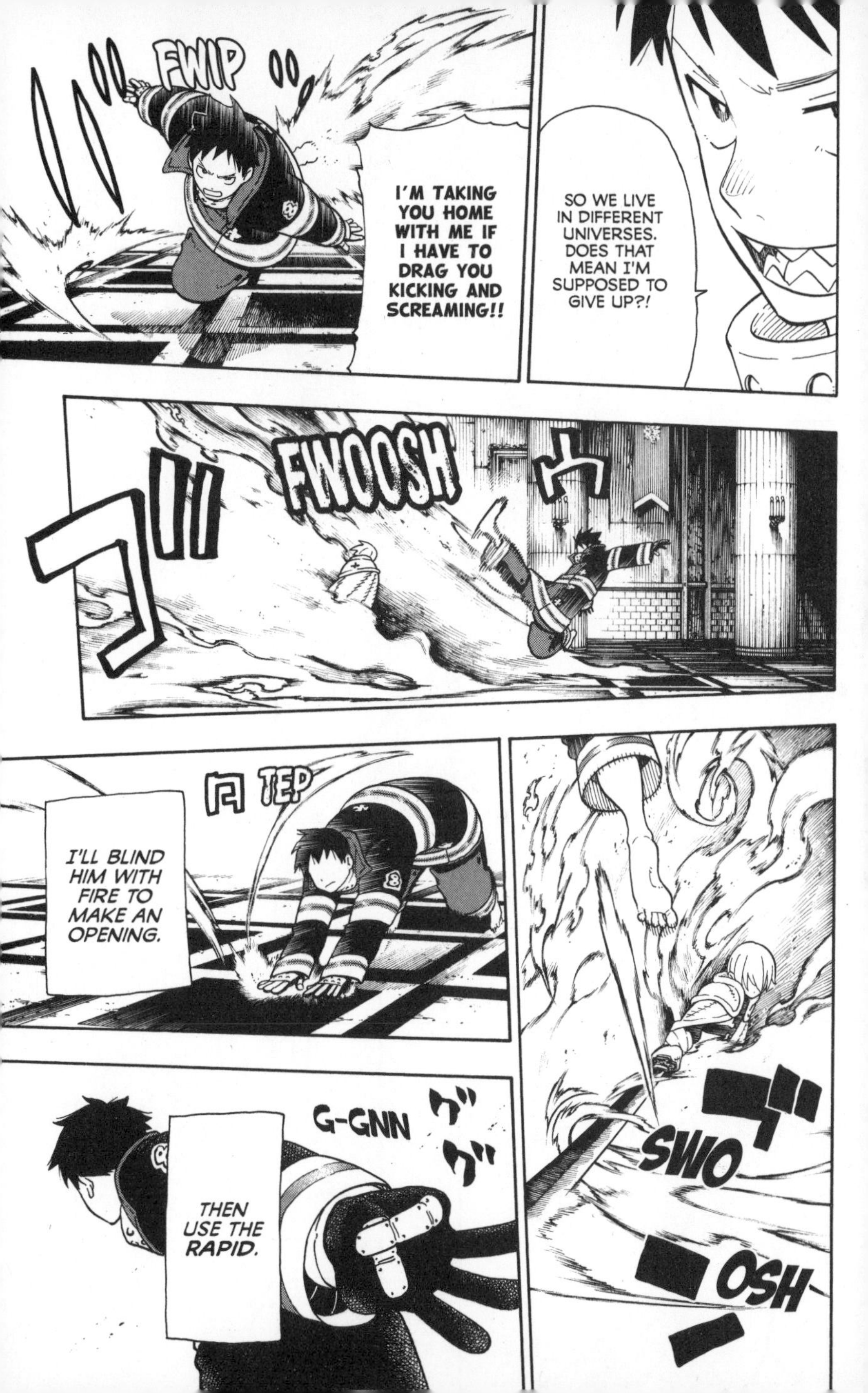
SO WE LIVE IN DIFFERENT UNIVERSES. DOES THAT MEAN I'M SUPPOSED TO GIVE UP?!
FWIP
I'M TAKING YOU HOME WITH ME IF I HAVE TO DRAG YOU KICKING AND SCREAMING!!
FWOOSH
SWO
OSH
TEP
I'LL BLIND HIM WITH FIRE TO MAKE AN OPENING.
G-GNN
THEN USE THE RAPID.

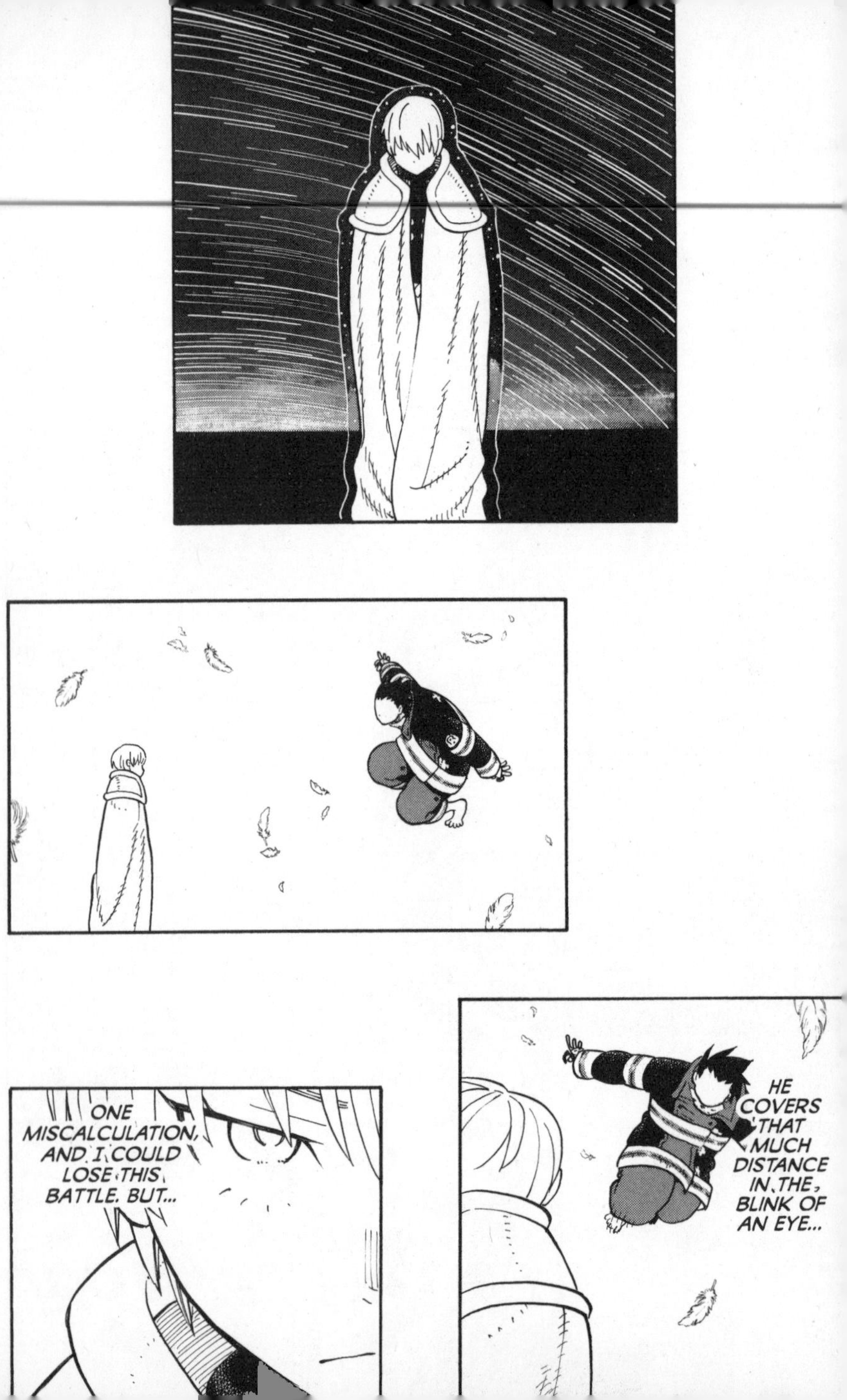
HE COVERS THAT MUCH DISTANCE IN THE BLINK OF AN EYE...
ONE MISCALCULATION, AND I COULD LOSE THIS BATTLE. BUT...

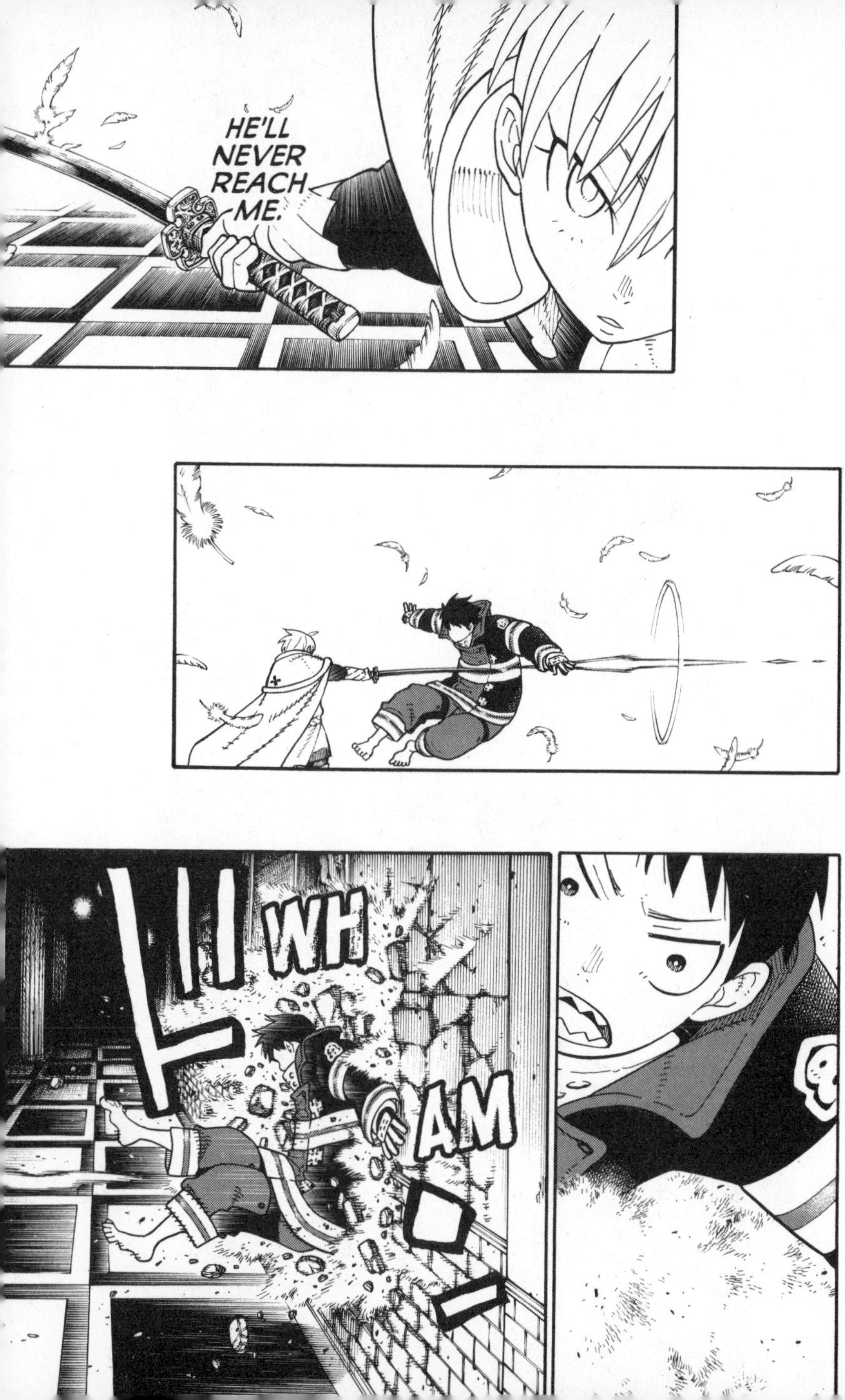
HE'LL NEVER REACH ME.
WHAM

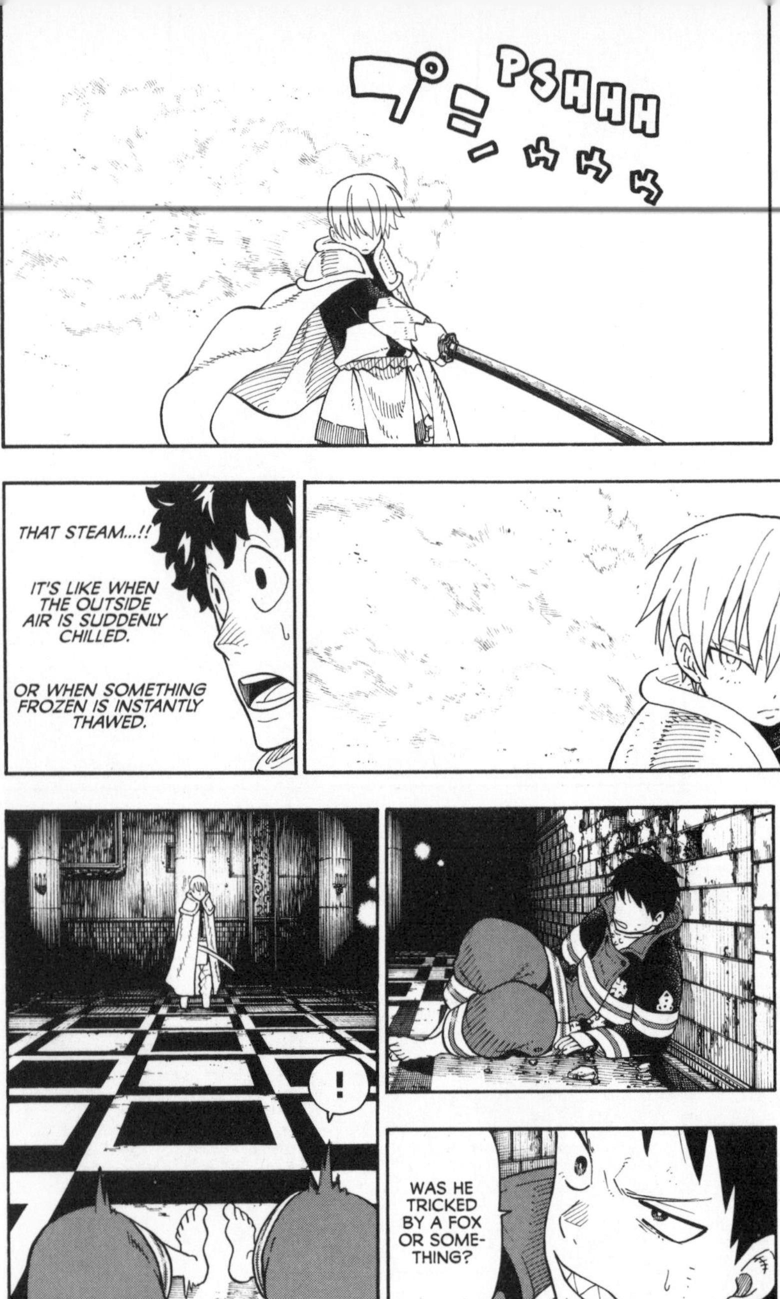
PSHHH
THAT STEAM...!!
IT'S LIKE WHEN THE OUTSIDE AIR IS SUDDENLY CHILLED.
OR WHEN SOMETHING FROZEN IS INSTANTLY THAWED.
WAS HE TRICKED BY A FOX OR SOME-THING?
!

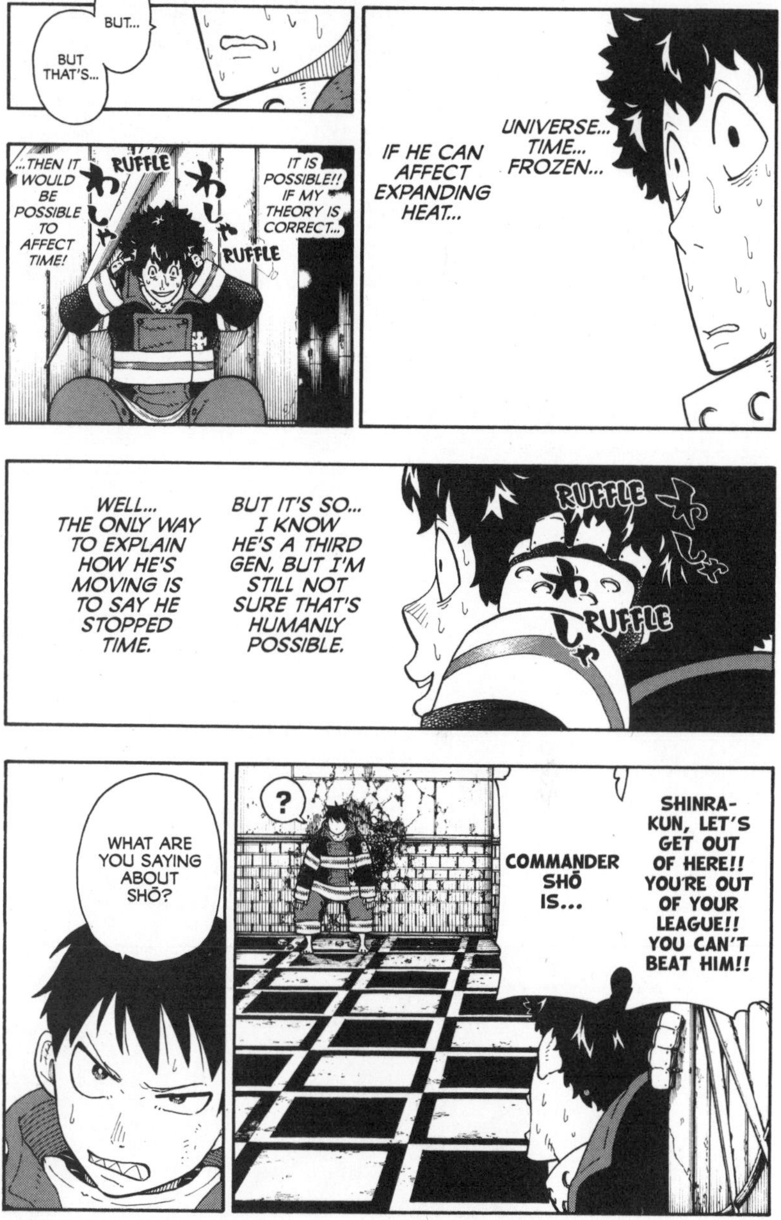
UNIVERSE... TIME... FROZEN...
IF HE CAN AFFECT EXPANDING HEAT...
BUT...
BUT THAT'S...
RUFFLE
IT IS POSSIBLE!! IF MY THEORY IS CORRECT...
RUFFLE
...THEN IT WOULD BE POSSIBLE TO AFFECT TIME!
RUFFLE
RUFFLE
BUT IT'S SO... I KNOW HE'S A THIRD GEN, BUT I'M STILL NOT SURE THAT'S HUMANLY POSSIBLE.
WELL... THE ONLY WAY TO EXPLAIN HOW HE'S MOVING IS TO SAY HE STOPPED TIME.
SHINRA-KUN, LET'S GET OUT OF HERE!! YOU'RE OUT OF YOUR LEAGUE!! YOU CAN'T BEAT HIM!!
COMMANDER SHŌ IS...
?
WHAT ARE YOU SAYING ABOUT SHŌ?

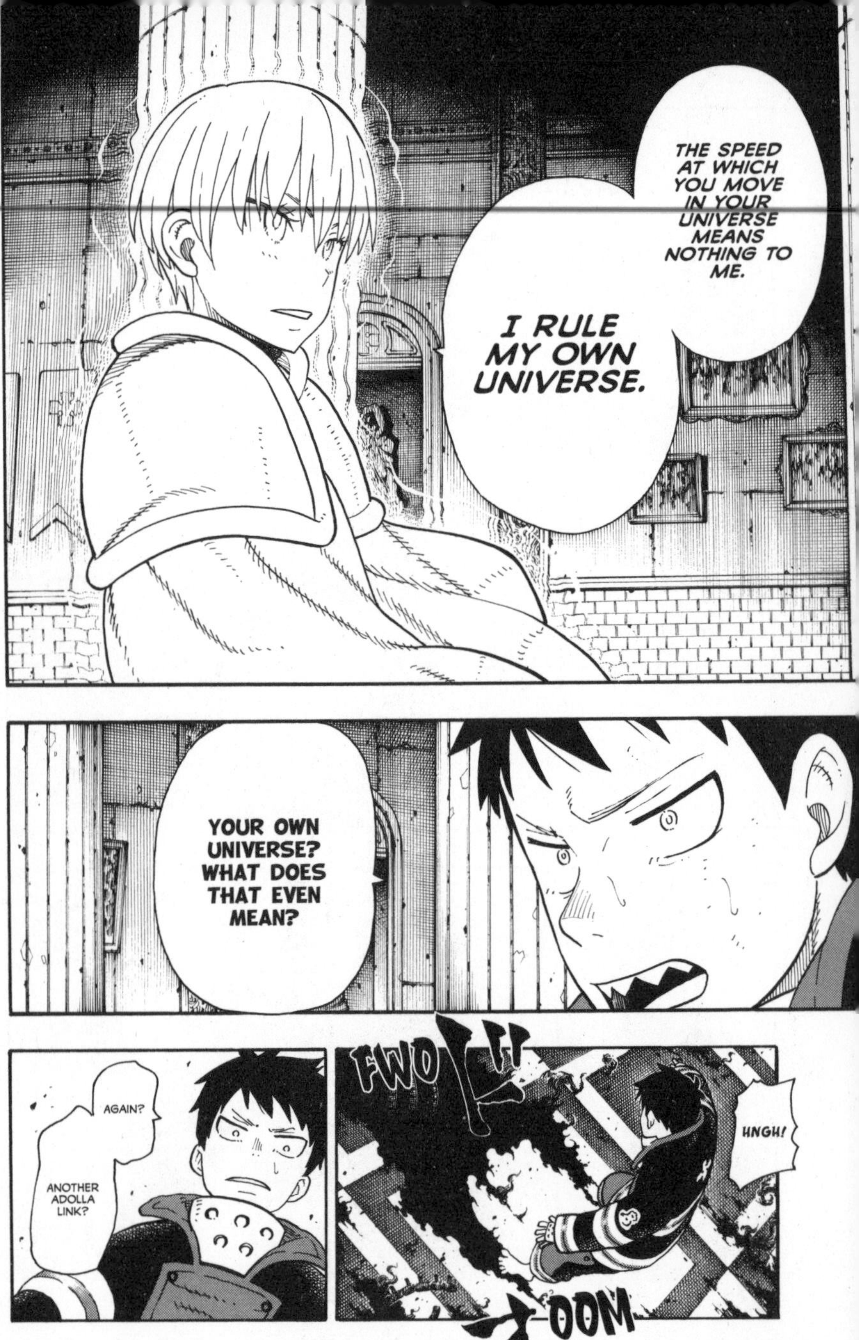
THE SPEED AT WHICH YOU MOVE IN YOUR UNIVERSE MEANS NOTHING TO ME.
I RULE MY OWN UNIVERSE.
YOUR OWN UNIVERSE? WHAT DOES THAT EVEN MEAN?
FWO
UNGH!
OOM
AGAIN?
ANOTHER ADOLLA LINK?

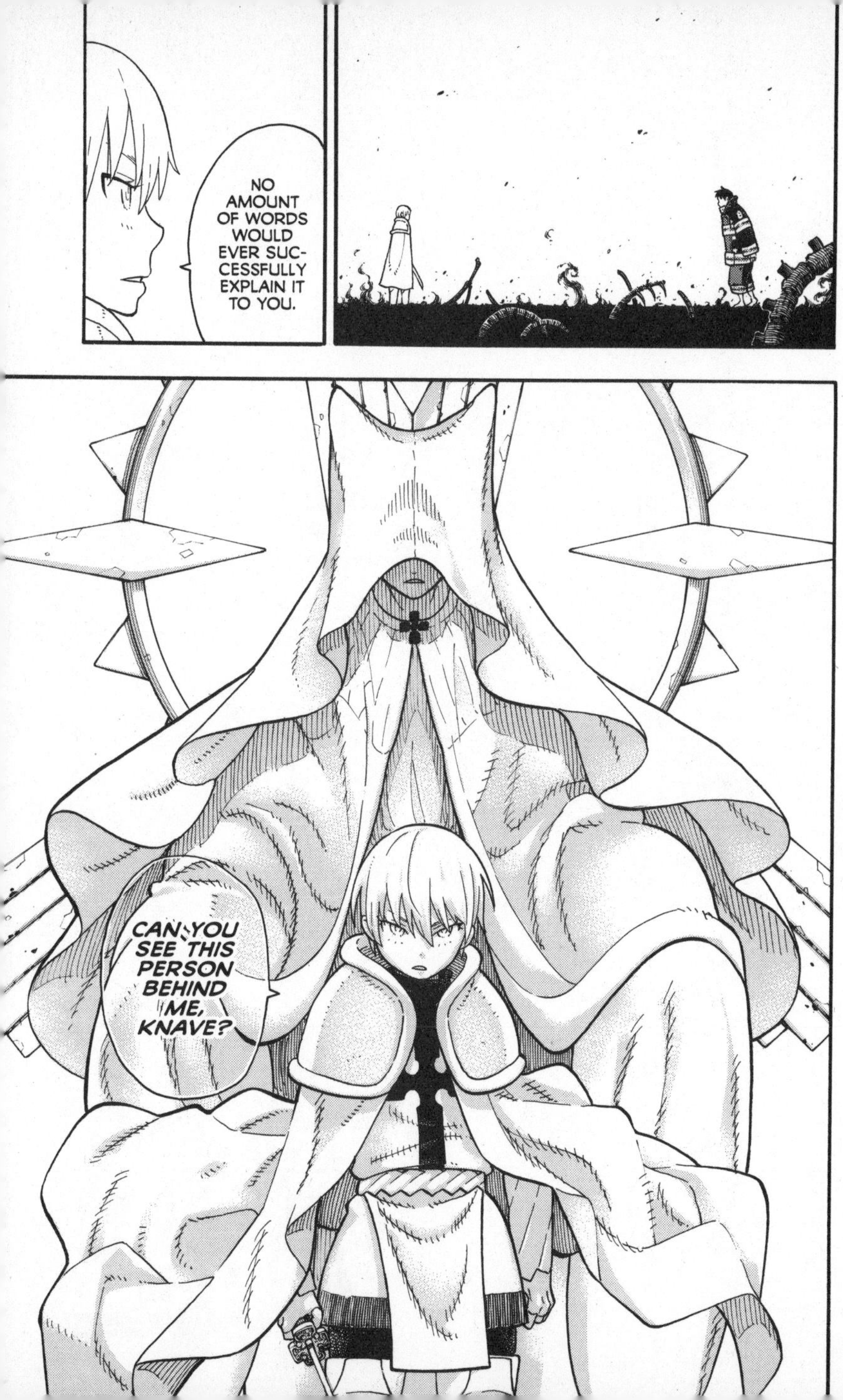
NO AMOUNT OF WORDS WOULD EVER SUCCESSFULLY EXPLAIN IT TO YOU.
CAN YOU SEE THIS PERSON BEHIND ME, KNAVE?

FIRE FORCE

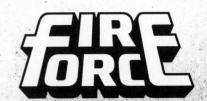

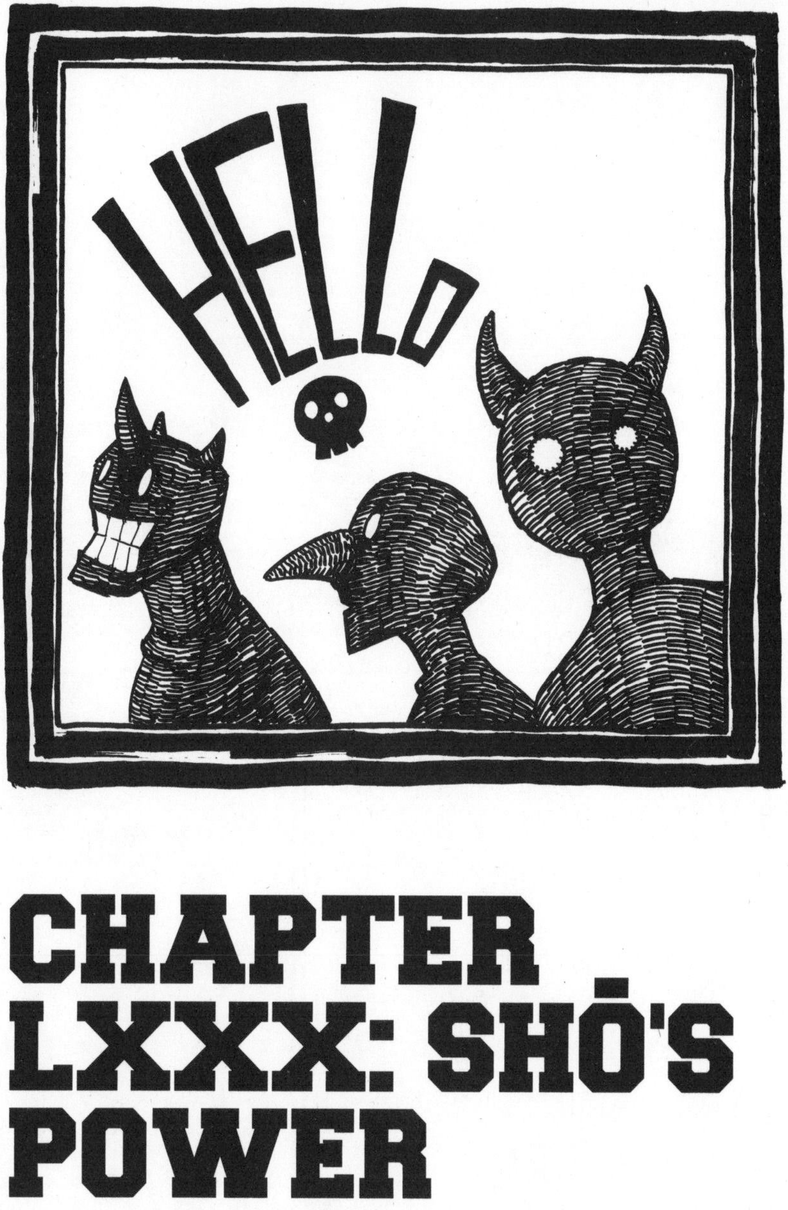
HELLO

CHAPTER LXXX: SHŌ'S POWER

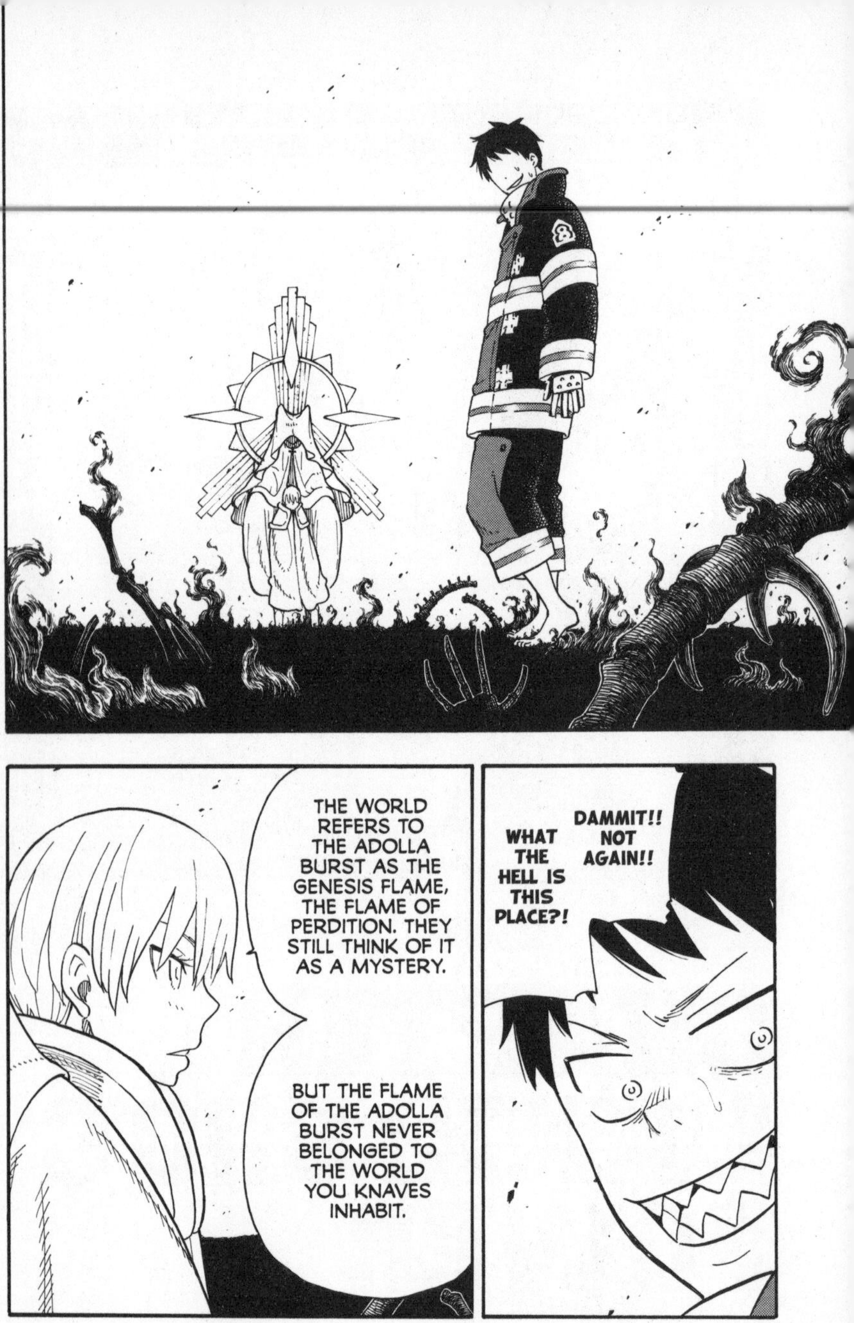
DAMMIT!! NOT AGAIN!!
WHAT THE HELL IS THIS PLACE?!
THE WORLD REFERS TO THE ADOLLA BURST AS THE GENESIS FLAME, THE FLAME OF PERDITION. THEY STILL THINK OF IT AS A MYSTERY.
BUT THE FLAME OF THE ADOLLA BURST NEVER BELONGED TO THE WORLD YOU KNAVES INHABIT.

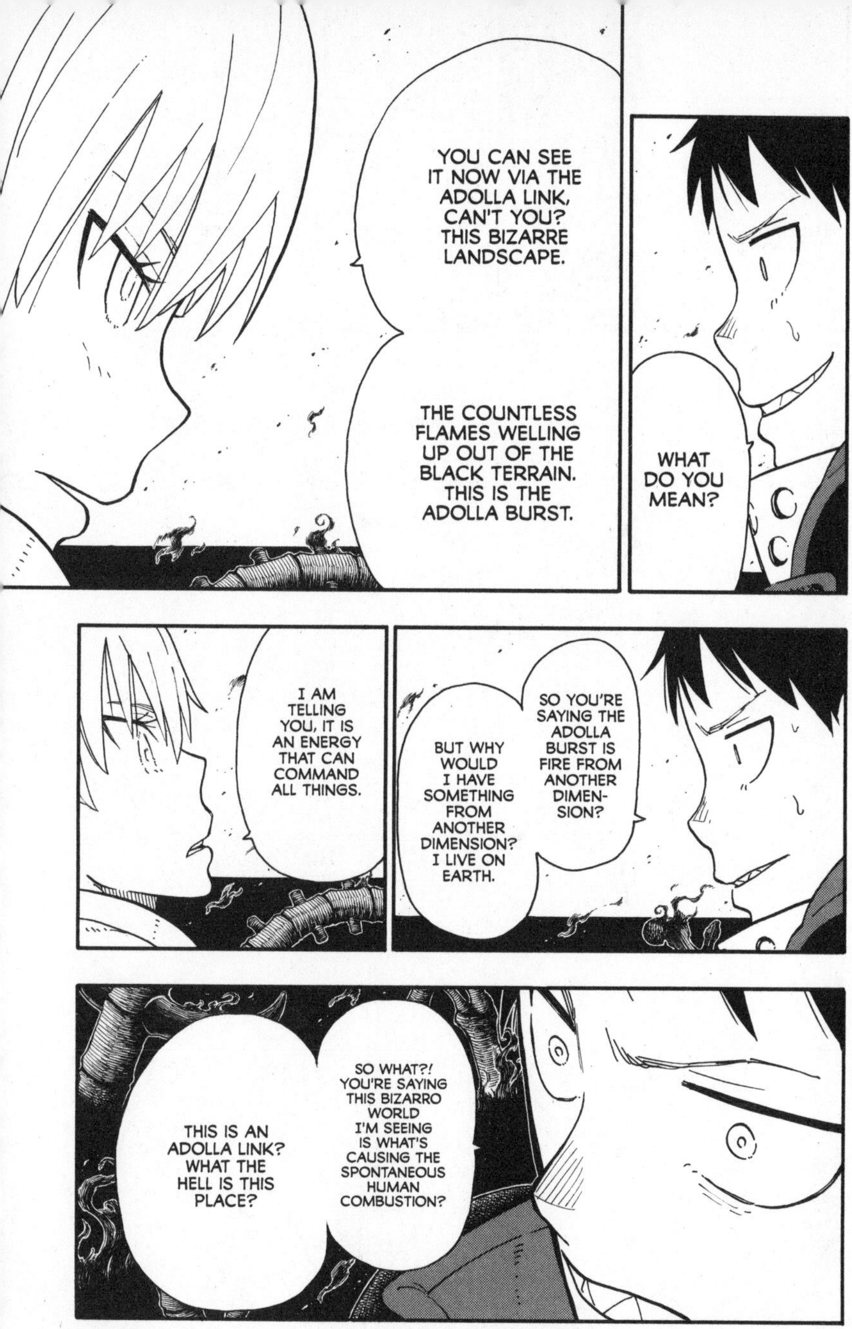
WHAT DO YOU MEAN?
YOU CAN SEE IT NOW VIA THE ADOLLA LINK, CAN'T YOU? THIS BIZARRE LANDSCAPE.
THE COUNTLESS FLAMES WELLING UP OUT OF THE BLACK TERRAIN. THIS IS THE ADOLLA BURST.
SO YOU'RE SAYING THE ADOLLA BURST IS FIRE FROM ANOTHER DIMENSION?
BUT WHY WOULD I HAVE SOMETHING FROM ANOTHER DIMENSION? I LIVE ON EARTH.
I AM TELLING YOU, IT IS AN ENERGY THAT CAN COMMAND ALL THINGS.
SO WHAT?! YOU'RE SAYING THIS BIZARRO WORLD I'M SEEING IS WHAT'S CAUSING THE SPONTANEOUS HUMAN COMBUSTION?
THIS IS AN ADOLLA LINK? WHAT THE HELL IS THIS PLACE?

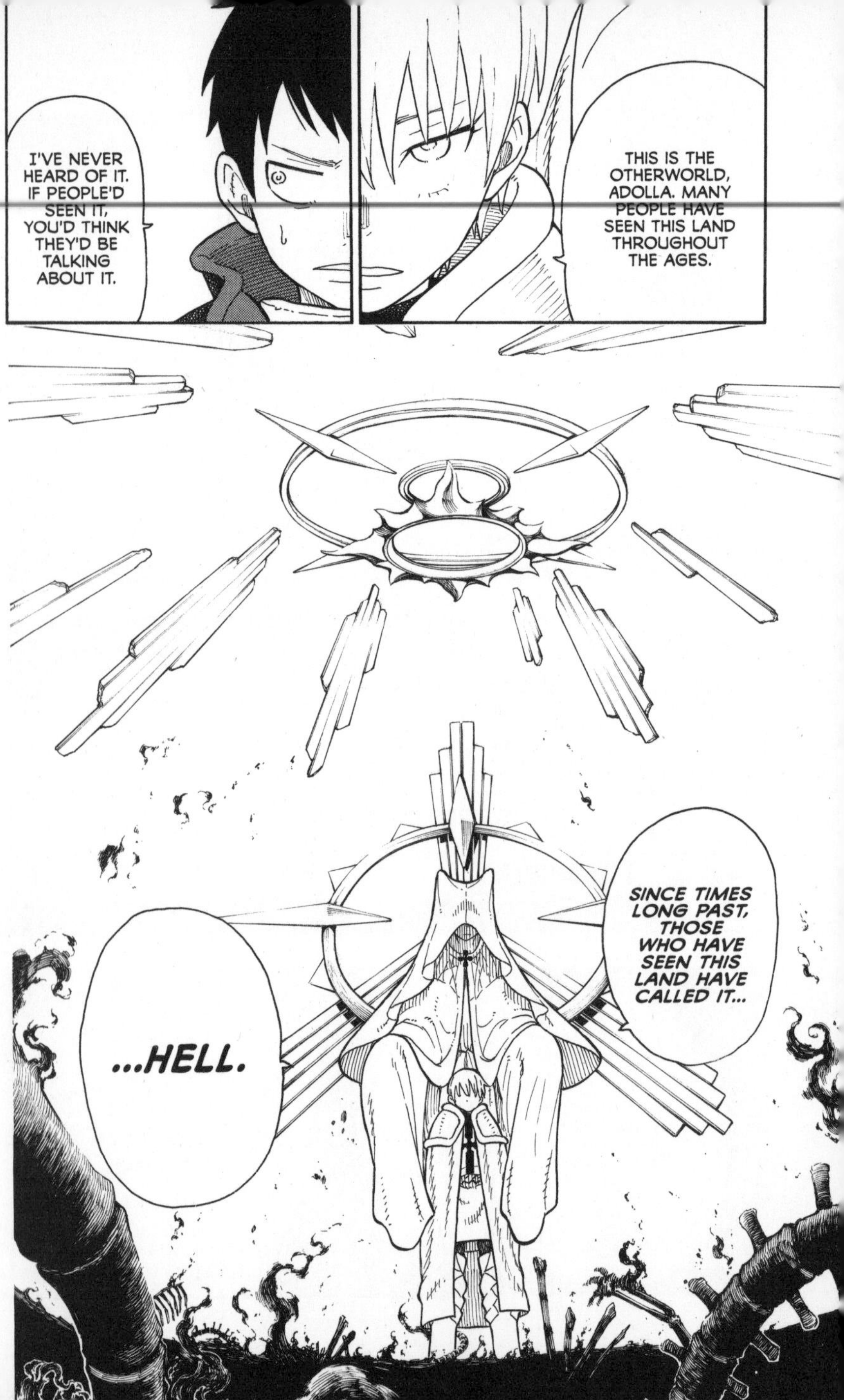
THIS IS THE OTHERWORLD, ADOLLA. MANY PEOPLE HAVE SEEN THIS LAND THROUGHOUT THE AGES.
I'VE NEVER HEARD OF IT. IF PEOPLE'D SEEN IT, YOU'D THINK THEY'D BE TALKING ABOUT IT.
SINCE TIMES LONG PAST, THOSE WHO HAVE SEEN THIS LAND HAVE CALLED IT...
...HELL.

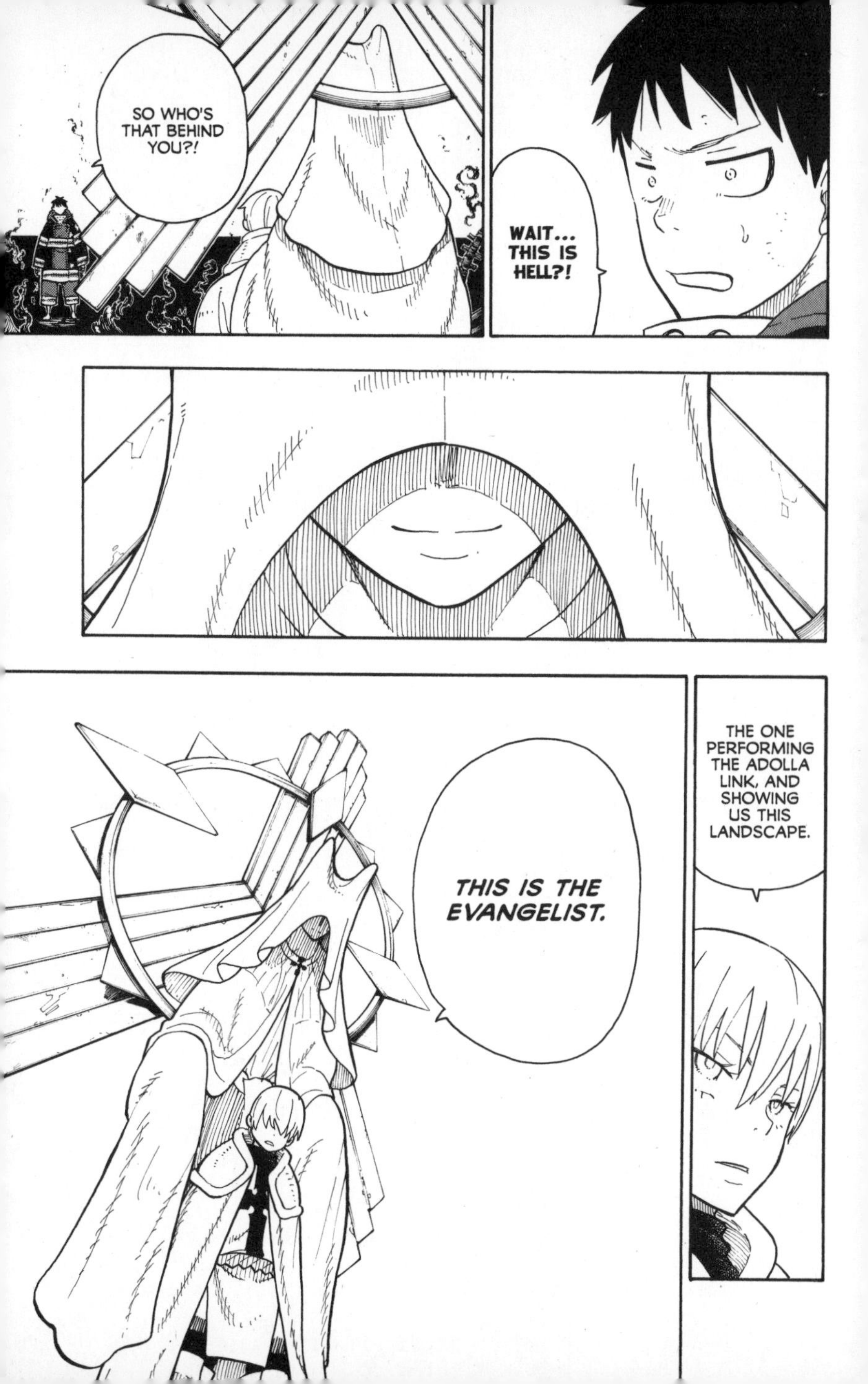
WAIT... THIS IS HELL?!
SO WHO'S THAT BEHIND YOU?!
THE ONE PERFORMING THE ADOLLA LINK, AND SHOWING US THIS LANDSCAPE.
THIS IS THE EVANGELIST.

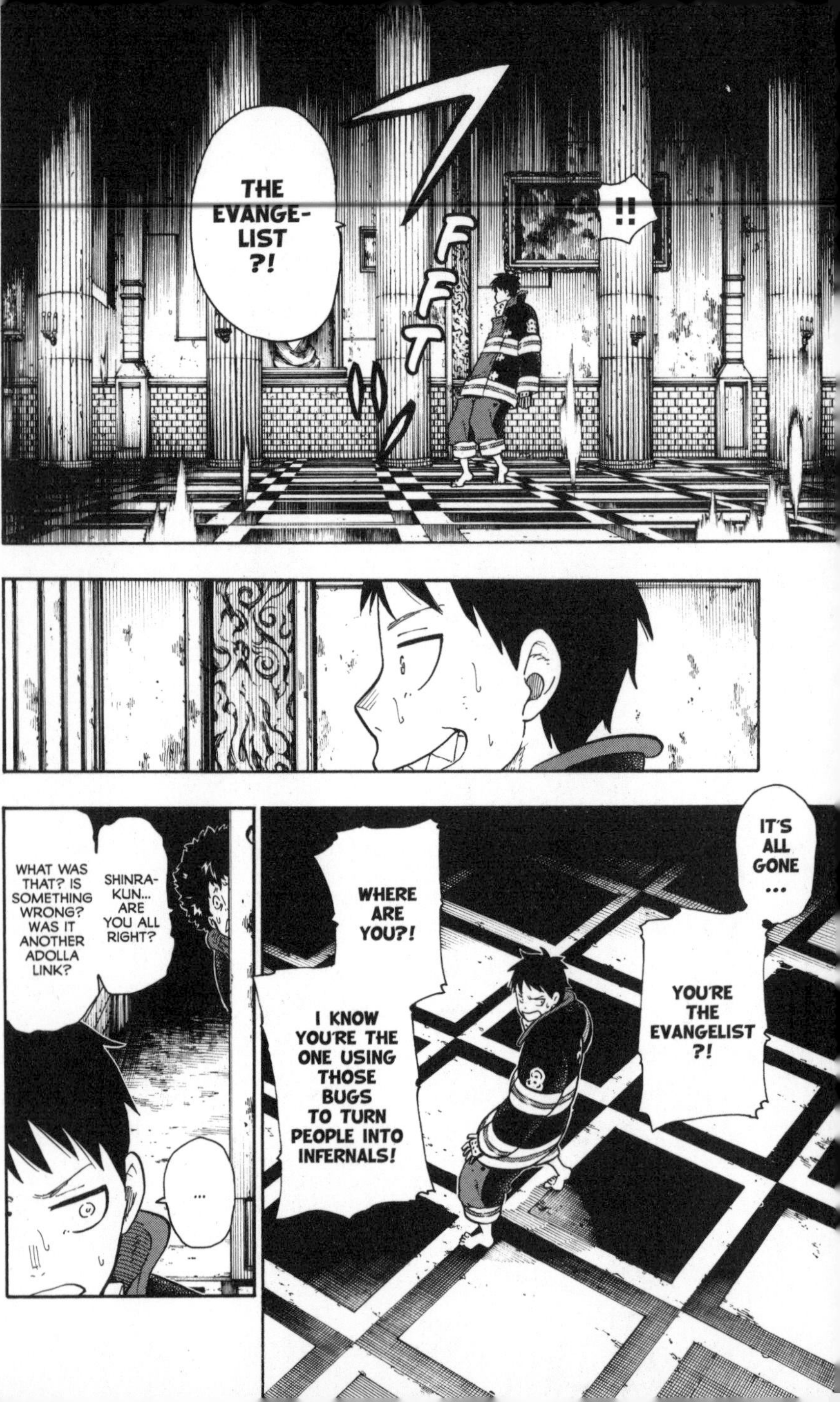
!!
FFT
THE EVANGE-LIST?!
IT'S ALL GONE...
YOU'RE THE EVANGELIST?!
WHERE ARE YOU?!
I KNOW YOU'RE THE ONE USING THOSE BUGS TO TURN PEOPLE INTO INFERNALS!
SHINRA-KUN... ARE YOU ALL RIGHT?
WHAT WAS THAT? IS SOMETHING WRONG? WAS IT ANOTHER ADOLLA LINK?
...

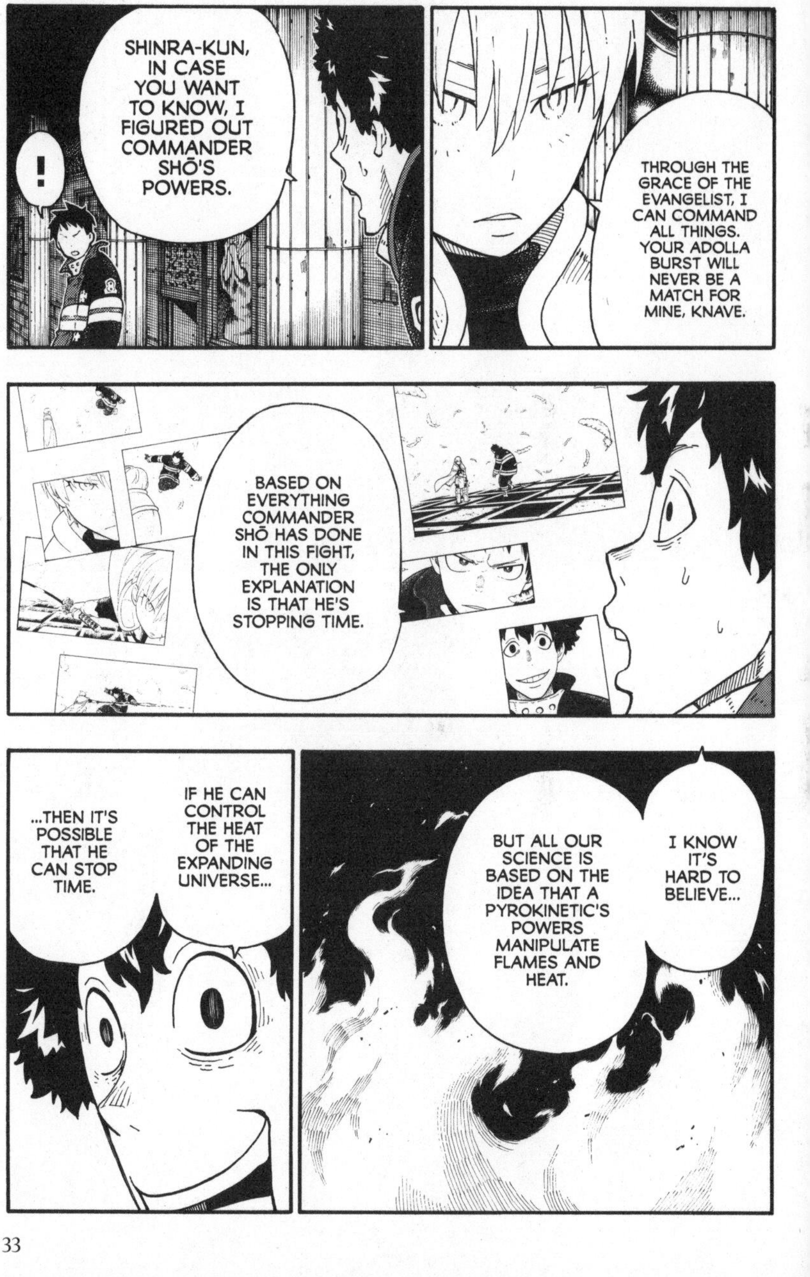
THROUGH THE GRACE OF THE EVANGELIST, I CAN COMMAND ALL THINGS. YOUR ADOLLA BURST WILL NEVER BE A MATCH FOR MINE, KNAVE.
SHINRA-KUN, IN CASE YOU WANT TO KNOW, I FIGURED OUT COMMANDER SHŌ'S POWERS.
!
BASED ON EVERYTHING COMMANDER SHŌ HAS DONE IN THIS FIGHT, THE ONLY EXPLANATION IS THAT HE'S STOPPING TIME.
I KNOW IT'S HARD TO BELIEVE...
BUT ALL OUR SCIENCE IS BASED ON THE IDEA THAT A PYROKINETIC'S POWERS MANIPULATE FLAMES AND HEAT.
IF HE CAN CONTROL THE HEAT OF THE EXPANDING UNIVERSE...
...THEN IT'S POSSIBLE THAT HE CAN STOP TIME.

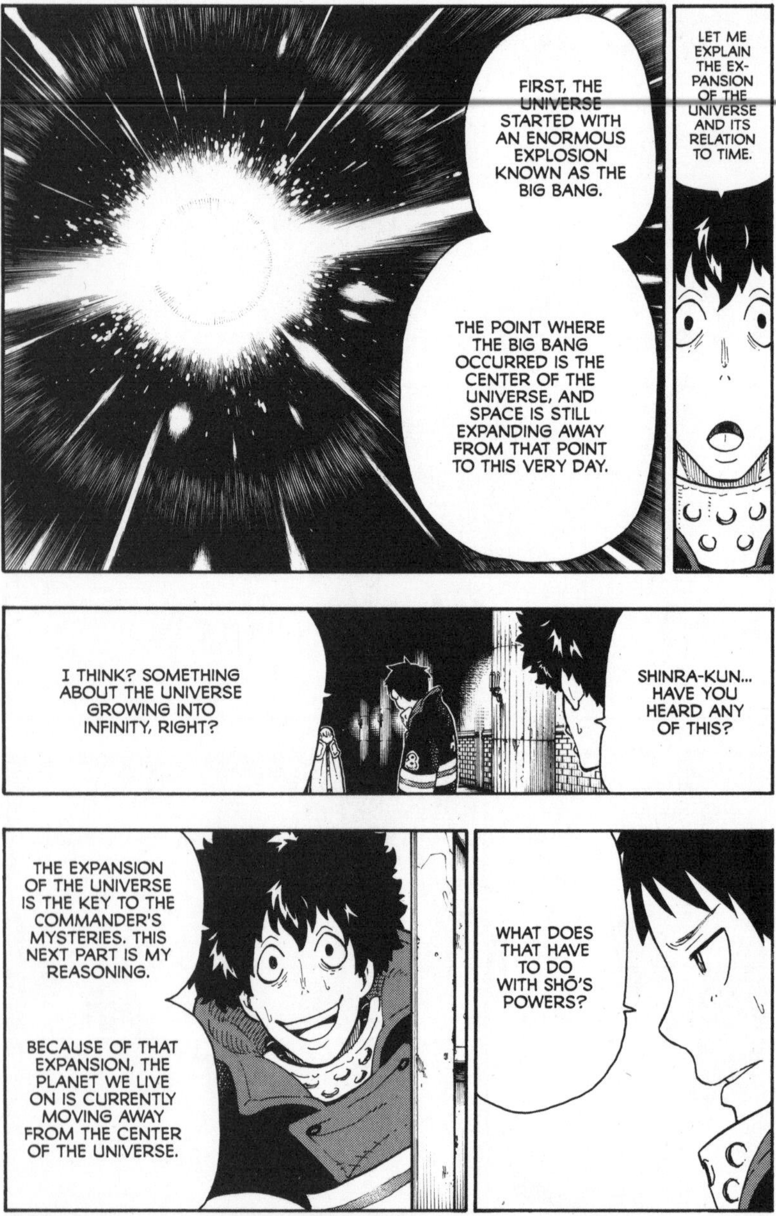
LET ME EXPLAIN THE EX-PANSION OF THE UNIVERSE AND ITS RELATION TO TIME.
FIRST, THE UNIVERSE STARTED WITH AN ENORMOUS EXPLOSION KNOWN AS THE BIG BANG.
THE POINT WHERE THE BIG BANG OCCURRED IS THE CENTER OF THE UNIVERSE, AND SPACE IS STILL EXPANDING AWAY FROM THAT POINT TO THIS VERY DAY.
SHINRA-KUN... HAVE YOU HEARD ANY OF THIS?
I THINK? SOMETHING ABOUT THE UNIVERSE GROWING INTO INFINITY, RIGHT?
WHAT DOES THAT HAVE TO DO WITH SHŌ'S POWERS?
THE EXPANSION OF THE UNIVERSE IS THE KEY TO THE COMMANDER'S MYSTERIES. THIS NEXT PART IS MY REASONING.
BECAUSE OF THAT EXPANSION, THE PLANET WE LIVE ON IS CURRENTLY MOVING AWAY FROM THE CENTER OF THE UNIVERSE.

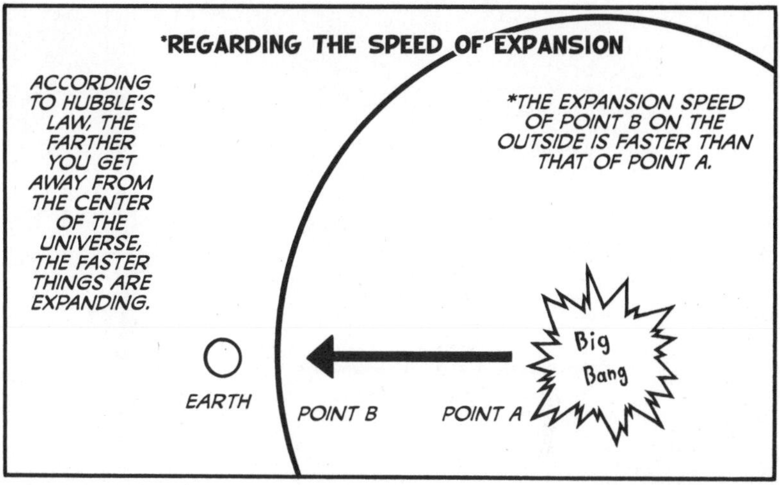
*REGARDING THE SPEED OF EXPANSION
*THE EXPANSION SPEED OF POINT B ON THE OUTSIDE IS FASTER THAN THAT OF POINT A.
ACCORDING TO HUBBLE'S LAW, THE FARTHER YOU GET AWAY FROM THE CENTER OF THE UNIVERSE, THE FASTER THINGS ARE EXPANDING.
Big Bang
POINT A
POINT B
EARTH

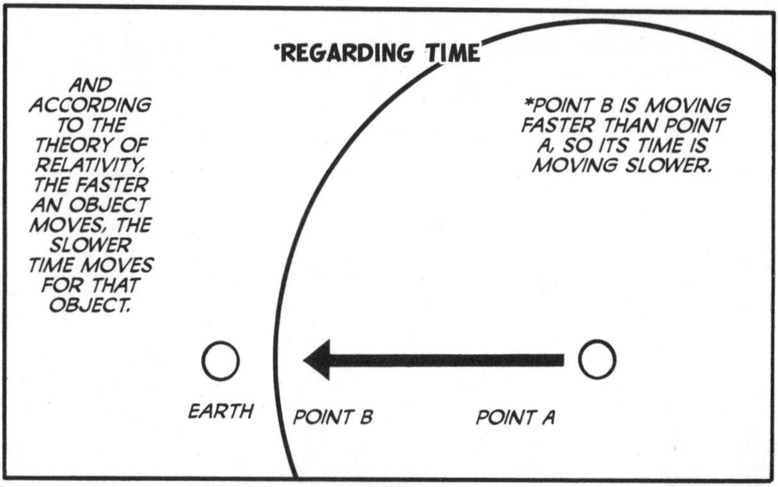
*REGARDING TIME
*POINT B IS MOVING FASTER THAN POINT A, SO ITS TIME IS MOVING SLOWER.
AND ACCORDING TO THE THEORY OF RELATIVITY, THE FASTER AN OBJECT MOVES, THE SLOWER TIME MOVES FOR THAT OBJECT.
POINT A
POINT B
EARTH

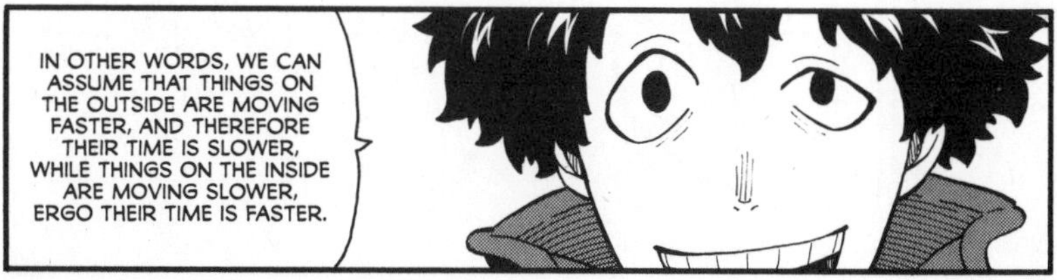
IN OTHER WORDS, WE CAN ASSUME THAT THINGS ON THE OUTSIDE ARE MOVING FASTER, AND THEREFORE THEIR TIME IS SLOWER, WHILE THINGS ON THE INSIDE ARE MOVING SLOWER, ERGO THEIR TIME IS FASTER.

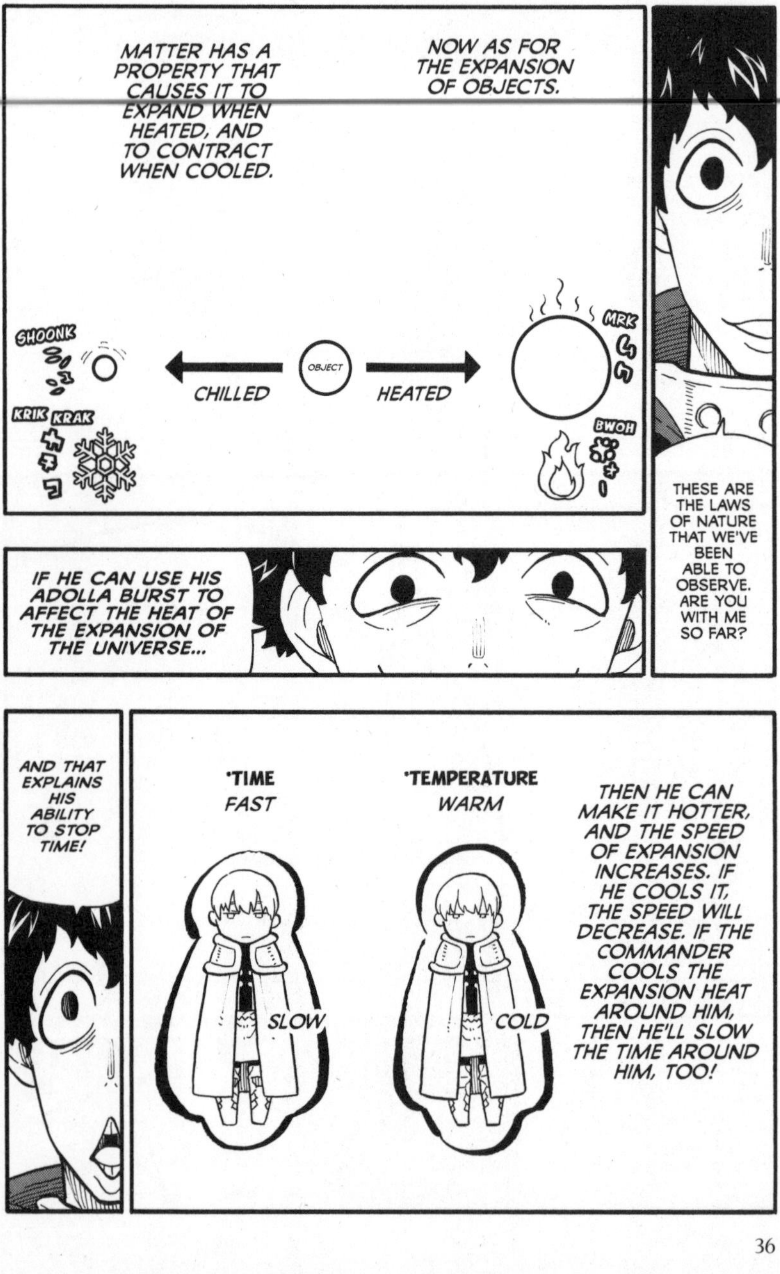
THESE ARE THE LAWS OF NATURE THAT WE'VE BEEN ABLE TO OBSERVE. ARE YOU WITH ME SO FAR?
NOW AS FOR THE EXPANSION OF OBJECTS.
MATTER HAS A PROPERTY THAT CAUSES IT TO EXPAND WHEN HEATED, AND TO CONTRACT WHEN COOLED.
MRK
BWOH
HEATED
OBJECT
CHILLED
SHOONK
KRIK KRAK
IF HE CAN USE HIS ADOLLA BURST TO AFFECT THE HEAT OF THE EXPANSION OF THE UNIVERSE...
THEN HE CAN MAKE IT HOTTER, AND THE SPEED OF EXPANSION INCREASES. IF HE COOLS IT, THE SPEED WILL DECREASE. IF THE COMMANDER COOLS THE EXPANSION HEAT AROUND HIM, THEN HE'LL SLOW THE TIME AROUND HIM, TOO!
•TEMPERATURE
WARM
COLD
•TIME
FAST
SLOW
AND THAT EXPLAINS HIS ABILITY TO STOP TIME!

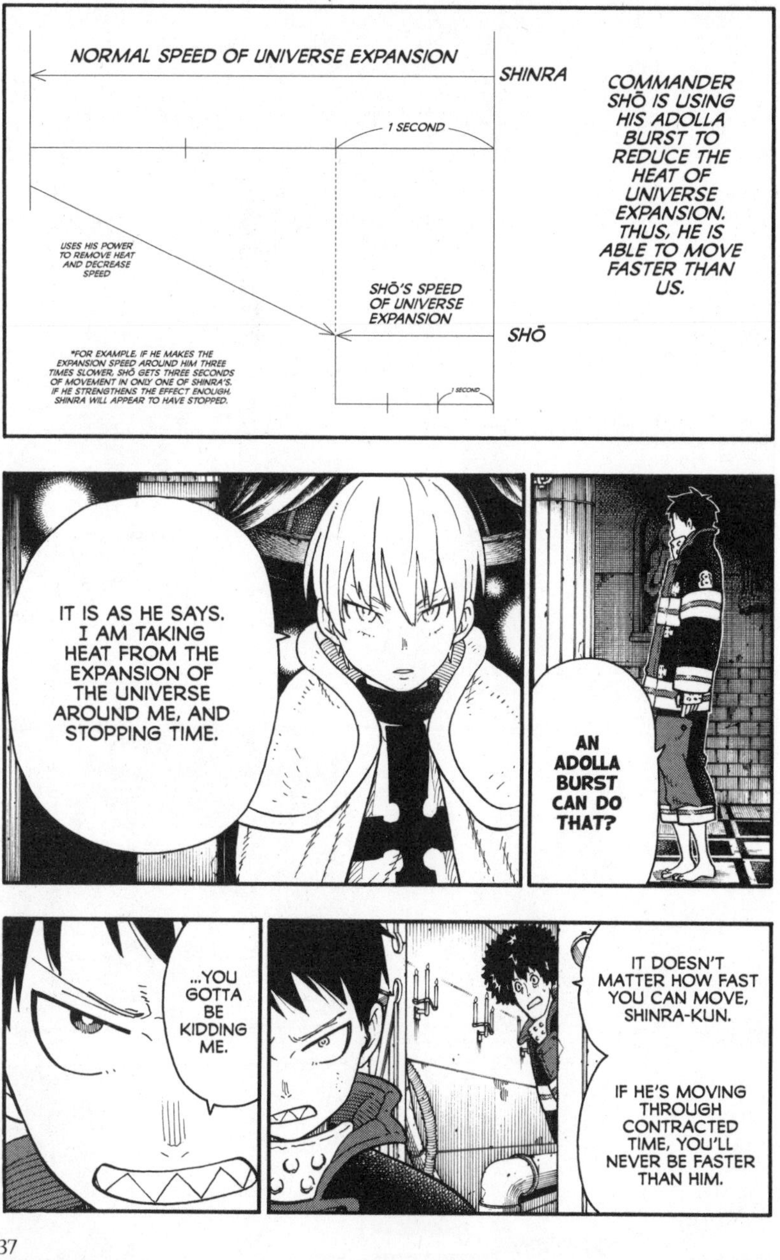
COMMANDER SHŌ IS USING HIS ADOLLA BURST TO REDUCE THE HEAT OF UNIVERSE EXPANSION. THUS, HE IS ABLE TO MOVE FASTER THAN US.
NORMAL SPEED OF UNIVERSE EXPANSION
SHINRA
1 SECOND
USES HIS POWER TO REMOVE HEAT AND DECREASE SPEED
SHŌ'S SPEED OF UNIVERSE EXPANSION
SHŌ
*FOR EXAMPLE, IF HE MAKES THE EXPANSION SPEED AROUND HIM THREE TIMES SLOWER, SHŌ GETS THREE SECONDS OF MOVEMENT IN ONLY ONE OF SHINRA'S. IF HE STRENGTHENS THE EFFECT ENOUGH, SHINRA WILL APPEAR TO HAVE STOPPED.
1 SECOND
AN ADOLLA BURST CAN DO THAT?
IT IS AS HE SAYS. I AM TAKING HEAT FROM THE EXPANSION OF THE UNIVERSE AROUND ME, AND STOPPING TIME.
IT DOESN'T MATTER HOW FAST YOU CAN MOVE, SHINRA-KUN.
IF HE'S MOVING THROUGH CONTRACTED TIME, YOU'LL NEVER BE FASTER THAN HIM.
...YOU GOTTA BE KIDDING ME.

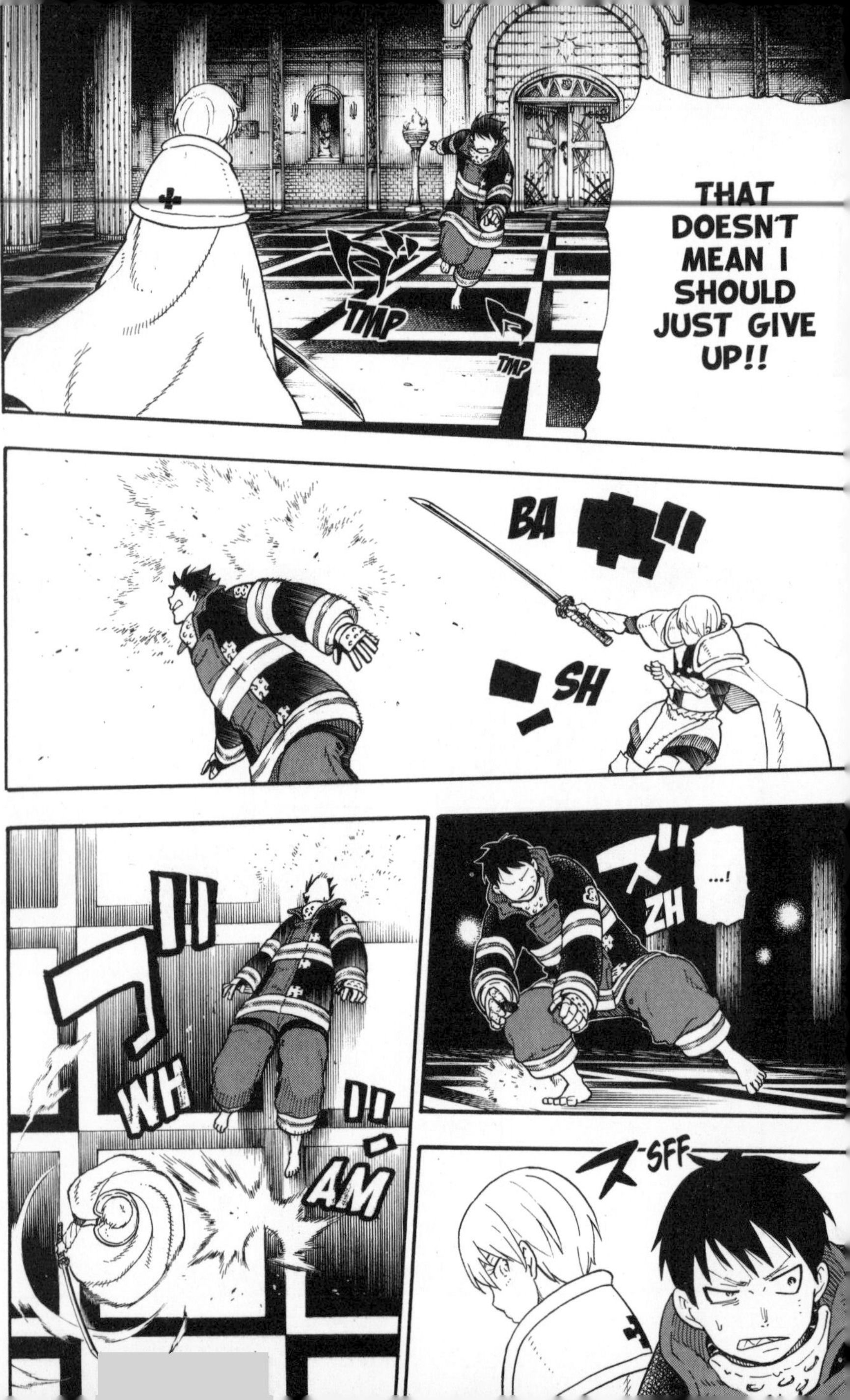
THAT DOESN'T MEAN I SHOULD JUST GIVE UP!!
TMP
TMP
BA
SH
...!
ZH
WH
AM
SFF

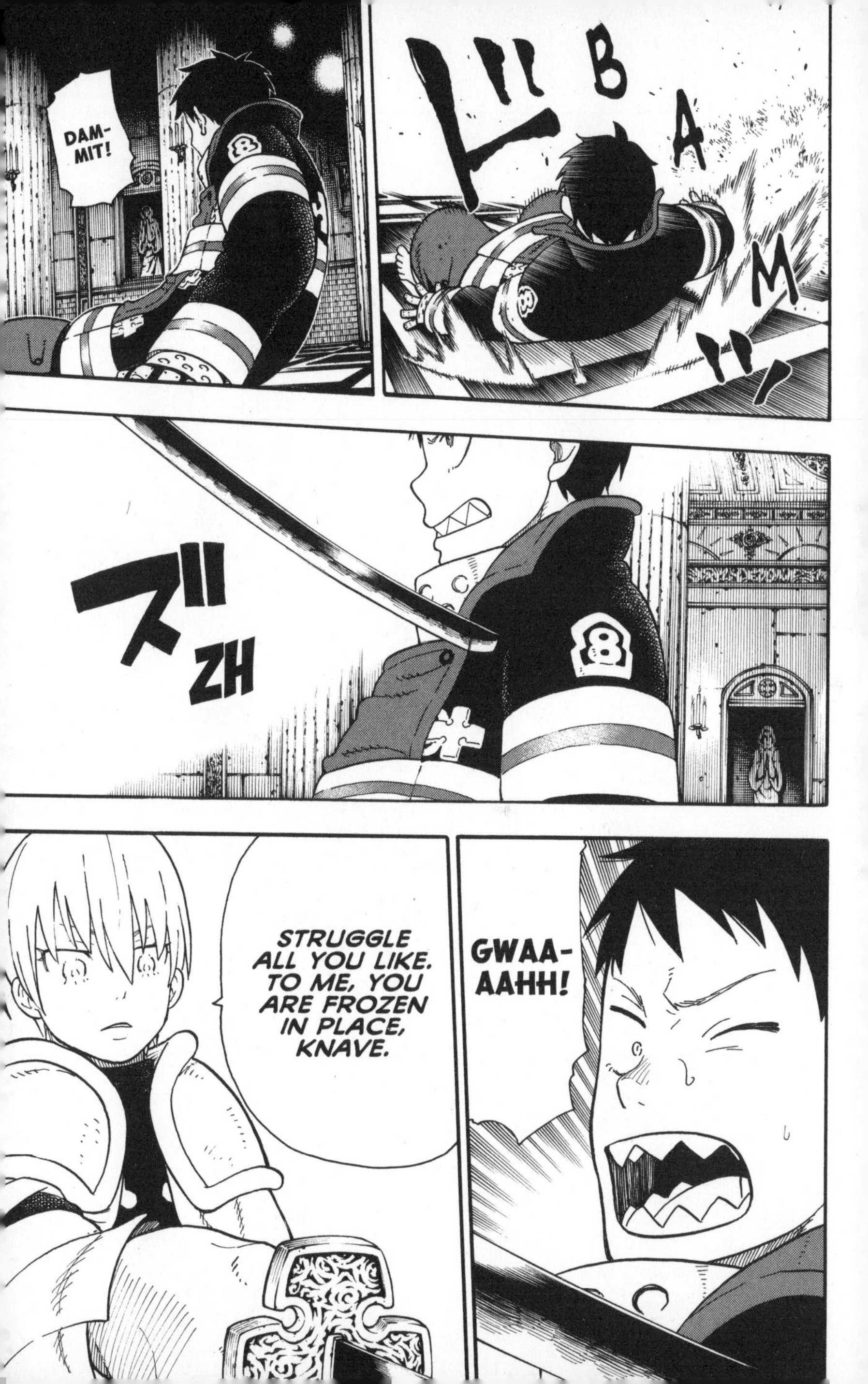
BAM
DAM-MIT!
ズ
ZH
GWAA-AAHH!
STRUGGLE ALL YOU LIKE. TO ME, YOU ARE FROZEN IN PLACE, KNAVE.

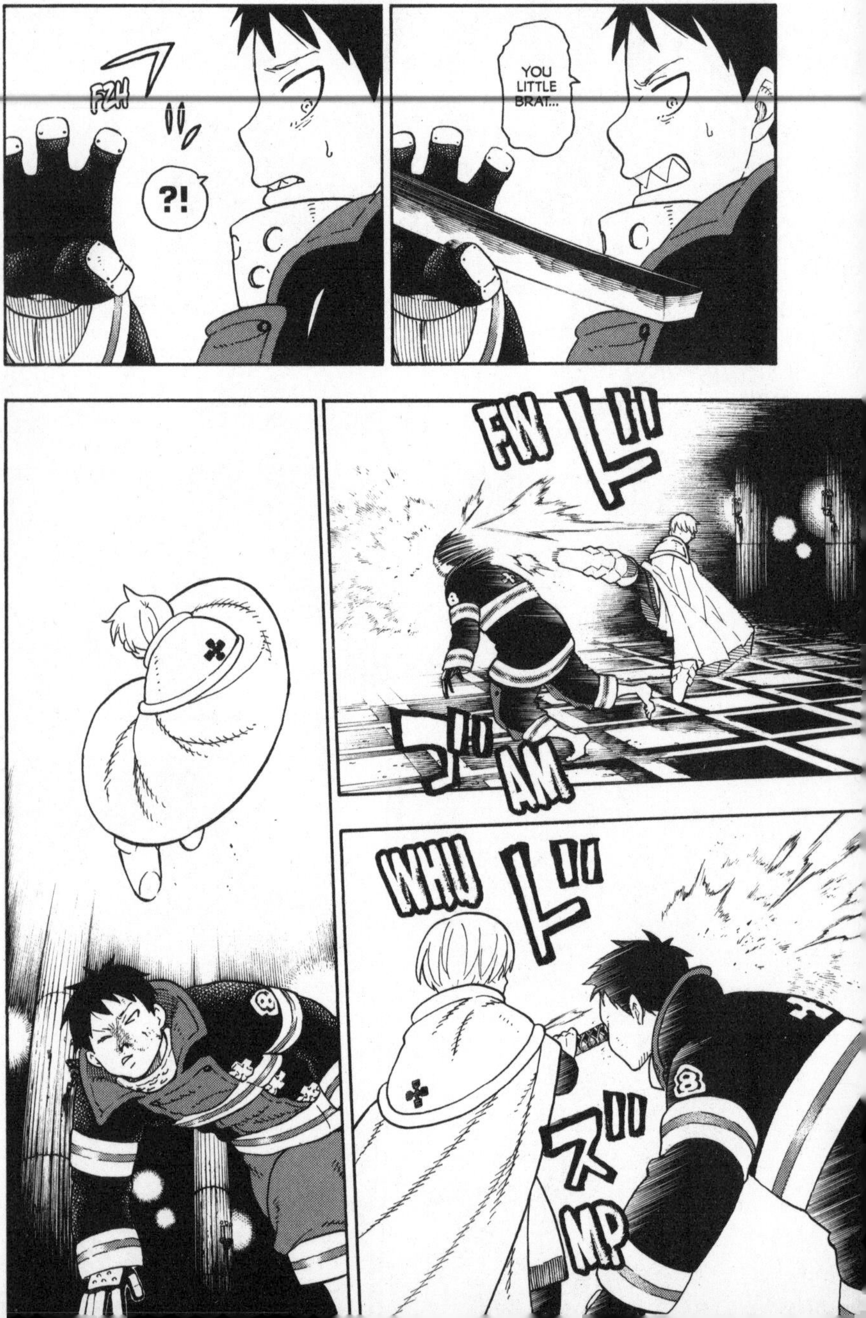
YOU LITTLE BRAT...
FZH
?!
FW
AM
WHU
MP

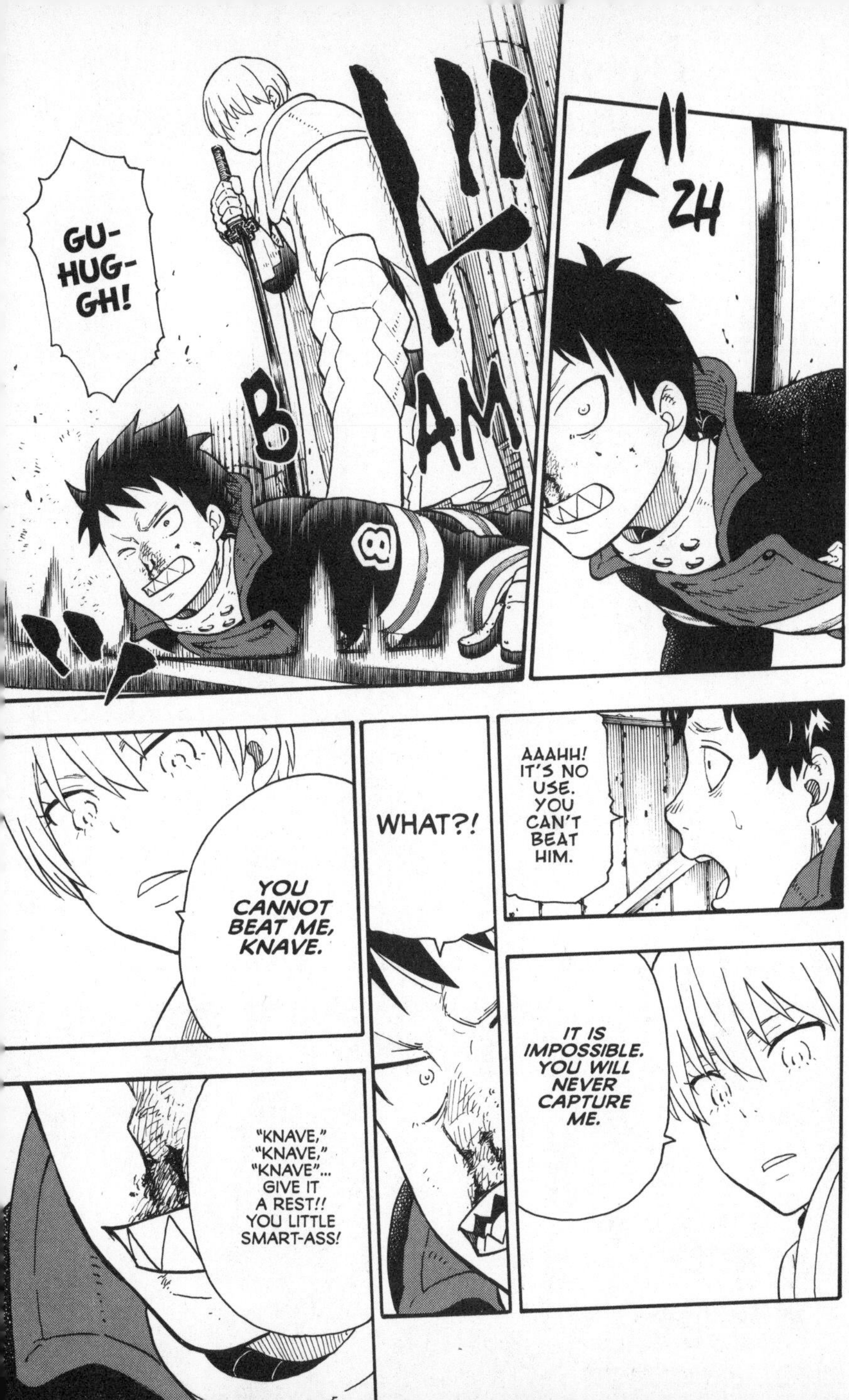
ZUH
!!
GU-HUG-GH!
BAM
AAAHH! IT'S NO USE. YOU CAN'T BEAT HIM.
WHAT?!
YOU CANNOT BEAT ME, KNAVE.
IT IS IMPOSSIBLE. YOU WILL NEVER CAPTURE ME.
"KNAVE," "KNAVE," "KNAVE"... GIVE IT A REST!! YOU LITTLE SMART-ASS!

JUST ONCE IN YOUR LIFE, BE A CUTE LITTLE BROTHER AND CALL ME ONII-CHAN!!

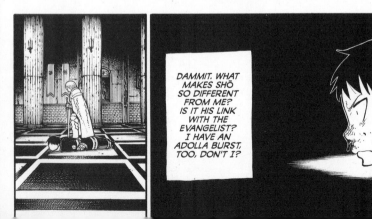

DAMMIT. WHAT MAKES SHŌ SO DIFFERENT FROM ME? IS IT HIS LINK WITH THE EVANGELIST? I HAVE AN ADOLLA BURST, TOO, DON'T I?

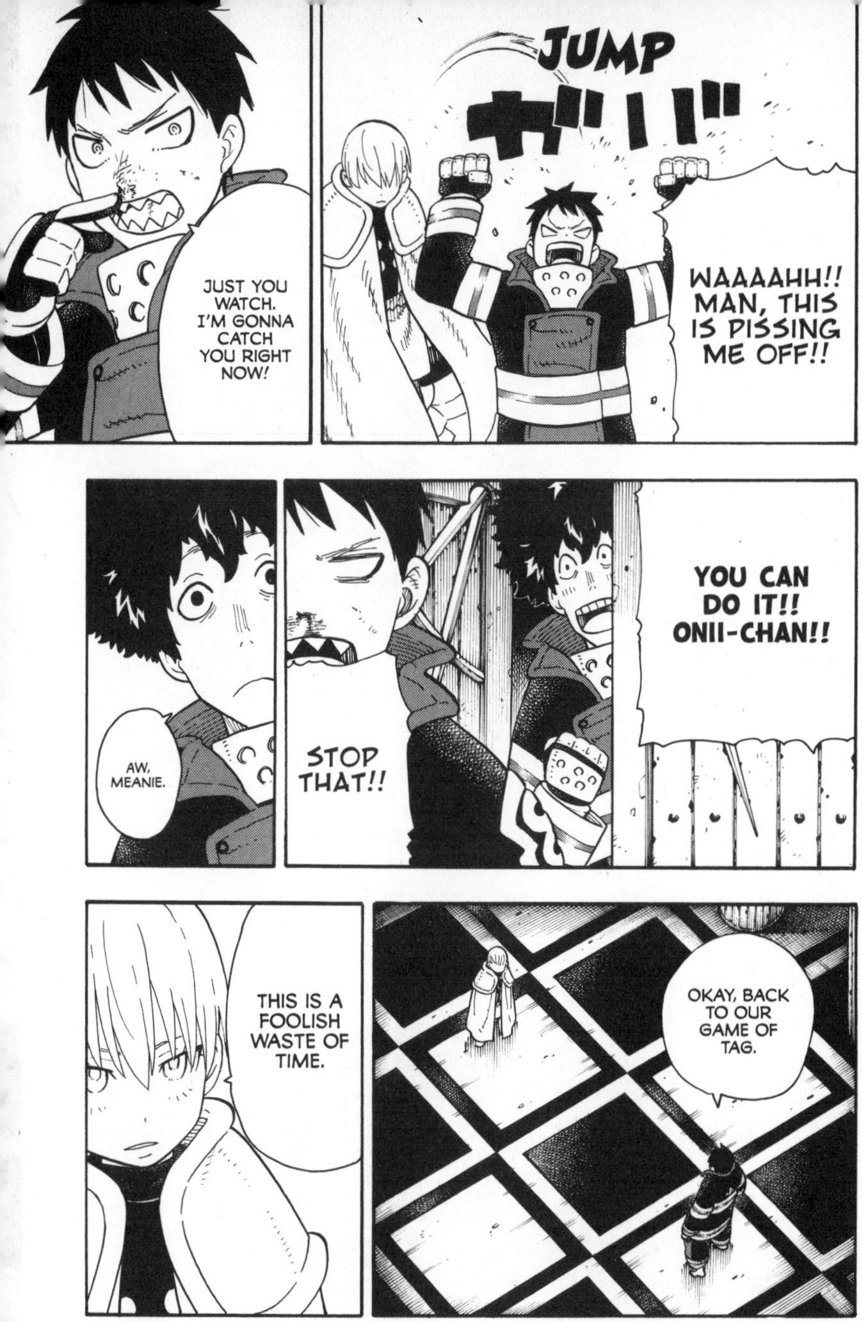
JUMP
WAAAAHH!! MAN, THIS IS PISSING ME OFF!!
JUST YOU WATCH. I'M GONNA CATCH YOU RIGHT NOW!
YOU CAN DO IT!! ONII-CHAN!!
STOP THAT!!
AW, MEANIE.
OKAY, BACK TO OUR GAME OF TAG.
THIS IS A FOOLISH WASTE OF TIME.

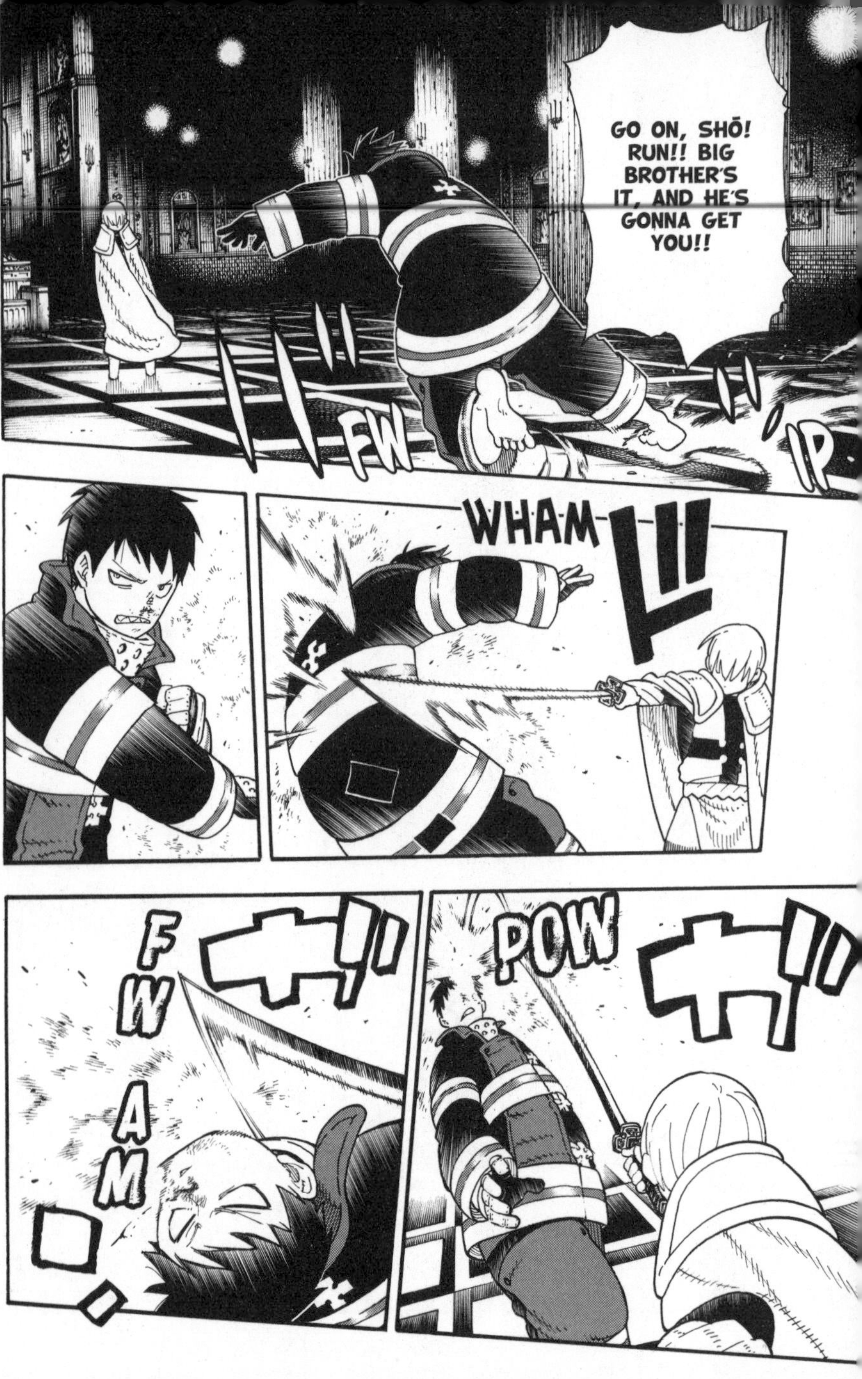
GO ON, SHŌ! RUN!! BIG BROTHER'S IT, AND HE'S GONNA GET YOU!!
FW
IP
WHAM
POW
FWAM

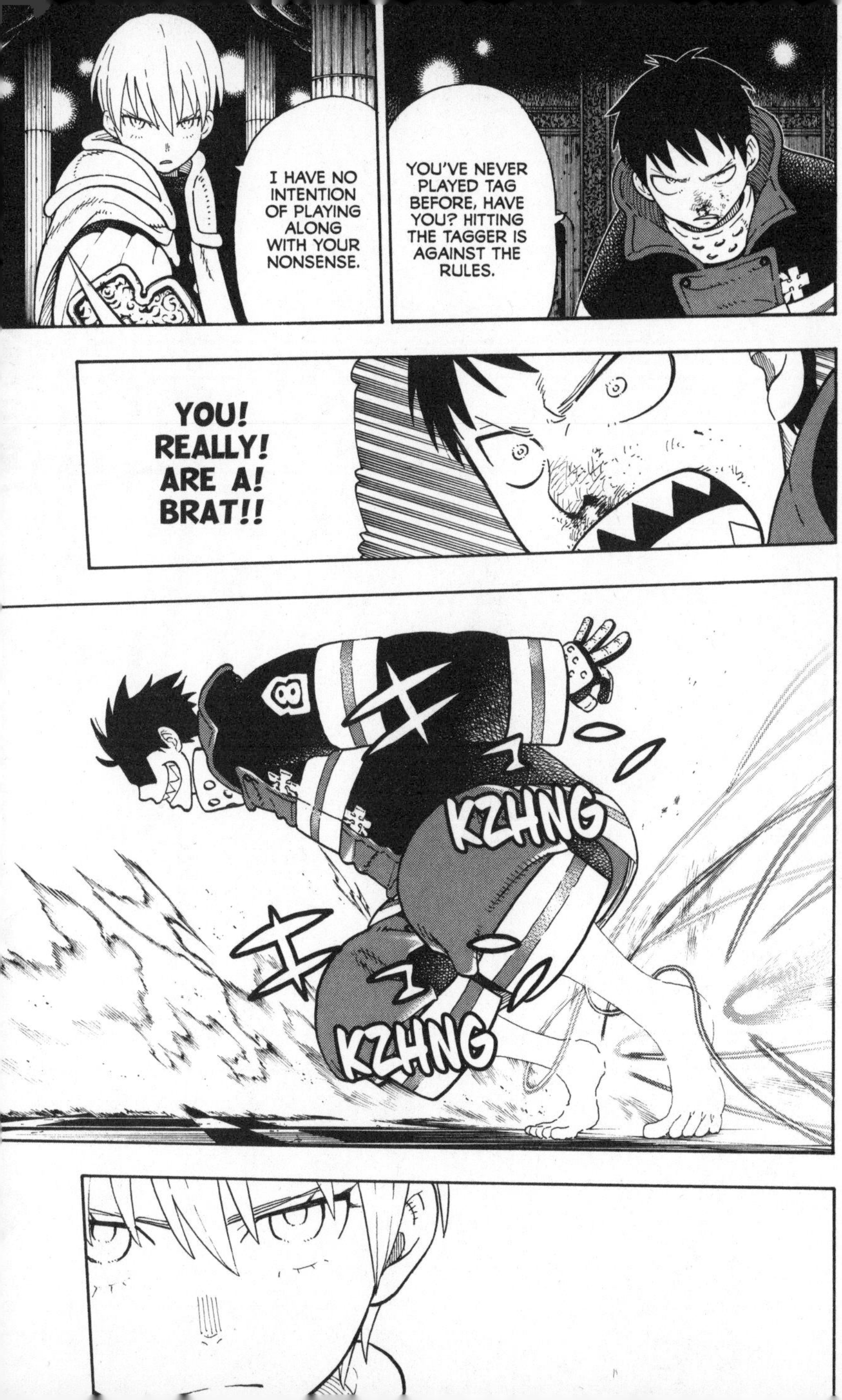
YOU'VE NEVER PLAYED TAG BEFORE, HAVE YOU? HITTING THE TAGGER IS AGAINST THE RULES.
I HAVE NO INTENTION OF PLAYING ALONG WITH YOUR NONSENSE.
YOU! REALLY! ARE A! BRAT!!
KZHNG
KZHNG

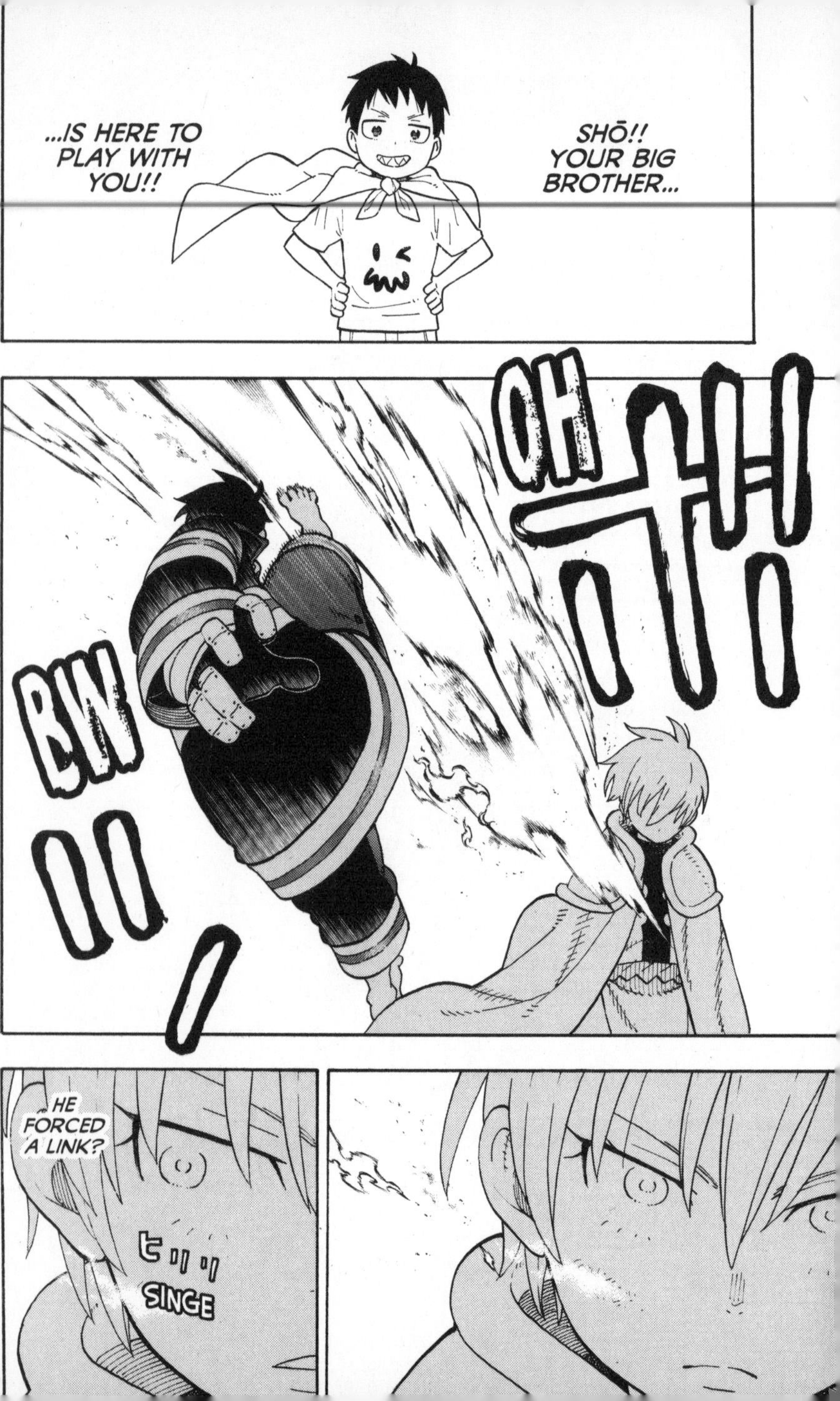
SHŌ!! YOUR BIG BROTHER...
...IS HERE TO PLAY WITH YOU!!
OH
BW
HE FORCED A LINK?
ヒリリ
SINGE

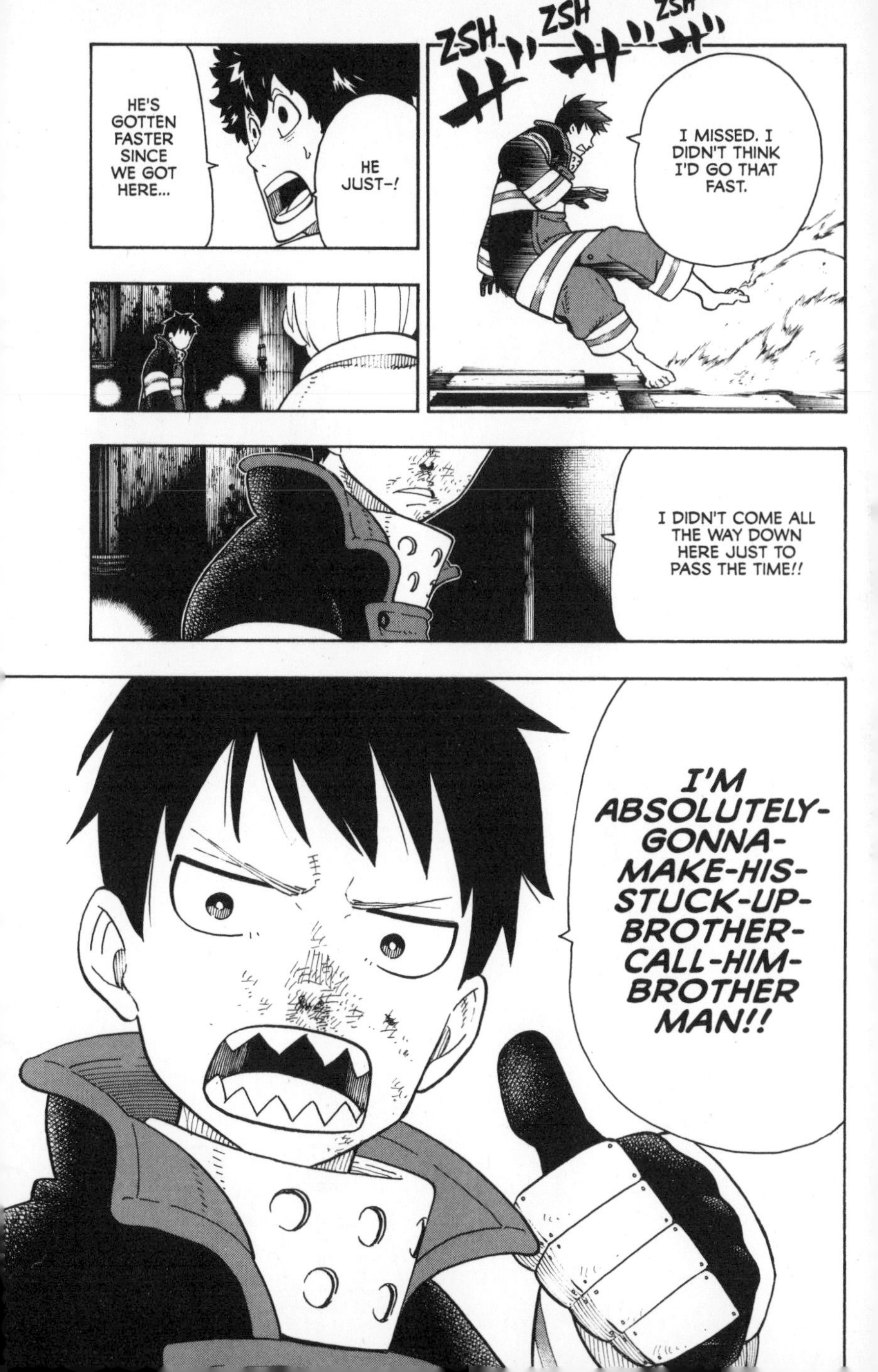
ZSH ZSH ZSH
I MISSED. I DIDN'T THINK I'D GO THAT FAST.
HE JUST-!
HE'S GOTTEN FASTER SINCE WE GOT HERE...
I DIDN'T COME ALL THE WAY DOWN HERE JUST TO PASS THE TIME!!
I'M ABSOLUTELY-GONNA-MAKE-HIS-STUCK-UP-BROTHER-CALL-HIM-BROTHER MAN!!

FIRE FORCE

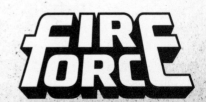

CHAPTER LXXXI: A BIG BROTHER'S DETERMINATION

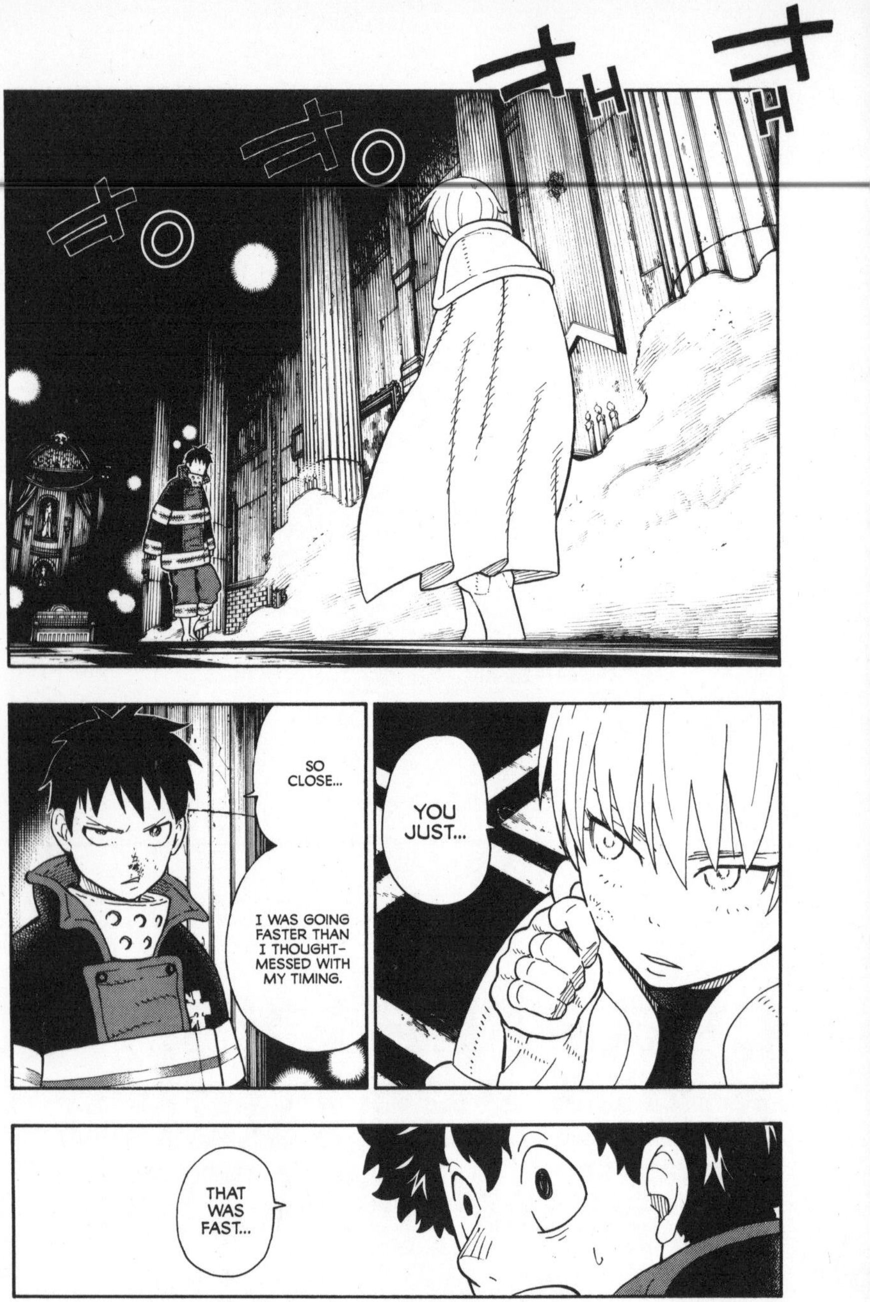
YOU JUST...
SO CLOSE...
I WAS GOING FASTER THAN I THOUGHT— MESSED WITH MY TIMING.
THAT WAS FAST...

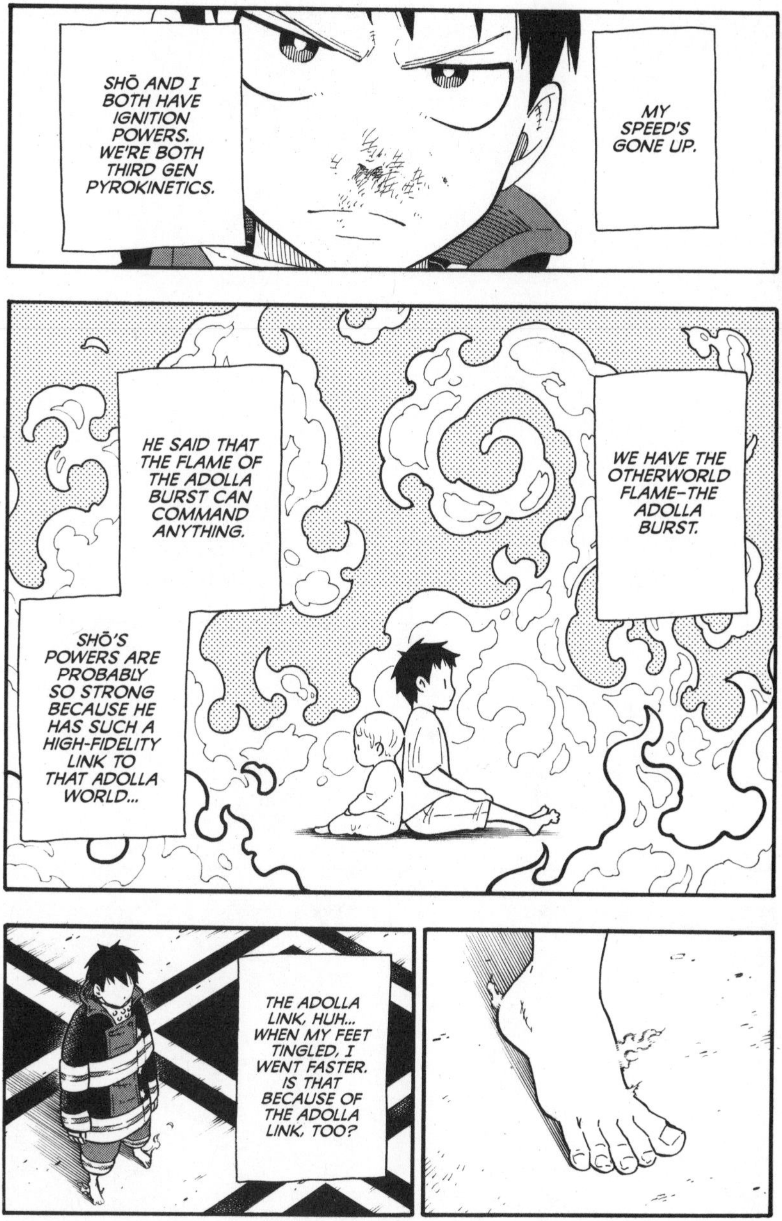
MY SPEED'S GONE UP.
SHŌ AND I BOTH HAVE IGNITION POWERS. WE'RE BOTH THIRD GEN PYROKINETICS.
WE HAVE THE OTHERWORLD FLAME—THE ADOLLA BURST.
HE SAID THAT THE FLAME OF THE ADOLLA BURST CAN COMMAND ANYTHING.
SHŌ'S POWERS ARE PROBABLY SO STRONG BECAUSE HE HAS SUCH A HIGH-FIDELITY LINK TO THAT ADOLLA WORLD...
THE ADOLLA LINK, HUH... WHEN MY FEET TINGLED, I WENT FASTER. IS THAT BECAUSE OF THE ADOLLA LINK, TOO?

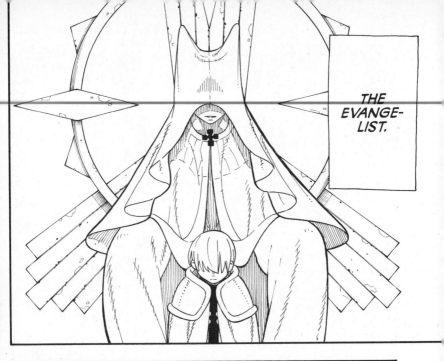

THE EVANGE-LIST.

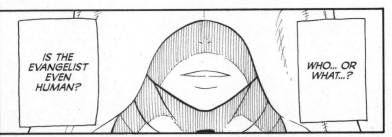

IS THE EVANGELIST EVEN HUMAN?

WHO... OR WHAT...?

BUT... HOW?

IF MY ADOLLA BURST CAN GET ME THE "GRACE OF THE EVANGELIST" OR WHATEVER IT IS, THEN I'LL BE STRONGER.

POP

IF I CAN GET ENOUGH SPEED TO OUTRUN SHŌ'S...

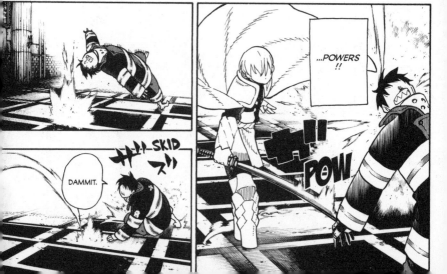

...POWERS!!

SKID

DAMMIT.

POW

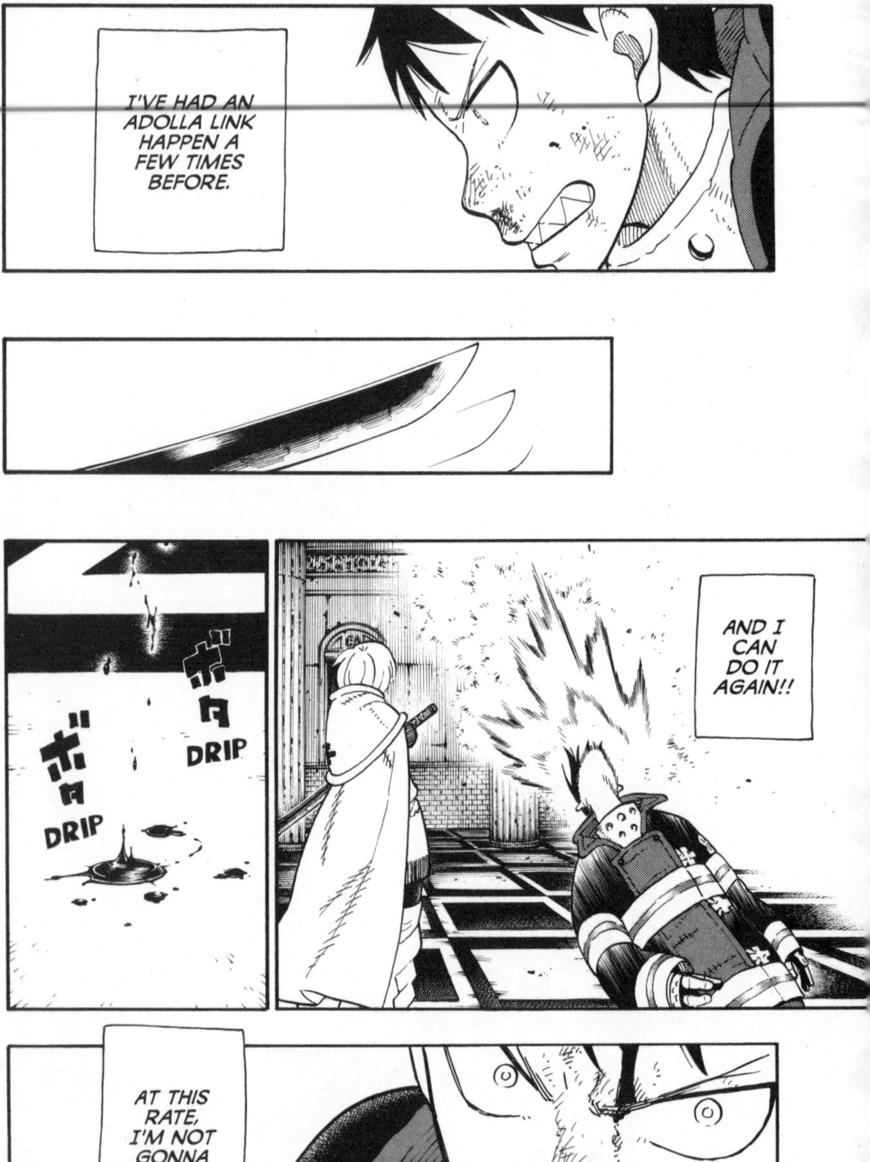
I'VE HAD AN ADOLLA LINK HAPPEN A FEW TIMES BEFORE.
AND I CAN DO IT AGAIN!!
ボタ
DRIP
ボタ
DRIP
AT THIS RATE, I'M NOT GONNA LAST.

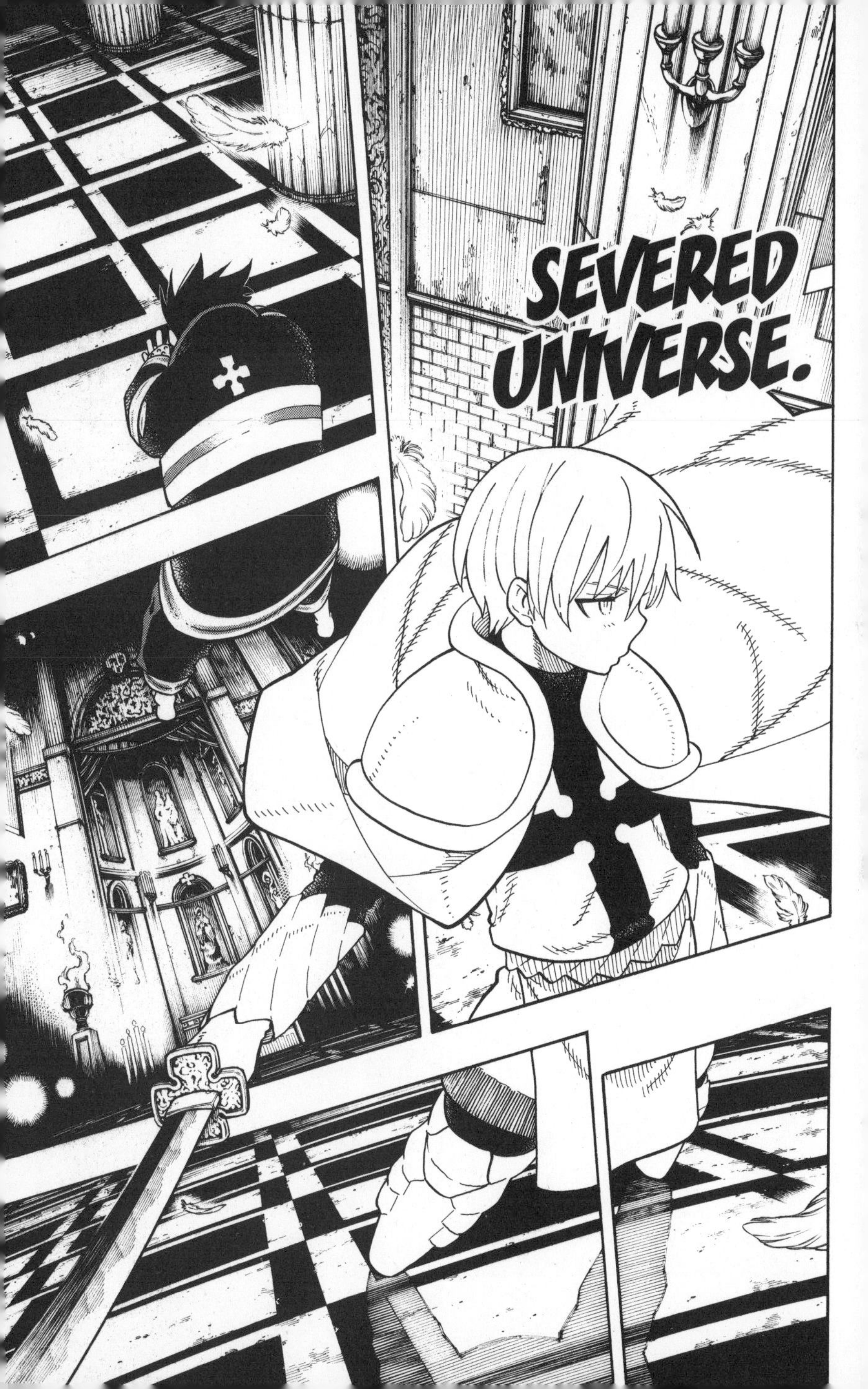
SEVERED UNIVERSE.

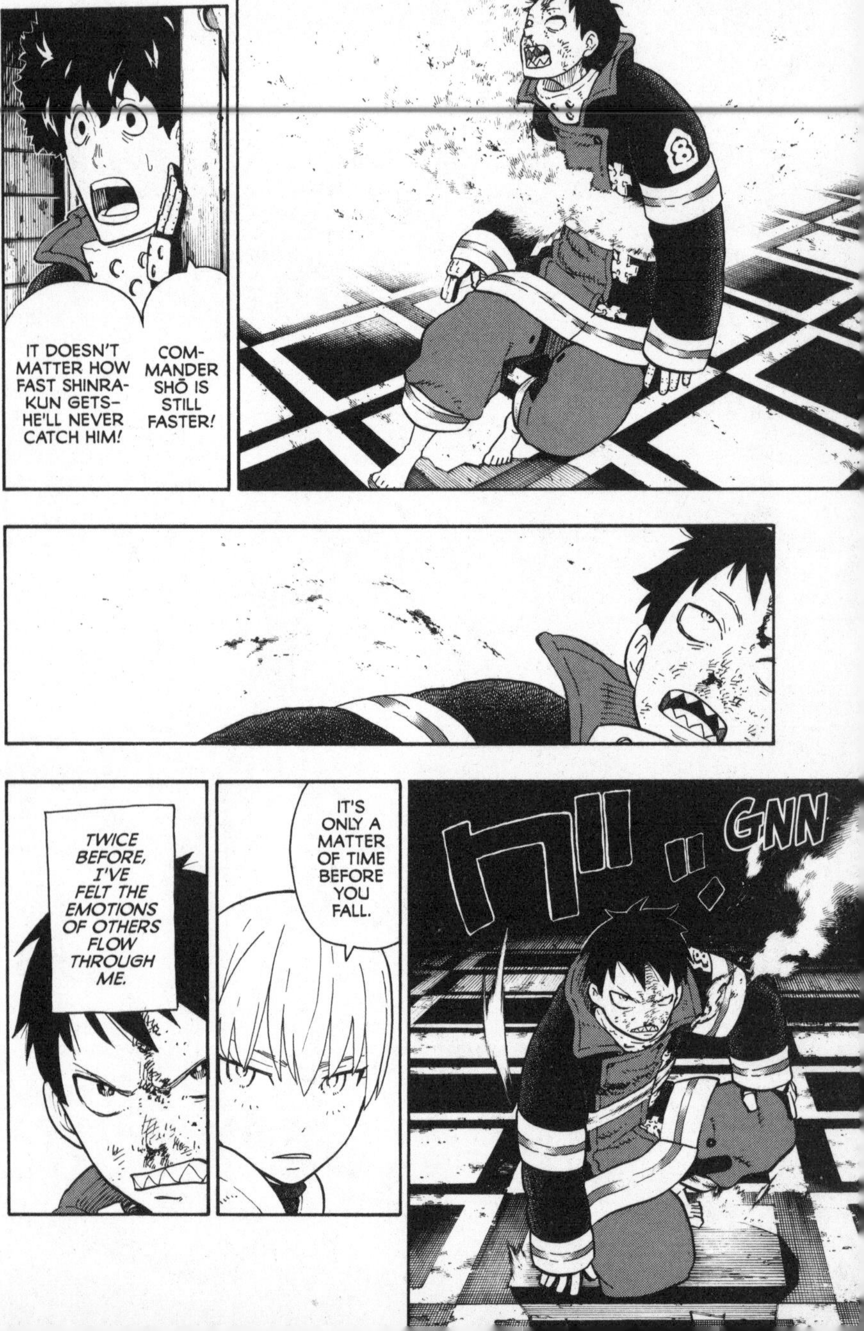
IT DOESN'T MATTER HOW FAST SHINRA-KUN GETS—HE'LL NEVER CATCH HIM!
COMMANDER SHŌ IS STILL FASTER!
GNN
IT'S ONLY A MATTER OF TIME BEFORE YOU FALL.
TWICE BEFORE, I'VE FELT THE EMOTIONS OF OTHERS FLOW THROUGH ME.

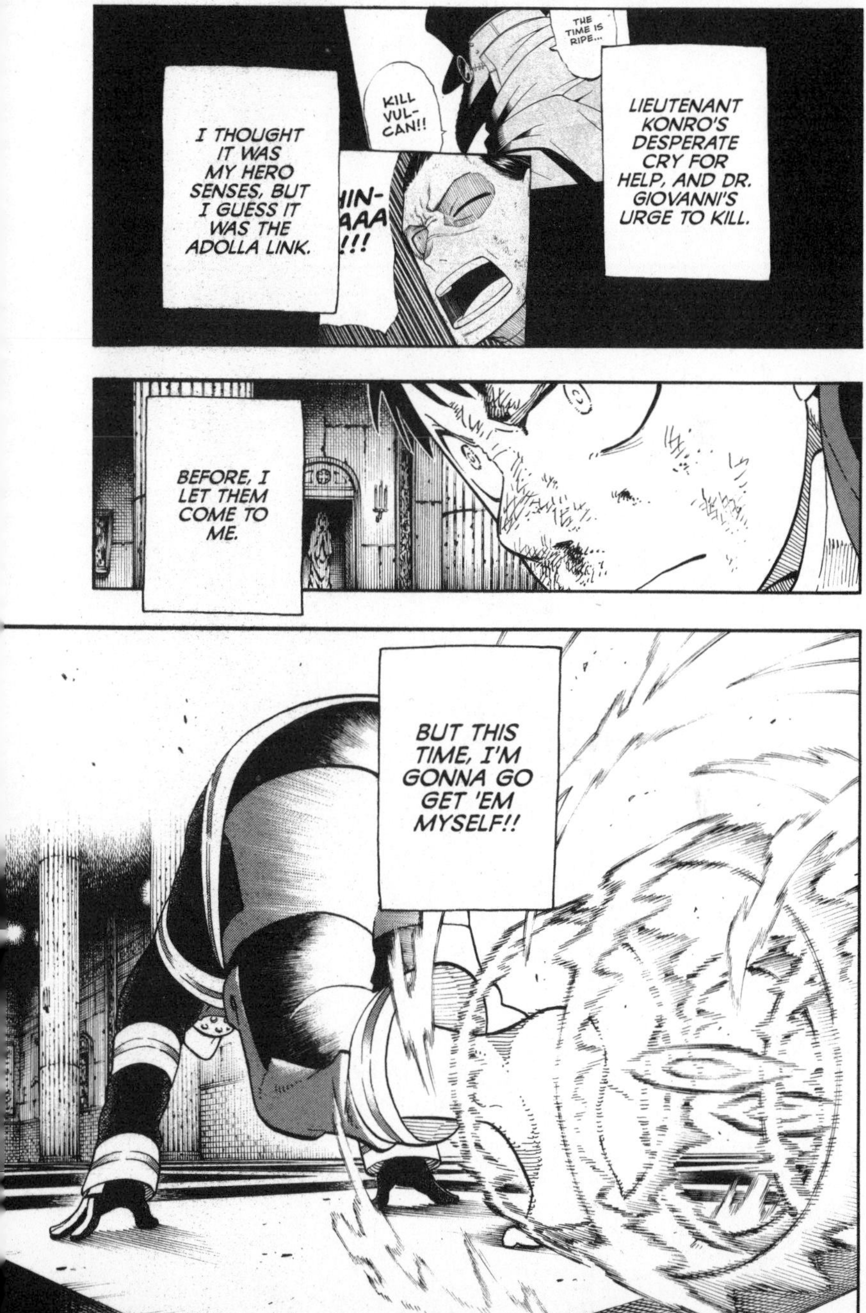
THE TIME IS RIPE...
LIEUTENANT KONRO'S DESPERATE CRY FOR HELP, AND DR. GIOVANNI'S URGE TO KILL.
KILL VUL-CAN!!
HIN-AAA!!!
I THOUGHT IT WAS MY HERO SENSES, BUT I GUESS IT WAS THE ADOLLA LINK.
BEFORE, I LET THEM COME TO ME.
BUT THIS TIME, I'M GONNA GO GET 'EM MYSELF!!

YOU CAN'T DO IT WITHOUT THE GRACE OF THE EVANGELIST.

I KNOW THAT.

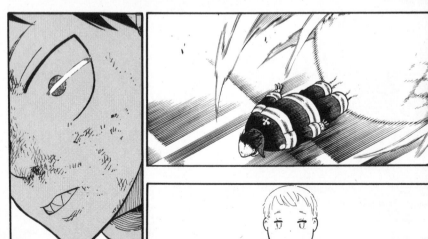

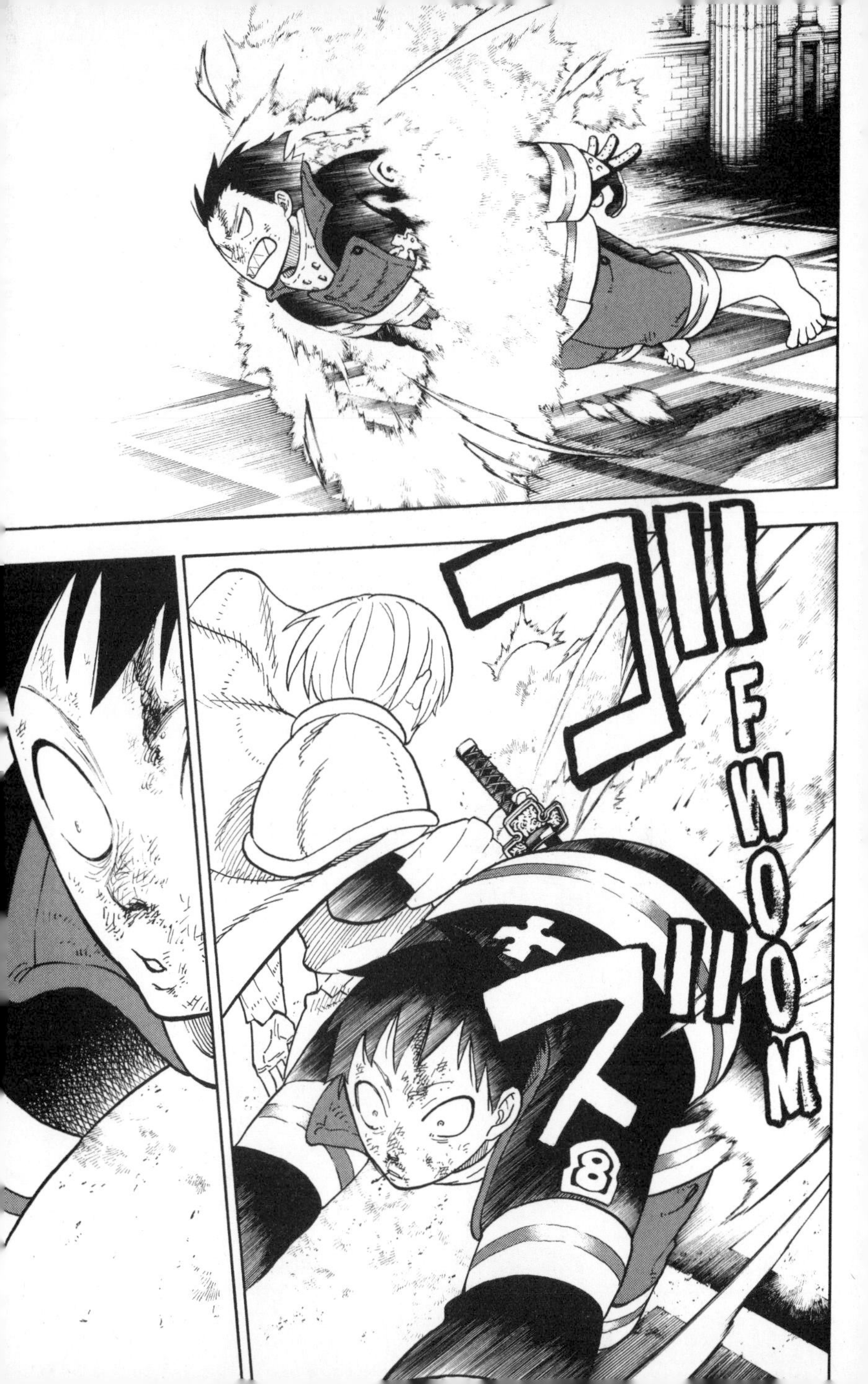
ゴッ
FWOOOM

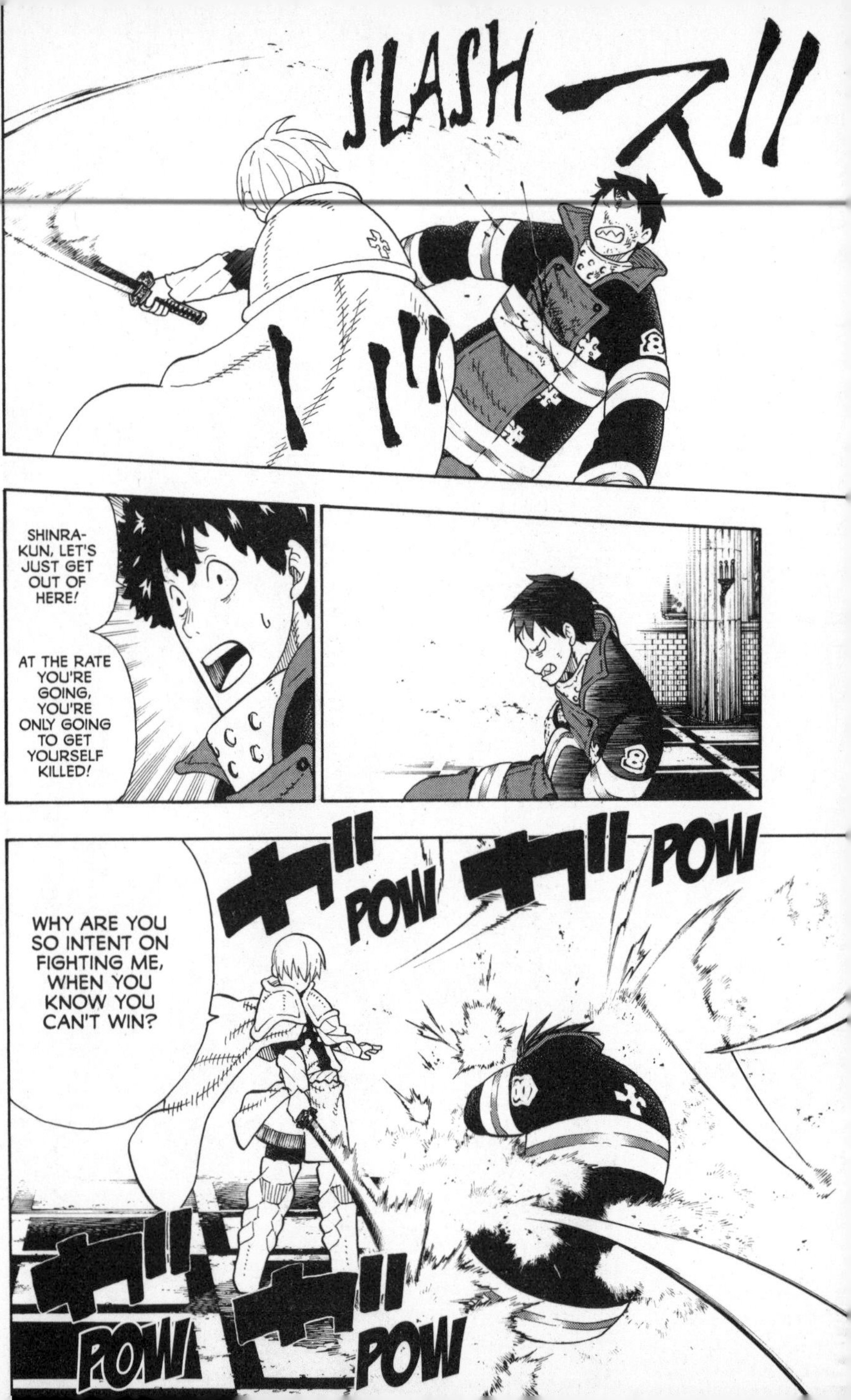
SLASH
SHINRA-KUN, LET'S JUST GET OUT OF HERE!
AT THE RATE YOU'RE GOING, YOU'RE ONLY GOING TO GET YOURSELF KILLED!
POW
POW
WHY ARE YOU SO INTENT ON FIGHTING ME, WHEN YOU KNOW YOU CAN'T WIN?
POW
POW

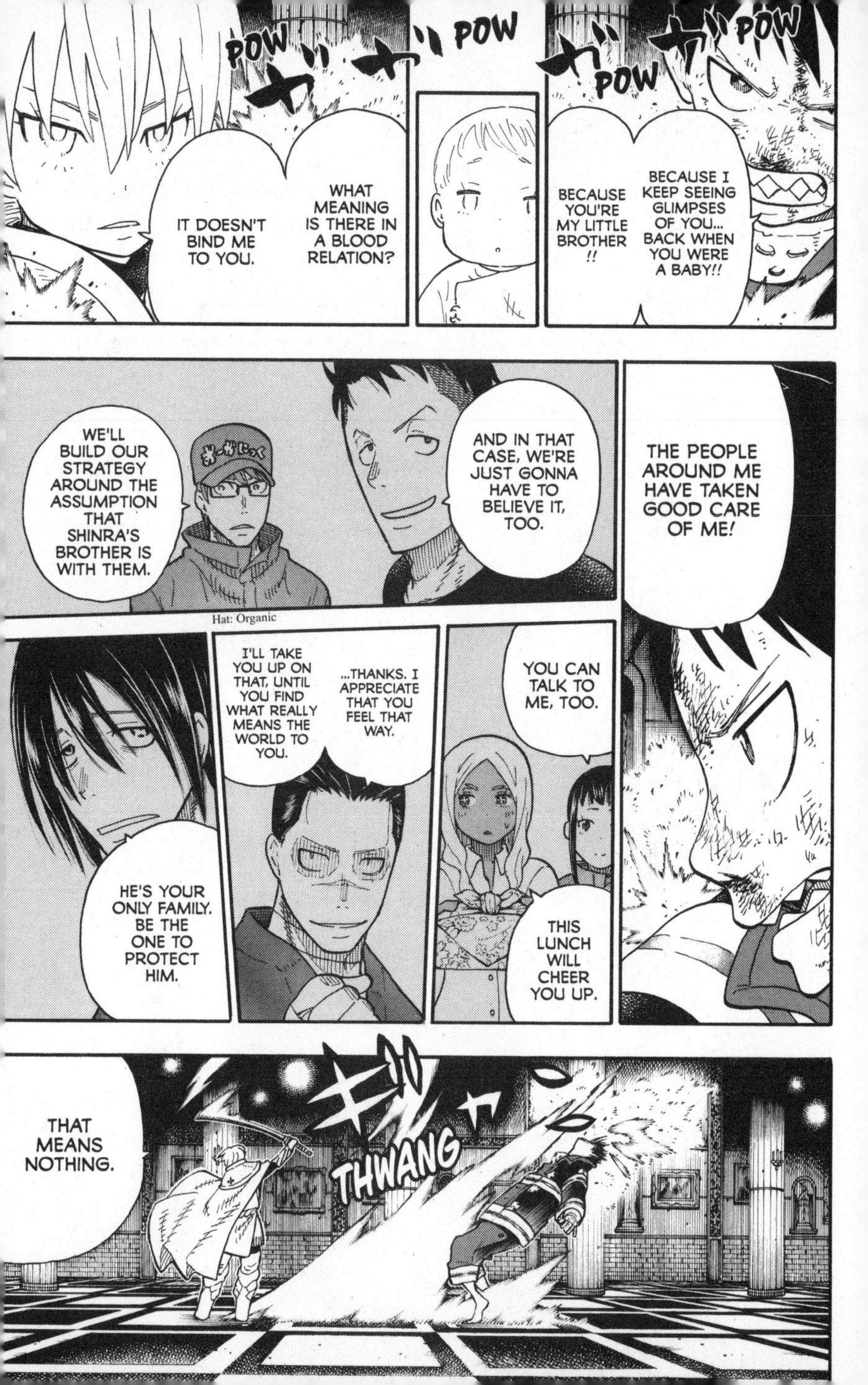
POW
POW
POW
POW
BECAUSE I KEEP SEEING GLIMPSES OF YOU... BACK WHEN YOU WERE A BABY!!
BECAUSE YOU'RE MY LITTLE BROTHER!!
WHAT MEANING IS THERE IN A BLOOD RELATION?
IT DOESN'T BIND ME TO YOU.
THE PEOPLE AROUND ME HAVE TAKEN GOOD CARE OF ME!
WE'LL BUILD OUR STRATEGY AROUND THE ASSUMPTION THAT SHINRA'S BROTHER IS WITH THEM.
AND IN THAT CASE, WE'RE JUST GONNA HAVE TO BELIEVE IT, TOO.
Hat: Organic
YOU CAN TALK TO ME, TOO.
THIS LUNCH WILL CHEER YOU UP.
...THANKS. I APPRECIATE THAT YOU FEEL THAT WAY.
I'LL TAKE YOU UP ON THAT, UNTIL YOU FIND WHAT REALLY MEANS THE WORLD TO YOU.
HE'S YOUR ONLY FAMILY. BE THE ONE TO PROTECT HIM.
THWANG
THAT MEANS NOTHING.

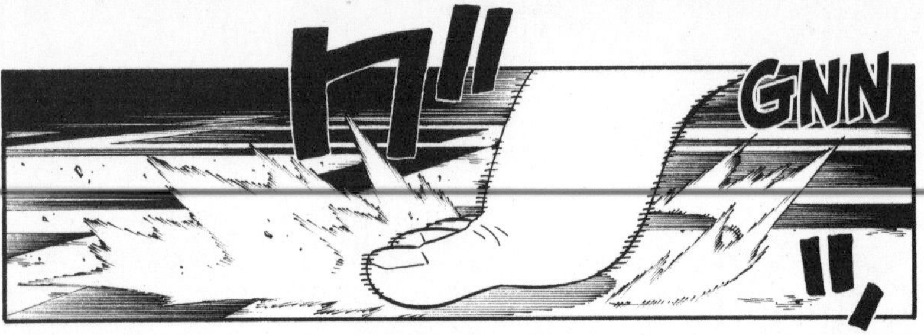
GNN

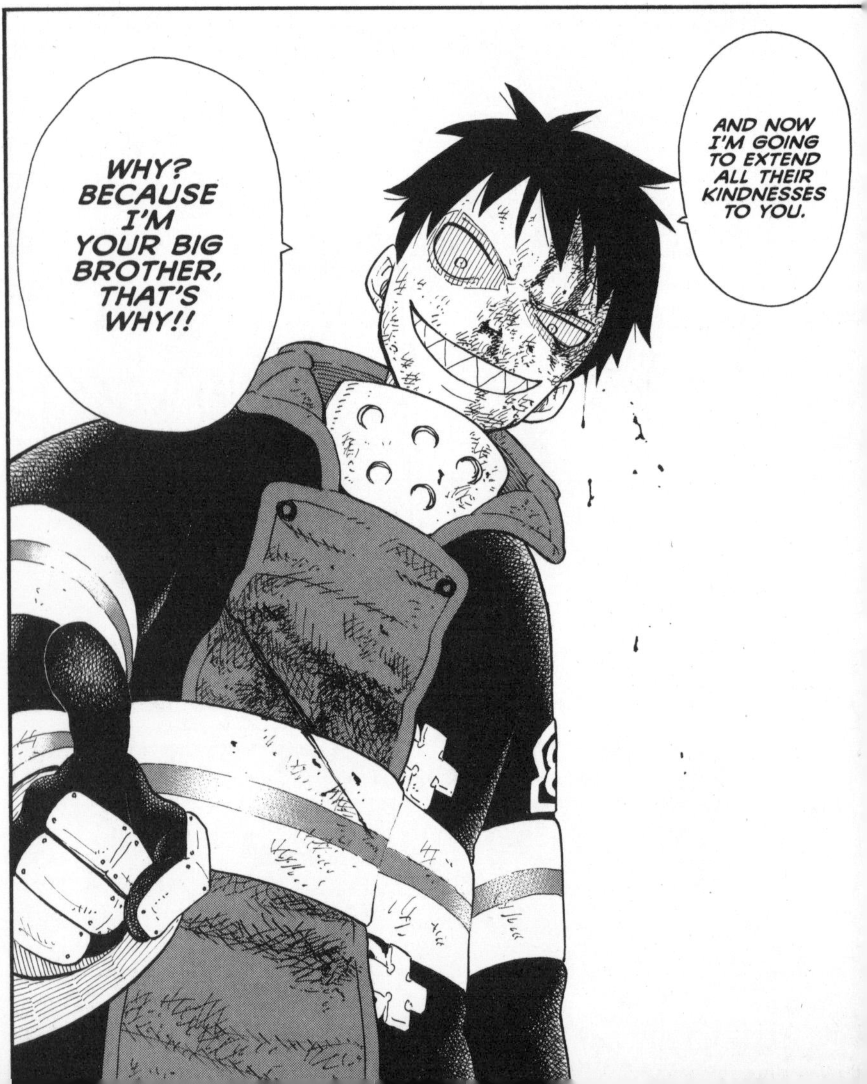
AND NOW I'M GOING TO EXTEND ALL THEIR KINDNESSES TO YOU.
WHY? BECAUSE I'M YOUR BIG BROTHER, THAT'S WHY!!

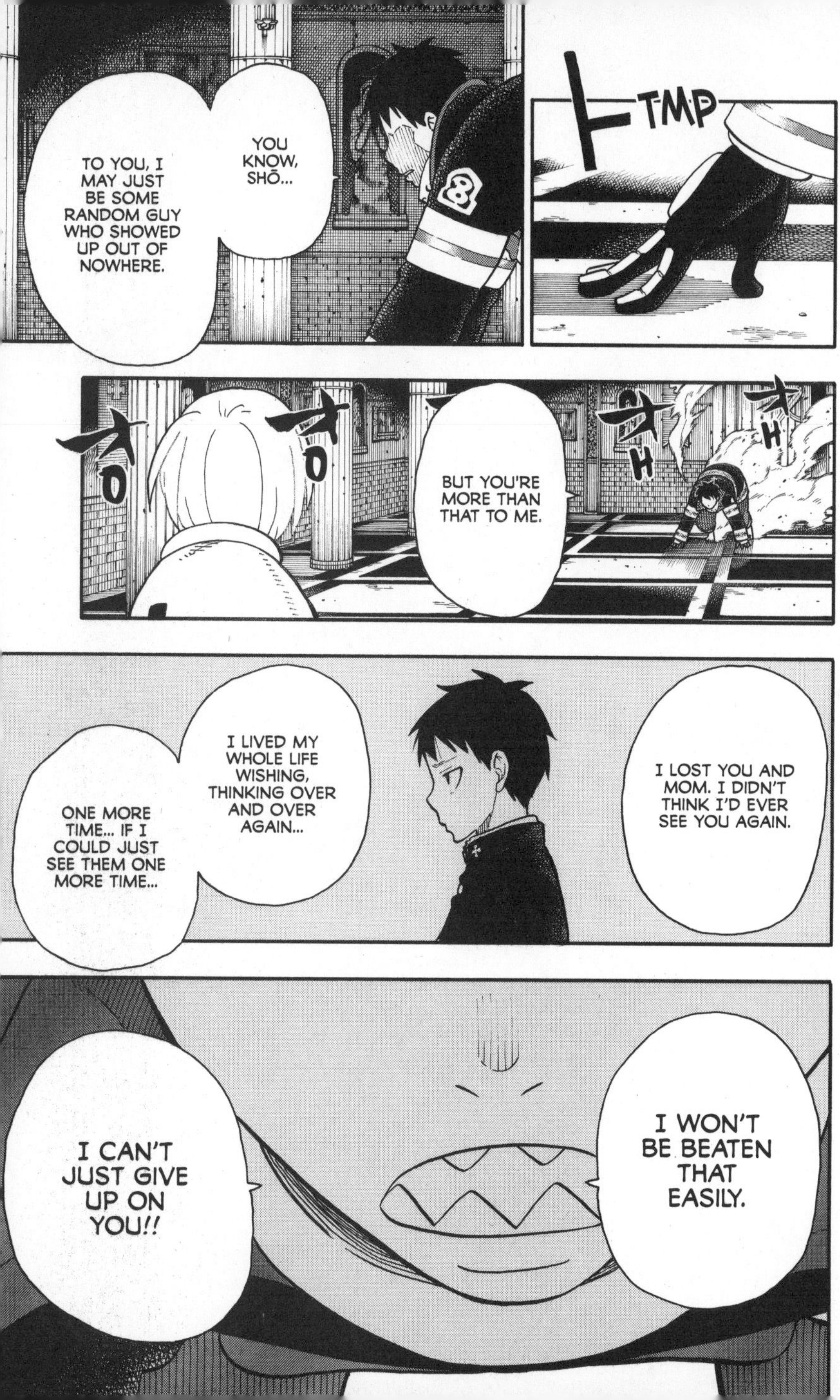
TMP
YOU KNOW, SHŌ...
TO YOU, I MAY JUST BE SOME RANDOM GUY WHO SHOWED UP OUT OF NOWHERE.
H
H
BUT YOU'RE MORE THAN THAT TO ME.
O
O
I LOST YOU AND MOM. I DIDN'T THINK I'D EVER SEE YOU AGAIN.
I LIVED MY WHOLE LIFE WISHING, THINKING OVER AND OVER AGAIN...
ONE MORE TIME... IF I COULD JUST SEE THEM ONE MORE TIME...
I WON'T BE BEATEN THAT EASILY.
I CAN'T JUST GIVE UP ON YOU!!

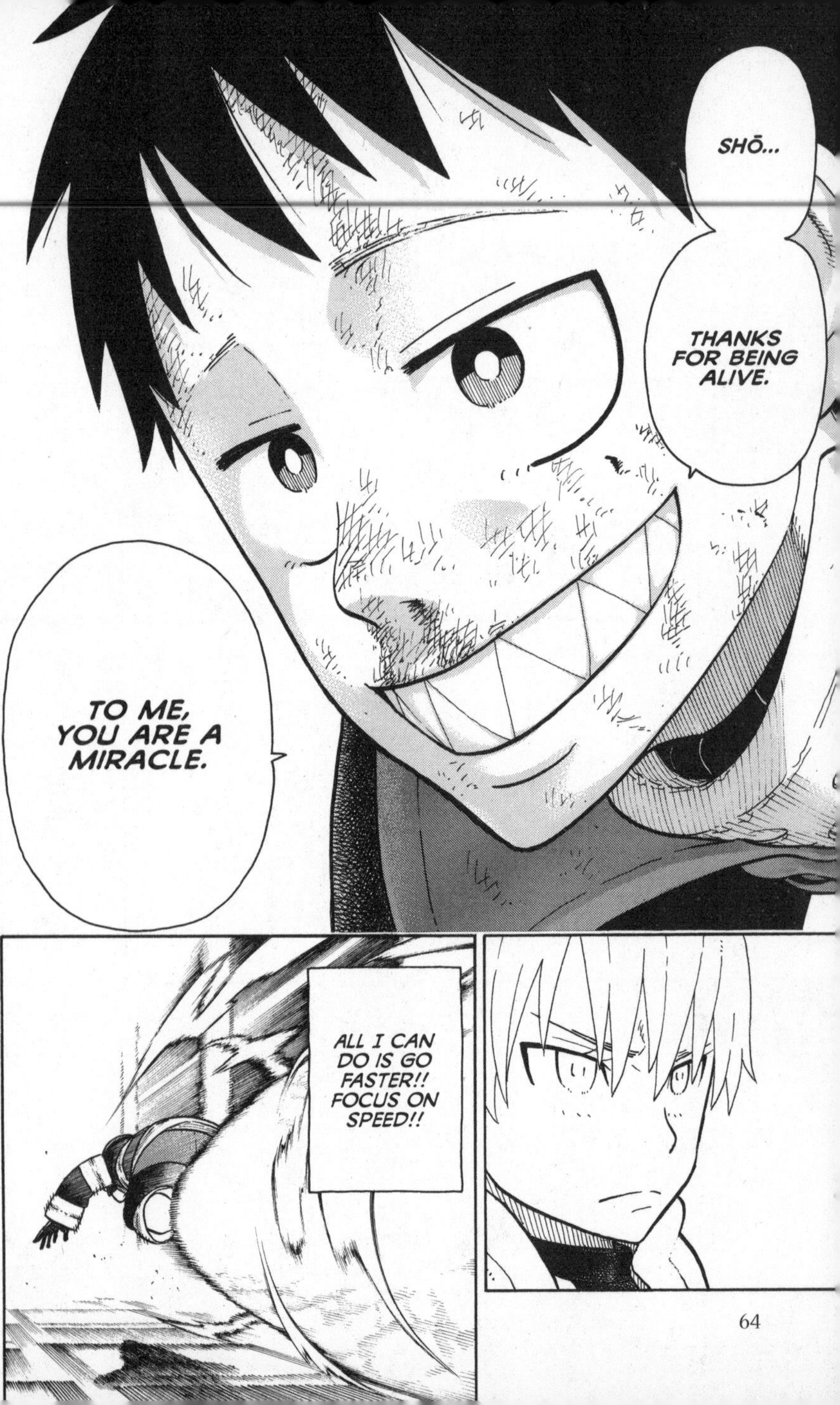
SHŌ...
THANKS FOR BEING ALIVE.
TO ME, YOU ARE A MIRACLE.
ALL I CAN DO IS GO FASTER!! FOCUS ON SPEED!!

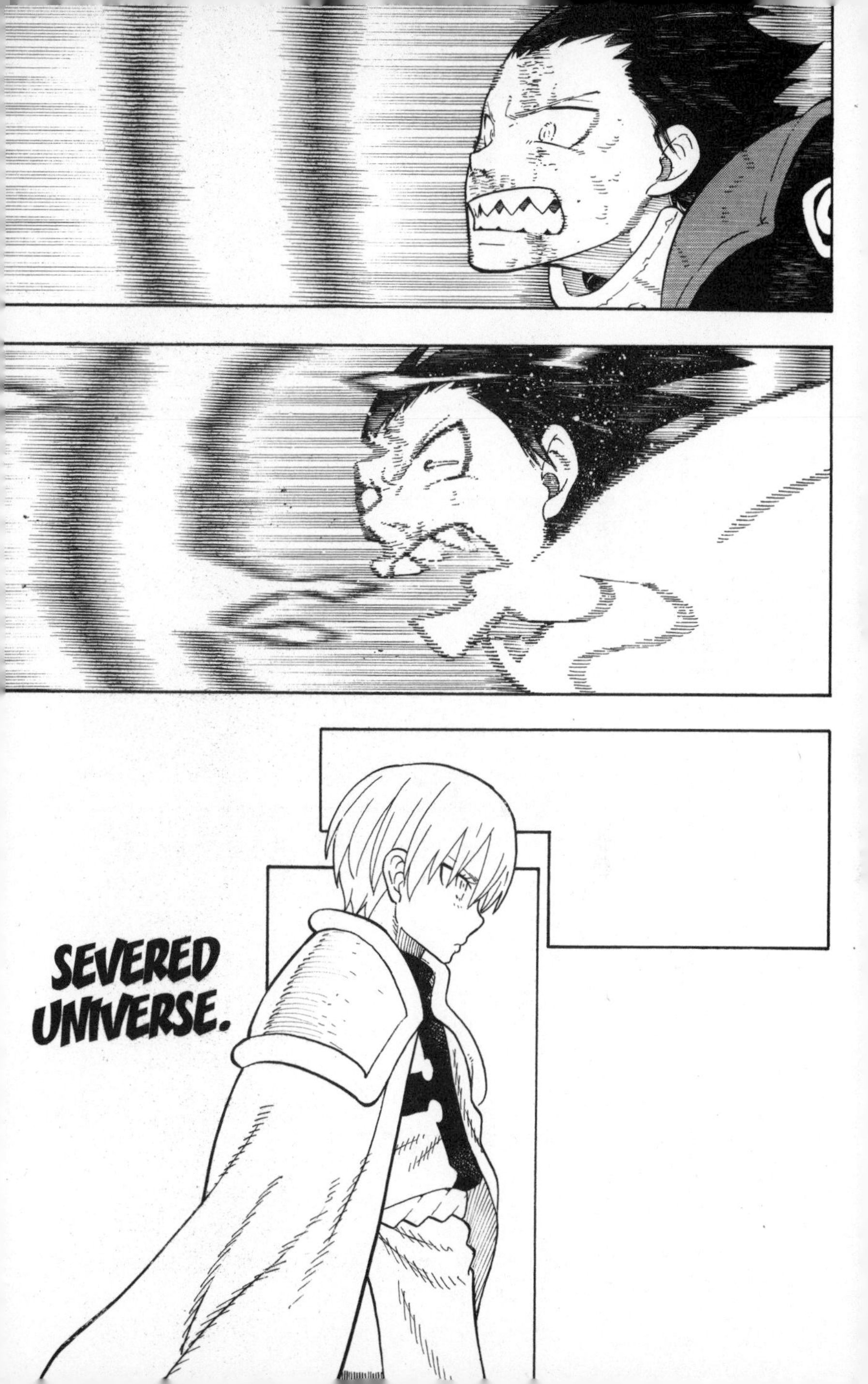
SEVERED UNIVERSE.

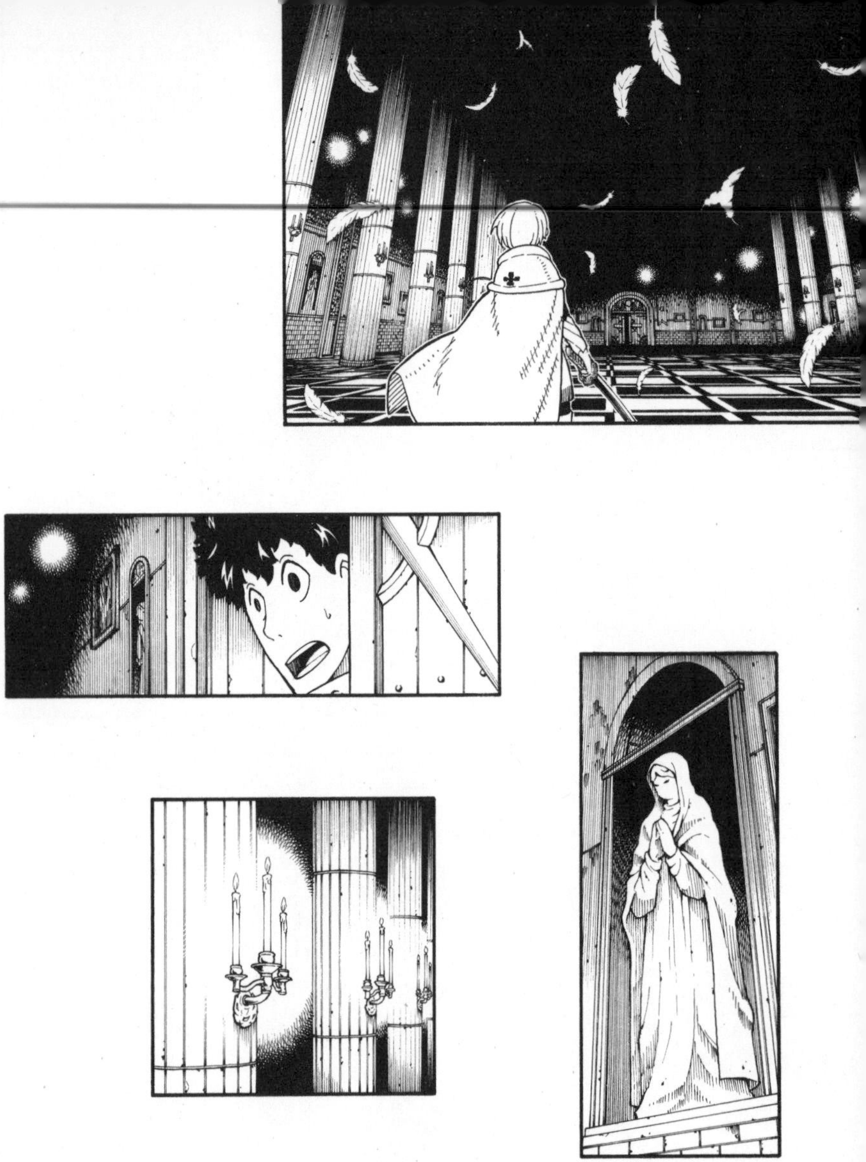

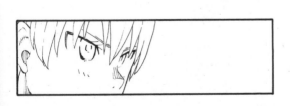

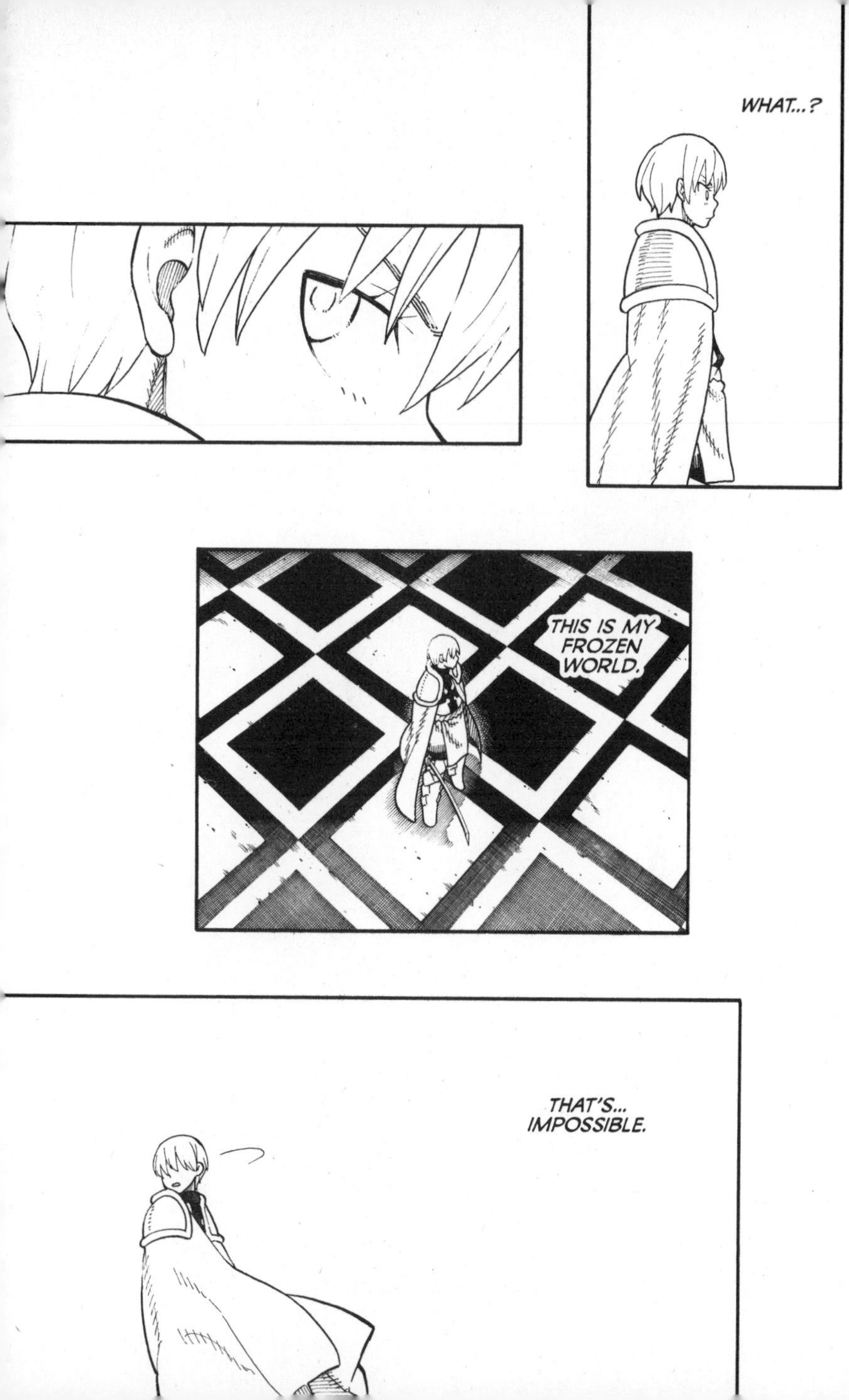
WHAT...?
THIS IS MY FROZEN WORLD.
THAT'S... IMPOSSIBLE.

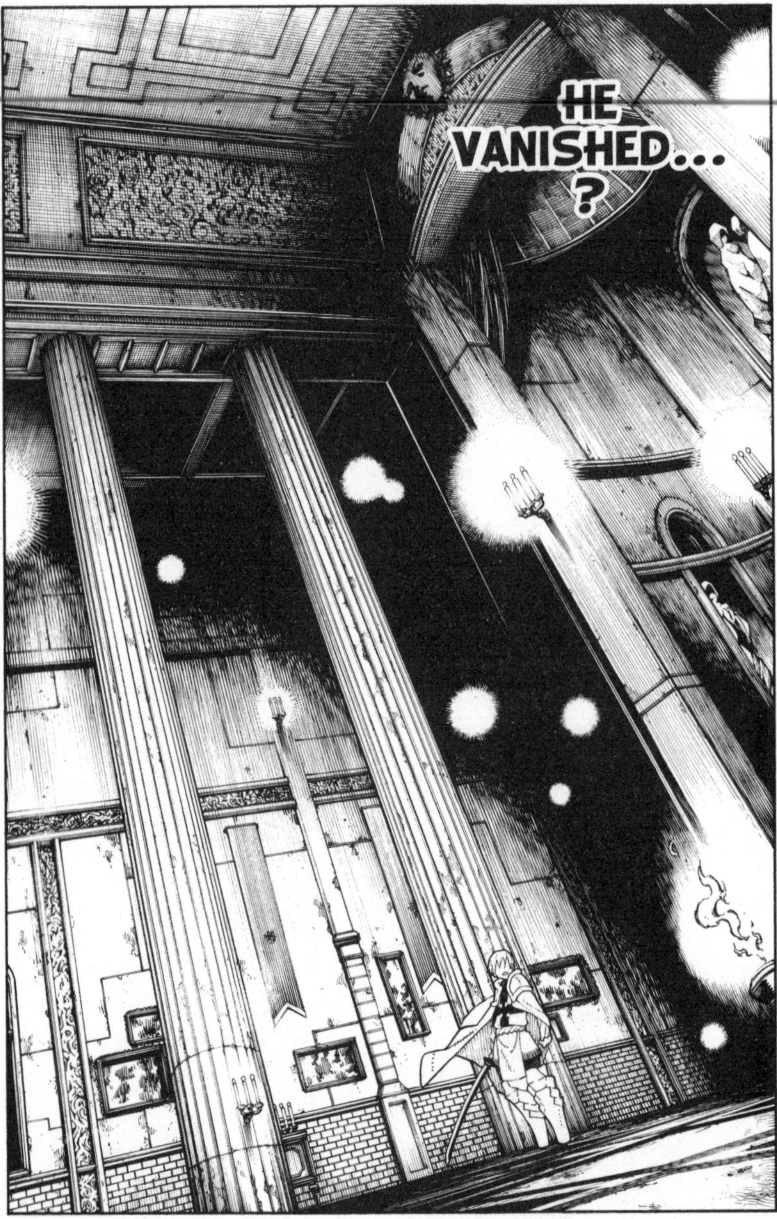
HE VANISHED...?

FIRE FORCE

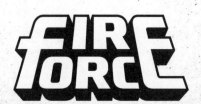

FIRE FORCE

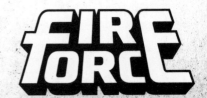

THEORY OF RELATIVITY

CHAPTER LXXXII: THE GRACE OF THE EVANGELIST

THAT'S... IMPOSSIBLE.

HE VANISHED...?

WHERE...?

...

WHERE IS SHINRA KUSAKABE?

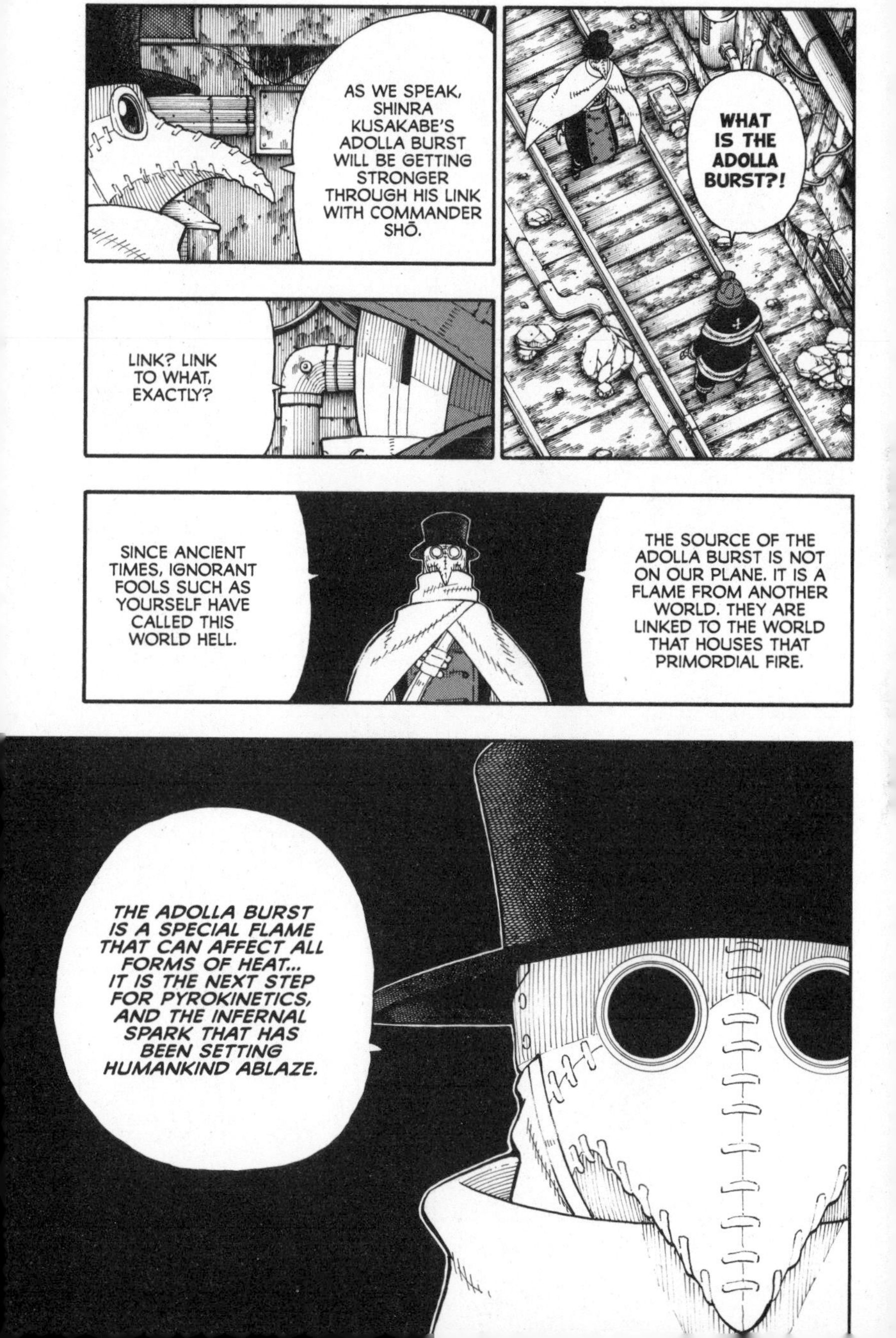
WHAT IS THE ADOLLA BURST?!
AS WE SPEAK, SHINRA KUSAKABE'S ADOLLA BURST WILL BE GETTING STRONGER THROUGH HIS LINK WITH COMMANDER SHŌ.
LINK? LINK TO WHAT, EXACTLY?
THE SOURCE OF THE ADOLLA BURST IS NOT ON OUR PLANE. IT IS A FLAME FROM ANOTHER WORLD. THEY ARE LINKED TO THE WORLD THAT HOUSES THAT PRIMORDIAL FIRE.
SINCE ANCIENT TIMES, IGNORANT FOOLS SUCH AS YOURSELF HAVE CALLED THIS WORLD HELL.
THE ADOLLA BURST IS A SPECIAL FLAME THAT CAN AFFECT ALL FORMS OF HEAT... IT IS THE NEXT STEP FOR PYROKINETICS, AND THE INFERNAL SPARK THAT HAS BEEN SETTING HUMANKIND ABLAZE.

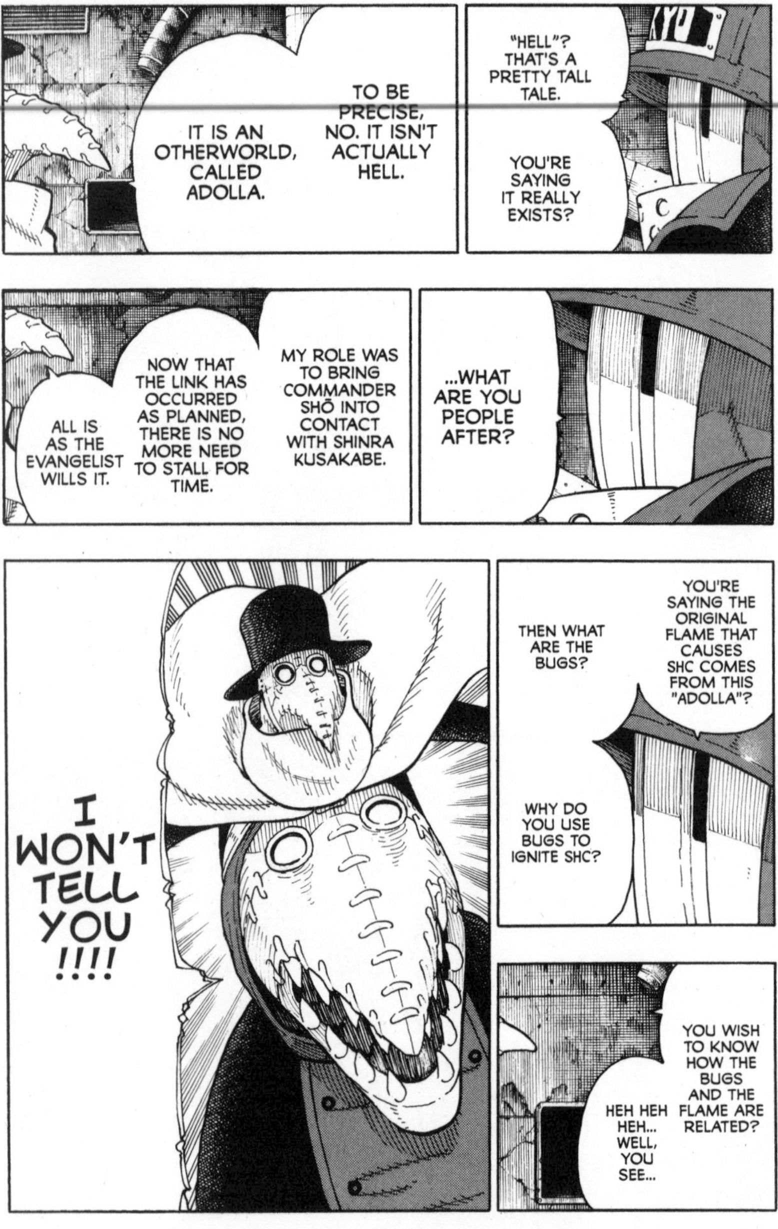
"HELL"? THAT'S A PRETTY TALL TALE.
YOU'RE SAYING IT REALLY EXISTS?
TO BE PRECISE, NO. IT ISN'T ACTUALLY HELL.
IT IS AN OTHERWORLD, CALLED ADOLLA.
...WHAT ARE YOU PEOPLE AFTER?
MY ROLE WAS TO BRING COMMANDER SHŌ INTO CONTACT WITH SHINRA KUSAKABE.
NOW THAT THE LINK HAS OCCURRED AS PLANNED, THERE IS NO MORE NEED TO STALL FOR TIME.
ALL IS AS THE EVANGELIST WILLS IT.
YOU'RE SAYING THE ORIGINAL FLAME THAT CAUSES SHC COMES FROM THIS "ADOLLA"?
THEN WHAT ARE THE BUGS?
WHY DO YOU USE BUGS TO IGNITE SHC?
YOU WISH TO KNOW HOW THE BUGS AND THE FLAME ARE RELATED?
HEH HEH HEH... WELL, YOU SEE...
I WON'T TELL YOU!!!!

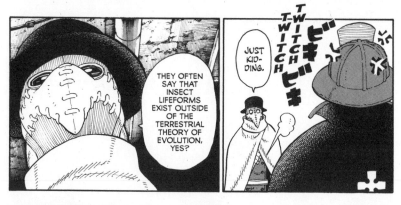

T-WITCH T-WITCH
ビキビキ
JUST KID-DING.
THEY OFTEN SAY THAT INSECT LIFEFORMS EXIST OUTSIDE OF THE TERRESTRIAL THEORY OF EVOLUTION, YES?
WHERE DO THE BUGS COME FROM? THERE ARE EVEN THOSE AMONG RESEARCHERS WHO HYPOTHESIZE THAT THEY COME FROM OUTER SPACE.
THE ORIGINS OF INSECTS ARE UNKNOWN TO US... WHAT IF THEY CAME FROM ADOLLA?
"LIKE A MOTH TO A FLAME"... WHAT IF THOSE MOTHS ARE TRYING TO RETURN TO THEIR MOTHER FLAME?
...

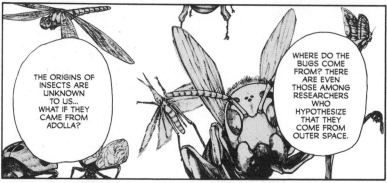

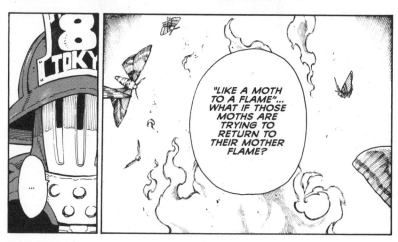

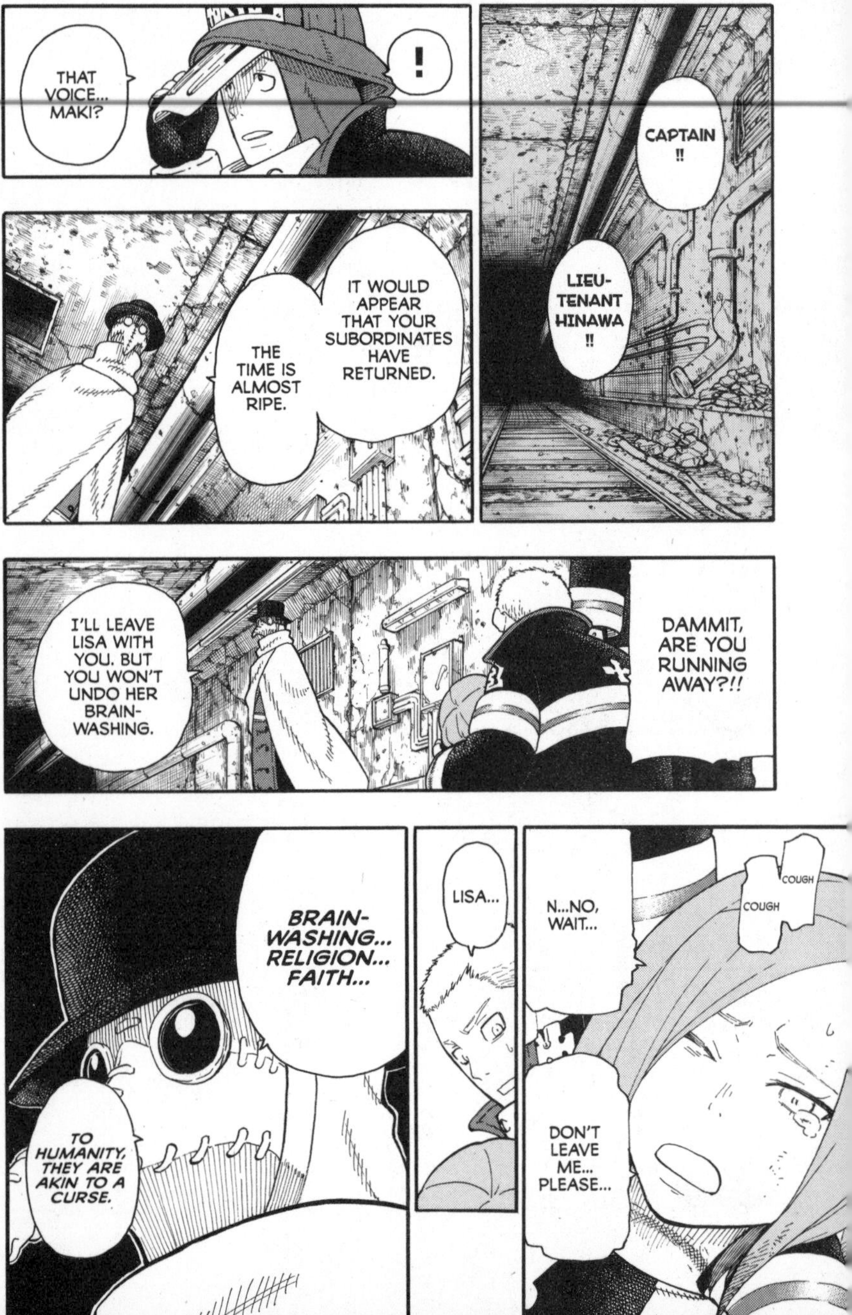
CAPTAIN!!
LIEUTENANT HINAWA!!
!
THAT VOICE... MAKI?
IT WOULD APPEAR THAT YOUR SUBORDINATES HAVE RETURNED.
THE TIME IS ALMOST RIPE.
DAMMIT, ARE YOU RUNNING AWAY?!!
I'LL LEAVE LISA WITH YOU. BUT YOU WON'T UNDO HER BRAIN-WASHING.
COUGH
COUGH
N...NO, WAIT...
DON'T LEAVE ME... PLEASE...
LISA...
BRAIN-WASHING... RELIGION... FAITH...
TO HUMANITY, THEY ARE AKIN TO A CURSE.

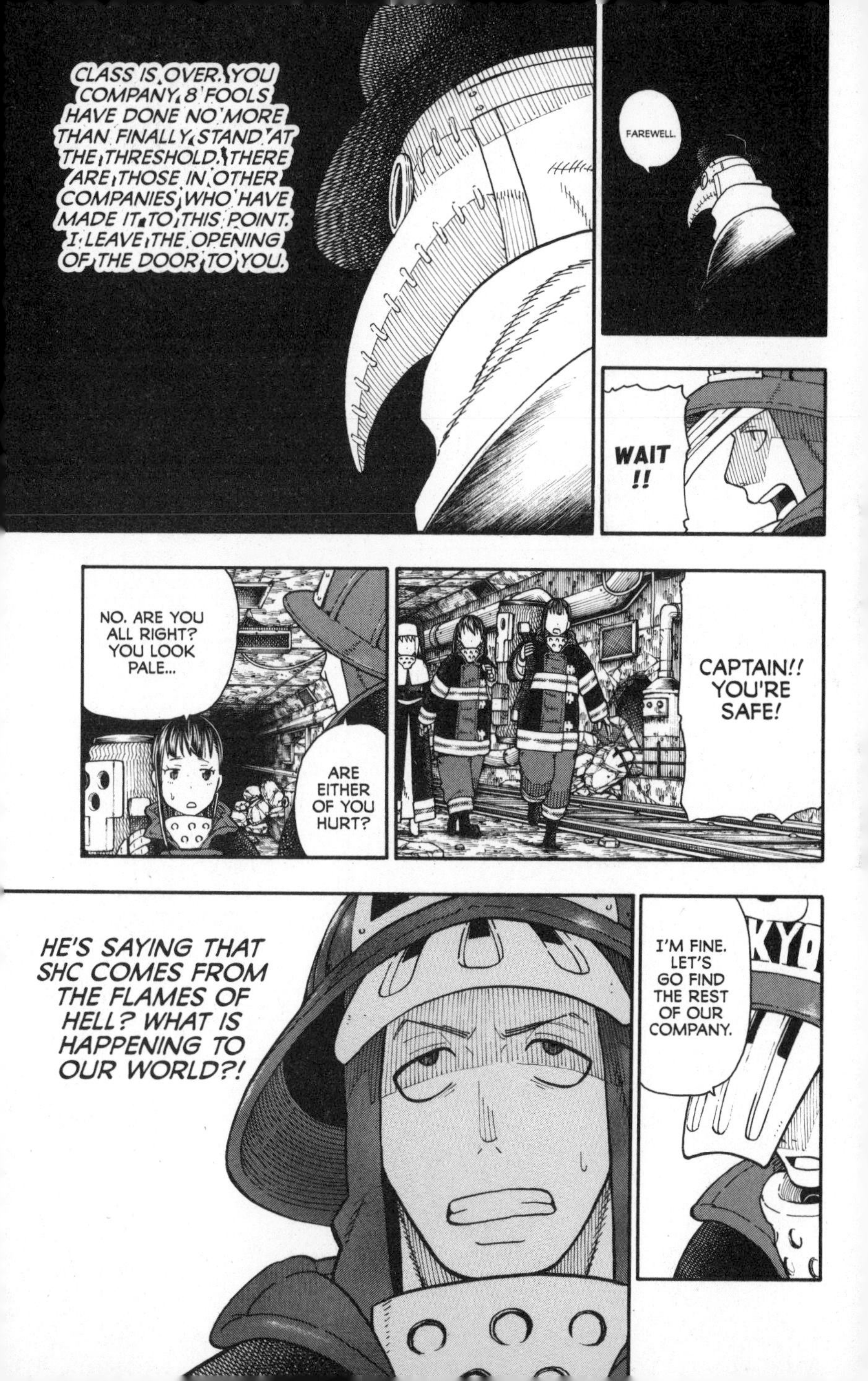
FAREWELL.
WAIT!!
CLASS IS OVER. YOU COMPANY 8 FOOLS HAVE DONE NO MORE THAN FINALLY STAND AT THE THRESHOLD. THERE ARE THOSE IN OTHER COMPANIES WHO HAVE MADE IT TO THIS POINT. I LEAVE THE OPENING OF THE DOOR TO YOU.
CAPTAIN!! YOU'RE SAFE!
ARE EITHER OF YOU HURT?
NO. ARE YOU ALL RIGHT? YOU LOOK PALE...
I'M FINE. LET'S GO FIND THE REST OF OUR COMPANY.
HE'S SAYING THAT SHC COMES FROM THE FLAMES OF HELL? WHAT IS HAPPENING TO OUR WORLD?!

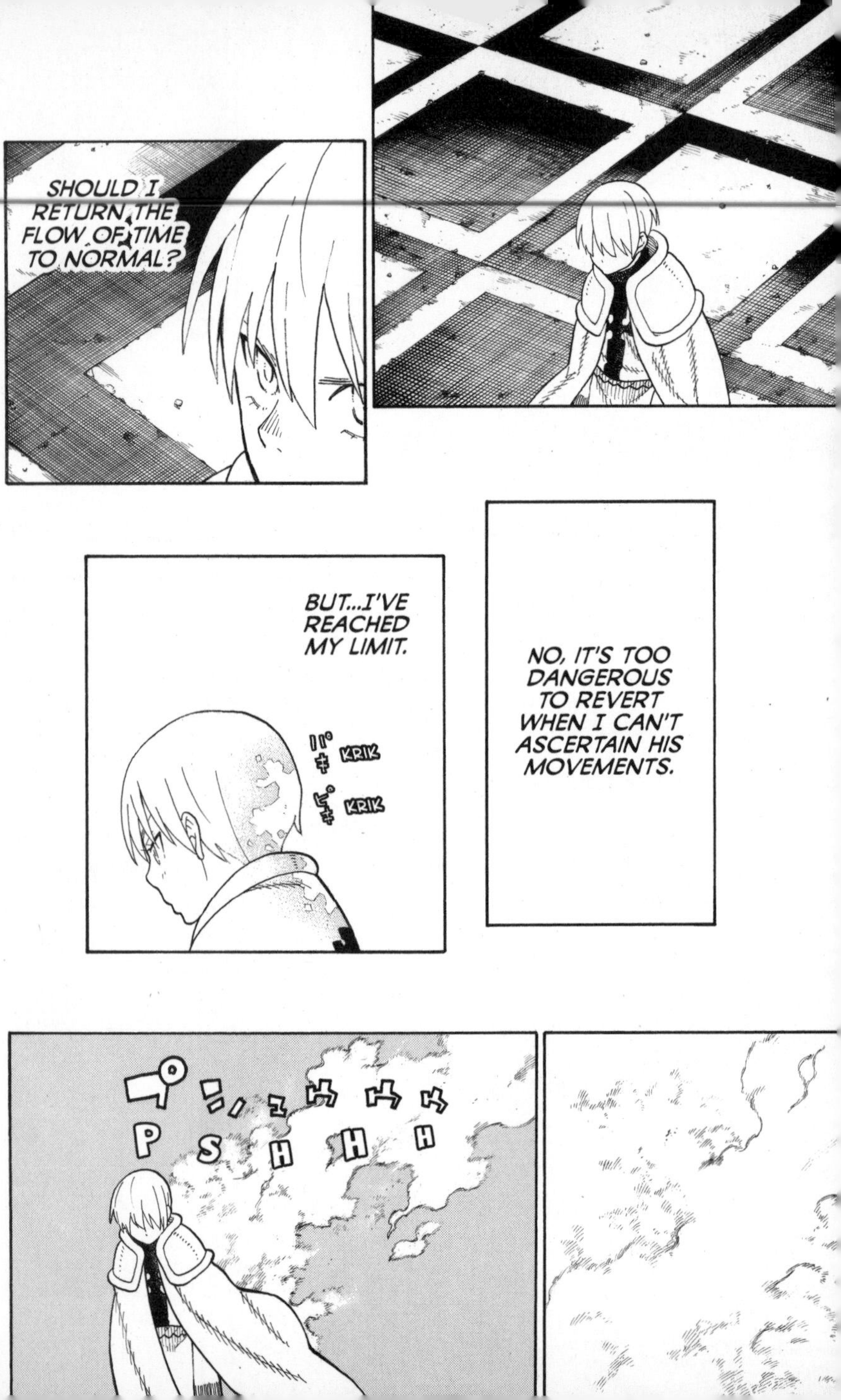
SHOULD I RETURN THE FLOW OF TIME TO NORMAL?
NO, IT'S TOO DANGEROUS TO REVERT WHEN I CAN'T ASCERTAIN HIS MOVEMENTS.
BUT...I'VE REACHED MY LIMIT.
KRIK
KRIK
PSHHH

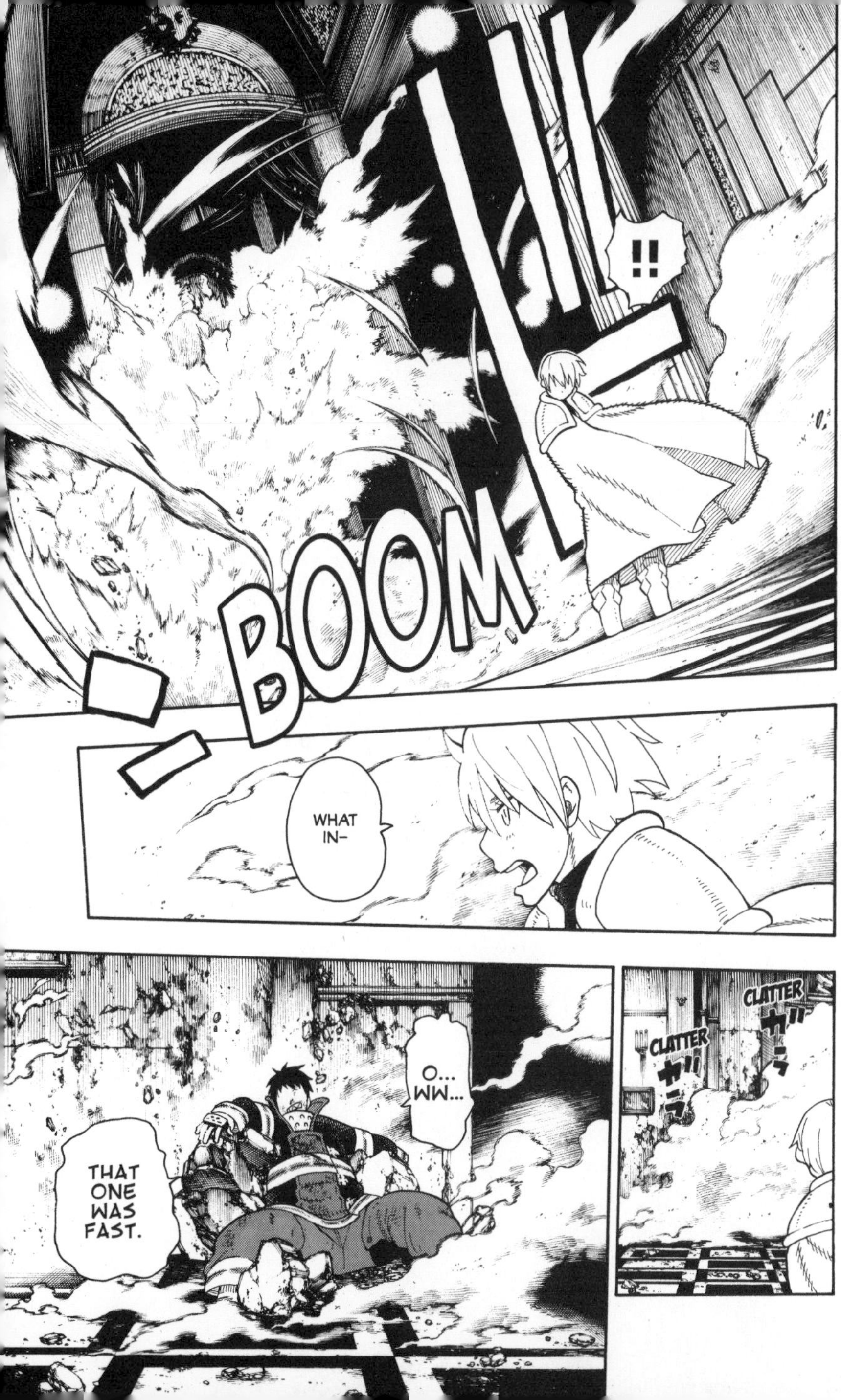
!!
BOOM
WHAT IN–
CLATTER
CLATTER
O... WW...
THAT ONE WAS FAST.

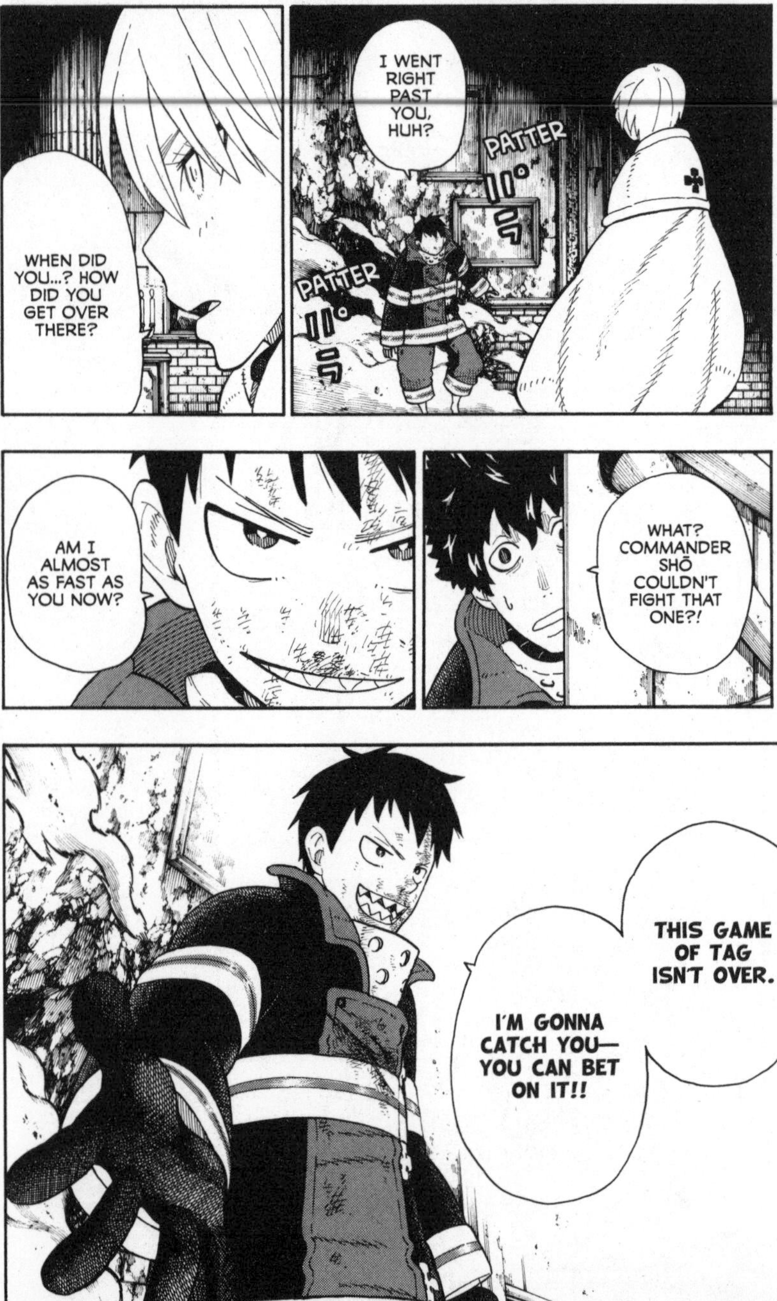
I WENT RIGHT PAST YOU, HUH?
PATTER
PATTER
WHEN DID YOU...? HOW DID YOU GET OVER THERE?
WHAT? COMMANDER SHŌ COULDN'T FIGHT THAT ONE?!
AM I ALMOST AS FAST AS YOU NOW?
THIS GAME OF TAG ISN'T OVER.
I'M GONNA CATCH YOU—YOU CAN BET ON IT!!

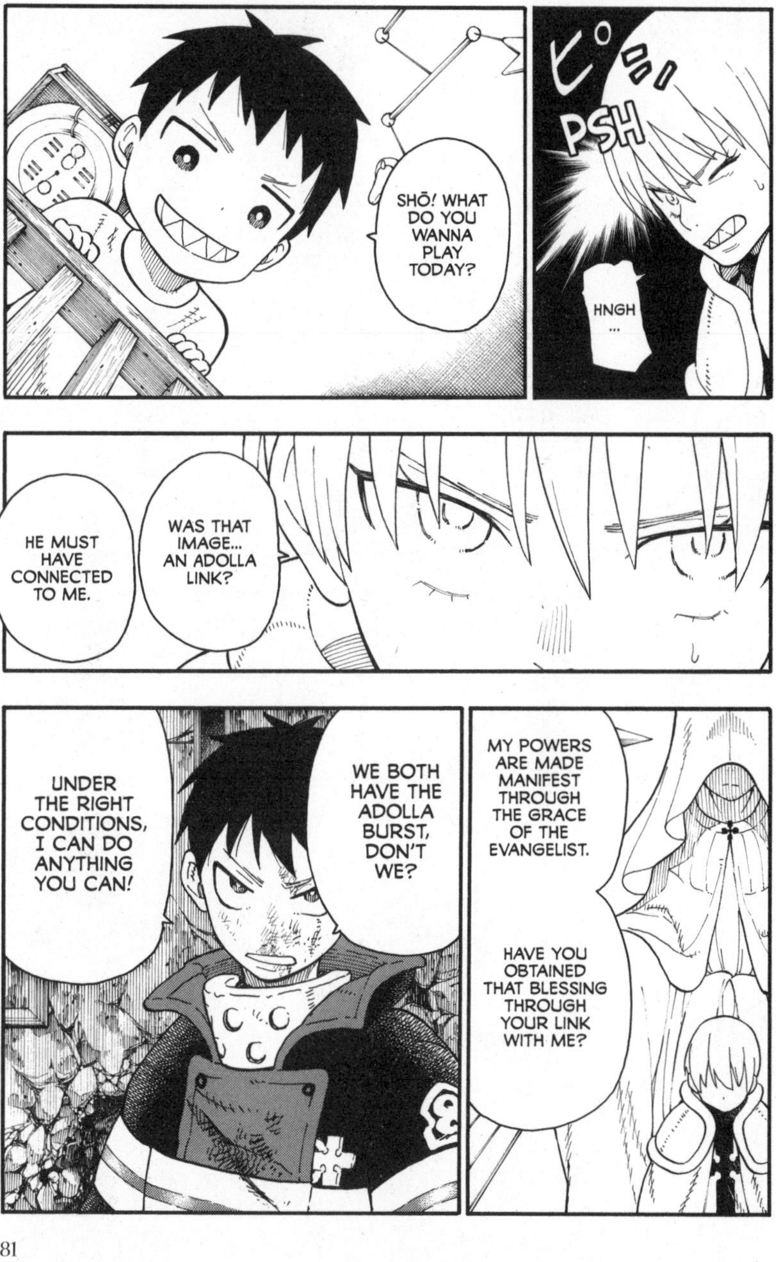
ピ
PSH
HNGH...
SHŌ! WHAT DO YOU WANNA PLAY TODAY?
WAS THAT IMAGE... AN ADOLLA LINK?
HE MUST HAVE CONNECTED TO ME.
MY POWERS ARE MADE MANIFEST THROUGH THE GRACE OF THE EVANGELIST.
HAVE YOU OBTAINED THAT BLESSING THROUGH YOUR LINK WITH ME?
WE BOTH HAVE THE ADOLLA BURST, DON'T WE?
UNDER THE RIGHT CONDITIONS, I CAN DO ANYTHING YOU CAN!

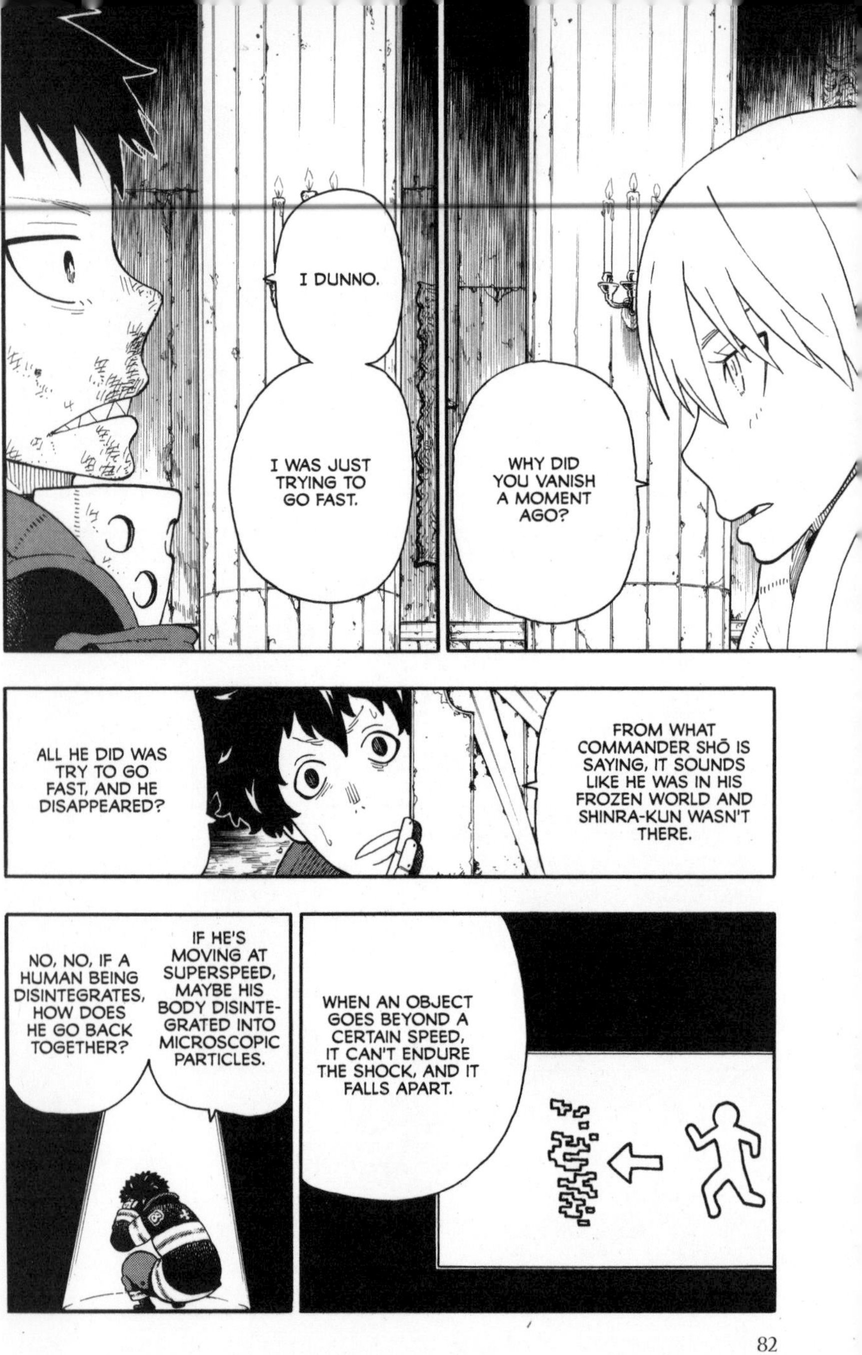
WHY DID YOU VANISH A MOMENT AGO?
I DUNNO.
I WAS JUST TRYING TO GO FAST.
FROM WHAT COMMANDER SHŌ IS SAYING, IT SOUNDS LIKE HE WAS IN HIS FROZEN WORLD AND SHINRA-KUN WASN'T THERE.
ALL HE DID WAS TRY TO GO FAST, AND HE DISAPPEARED?
WHEN AN OBJECT GOES BEYOND A CERTAIN SPEED, IT CAN'T ENDURE THE SHOCK, AND IT FALLS APART.
IF HE'S MOVING AT SUPERSPEED, MAYBE HIS BODY DISINTEGRATED INTO MICROSCOPIC PARTICLES.
NO, NO, IF A HUMAN BEING DISINTEGRATES, HOW DOES HE GO BACK TOGETHER?

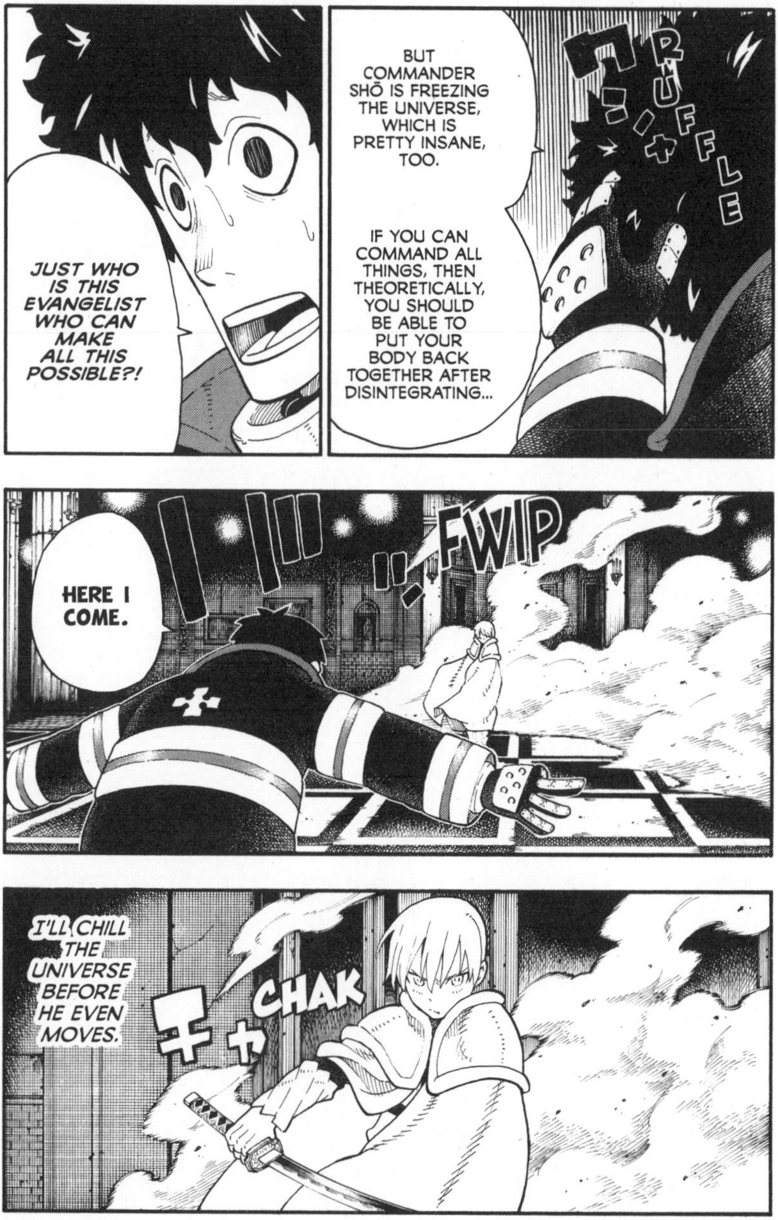
BUT COMMANDER SHŌ IS FREEZING THE UNIVERSE, WHICH IS PRETTY INSANE, TOO.
IF YOU CAN COMMAND ALL THINGS, THEN THEORETICALLY, YOU SHOULD BE ABLE TO PUT YOUR BODY BACK TOGETHER AFTER DISINTEGRATING...
RUFFLE
JUST WHO IS THIS EVANGELIST WHO CAN MAKE ALL THIS POSSIBLE?!
FWIP
HERE I COME.
I'LL CHILL THE UNIVERSE BEFORE HE EVEN MOVES.
CHAK

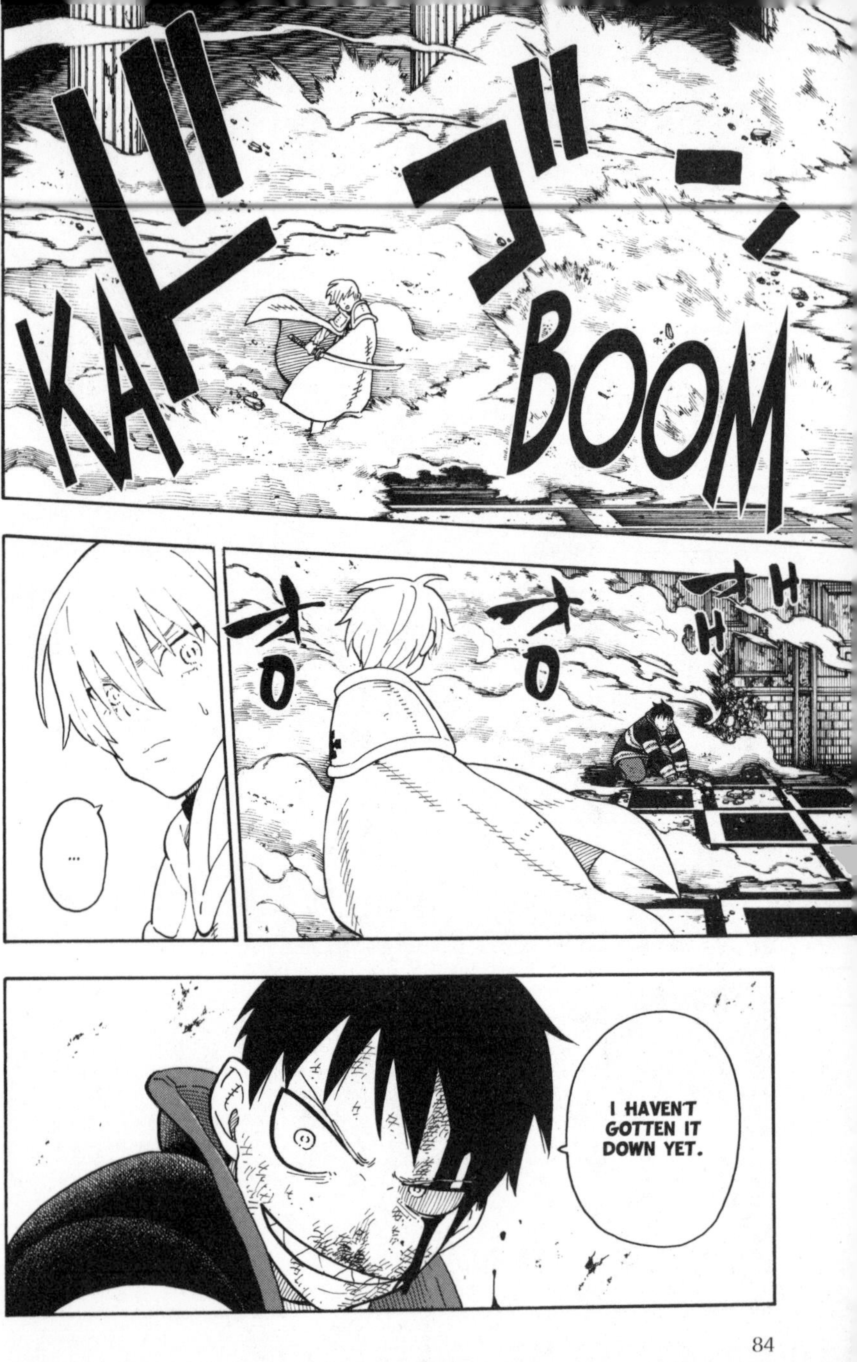
KA
BOOM
...
I HAVEN'T GOTTEN IT DOWN YET.

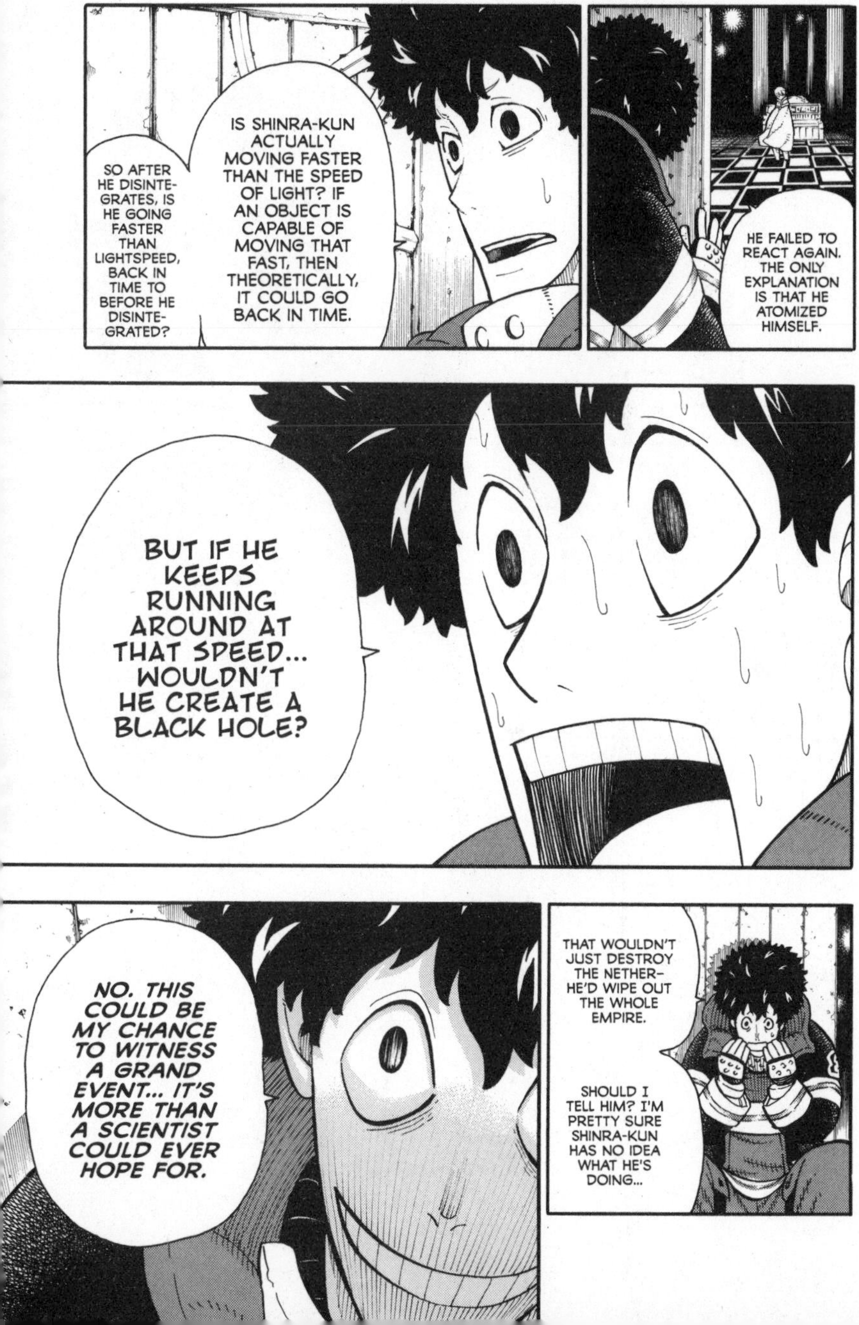
HE FAILED TO REACT AGAIN. THE ONLY EXPLANATION IS THAT HE ATOMIZED HIMSELF.
IS SHINRA-KUN ACTUALLY MOVING FASTER THAN THE SPEED OF LIGHT? IF AN OBJECT IS CAPABLE OF MOVING THAT FAST, THEN THEORETICALLY, IT COULD GO BACK IN TIME.
SO AFTER HE DISINTE-GRATES, IS HE GOING FASTER THAN LIGHTSPEED, BACK IN TIME TO BEFORE HE DISINTE-GRATED?
BUT IF HE KEEPS RUNNING AROUND AT THAT SPEED... WOULDN'T HE CREATE A BLACK HOLE?
THAT WOULDN'T JUST DESTROY THE NETHER– HE'D WIPE OUT THE WHOLE EMPIRE.
SHOULD I TELL HIM? I'M PRETTY SURE SHINRA-KUN HAS NO IDEA WHAT HE'S DOING...
NO. THIS COULD BE MY CHANCE TO WITNESS A GRAND EVENT... IT'S MORE THAN A SCIENTIST COULD EVER HOPE FOR.

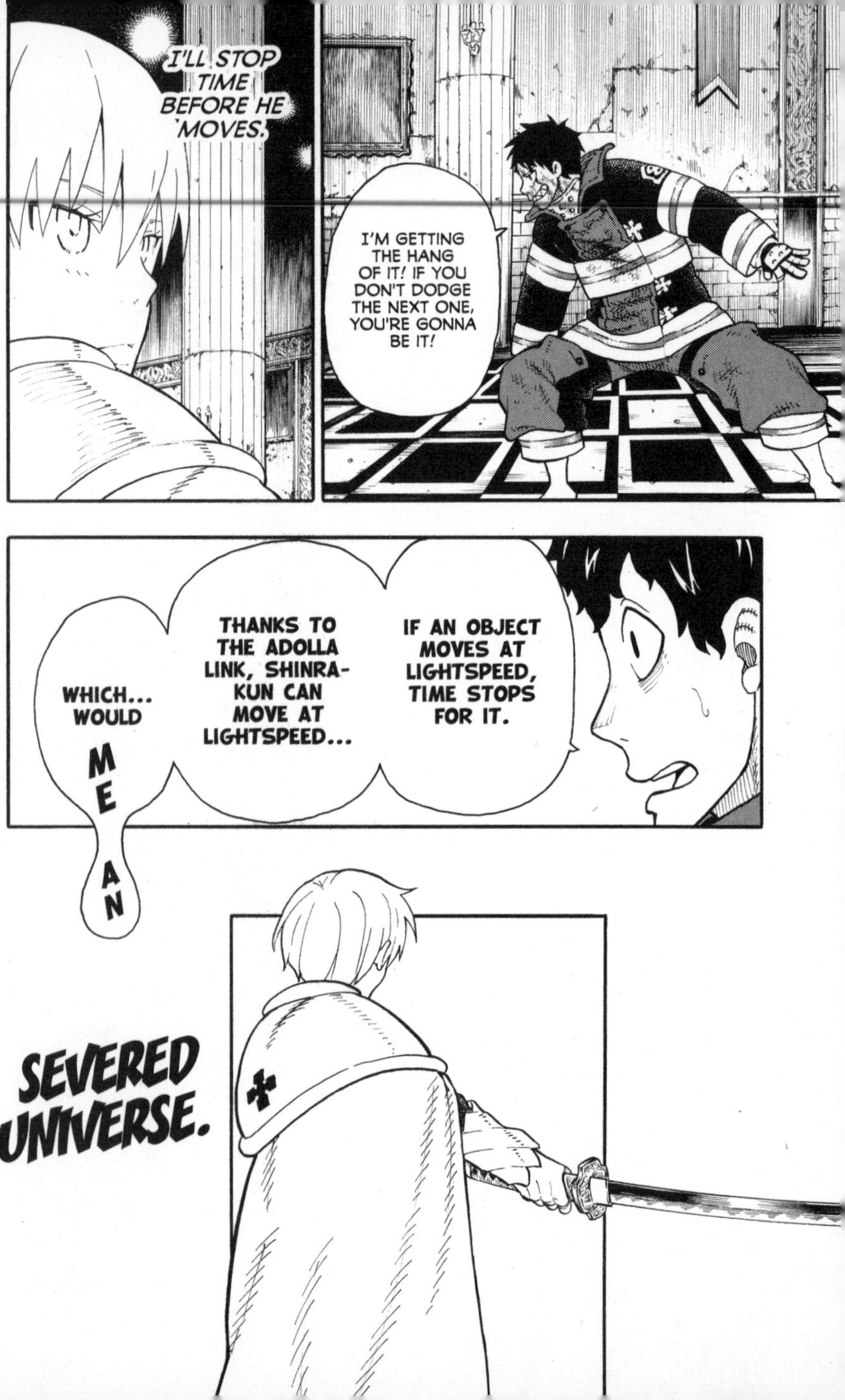
I'M GETTING THE HANG OF IT! IF YOU DON'T DODGE THE NEXT ONE, YOU'RE GONNA BE IT!
I'LL STOP TIME BEFORE HE MOVES.
IF AN OBJECT MOVES AT LIGHTSPEED, TIME STOPS FOR IT.
THANKS TO THE ADOLLA LINK, SHINRA-KUN CAN MOVE AT LIGHTSPEED...
WHICH... WOULD MEAN
SEVERED UNIVERSE.

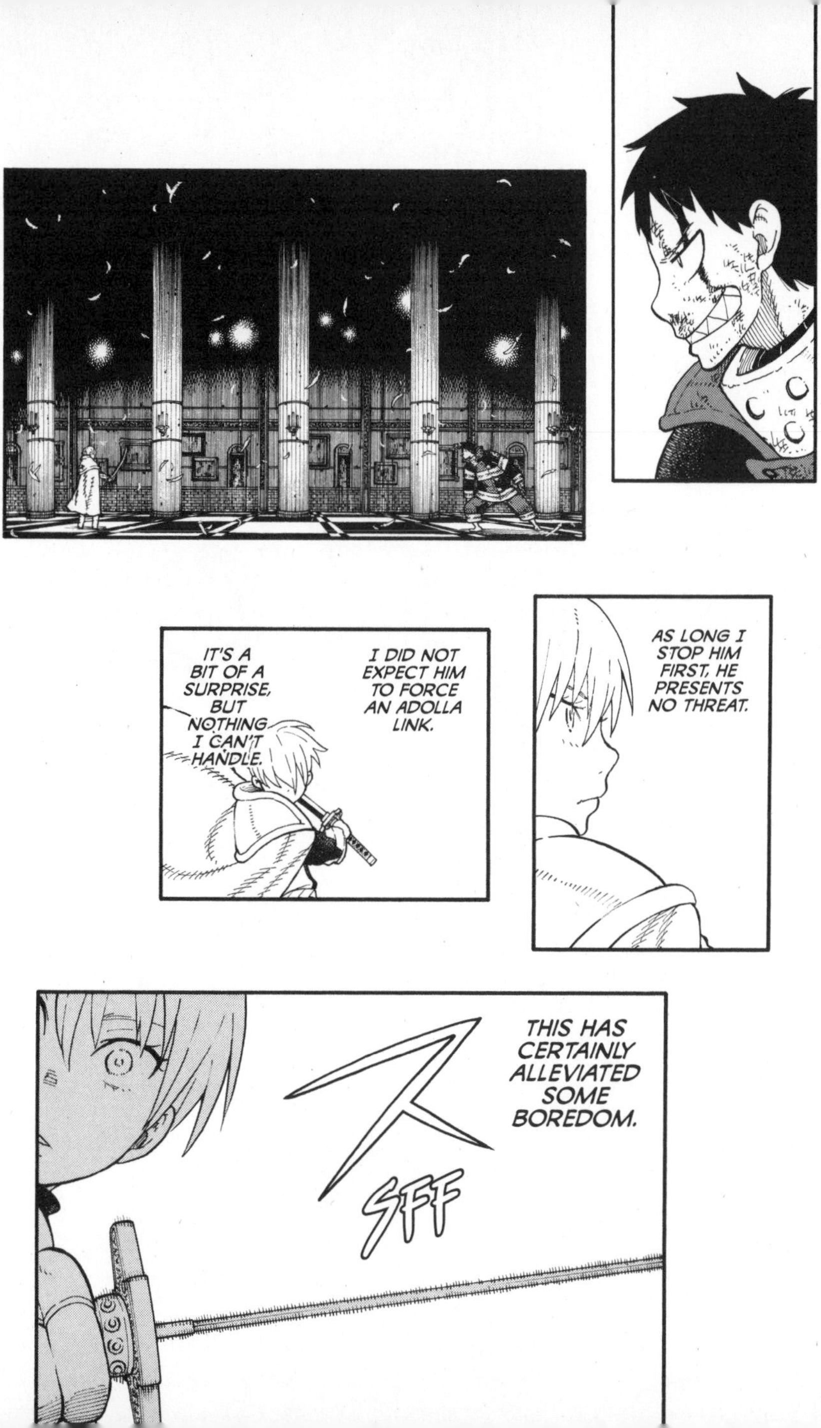
I DID NOT EXPECT HIM TO FORCE AN ADOLLA LINK.
IT'S A BIT OF A SURPRISE, BUT NOTHING I CAN'T HANDLE.
AS LONG I STOP HIM FIRST, HE PRESENTS NO THREAT.
THIS HAS CERTAINLY ALLEVIATED SOME BOREDOM.
SFF

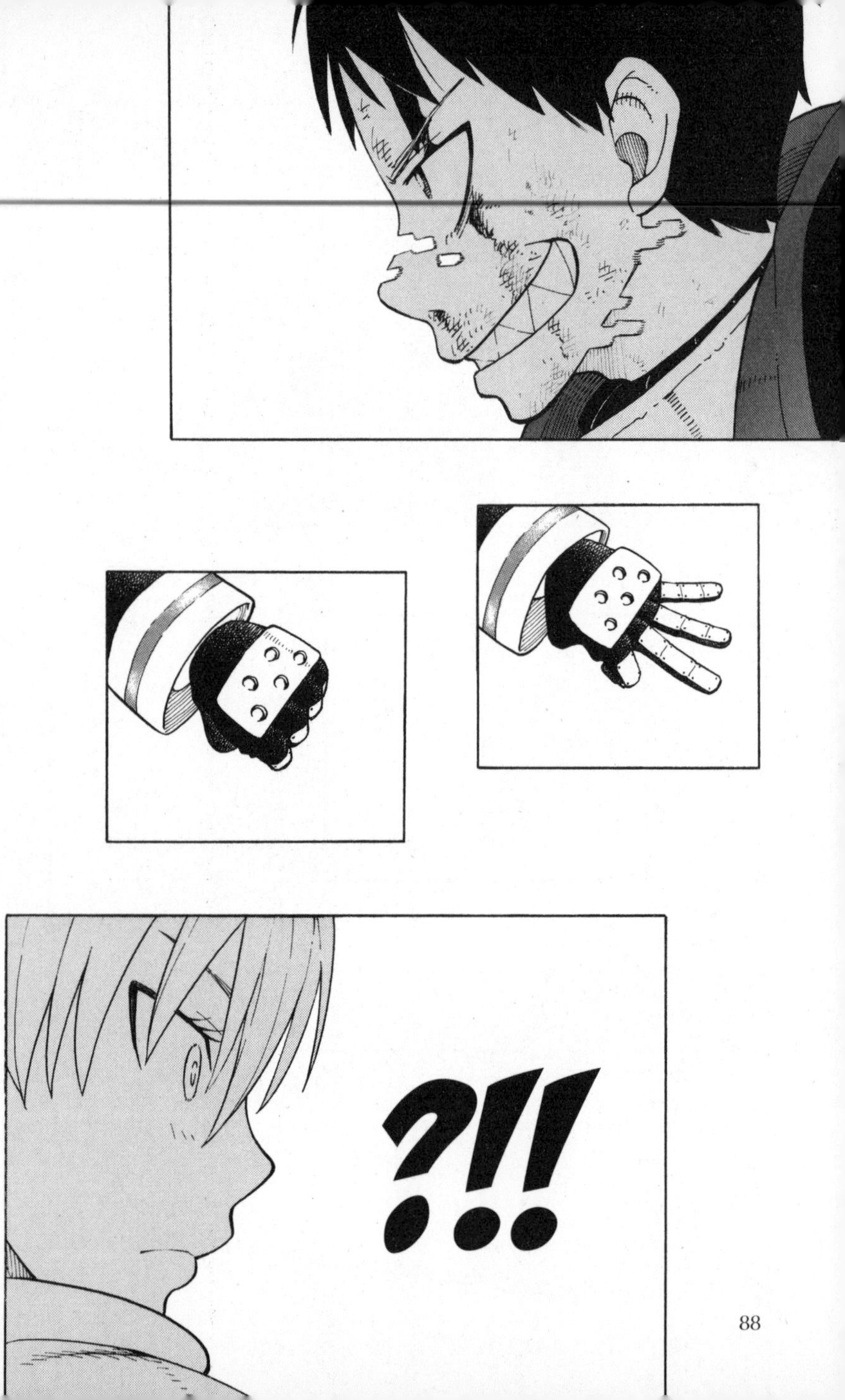
?!!

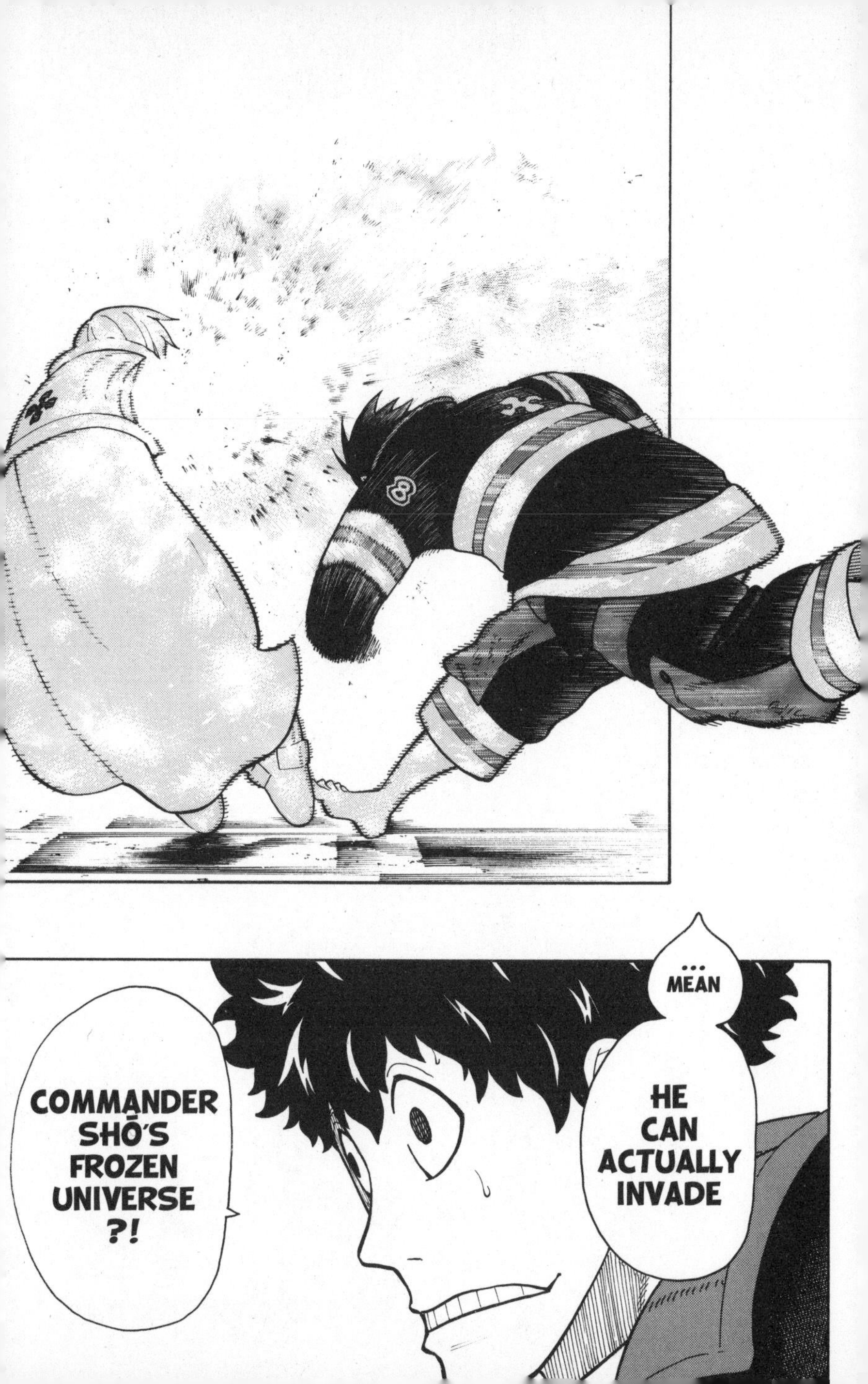
...MEAN
HE CAN ACTUALLY INVADE
COMMANDER SHŌ'S FROZEN UNIVERSE ?!

FIRE FORCE

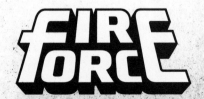

CHAPTER LXXXIII: FOURTH GENERATION

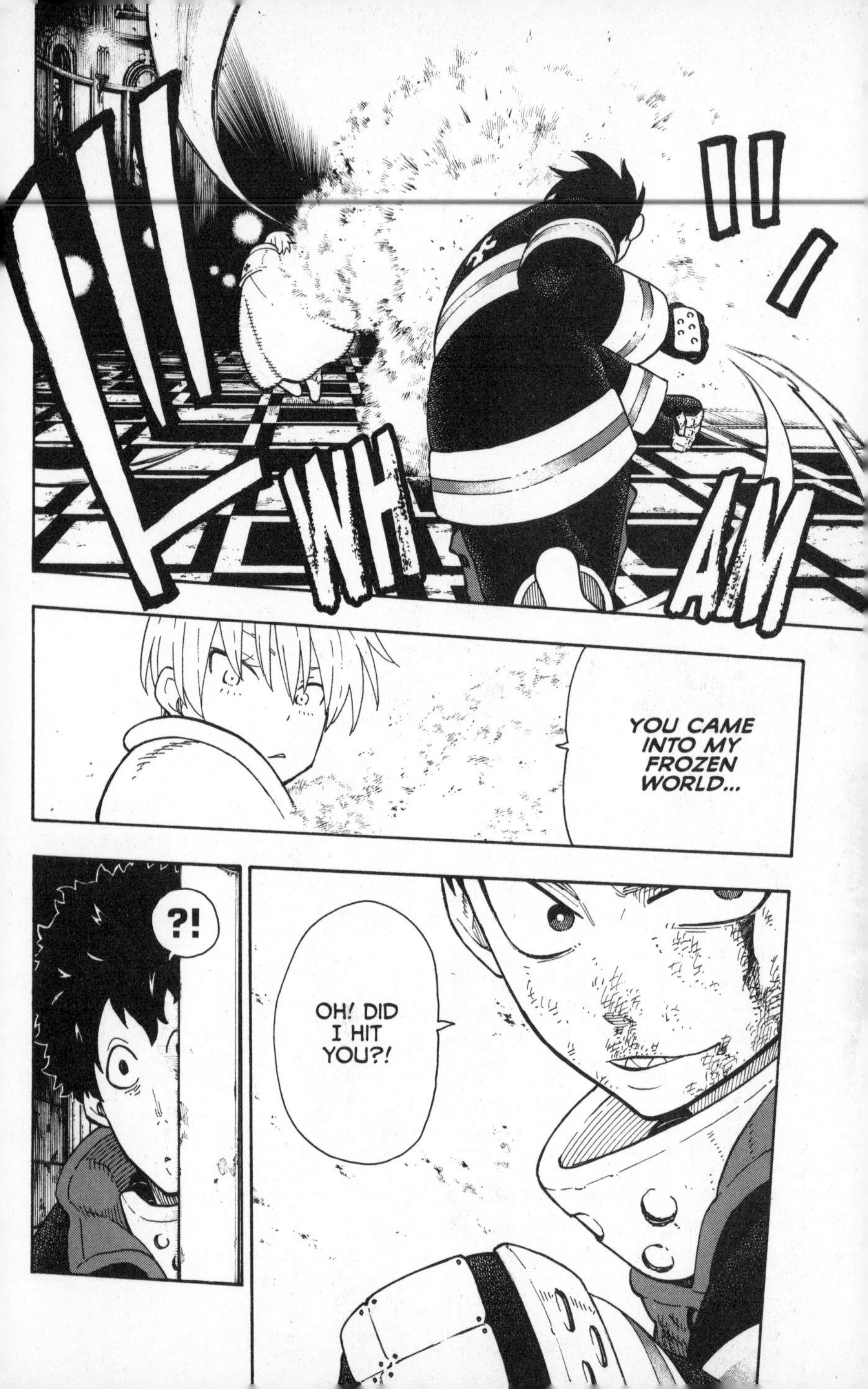
WHAM!!!
YOU CAME INTO MY FROZEN WORLD...
OH! DID I HIT YOU?!
?!

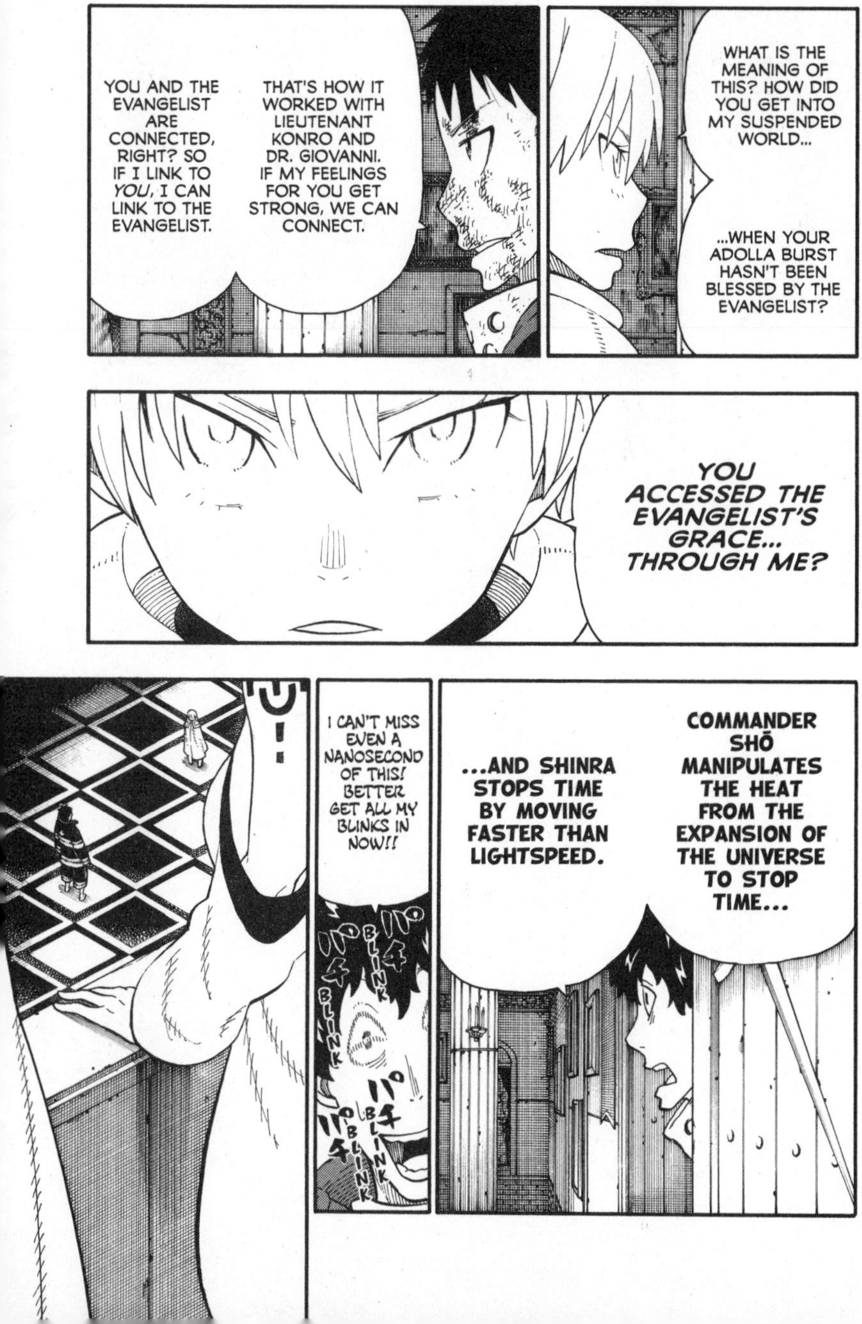
WHAT IS THE MEANING OF THIS? HOW DID YOU GET INTO MY SUSPENDED WORLD...
...WHEN YOUR ADOLLA BURST HASN'T BEEN BLESSED BY THE EVANGELIST?
THAT'S HOW IT WORKED WITH LIEUTENANT KONRO AND DR. GIOVANNI. IF MY FEELINGS FOR YOU GET STRONG, WE CAN CONNECT.
YOU AND THE EVANGELIST ARE CONNECTED, RIGHT? SO IF I LINK TO *YOU*, I CAN LINK TO THE EVANGELIST.
YOU ACCESSED THE EVANGELIST'S GRACE... THROUGH ME?
COMMANDER SHŌ MANIPULATES THE HEAT FROM THE EXPANSION OF THE UNIVERSE TO STOP TIME...
...AND SHINRA STOPS TIME BY MOVING FASTER THAN LIGHTSPEED.
I CAN'T MISS EVEN A NANOSECOND OF THIS! BETTER GET ALL MY BLINKS IN NOW!!
BLINK BLINK
BLINK BLINK

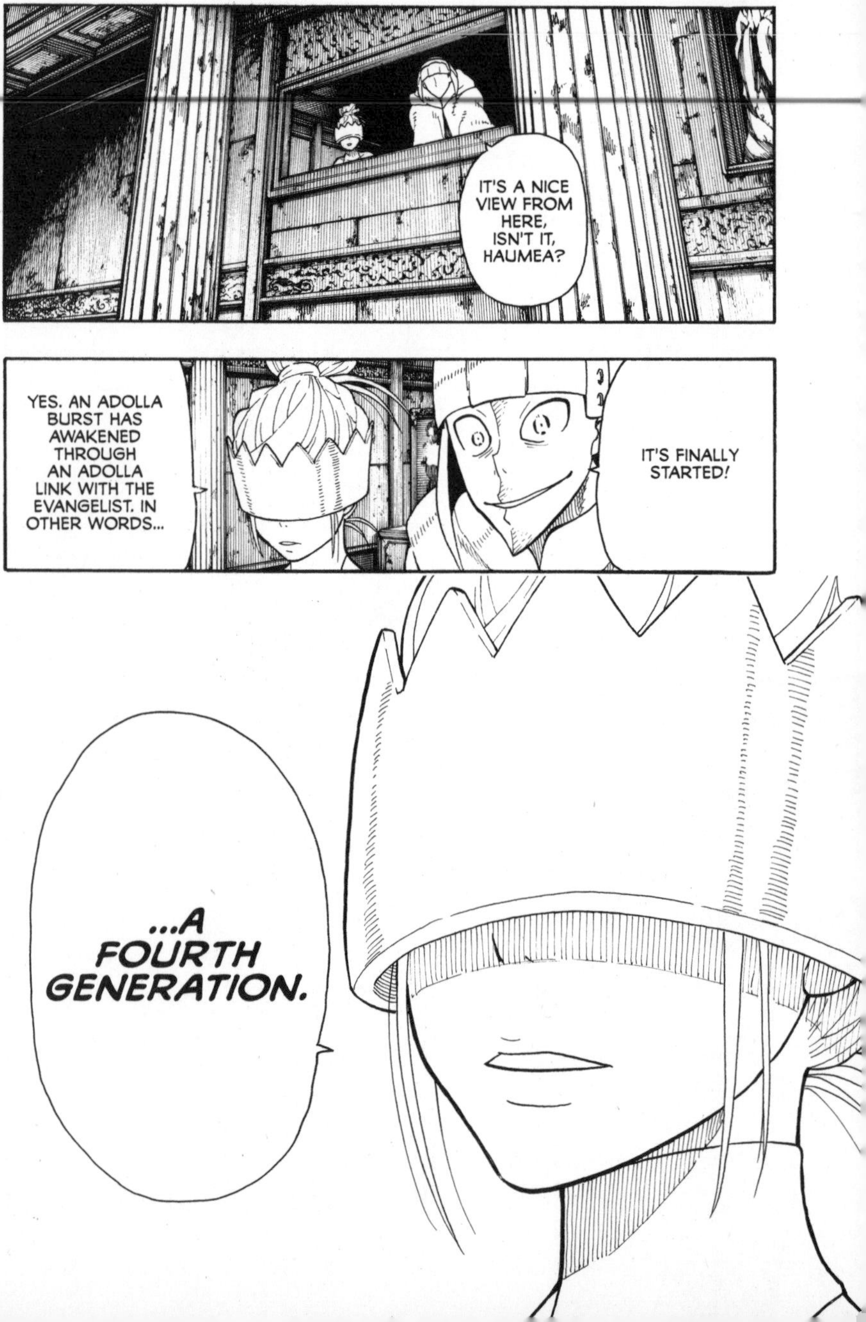
IT'S A NICE VIEW FROM HERE, ISN'T IT, HAUMEA?
IT'S FINALLY STARTED!
YES. AN ADOLLA BURST HAS AWAKENED THROUGH AN ADOLLA LINK WITH THE EVANGELIST. IN OTHER WORDS...
...A FOURTH GENERATION.

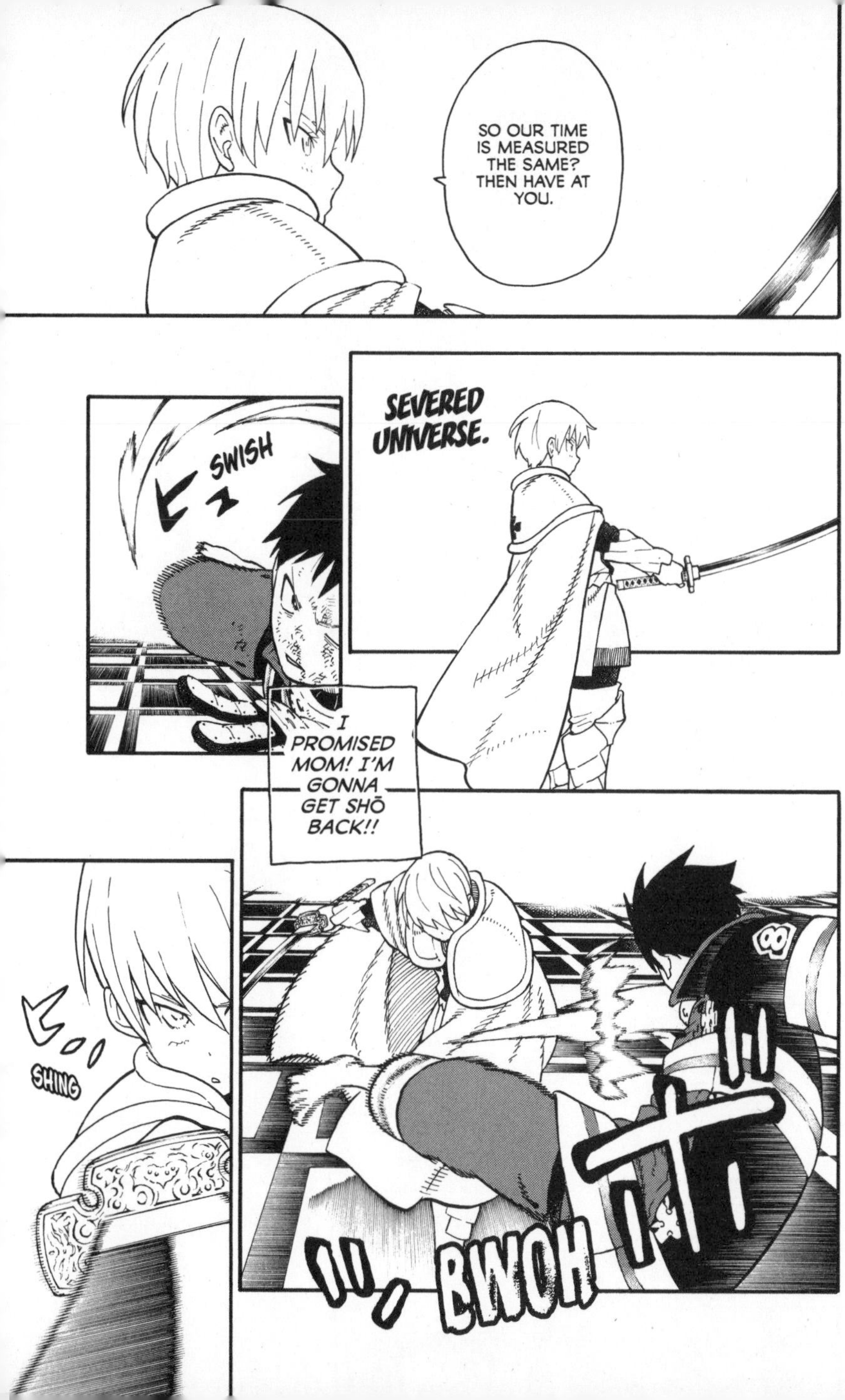
SO OUR TIME IS MEASURED THE SAME? THEN HAVE AT YOU.
SEVERED UNIVERSE.
SWISH
I PROMISED MOM! I'M GONNA GET SHŌ BACK!!
BWOH
SHING

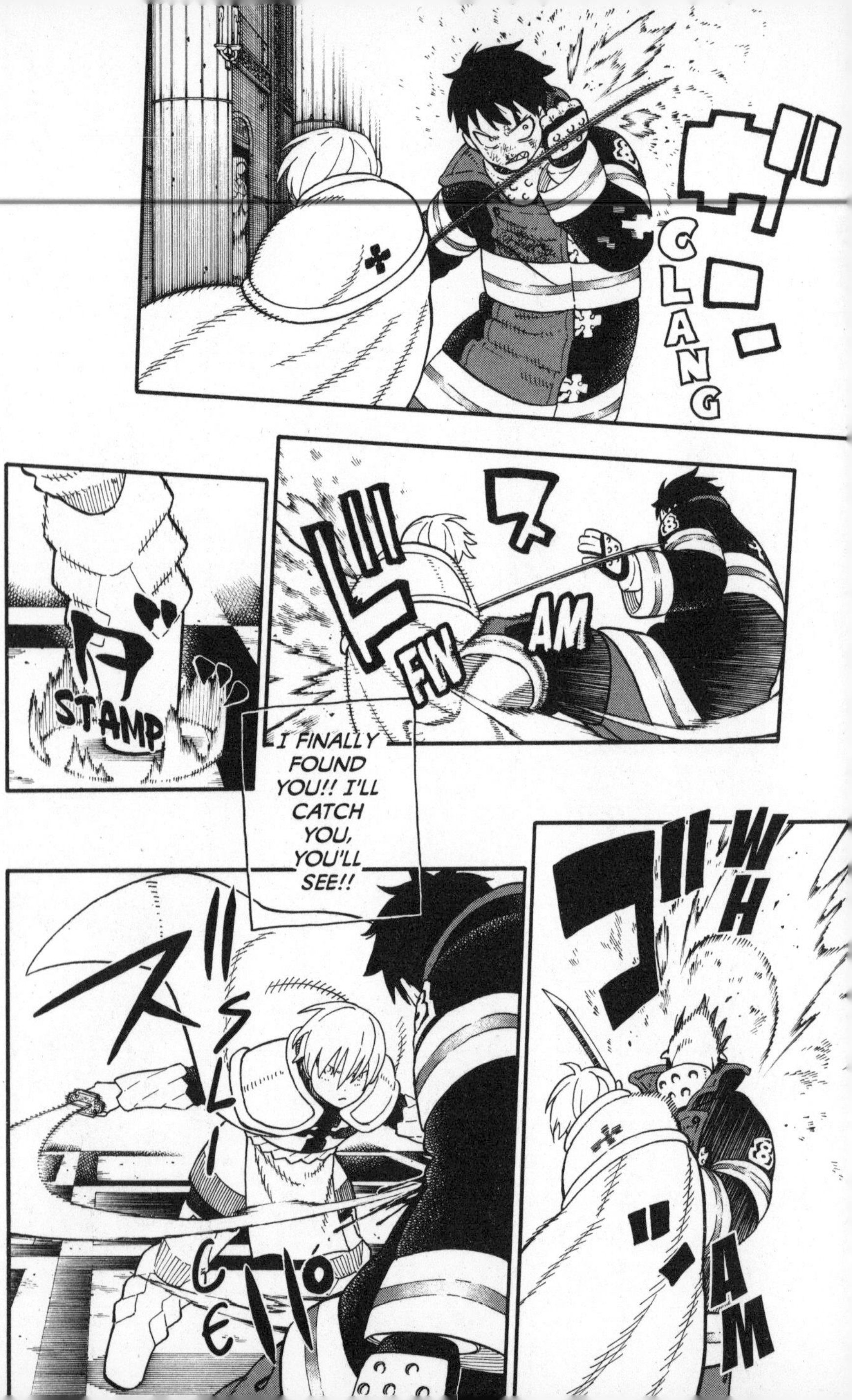
CLANG
FWAM
STAMP
I FINALLY FOUND YOU!! I'LL CATCH YOU, YOU'LL SEE!!
WHAM
SLICE

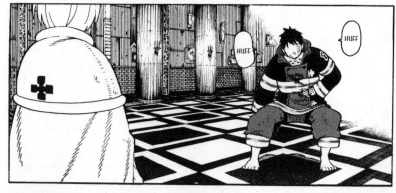

HUFF
HUFF
JUST...
...ONE BLINK...
...AND EVERYTHING HAS CHANGED.
IN THE TIME IT TAKES...
...TO CLOSE AND OPEN MY EYES...
...SO MUCH HAS HAPPENED!
BLINK

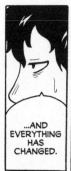

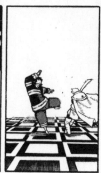

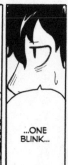

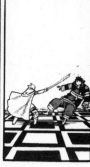

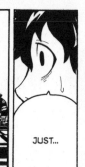

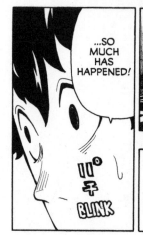

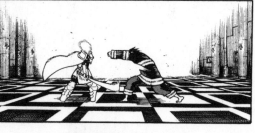

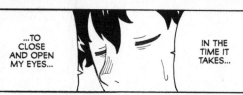

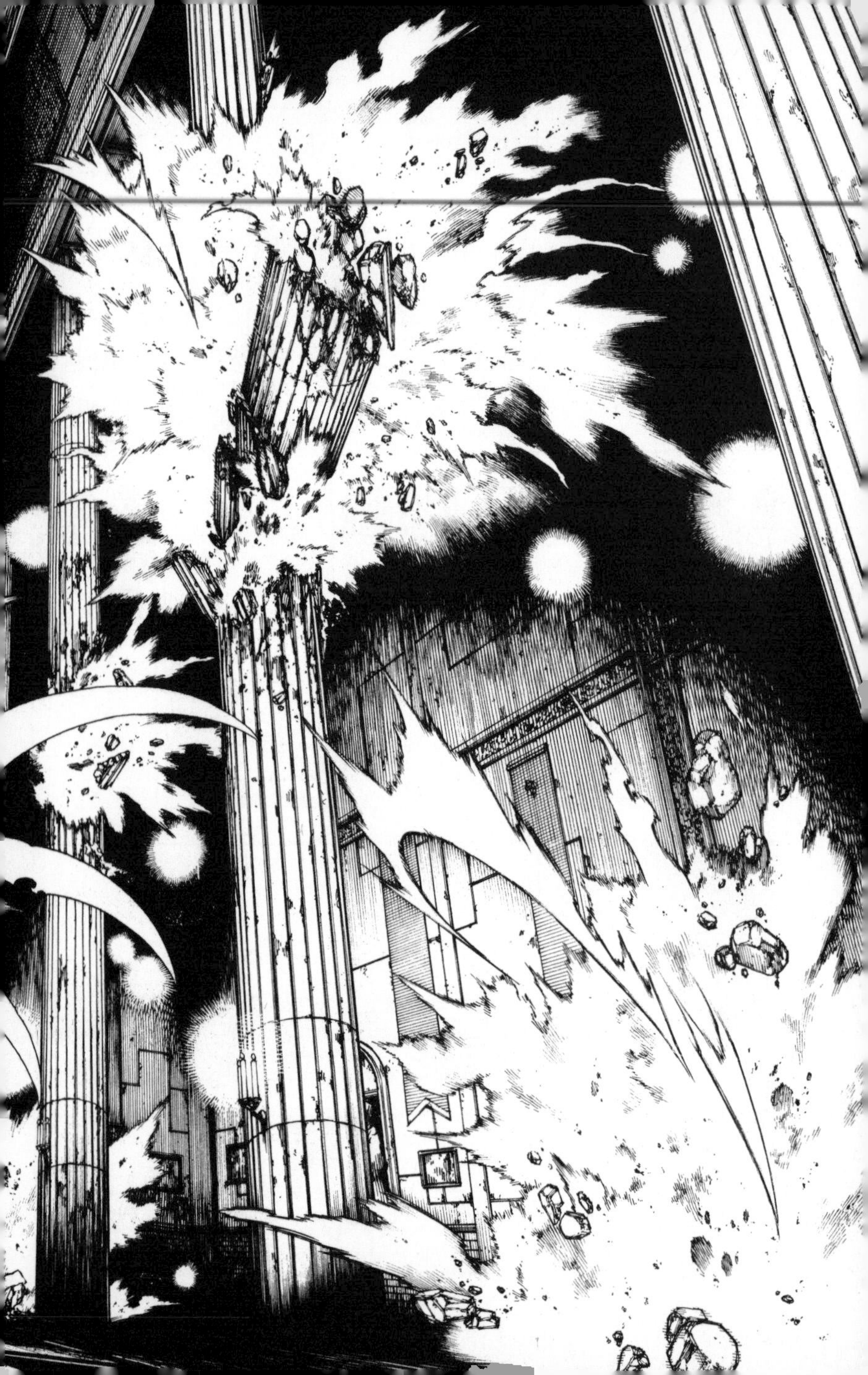

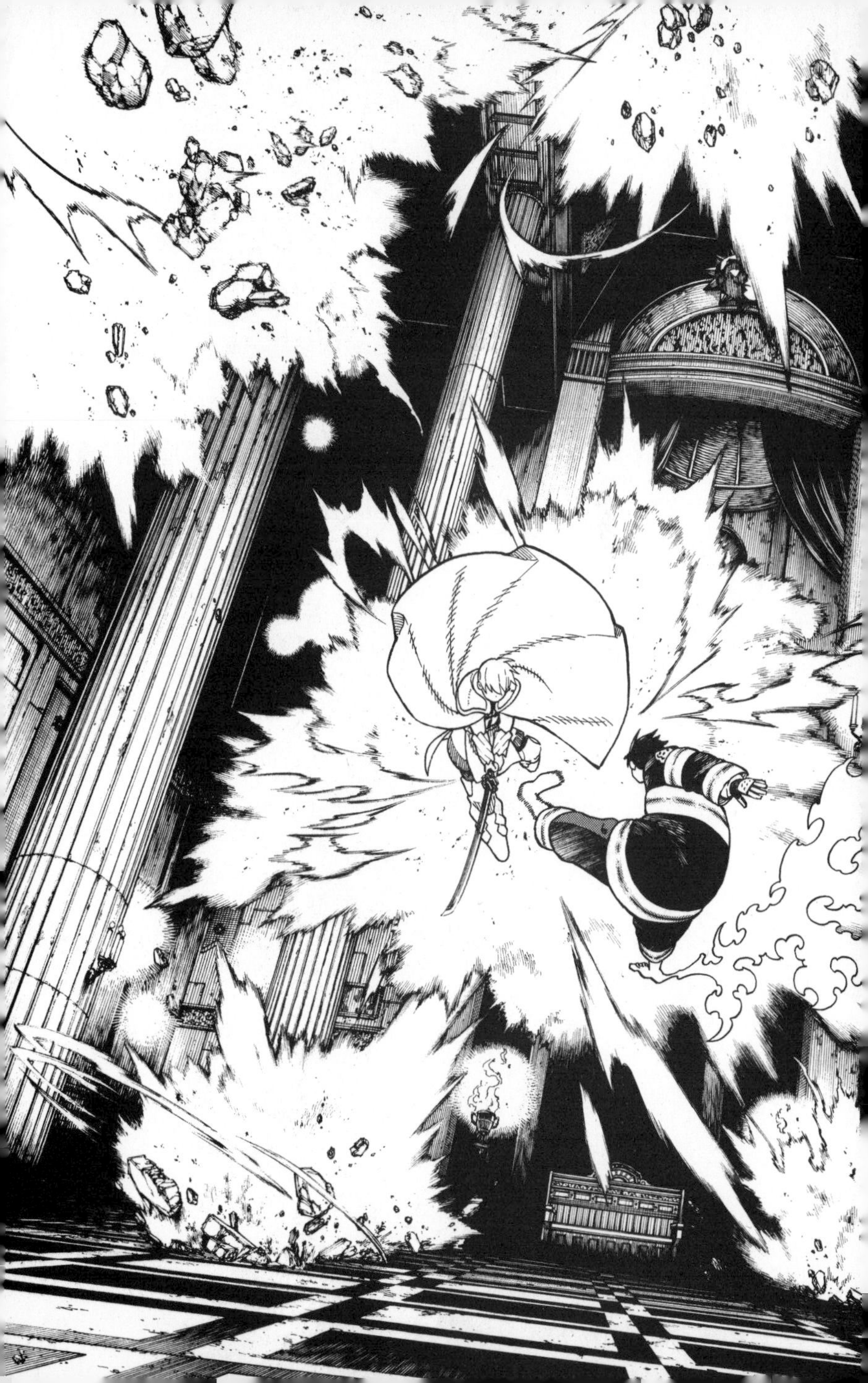

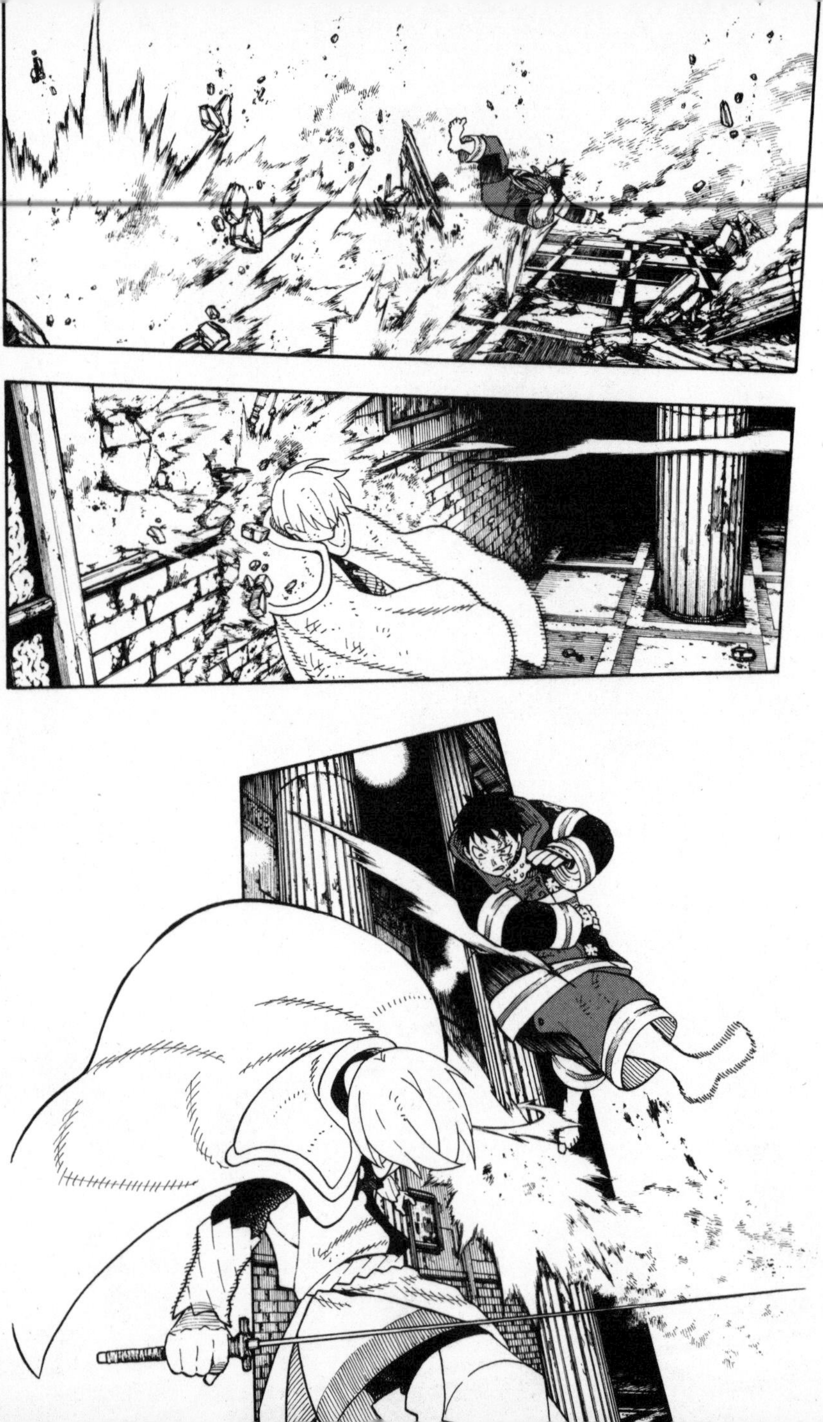

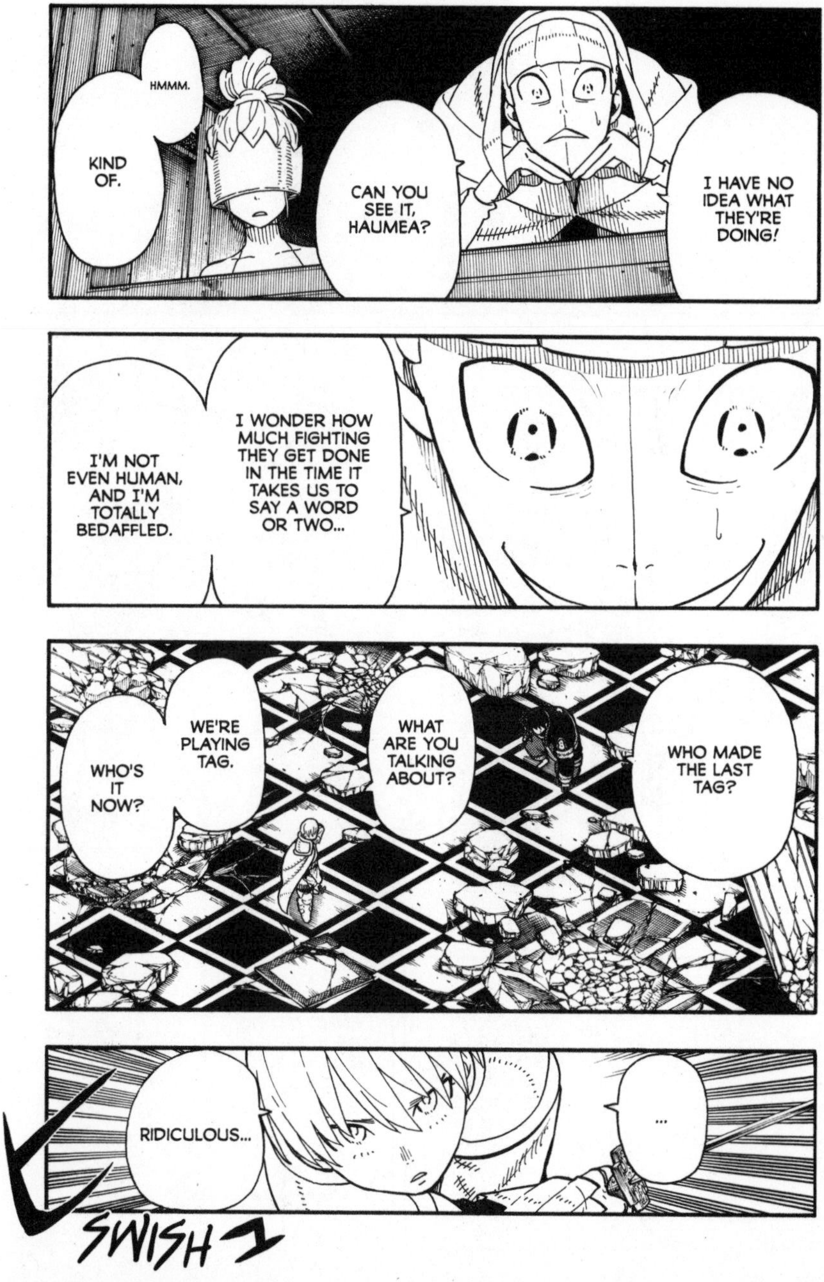
I HAVE NO IDEA WHAT THEY'RE DOING!
CAN YOU SEE IT, HAUMEA?
HMMM.
KIND OF.
I WONDER HOW MUCH FIGHTING THEY GET DONE IN THE TIME IT TAKES US TO SAY A WORD OR TWO...
I'M NOT EVEN HUMAN, AND I'M TOTALLY BEDAFFLED.
WHO MADE THE LAST TAG?
WHAT ARE YOU TALKING ABOUT?
WE'RE PLAYING TAG.
WHO'S IT NOW?
...
RIDICULOUS...
SWISH

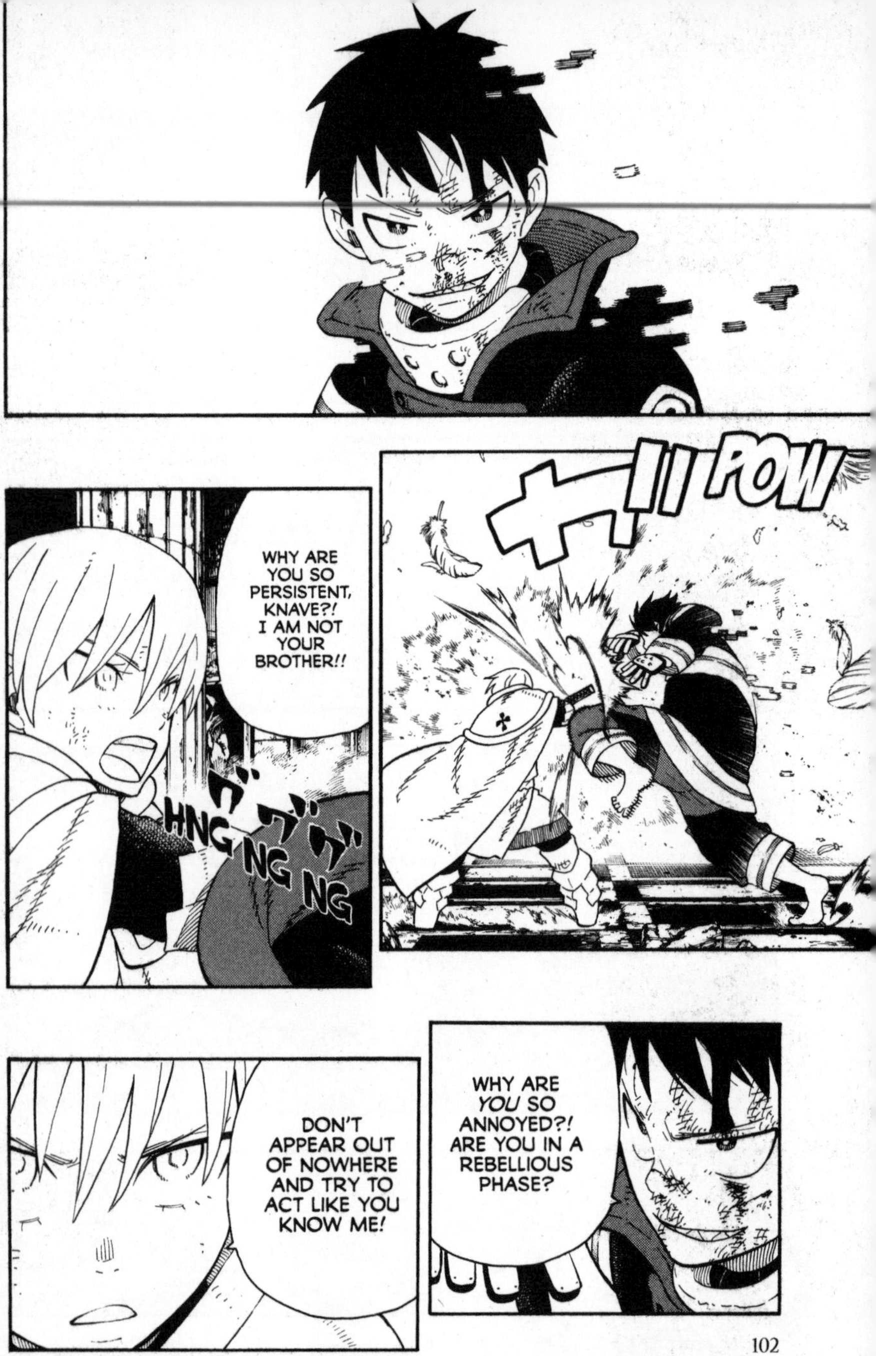
POW
WHY ARE YOU SO PERSISTENT, KNAVE?! I AM NOT YOUR BROTHER!!
HNG NG NG
WHY ARE *YOU* SO ANNOYED?! ARE YOU IN A REBELLIOUS PHASE?
DON'T APPEAR OUT OF NOWHERE AND TRY TO ACT LIKE YOU KNOW ME!

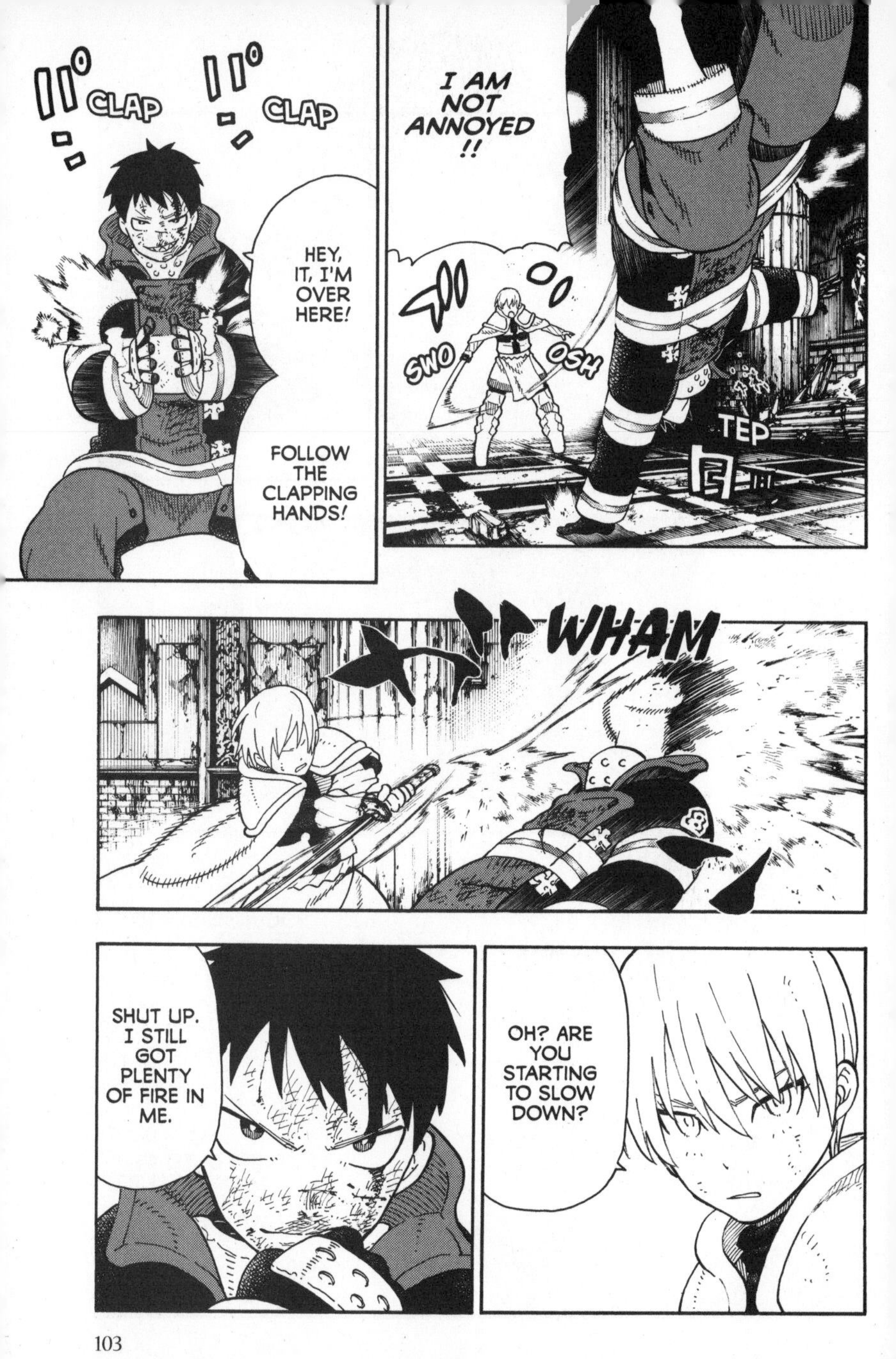
I AM NOT ANNOYED!!
SWOOSH
TEP
CLAP
CLAP
HEY, IT, I'M OVER HERE!
FOLLOW THE CLAPPING HANDS!
WHAM
OH? ARE YOU STARTING TO SLOW DOWN?
SHUT UP. I STILL GOT PLENTY OF FIRE IN ME.

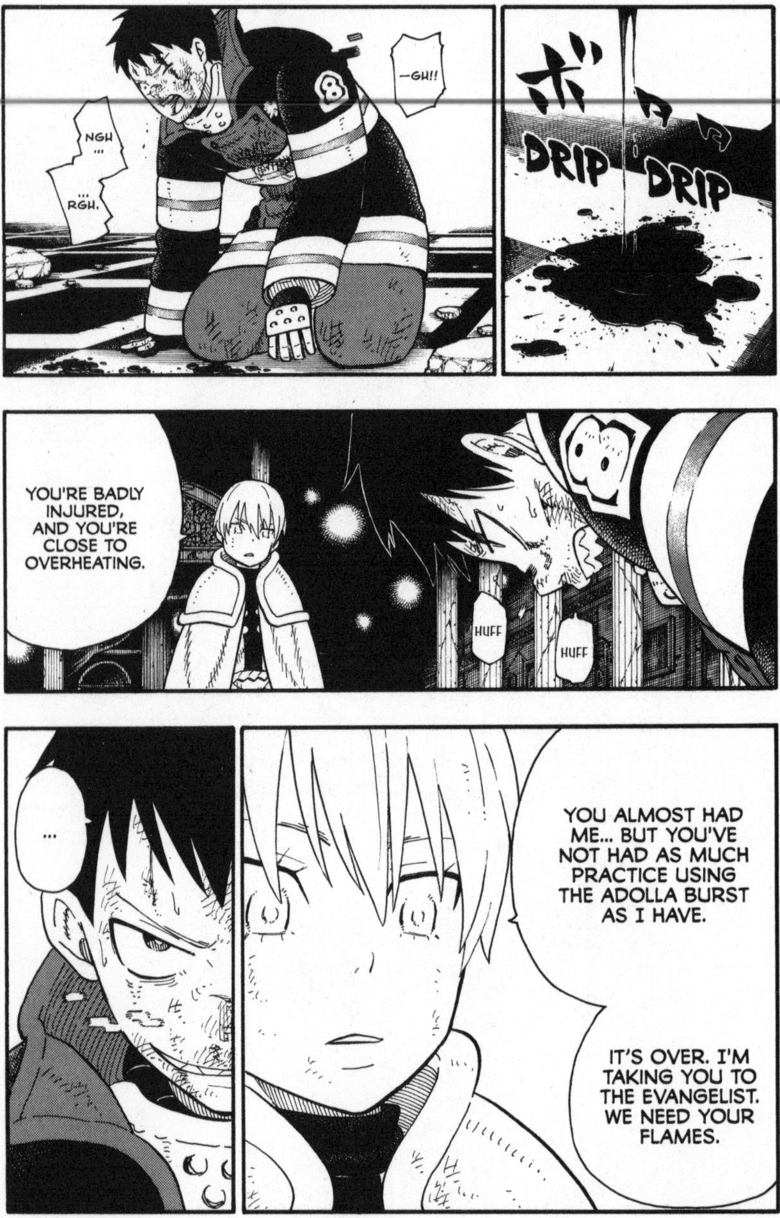
ボタッ
DRIP DRIP
—GH!!
NGH...
...RGH.
HUFF
HUFF
YOU'RE BADLY INJURED, AND YOU'RE CLOSE TO OVERHEATING.
YOU ALMOST HAD ME... BUT YOU'VE NOT HAD AS MUCH PRACTICE USING THE ADOLLA BURST AS I HAVE.
IT'S OVER. I'M TAKING YOU TO THE EVANGELIST. WE NEED YOUR FLAMES.
...

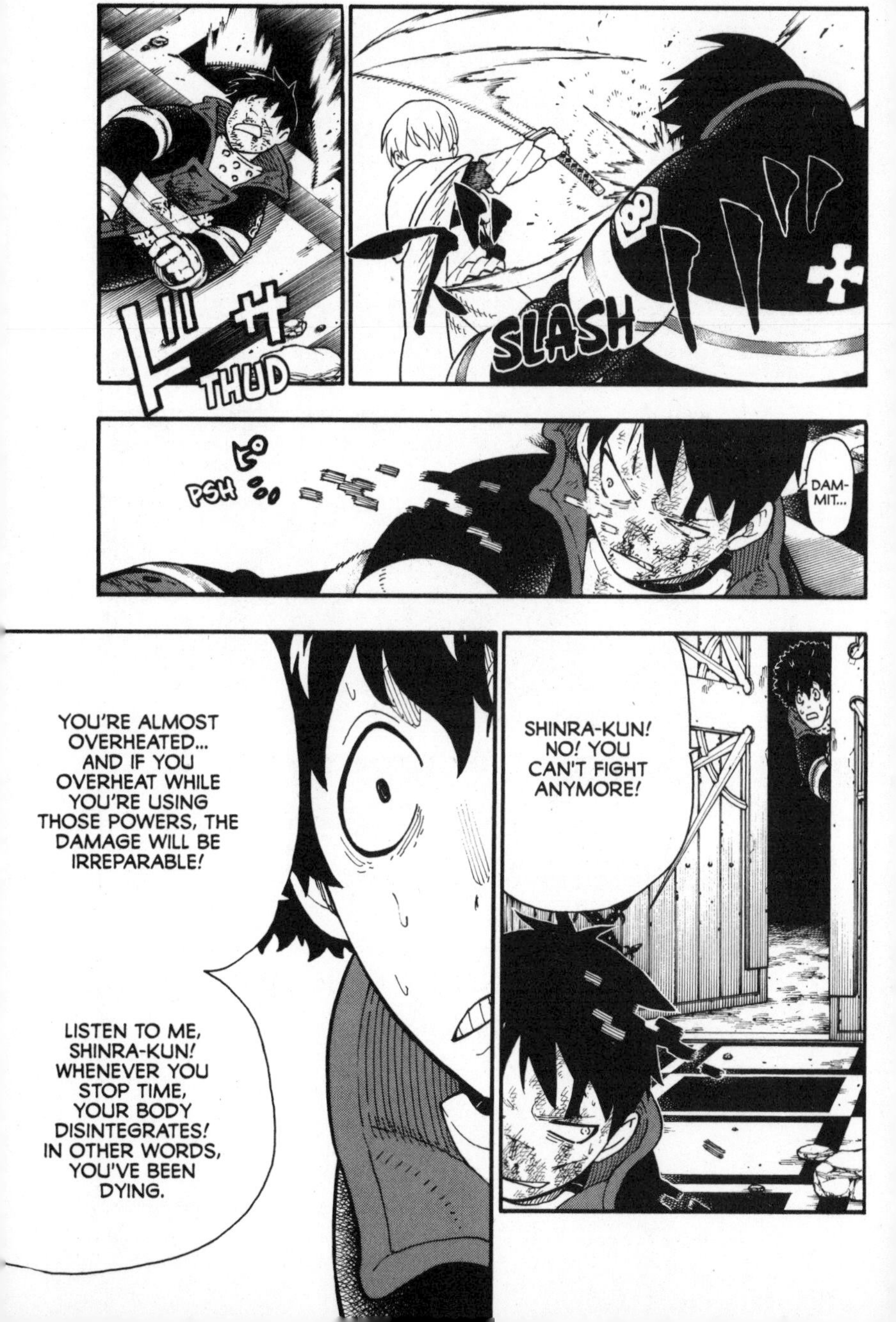
SLASH
THUD
DAM-MIT...
PSH
SHINRA-KUN! NO! YOU CAN'T FIGHT ANYMORE!
YOU'RE ALMOST OVERHEATED... AND IF YOU OVERHEAT WHILE YOU'RE USING THOSE POWERS, THE DAMAGE WILL BE IRREPARABLE!
LISTEN TO ME, SHINRA-KUN! WHENEVER YOU STOP TIME, YOUR BODY DISINTEGRATES! IN OTHER WORDS, YOU'VE BEEN DYING.

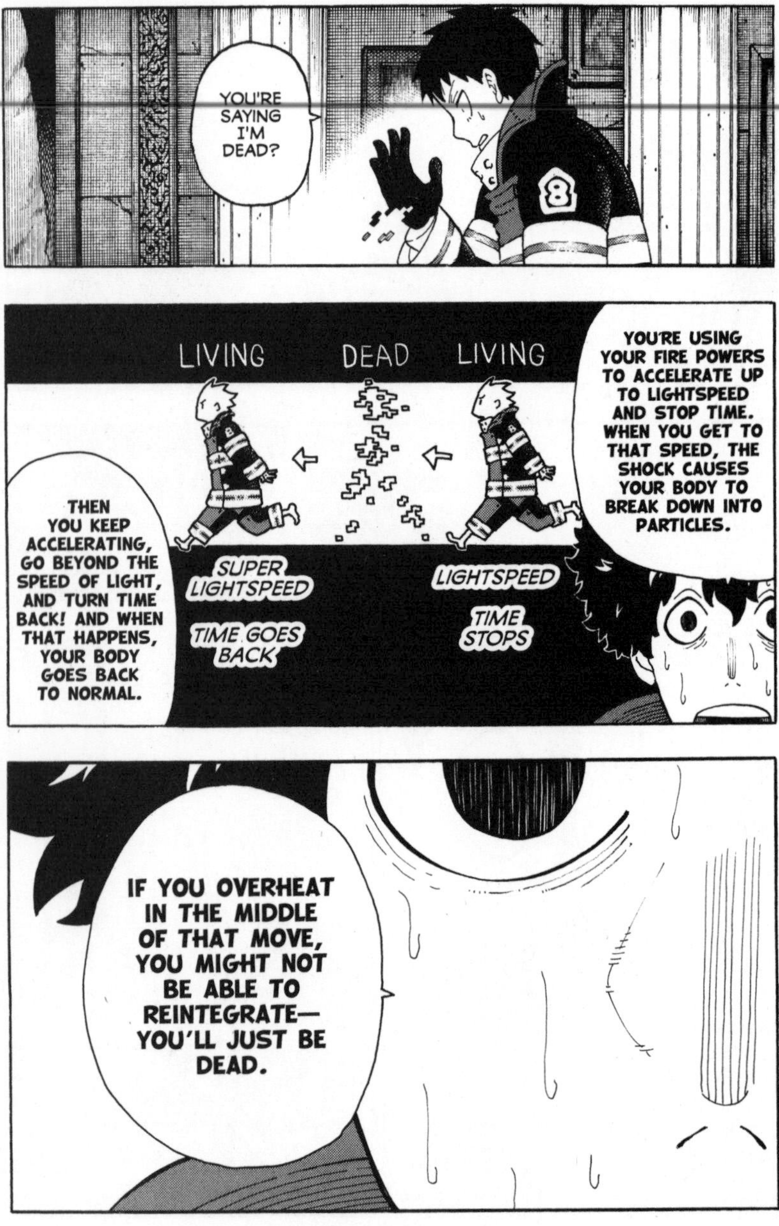
YOU'RE SAYING I'M DEAD?
YOU'RE USING YOUR FIRE POWERS TO ACCELERATE UP TO LIGHTSPEED AND STOP TIME. WHEN YOU GET TO THAT SPEED, THE SHOCK CAUSES YOUR BODY TO BREAK DOWN INTO PARTICLES.
LIVING
DEAD
LIVING
LIGHTSPEED
TIME STOPS
SUPER LIGHTSPEED
TIME GOES BACK
THEN YOU KEEP ACCELERATING, GO BEYOND THE SPEED OF LIGHT, AND TURN TIME BACK! AND WHEN THAT HAPPENS, YOUR BODY GOES BACK TO NORMAL.
IF YOU OVERHEAT IN THE MIDDLE OF THAT MOVE, YOU MIGHT NOT BE ABLE TO REINTEGRATE— YOU'LL JUST BE DEAD.

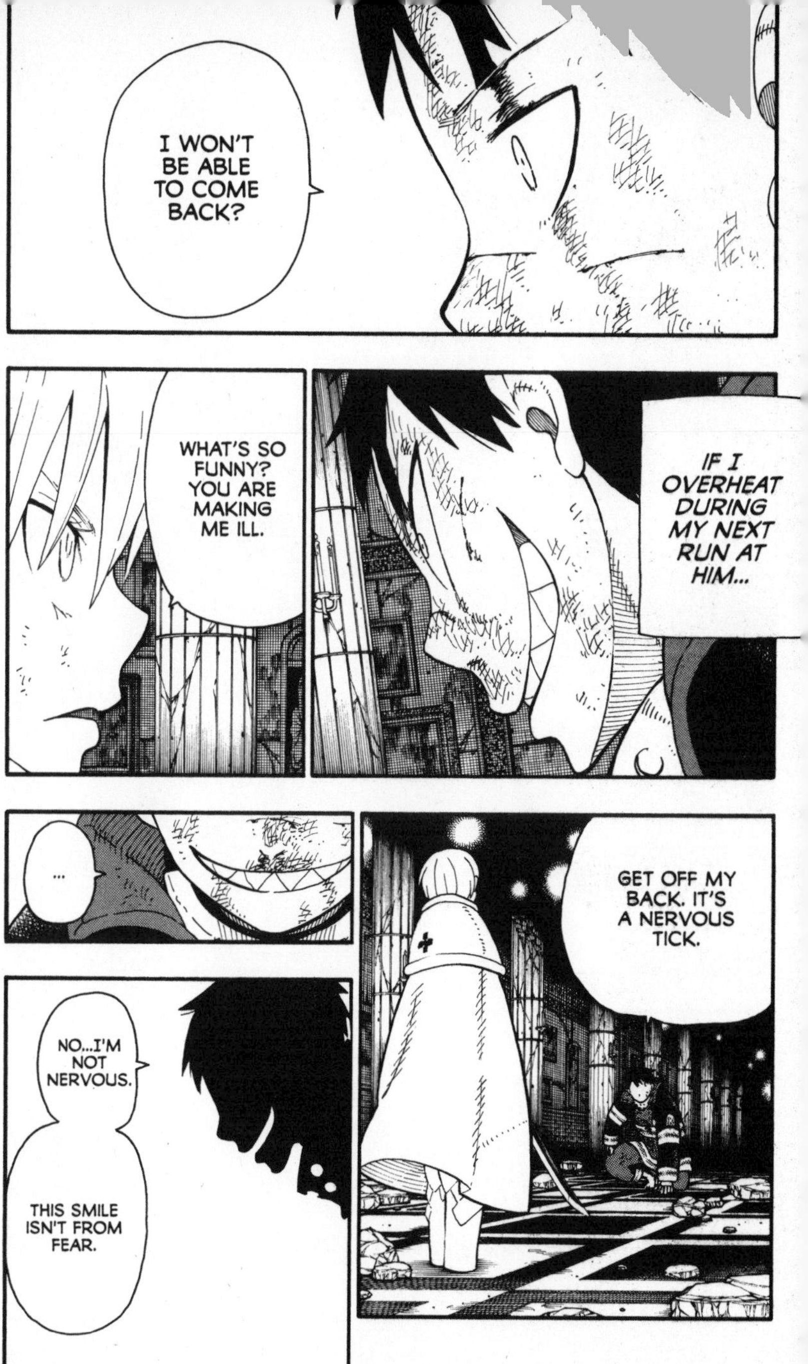
I WON'T BE ABLE TO COME BACK?
IF I OVERHEAT DURING MY NEXT RUN AT HIM...
WHAT'S SO FUNNY? YOU ARE MAKING ME ILL.
GET OFF MY BACK. IT'S A NERVOUS TICK.
...
NO...I'M NOT NERVOUS.
THIS SMILE ISN'T FROM FEAR.

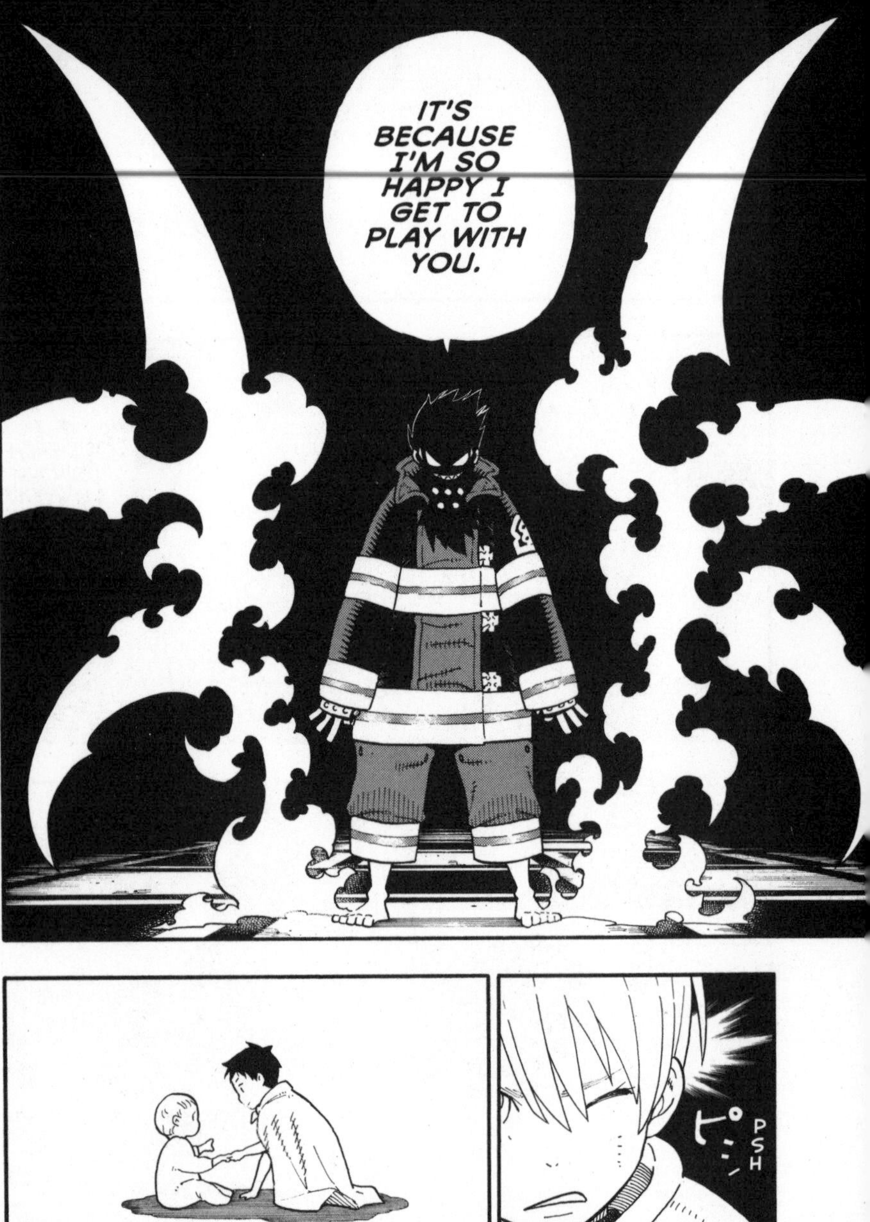
IT'S BECAUSE I'M SO HAPPY I GET TO PLAY WITH YOU.
PSH

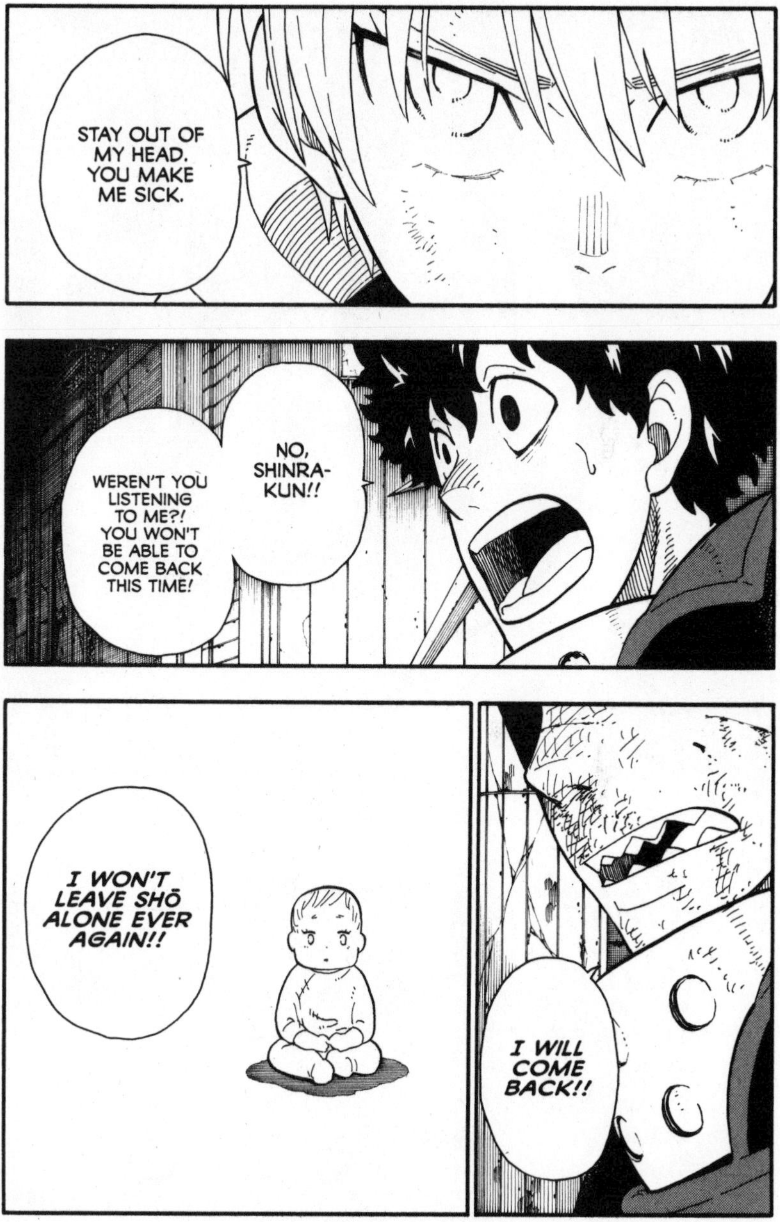
STAY OUT OF MY HEAD. YOU MAKE ME SICK.
NO, SHINRA-KUN!!
WEREN'T YOU LISTENING TO ME?! YOU WON'T BE ABLE TO COME BACK THIS TIME!
I WILL COME BACK!!
I WON'T LEAVE SHŌ ALONE EVER AGAIN!!

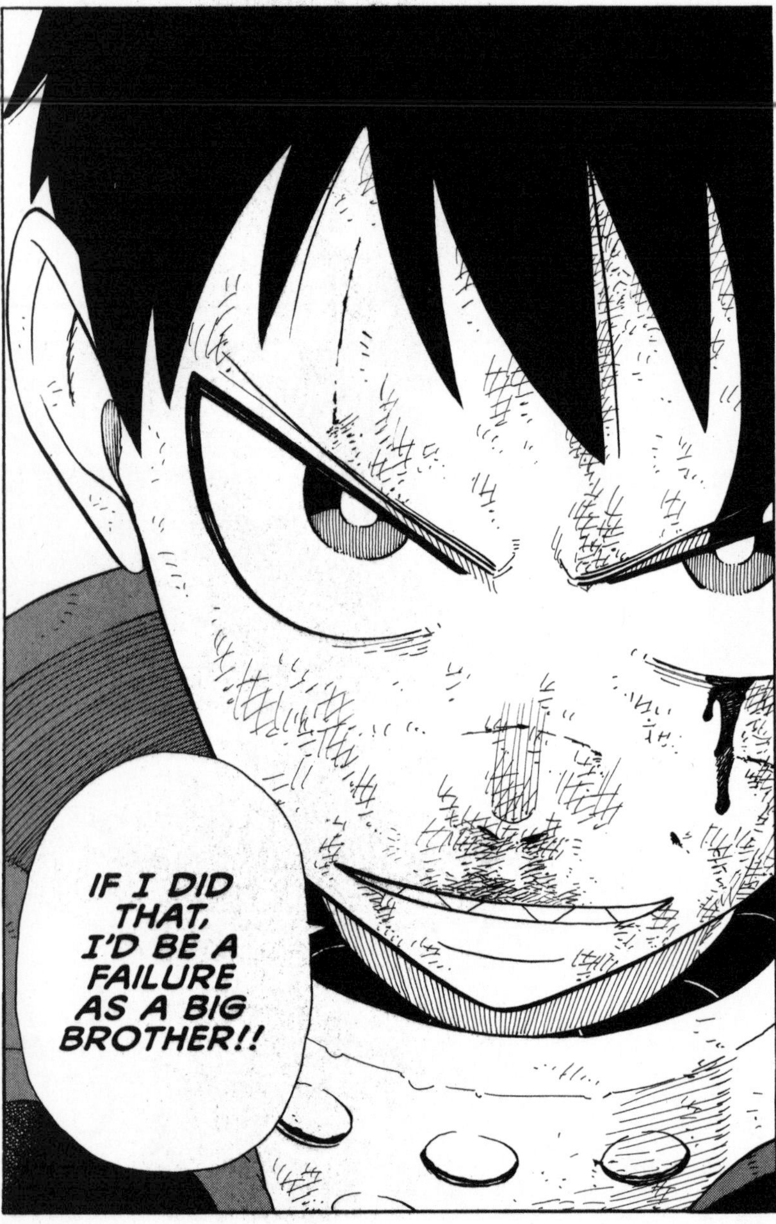
IF I DID THAT, I'D BE A FAILURE AS A BIG BROTHER!!

FIRE FORCE

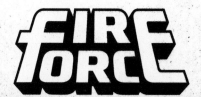

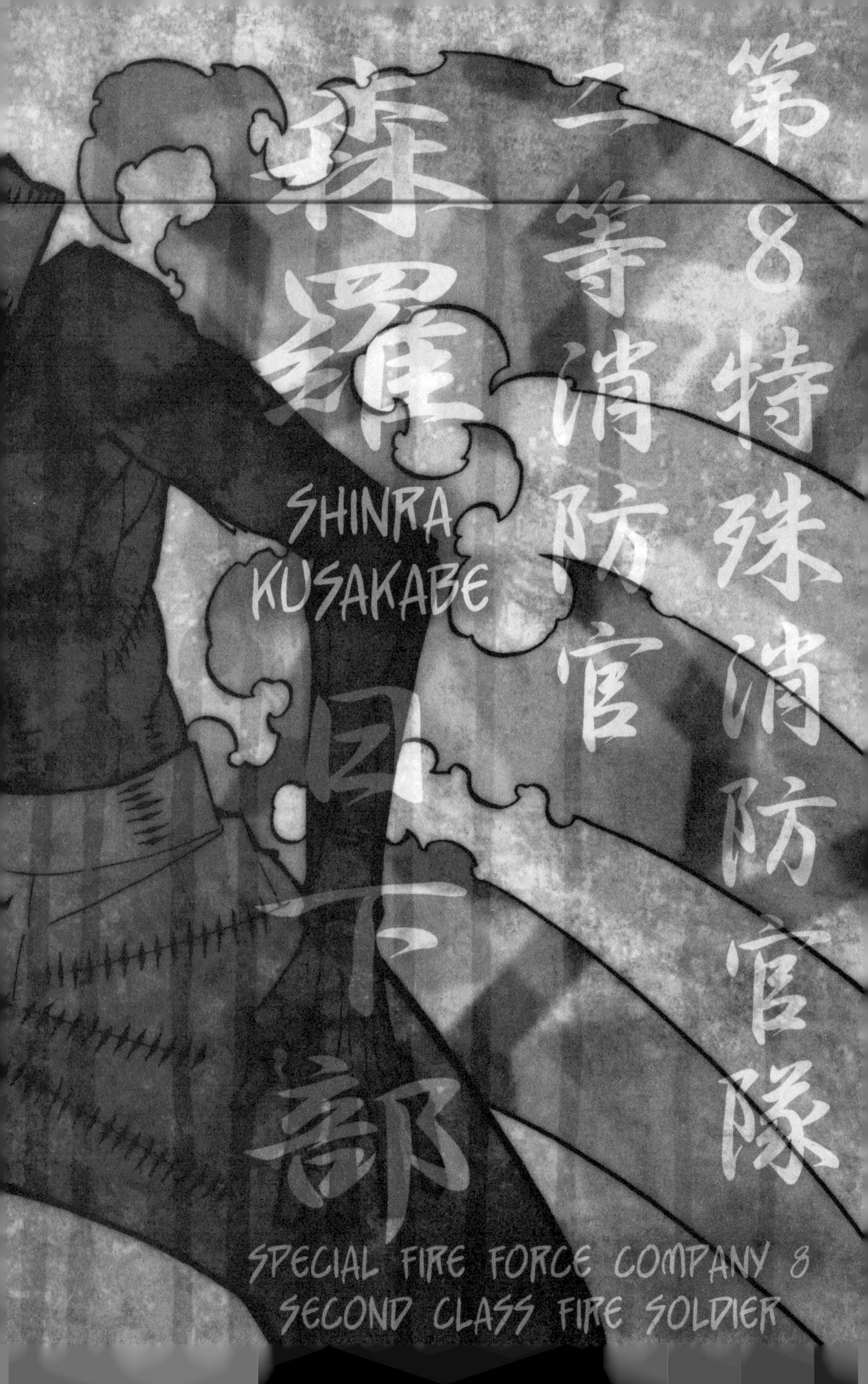
第8特殊消防隊
二等消防官
森羅
SHINRA
KUSAKABE
日下部
SPECIAL FIRE FORCE COMPANY 8
SECOND CLASS FIRE SOLDIER

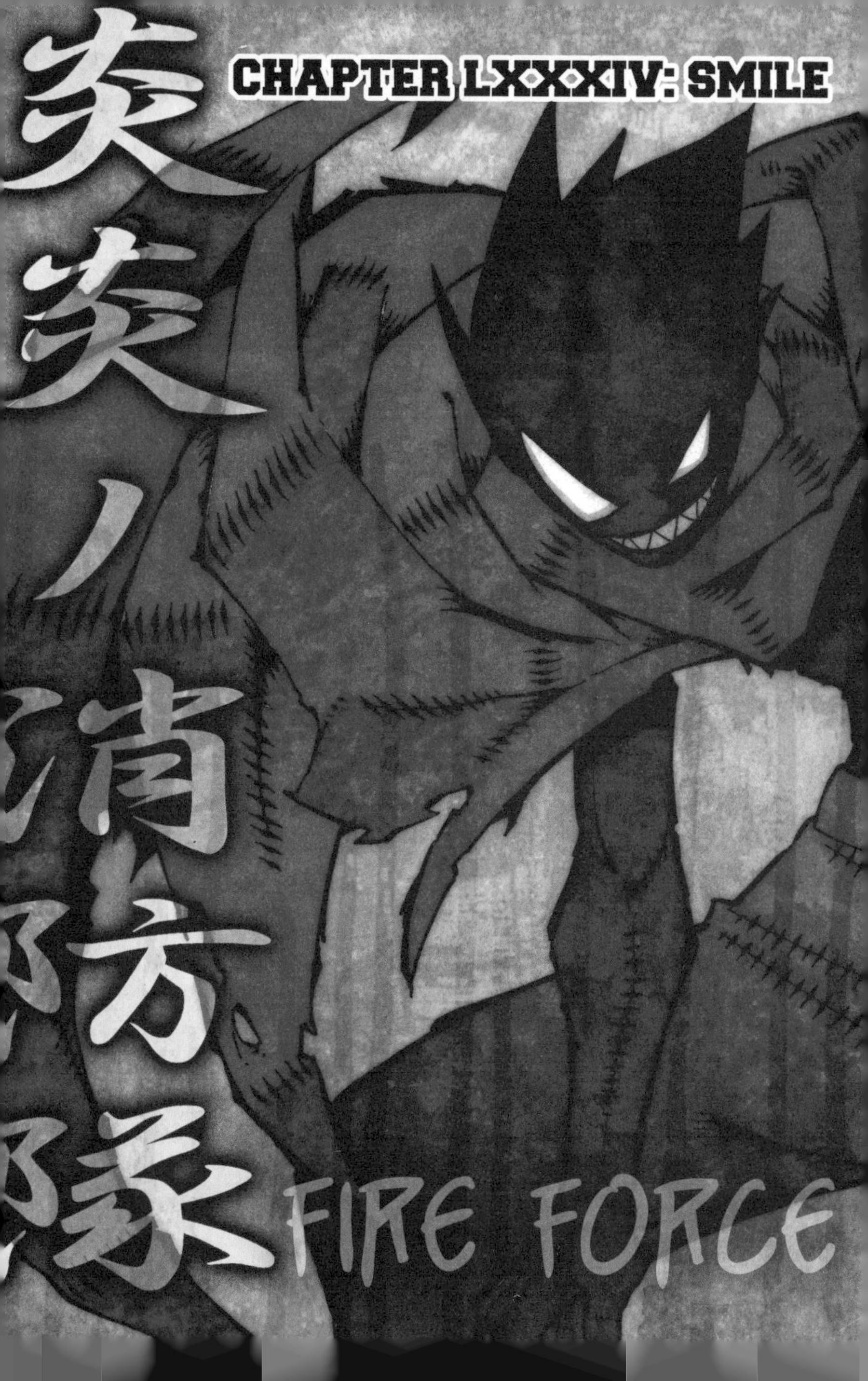
CHAPTER LXXXIV: SMILE
炎炎ノ消防隊
FIRE FORCE

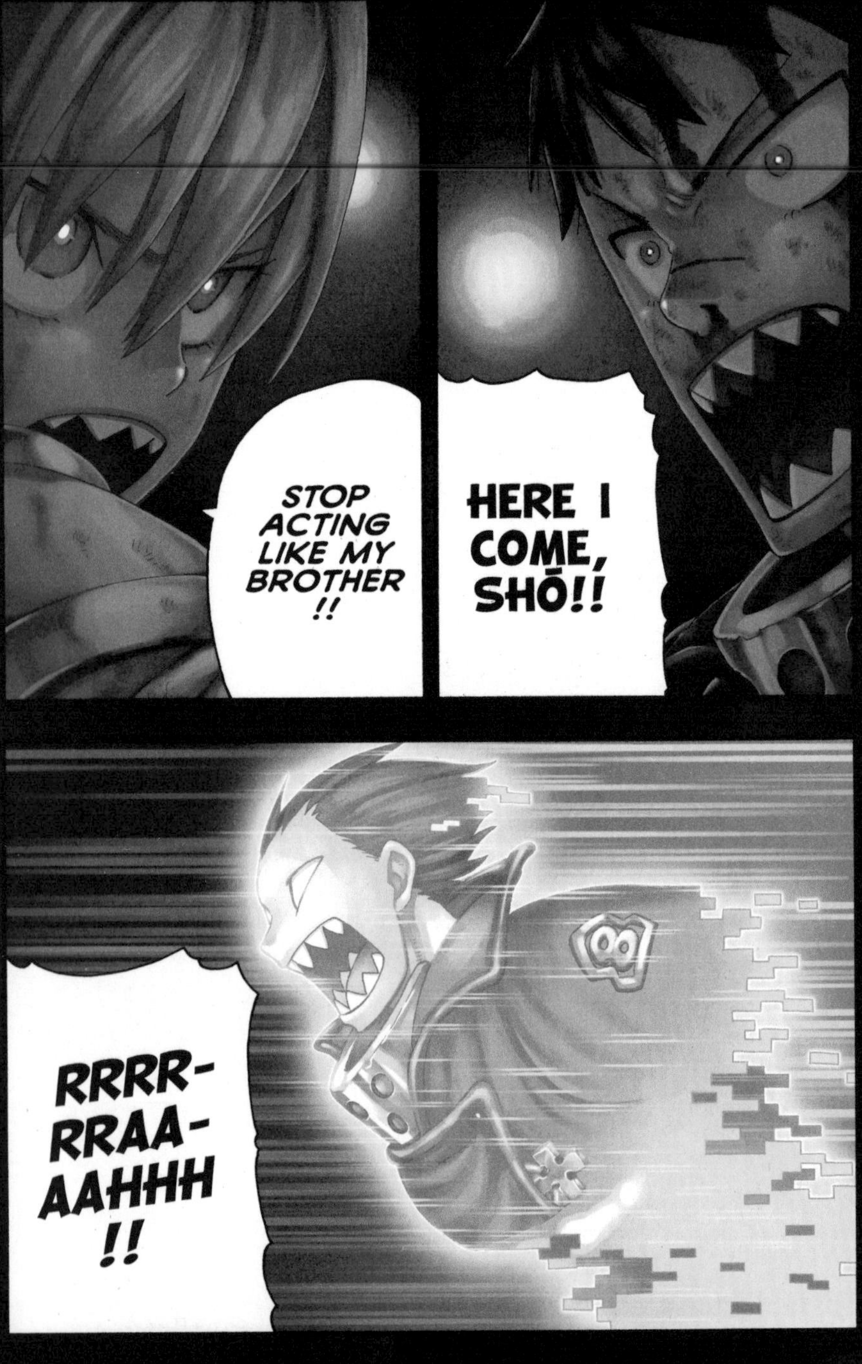
HERE I COME, SHŌ!!
STOP ACTING LIKE MY BROTHER !!
RRRR-RRAA-AAHHH !!

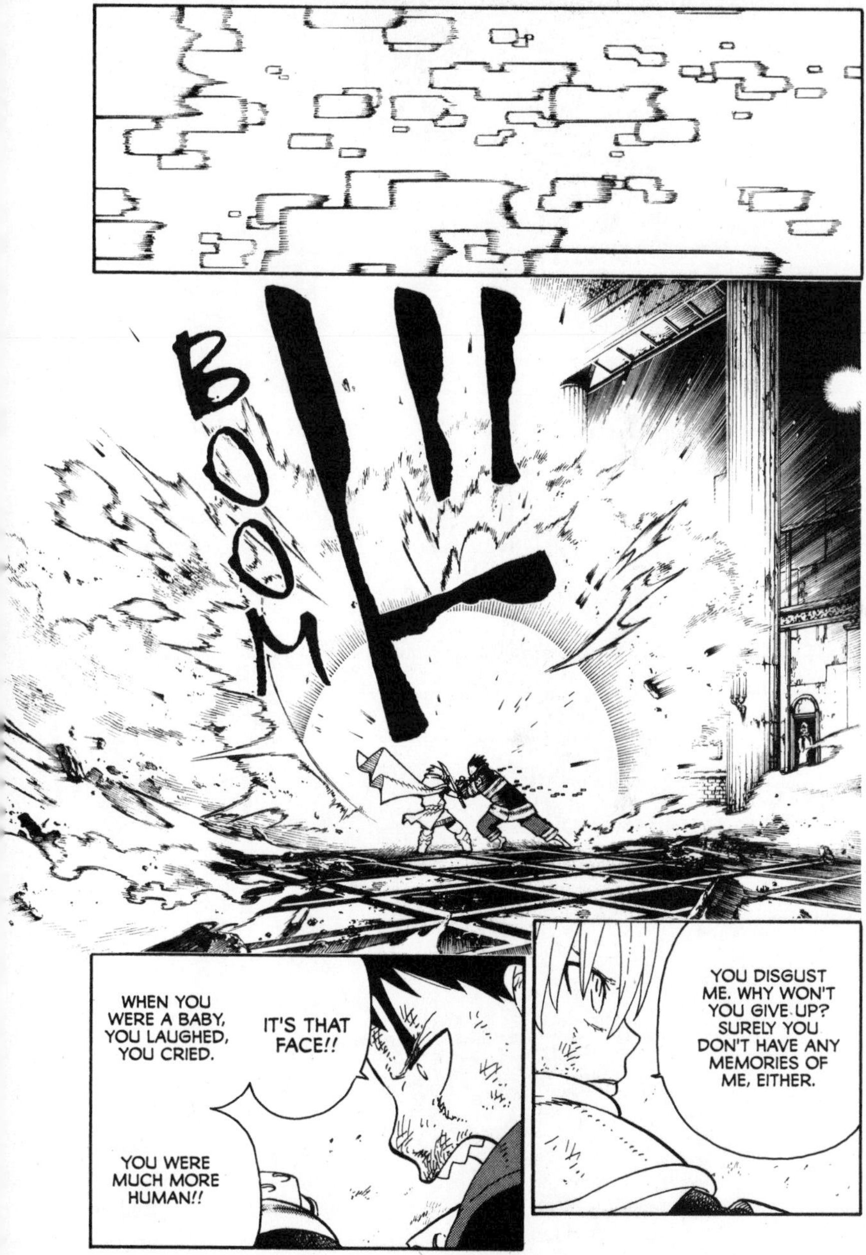
BOOM
YOU DISGUST ME. WHY WON'T YOU GIVE UP? SURELY YOU DON'T HAVE ANY MEMORIES OF ME, EITHER.
IT'S THAT FACE!!
WHEN YOU WERE A BABY, YOU LAUGHED, YOU CRIED.
YOU WERE MUCH MORE HUMAN!!

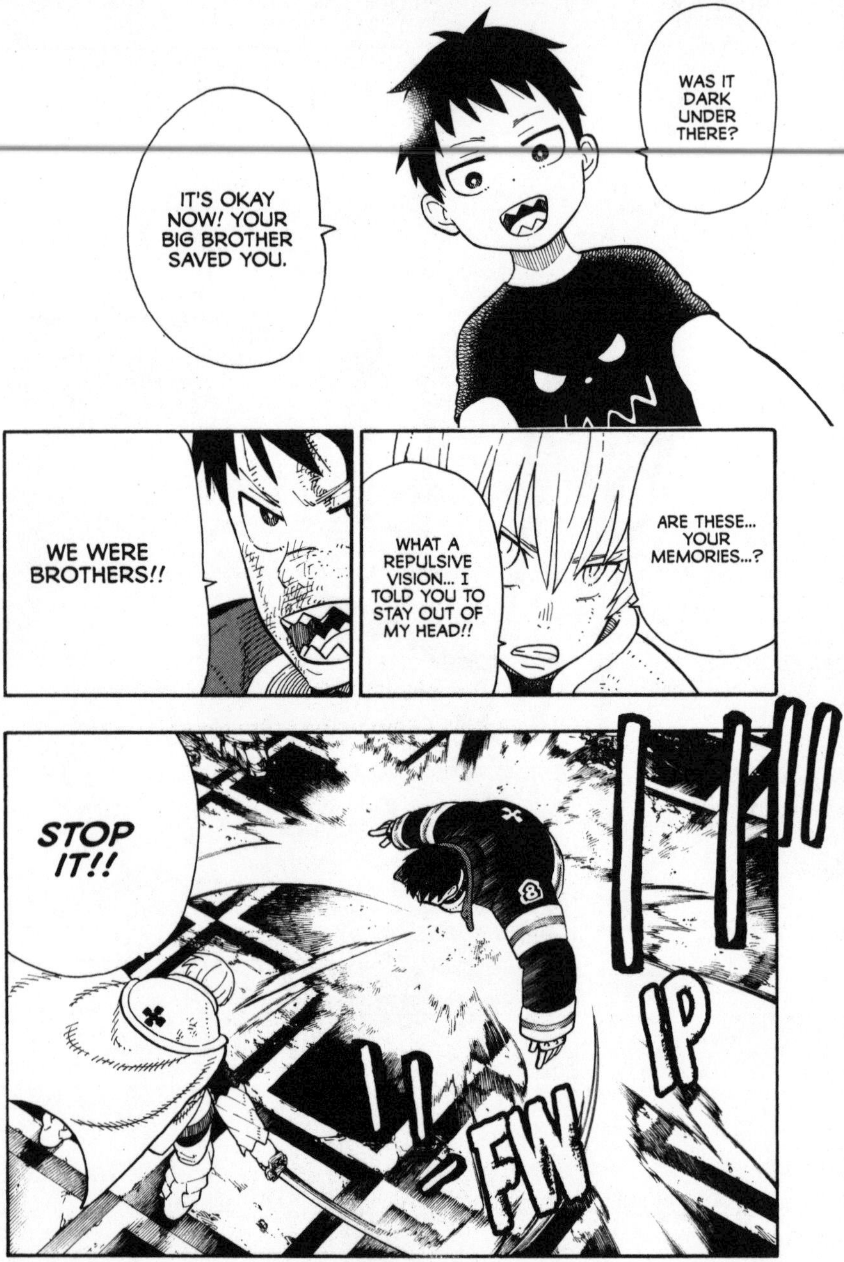
WAS IT DARK UNDER THERE?
IT'S OKAY NOW! YOUR BIG BROTHER SAVED YOU.
ARE THESE... YOUR MEMORIES...?
WHAT A REPULSIVE VISION... I TOLD YOU TO STAY OUT OF MY HEAD!!
WE WERE BROTHERS!!
FWIP
STOP IT!!

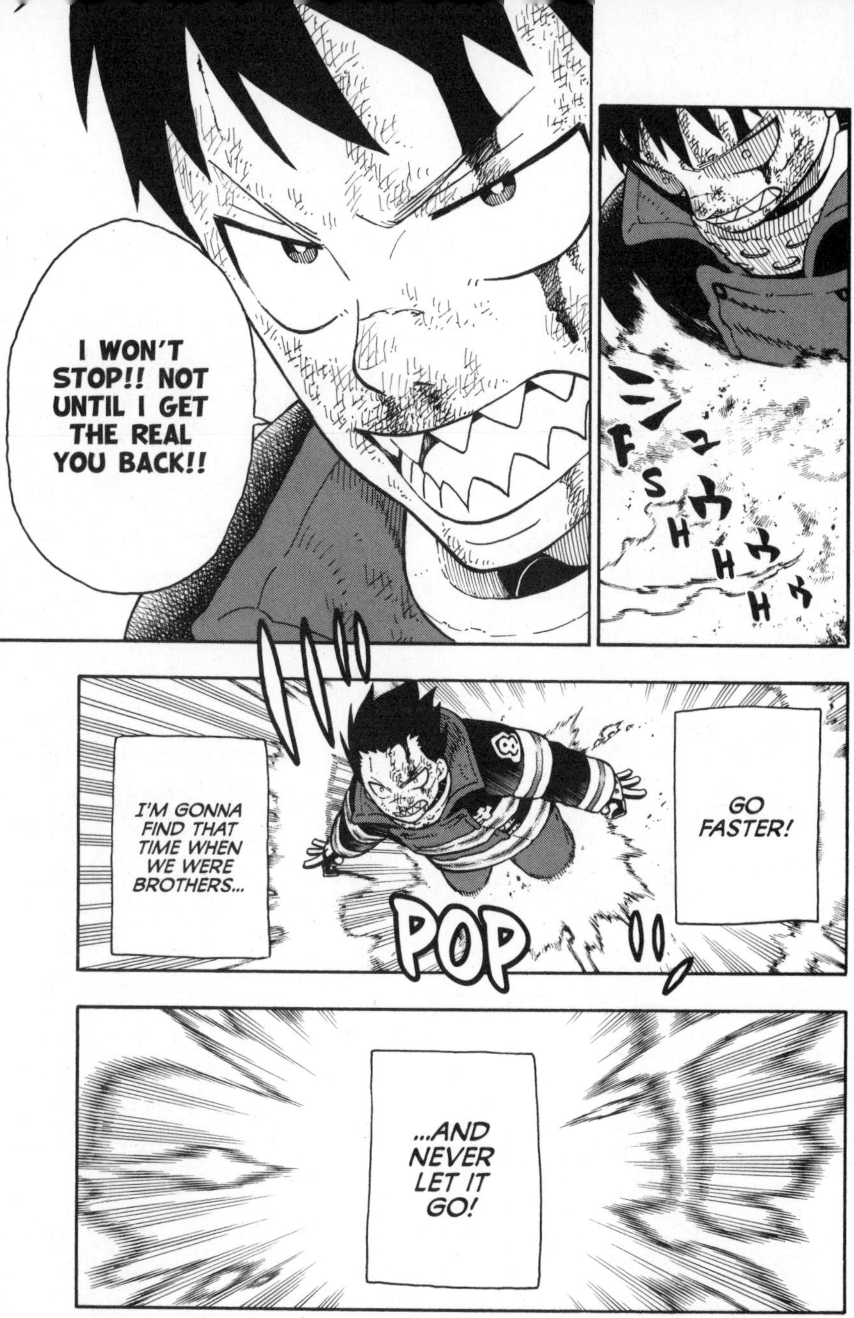
FSHHH
I WON'T STOP!! NOT UNTIL I GET THE REAL YOU BACK!!
GO FASTER!
I'M GONNA FIND THAT TIME WHEN WE WERE BROTHERS...
POP
...AND NEVER LET IT GO!

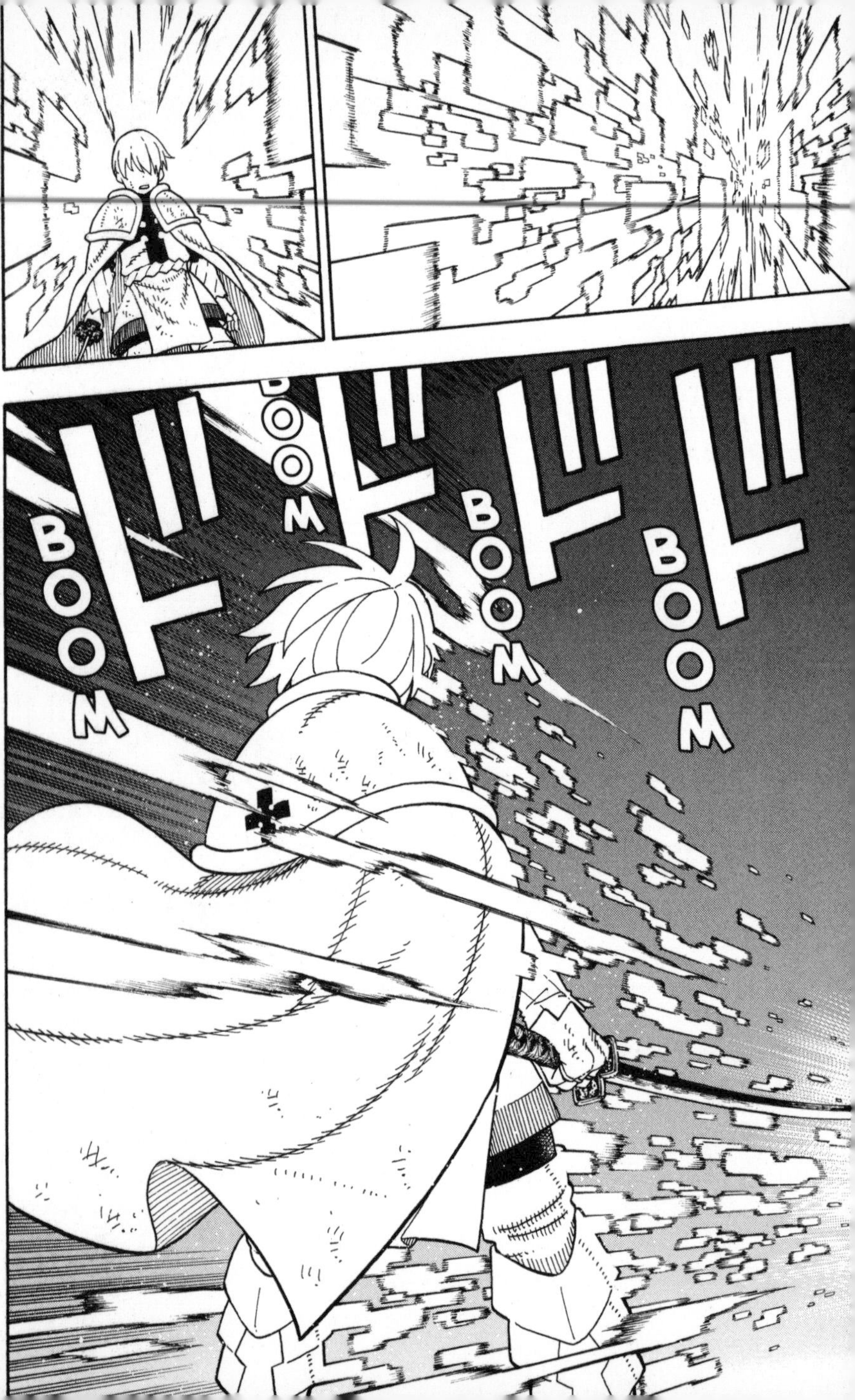

ドドドド
BOOM
BOOM
BOOM
BOOM

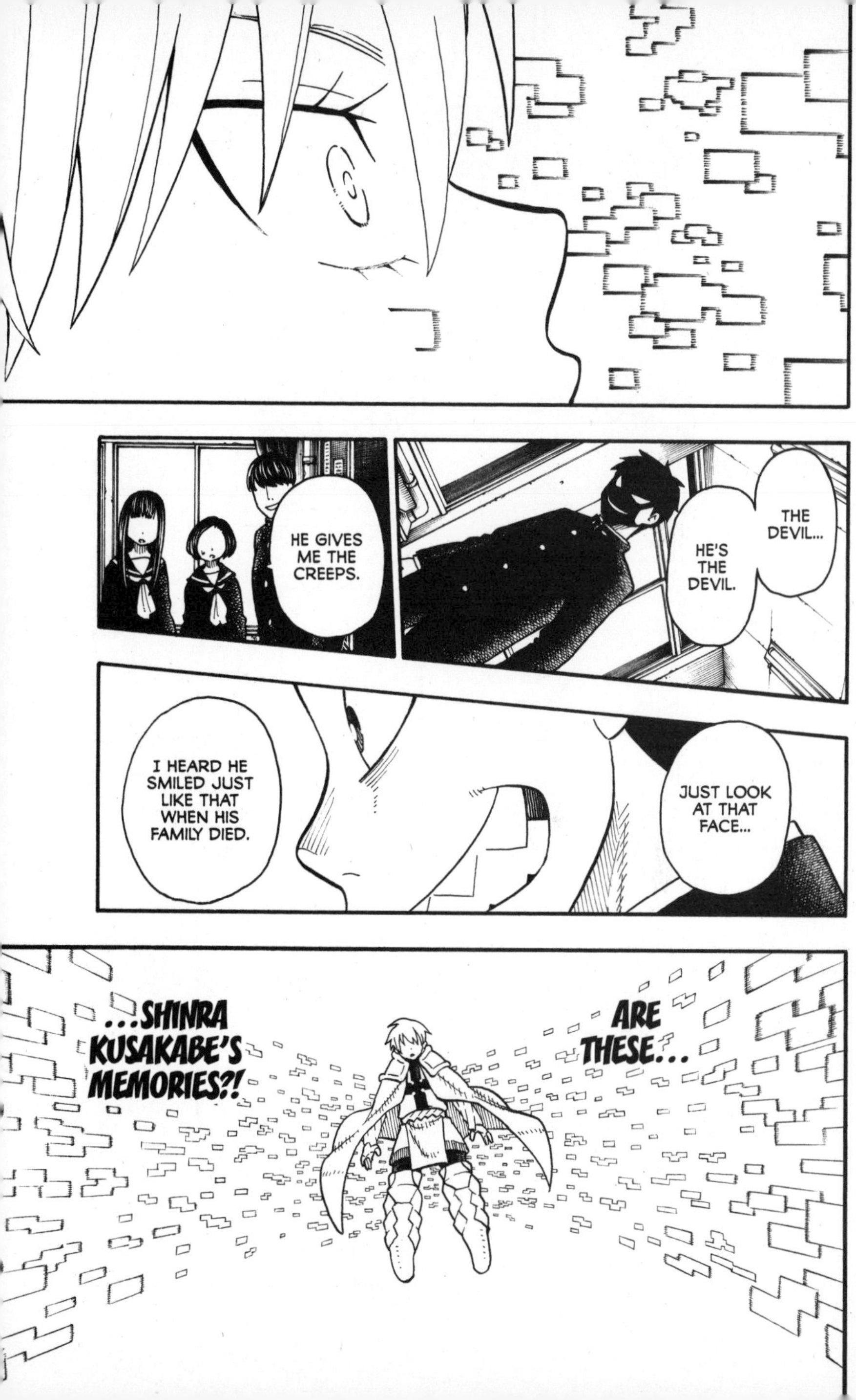
THE DEVIL...
HE'S THE DEVIL.
HE GIVES ME THE CREEPS.
JUST LOOK AT THAT FACE...
I HEARD HE SMILED JUST LIKE THAT WHEN HIS FAMILY DIED.
ARE THESE...
...SHINRA KUSAKABE'S MEMORIES?!

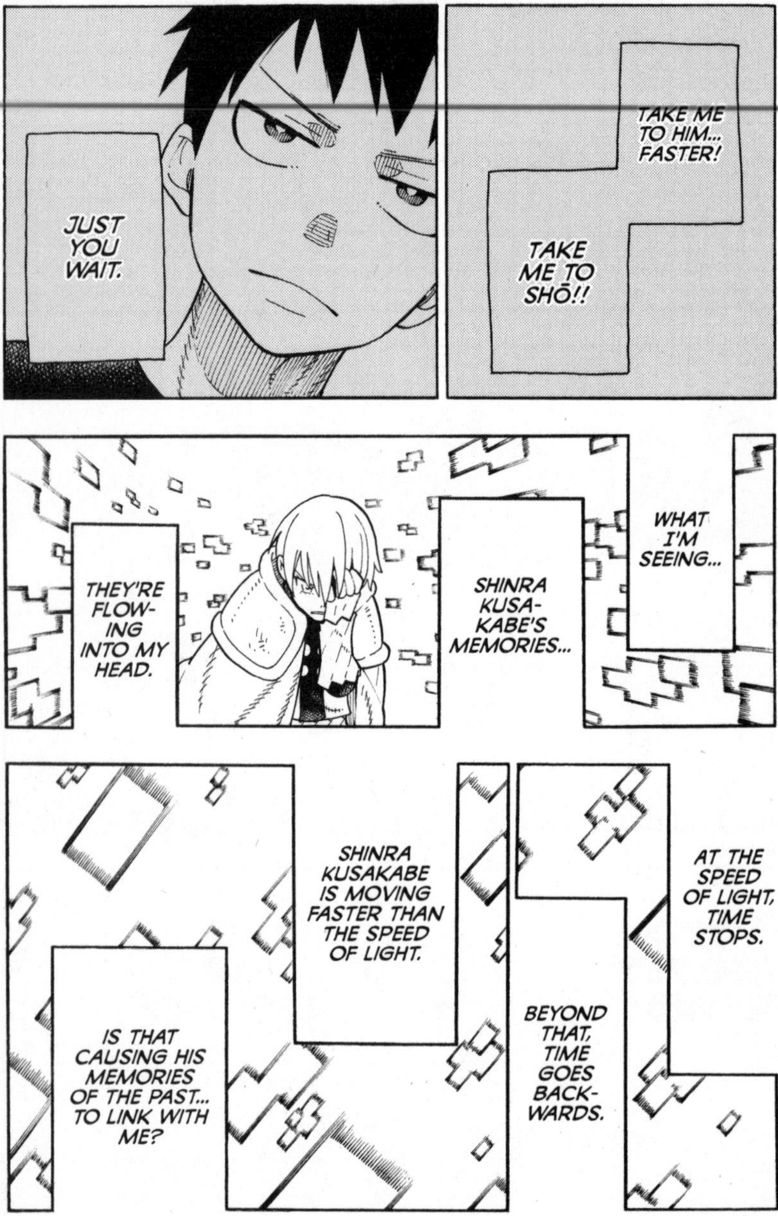
TAKE ME TO HIM... FASTER!
TAKE ME TO SHŌ!!
JUST YOU WAIT.
WHAT I'M SEEING...
SHINRA KUSAKABE'S MEMORIES...
THEY'RE FLOWING INTO MY HEAD.
AT THE SPEED OF LIGHT, TIME STOPS.
BEYOND THAT, TIME GOES BACKWARDS.
SHINRA KUSAKABE IS MOVING FASTER THAN THE SPEED OF LIGHT.
IS THAT CAUSING HIS MEMORIES OF THE PAST... TO LINK WITH ME?

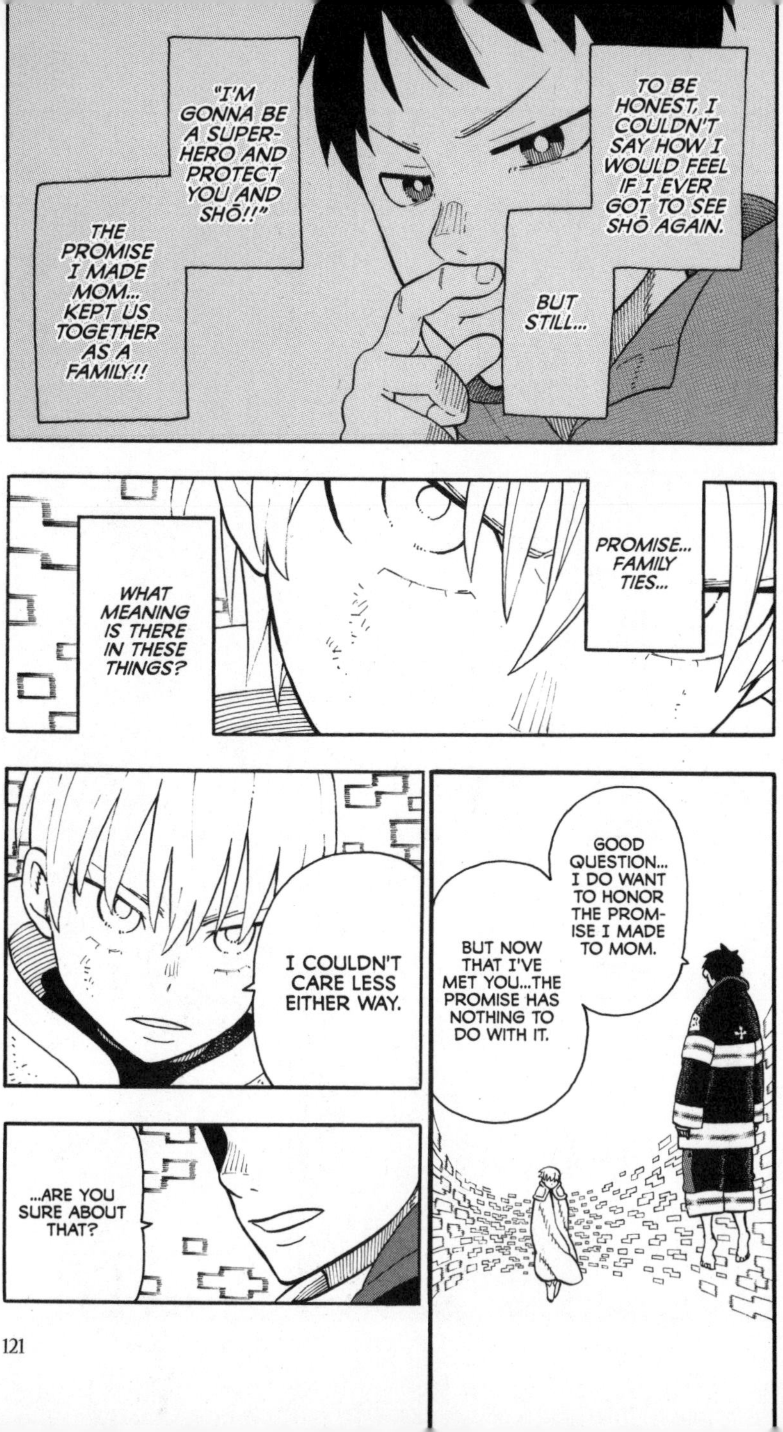
TO BE HONEST, I COULDN'T SAY HOW I WOULD FEEL IF I EVER GOT TO SEE SHŌ AGAIN.
BUT STILL...
"I'M GONNA BE A SUPER-HERO AND PROTECT YOU AND SHŌ!!"
THE PROMISE I MADE MOM... KEPT US TOGETHER AS A FAMILY!!
PROMISE... FAMILY TIES...
WHAT MEANING IS THERE IN THESE THINGS?
GOOD QUESTION... I DO WANT TO HONOR THE PROM-ISE I MADE TO MOM.
BUT NOW THAT I'VE MET YOU...THE PROMISE HAS NOTHING TO DO WITH IT.
I COULDN'T CARE LESS EITHER WAY.
...ARE YOU SURE ABOUT THAT?

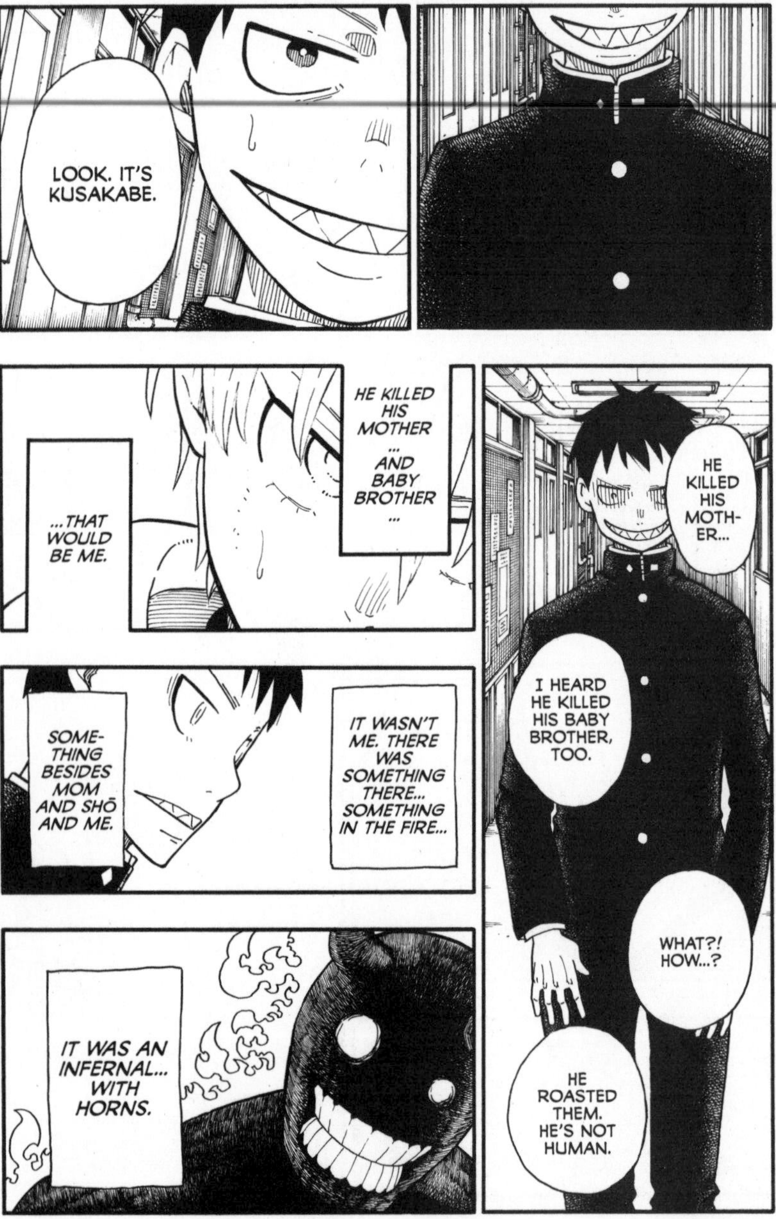
LOOK. IT'S KUSAKABE.
HE KILLED HIS MOTHER...
I HEARD HE KILLED HIS BABY BROTHER, TOO.
WHAT?! HOW...?
HE ROASTED THEM. HE'S NOT HUMAN.
HE KILLED HIS MOTHER ... AND BABY BROTHER ...
...THAT WOULD BE ME.
IT WASN'T ME. THERE WAS SOMETHING THERE... SOMETHING IN THE FIRE...
SOMETHING BESIDES MOM AND SHŌ AND ME.
IT WAS AN INFERNAL... WITH HORNS.

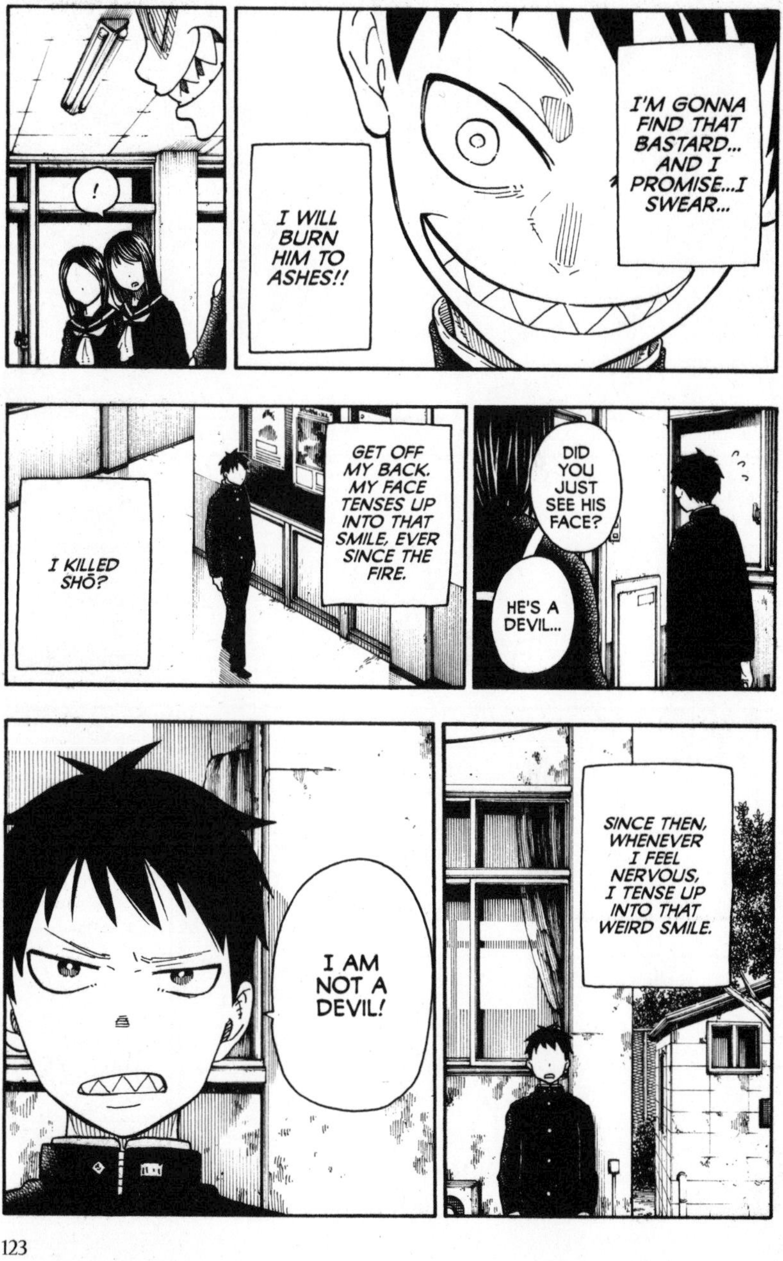
I'M GONNA FIND THAT BASTARD... AND I PROMISE...I SWEAR...
I WILL BURN HIM TO ASHES!!
!
DID YOU JUST SEE HIS FACE?
HE'S A DEVIL...
GET OFF MY BACK. MY FACE TENSES UP INTO THAT SMILE, EVER SINCE THE FIRE.
I KILLED SHŌ?
SINCE THEN, WHENEVER I FEEL NERVOUS, I TENSE UP INTO THAT WEIRD SMILE.
I AM NOT A DEVIL!

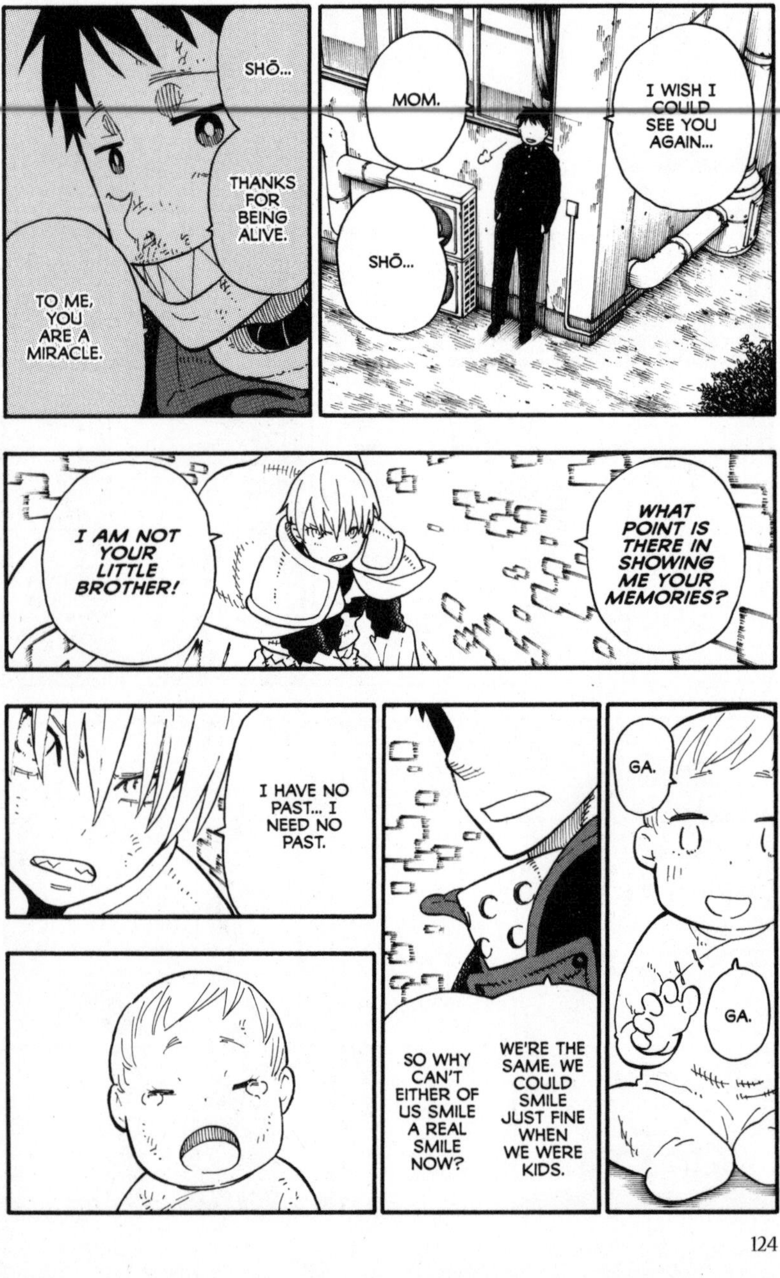
I WISH I COULD SEE YOU AGAIN...
MOM.
SHŌ...
SHŌ...
THANKS FOR BEING ALIVE.
TO ME, YOU ARE A MIRACLE.
WHAT POINT IS THERE IN SHOWING ME YOUR MEMORIES?
I AM NOT YOUR LITTLE BROTHER!
GA.
GA.
WE'RE THE SAME. WE COULD SMILE JUST FINE WHEN WE WERE KIDS.
SO WHY CAN'T EITHER OF US SMILE A REAL SMILE NOW?
I HAVE NO PAST... I NEED NO PAST.

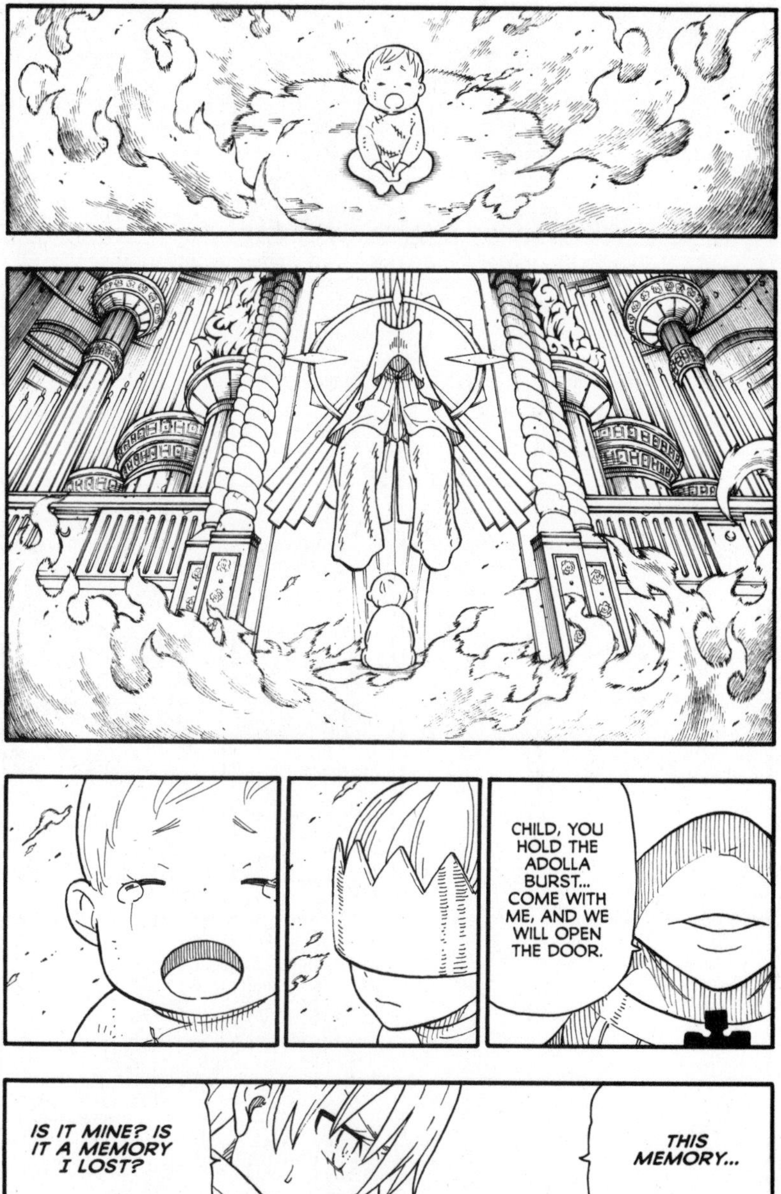
CHILD, YOU HOLD THE ADOLLA BURST... COME WITH ME, AND WE WILL OPEN THE DOOR.
THIS MEMORY...
IS IT MINE? IS IT A MEMORY I LOST?

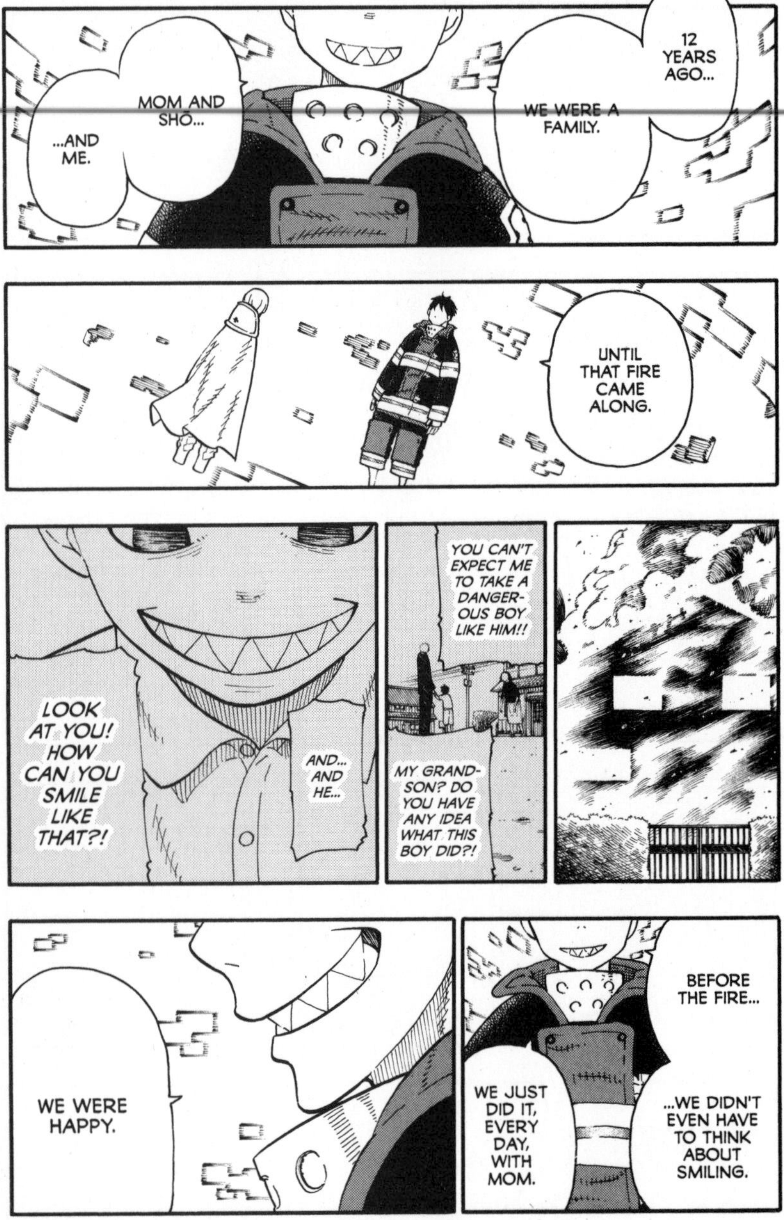
12 YEARS AGO...
WE WERE A FAMILY.
MOM AND SHO...
...AND ME.
UNTIL THAT FIRE CAME ALONG.
YOU CAN'T EXPECT ME TO TAKE A DANGEROUS BOY LIKE HIM!!
MY GRANDSON? DO YOU HAVE ANY IDEA WHAT THIS BOY DID?!
AND... AND HE...
LOOK AT YOU! HOW CAN YOU SMILE LIKE THAT?!
BEFORE THE FIRE...
...WE DIDN'T EVEN HAVE TO THINK ABOUT SMILING.
WE JUST DID IT, EVERY DAY, WITH MOM.
WE WERE HAPPY.

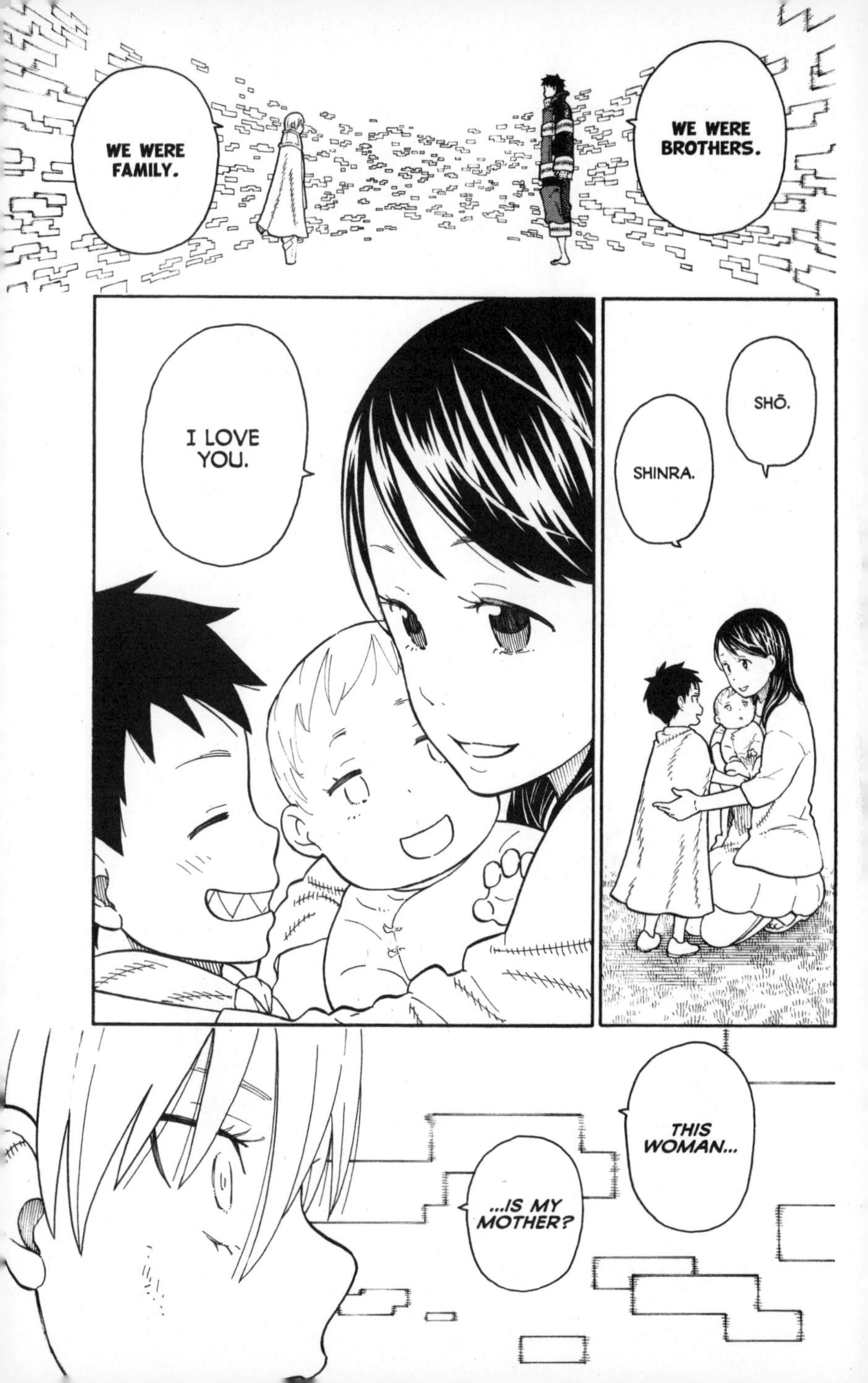
WE WERE BROTHERS.
WE WERE FAMILY.
SHŌ.
SHINRA.
I LOVE YOU.
THIS WOMAN...
...IS MY MOTHER?

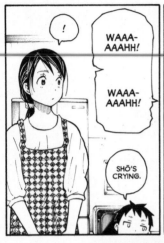

WHACHA MAKING, MOM?
HAMBURG STEAK!!
If you open it, close it!
YESSS!
!
WAAA-AAAHH!
WAAA-AAAHH!
SHŌ'S CRYING.
OH, MY, MY, WHAT DO I DO?
I *JUST* FED HIM AND PUT HIM TO SLEEP.
JUST HOLD ON A MINUTE! I'LL GO WASH MY HANDS!
I'LL DO IT, MOM!
I'LL GO SAVE THE DAY!
STOMP だ
I'M ON MY WAY, SHŌ!!
STOMP だ
STOMP だ
クス HEE HEE
WAAAA-AAHH!
ARE YOU OKAY?! YOU CAN RELAX NOW–YOUR BROTHER'S HERE!
ざざん ZA-ZAM

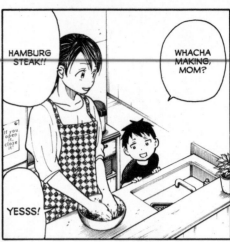

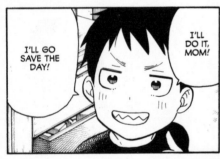

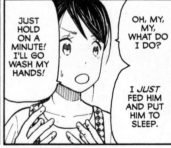

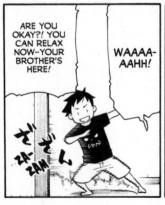

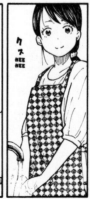

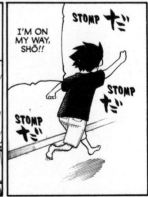

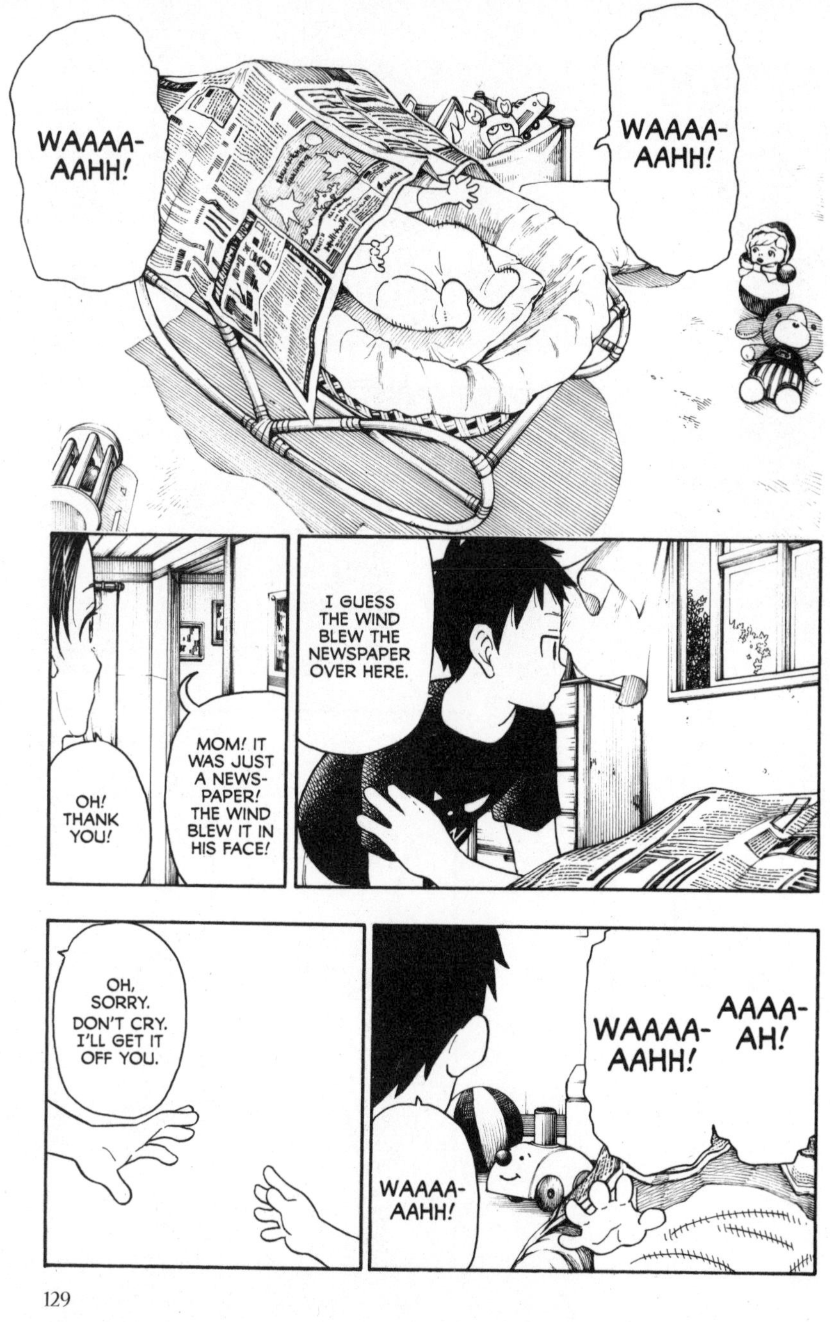
WAAAA-AAHH!
WAAAA-AAHH!
I GUESS THE WIND BLEW THE NEWSPAPER OVER HERE.
MOM! IT WAS JUST A NEWS-PAPER! THE WIND BLEW IT IN HIS FACE!
OH! THANK YOU!
AAAA-AH!
WAAAA-AAHH!
WAAAA-AAHH!
OH, SORRY. DON'T CRY. I'LL GET IT OFF YOU.

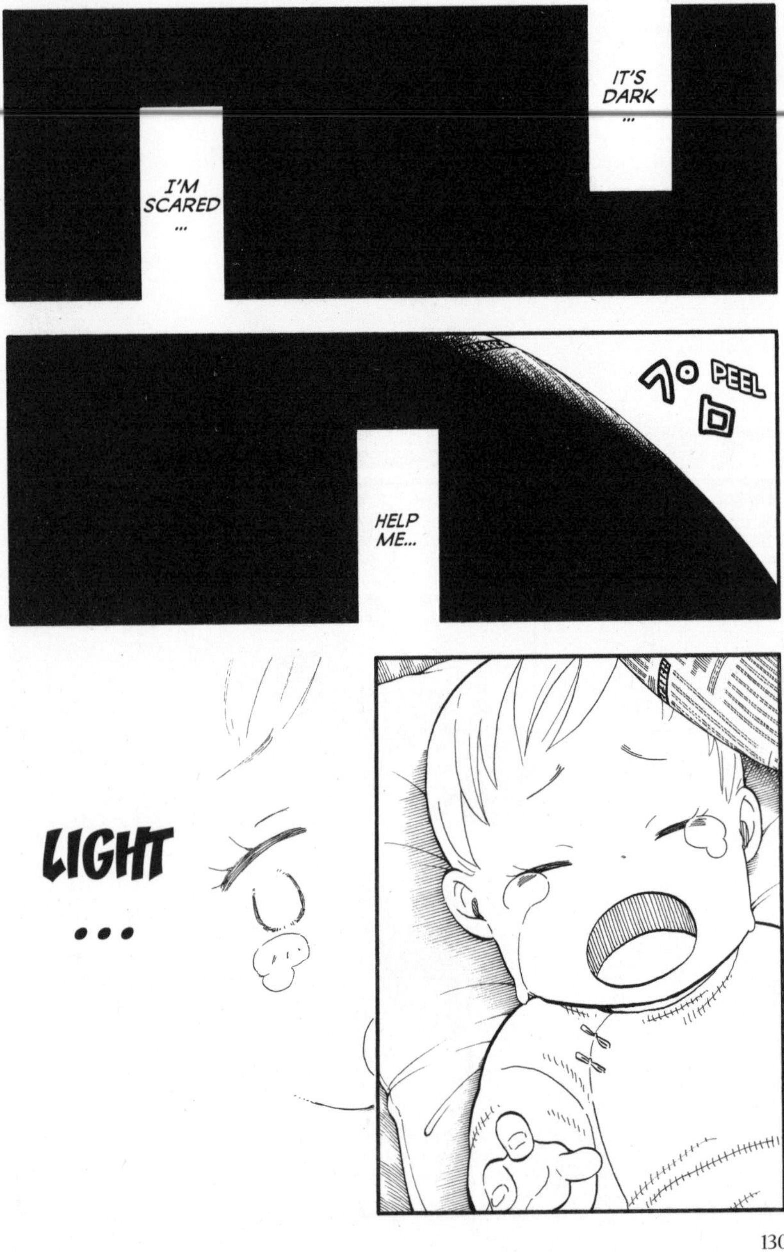
IT'S DARK ...
I'M SCARED ...
PEEL
HELP ME...
LIGHT ...

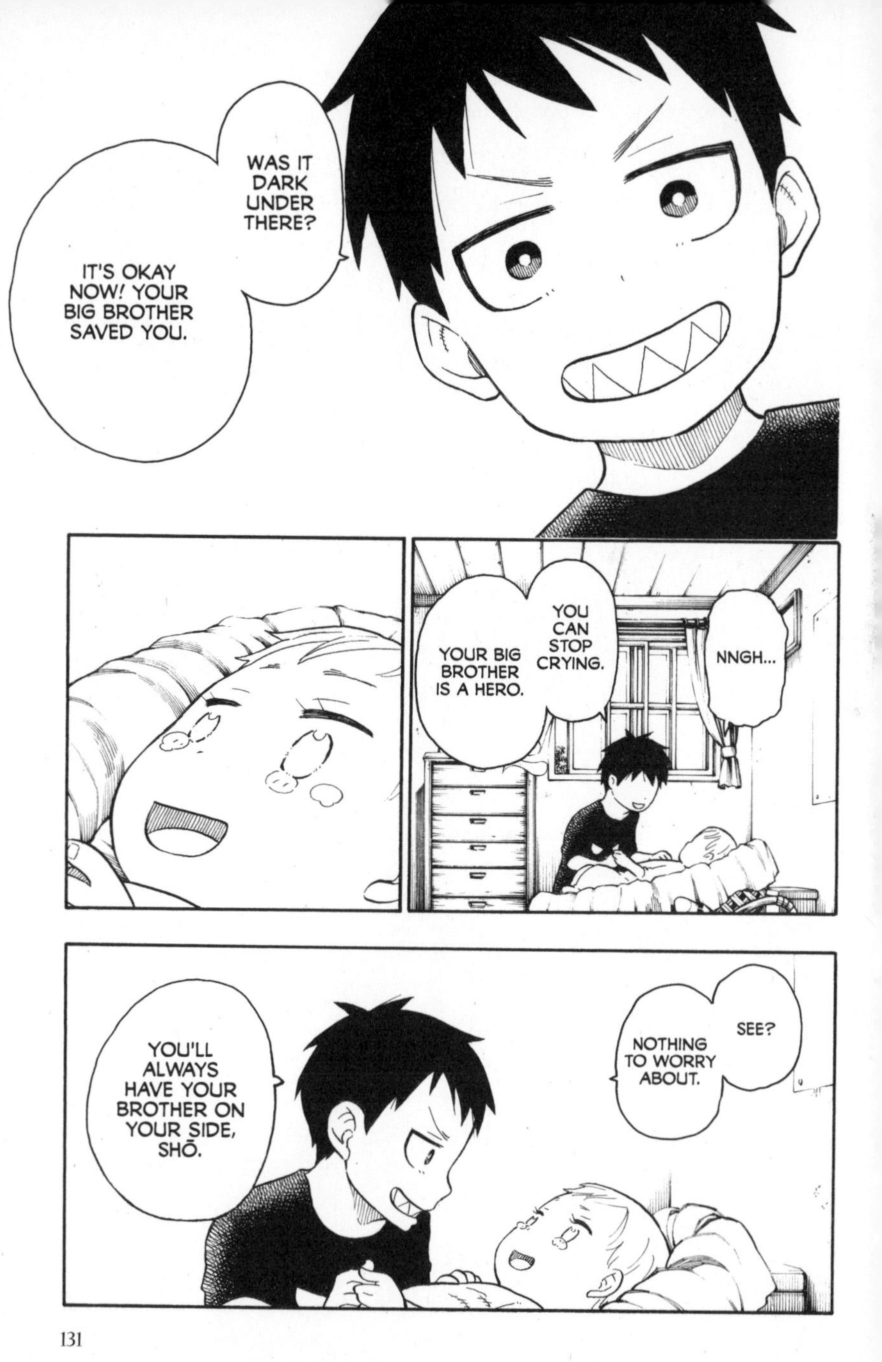
WAS IT DARK UNDER THERE?
IT'S OKAY NOW! YOUR BIG BROTHER SAVED YOU.
NNGH...
YOU CAN STOP CRYING.
YOUR BIG BROTHER IS A HERO.
SEE?
NOTHING TO WORRY ABOUT.
YOU'LL ALWAYS HAVE YOUR BROTHER ON YOUR SIDE, SHŌ.

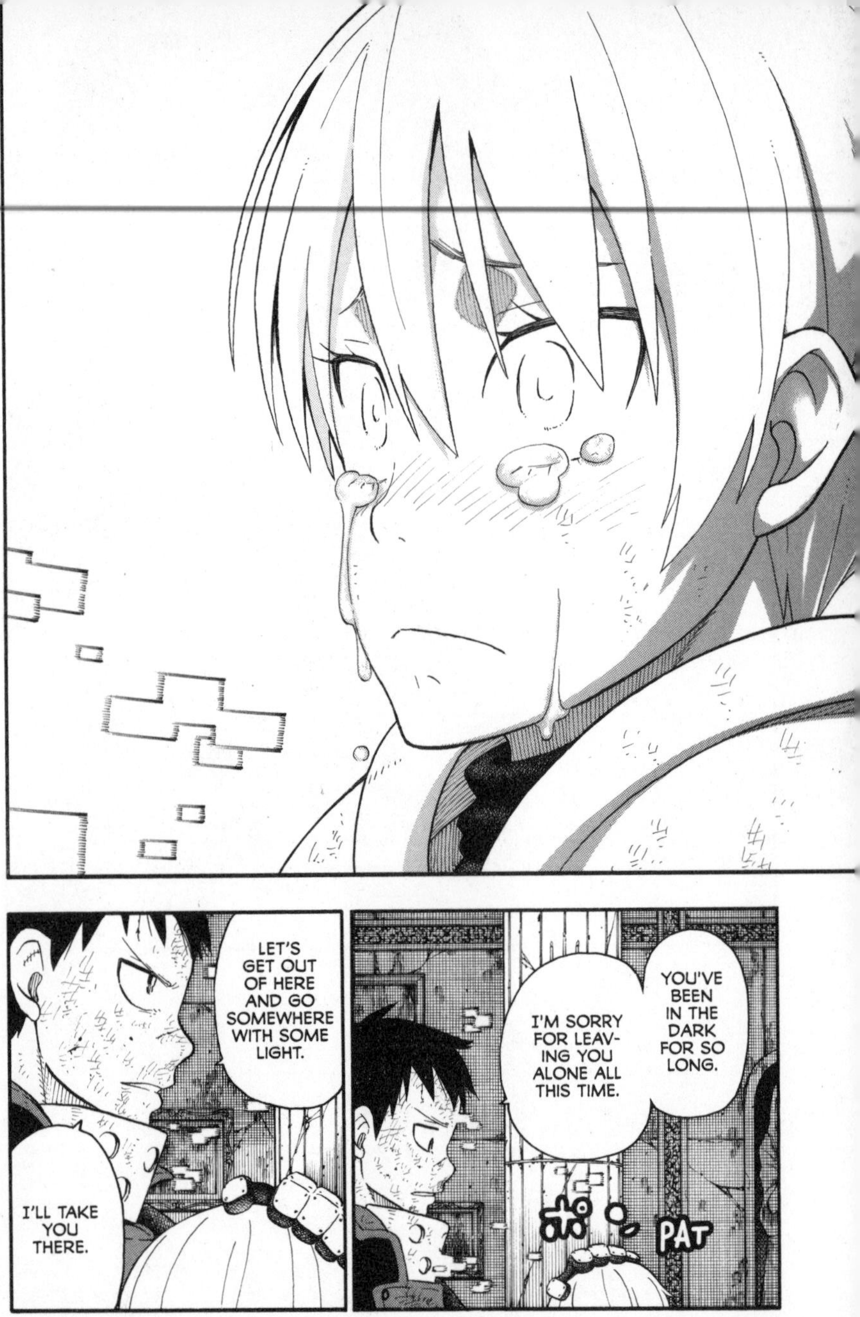
YOU'VE BEEN IN THE DARK FOR SO LONG.
I'M SORRY FOR LEAVING YOU ALONE ALL THIS TIME.
PAT
LET'S GET OUT OF HERE AND GO SOMEWHERE WITH SOME LIGHT.
I'LL TAKE YOU THERE.

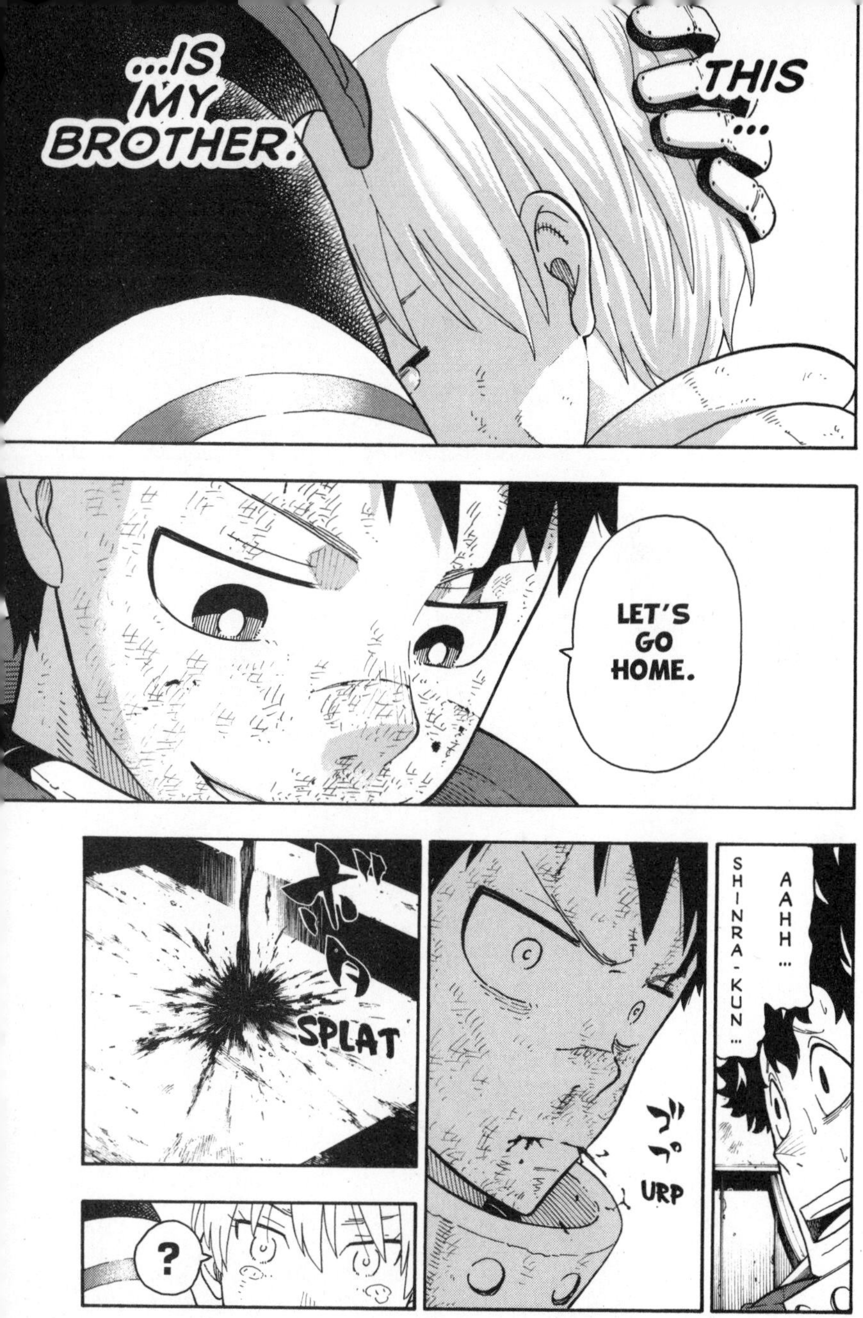
THIS...
...IS MY BROTHER.
LET'S GO HOME.
AAHH...
SHINRA-KUN...
URP
SPLAT
?

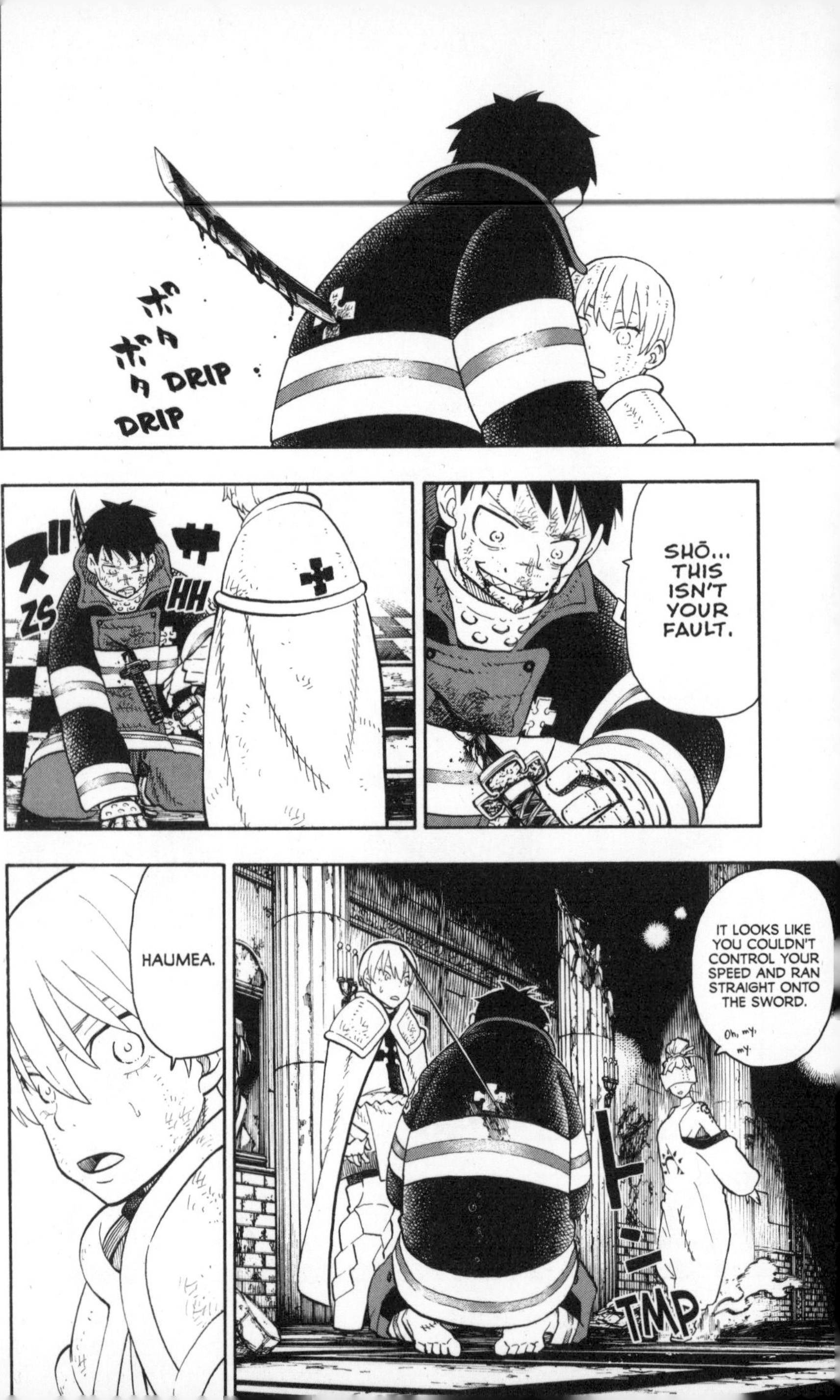
ポタ ポタ
DRIP DRIP
SHŌ... THIS ISN'T YOUR FAULT.
ズザ
ZS HH
IT LOOKS LIKE YOU COULDN'T CONTROL YOUR SPEED AND RAN STRAIGHT ONTO THE SWORD.
Oh, my, my.
TMP
HAUMEA.

FIRE FORCE

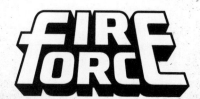

FIRE FORCE

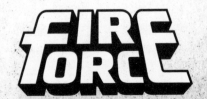

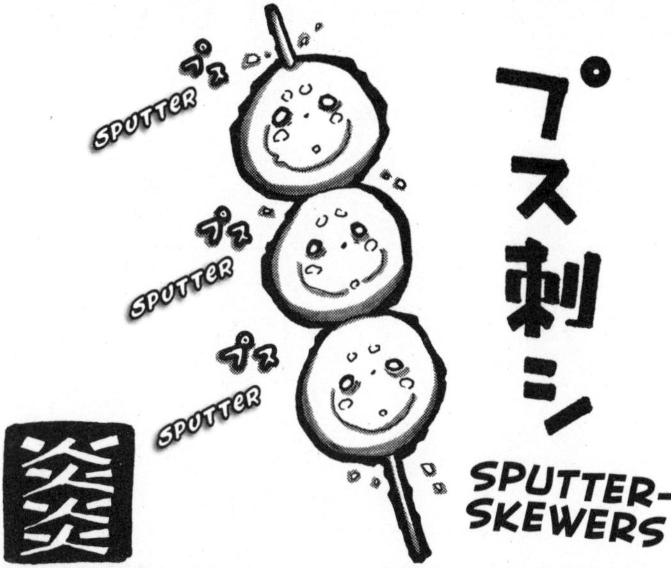
プス刺シ
SPUTTER-SKEWERS
プス
SPUTTER
プス
SPUTTER
プス
SPUTTER
炎
Stamp: Fire

CHAPTER LXXXV: A PLOT REVEALED

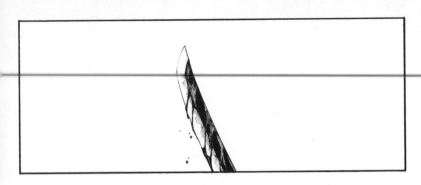

ALO-HELLO!

HAUMEA...

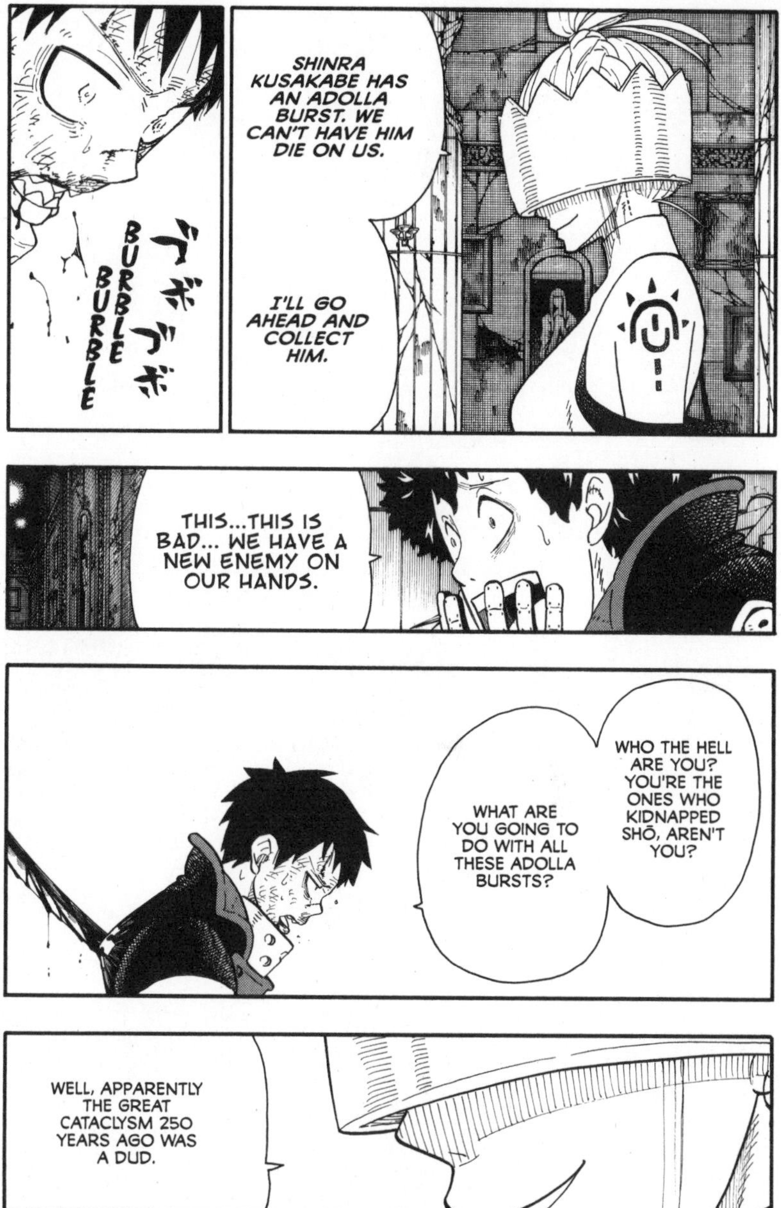
SHINRA KUSAKABE HAS AN ADOLLA BURST. WE CAN'T HAVE HIM DIE ON US.
I'LL GO AHEAD AND COLLECT HIM.
ゴボゴボ
BURBLE BURBLE
THIS...THIS IS BAD... WE HAVE A NEW ENEMY ON OUR HANDS.
WHO THE HELL ARE YOU? YOU'RE THE ONES WHO KIDNAPPED SHŌ, AREN'T YOU?
WHAT ARE YOU GOING TO DO WITH ALL THESE ADOLLA BURSTS?
WELL, APPARENTLY THE GREAT CATACLYSM 250 YEARS AGO WAS A DUD.

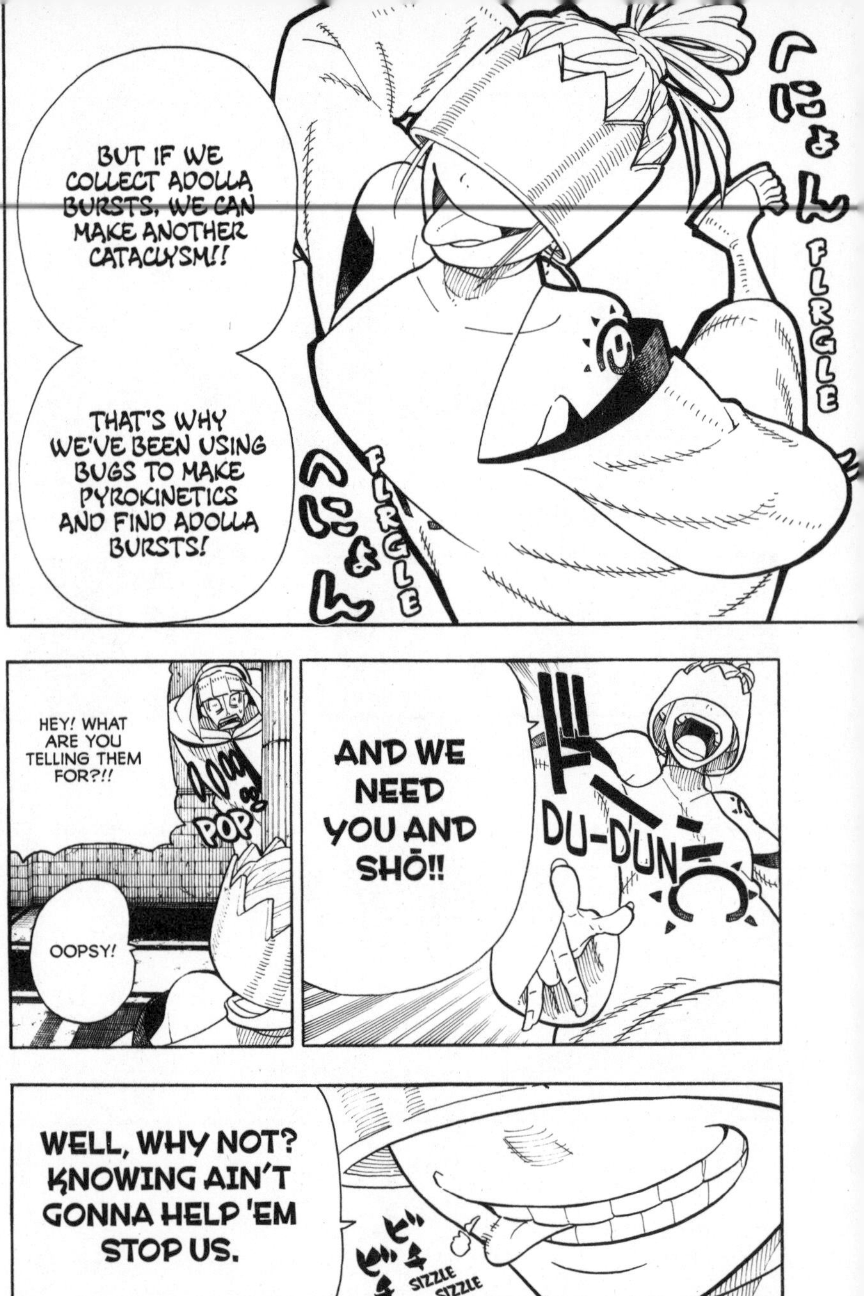
BUT IF WE COLLECT ADOLLA BURSTS, WE CAN MAKE ANOTHER CATACLYSM!!
THAT'S WHY WE'VE BEEN USING BUGS TO MAKE PYROKINETICS AND FIND ADOLLA BURSTS!
へにょん
FLRGLE
へにょん
FLRGLE
AND WE NEED YOU AND SHŌ!!
ドン
DU-DUN
HEY! WHAT ARE YOU TELLING THEM FOR?!!
POP
OOPSY!
WELL, WHY NOT? KNOWING AIN'T GONNA HELP 'EM STOP US.
SIZZLE SIZZLE

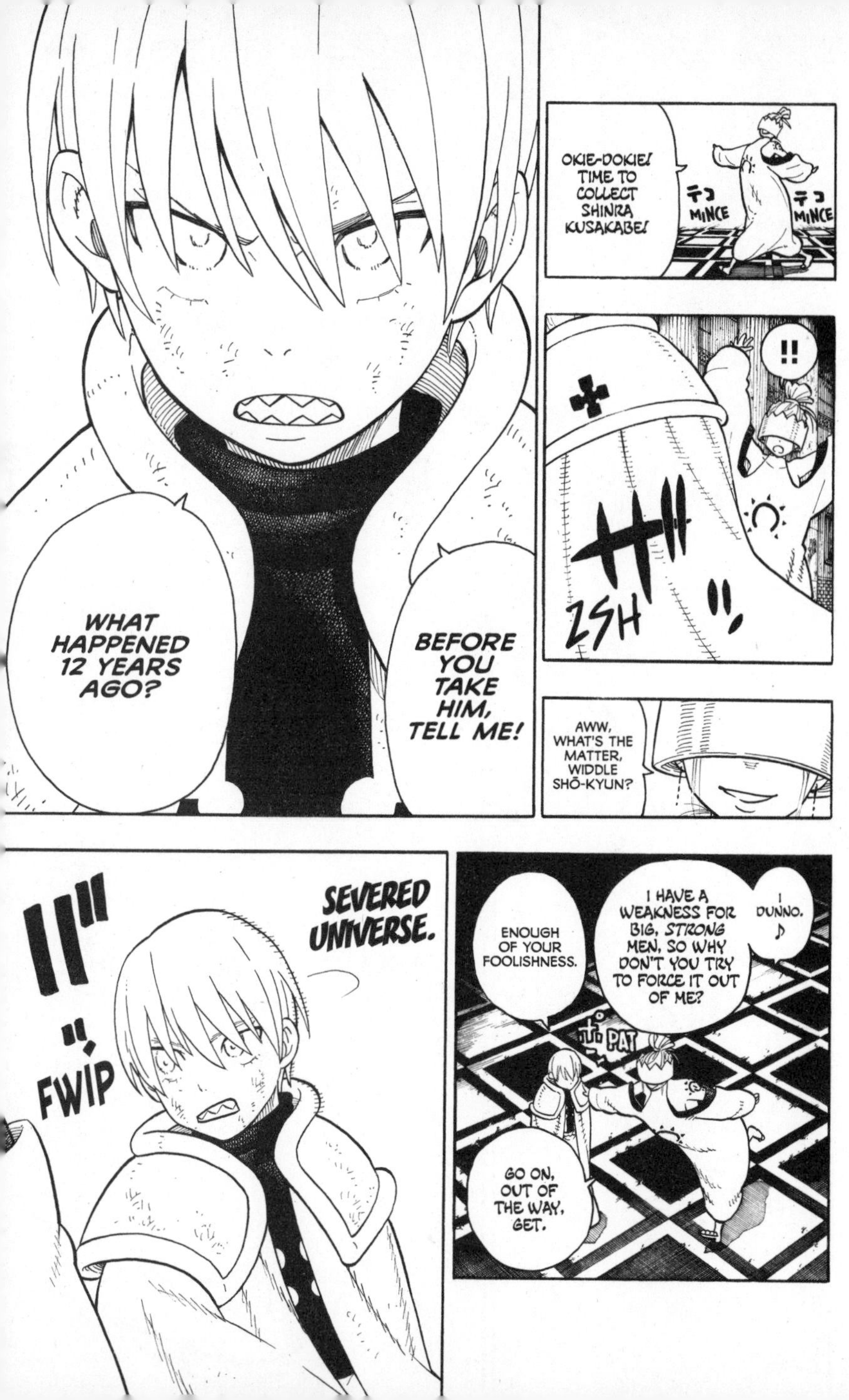
OKIE-DOKIE! TIME TO COLLECT SHINRA KUSAKABE!
テコ MINCE
テコ MINCE
!!
ZSH
AWW, WHAT'S THE MATTER, WIDDLE SHŌ-KYUN?
BEFORE YOU TAKE HIM, TELL ME!
WHAT HAPPENED 12 YEARS AGO?
I DUNNO. ♪
I HAVE A WEAKNESS FOR BIG, *STRONG* MEN, SO WHY DON'T YOU TRY TO FORCE IT OUT OF ME?
ENOUGH OF YOUR FOOLISHNESS.
PAT
GO ON, OUT OF THE WAY, GET.
SEVERED UNIVERSE.
FWIP

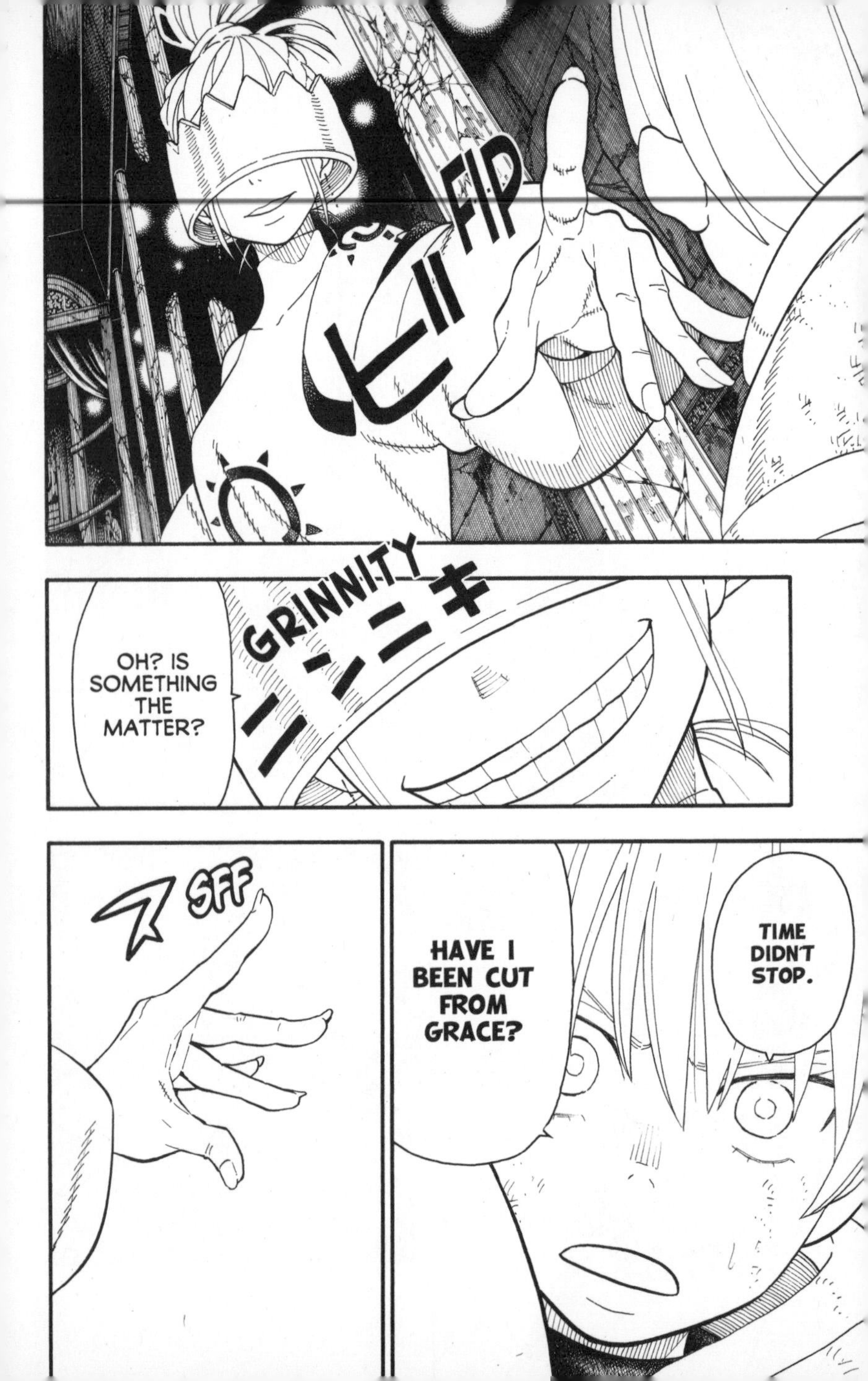
FIP
GRINNITY
OH? IS SOMETHING THE MATTER?
TIME DIDN'T STOP.
HAVE I BEEN CUT FROM GRACE?
SFF

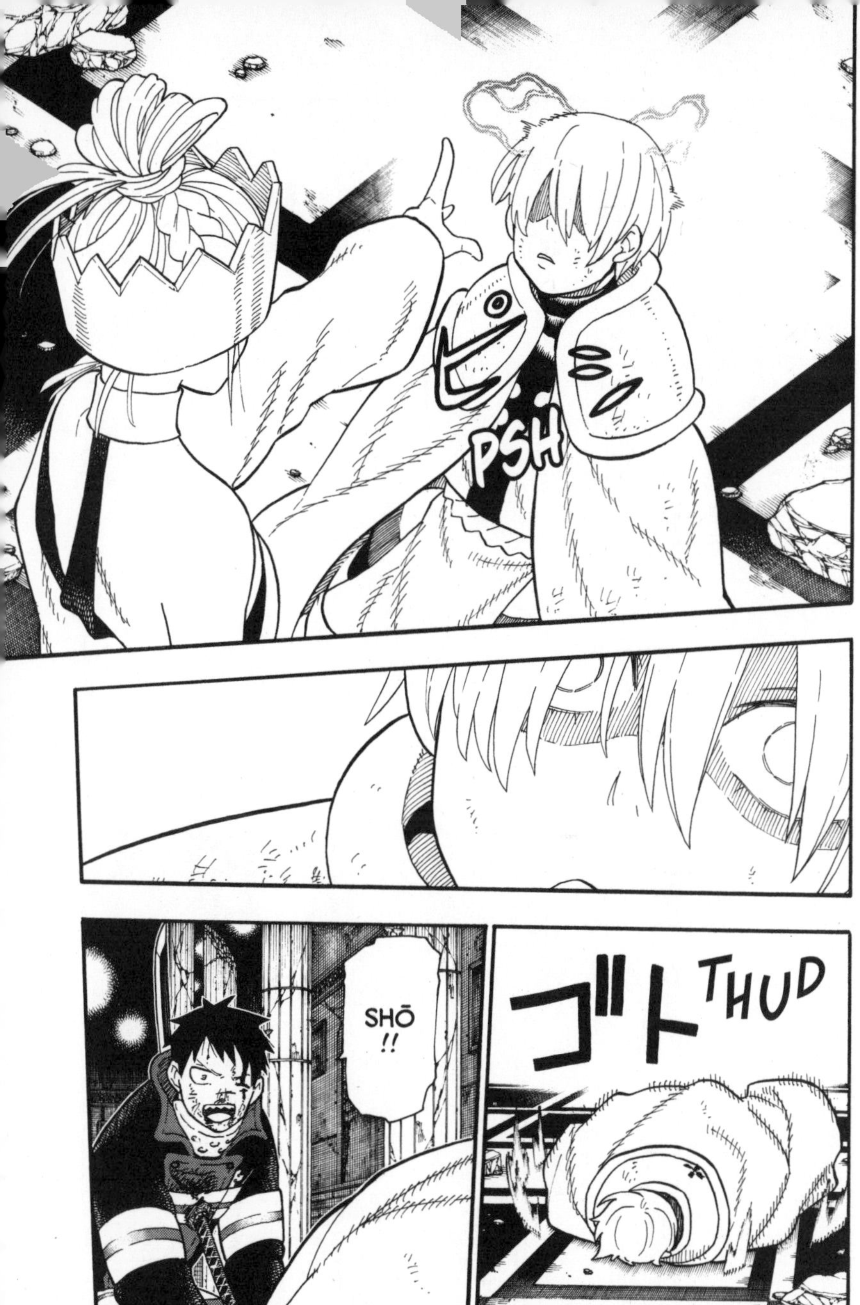
ピ
PSH
ゴト
THUD
SHŌ!!

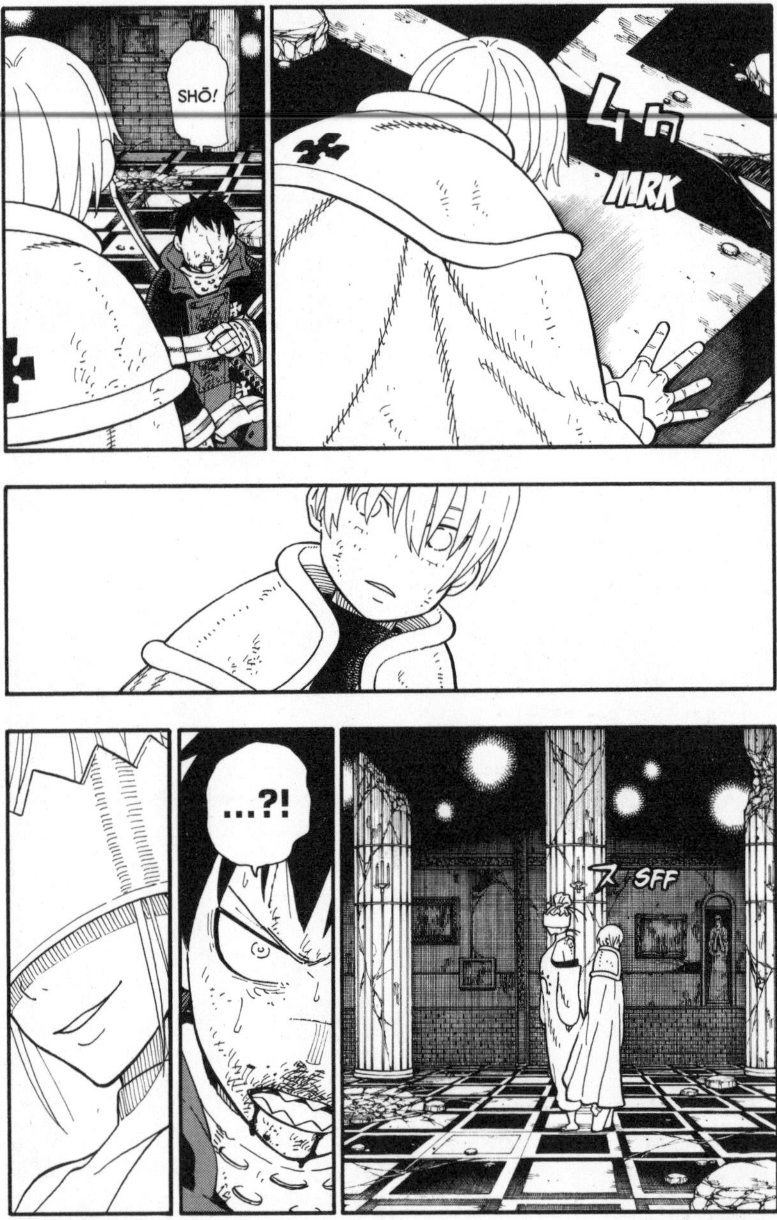
MRK
SHŌ!
ス SFF
...?!

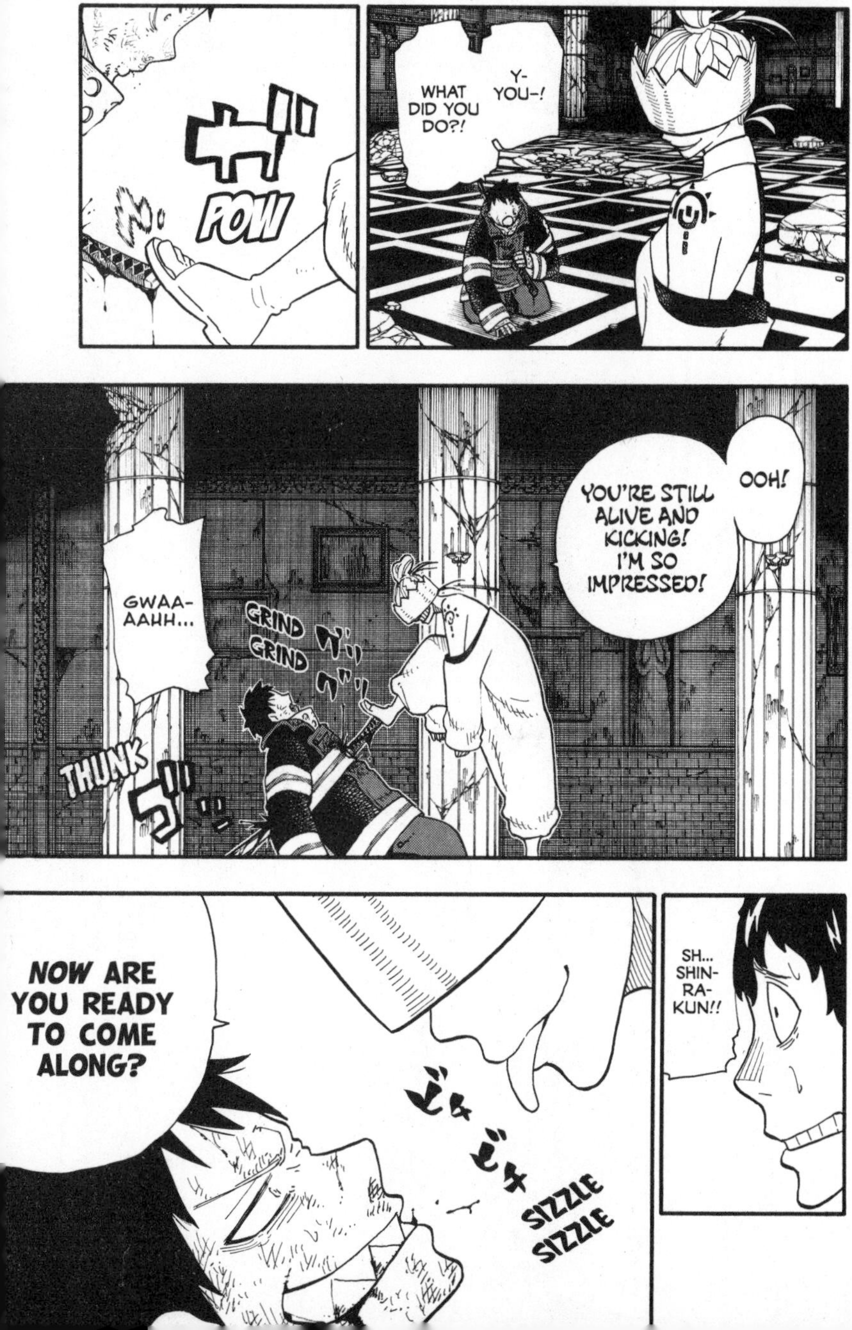
Y- YOU-!
WHAT DID YOU DO?!
POW
OOH!
YOU'RE STILL ALIVE AND KICKING! I'M SO IMPRESSED!
GRIND GRIND
GWAA-AAHH...
THUNK
SH... SHIN-RA-KUN!!
NOW ARE YOU READY TO COME ALONG?
SIZZLE SIZZLE

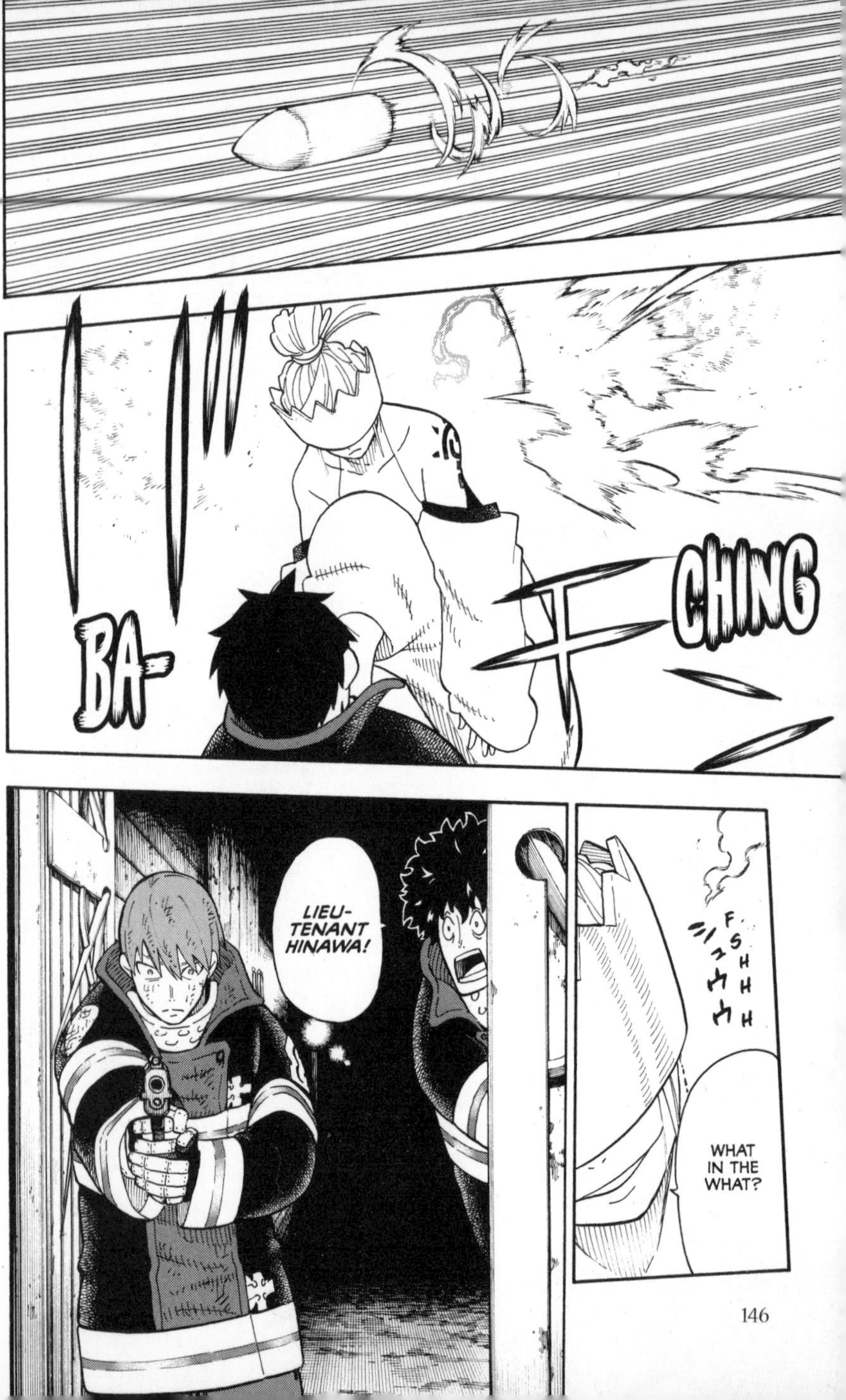
BA-
CHING
F S H H H
WHAT IN THE WHAT?
LIEU-TENANT HINAWA!

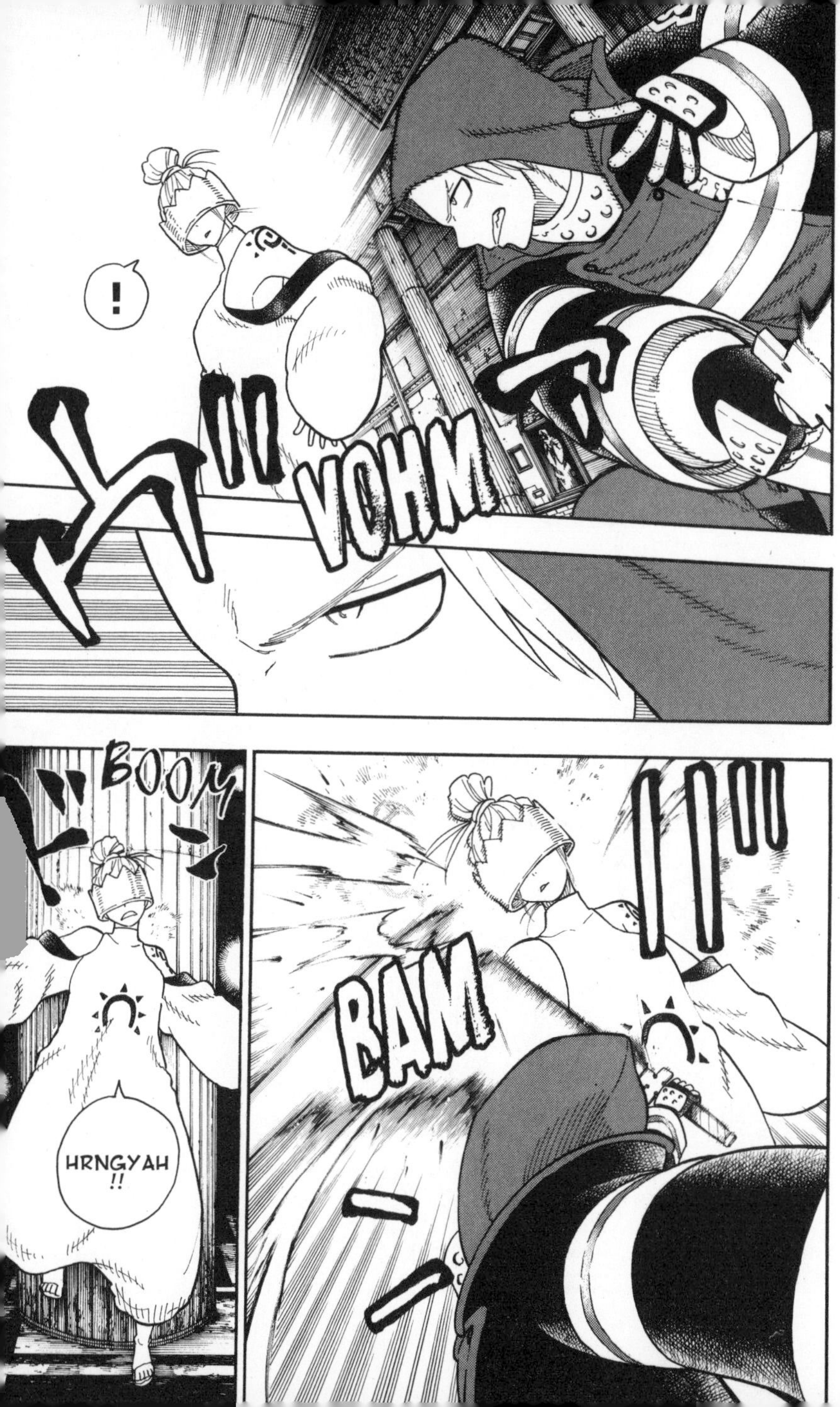
!
VOHM
BAM
BOOM
HRNGYAH !!

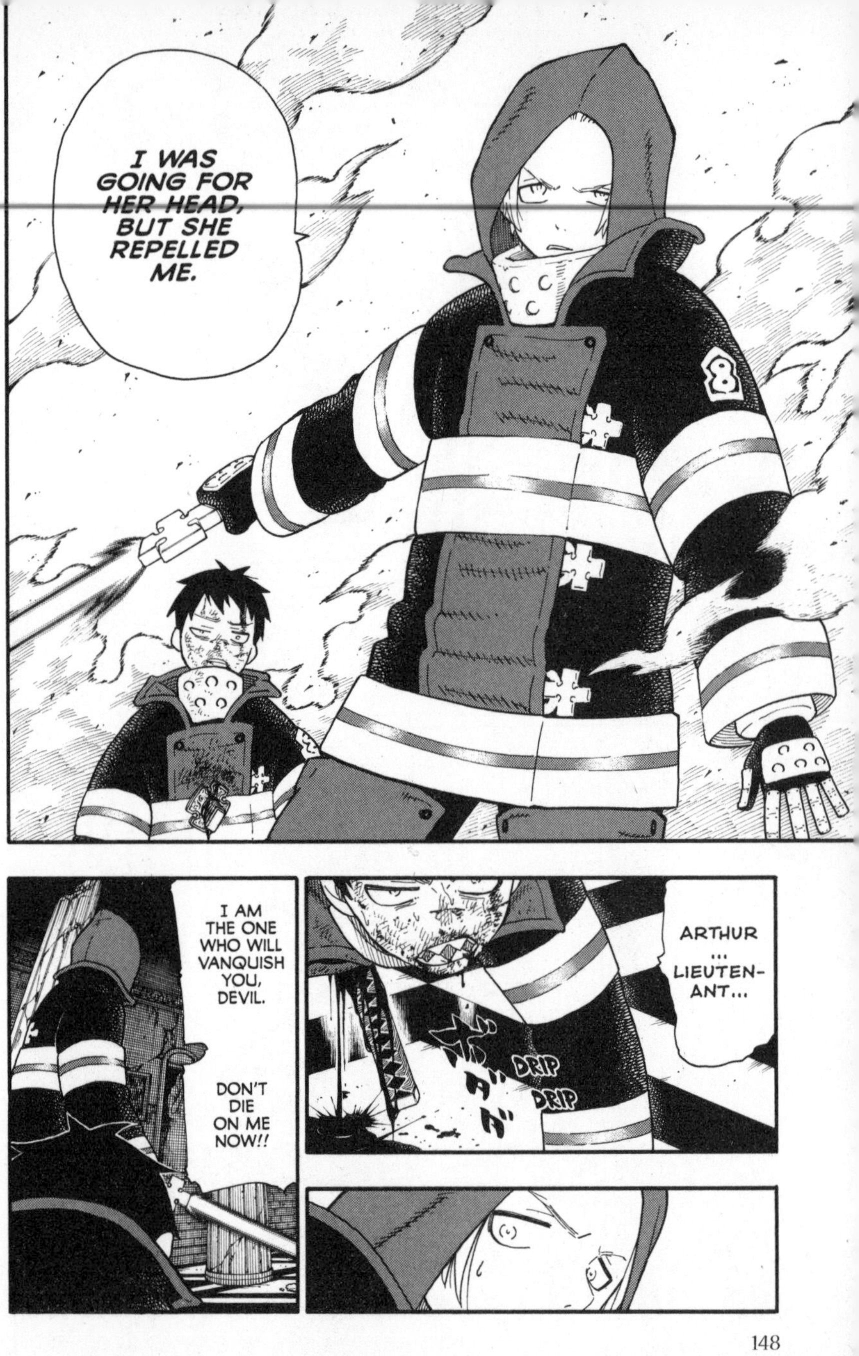
I WAS GOING FOR HER HEAD, BUT SHE REPELLED ME.
ARTHUR ... LIEUTEN-ANT...
DRIP
DRIP
I AM THE ONE WHO WILL VANQUISH YOU, DEVIL.
DON'T DIE ON ME NOW!!

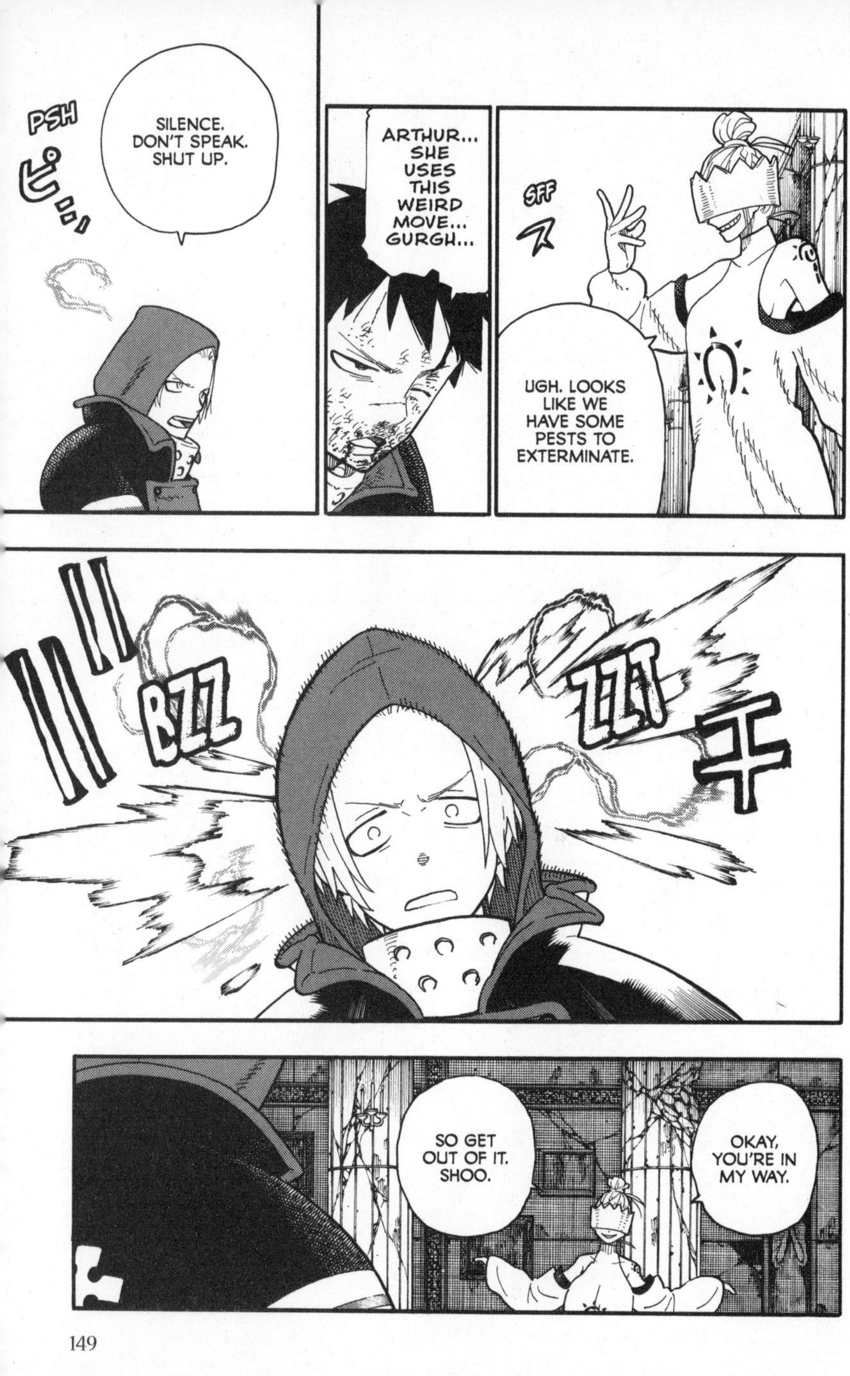
SFF
ス
UGH. LOOKS LIKE WE HAVE SOME PESTS TO EXTERMINATE.
ARTHUR... SHE USES THIS WEIRD MOVE... GURGH...
PSH
ピ
SILENCE. DON'T SPEAK. SHUT UP.
ZZT
キ
BZZ
OKAY, YOU'RE IN MY WAY.
SO GET OUT OF IT. SHOO.

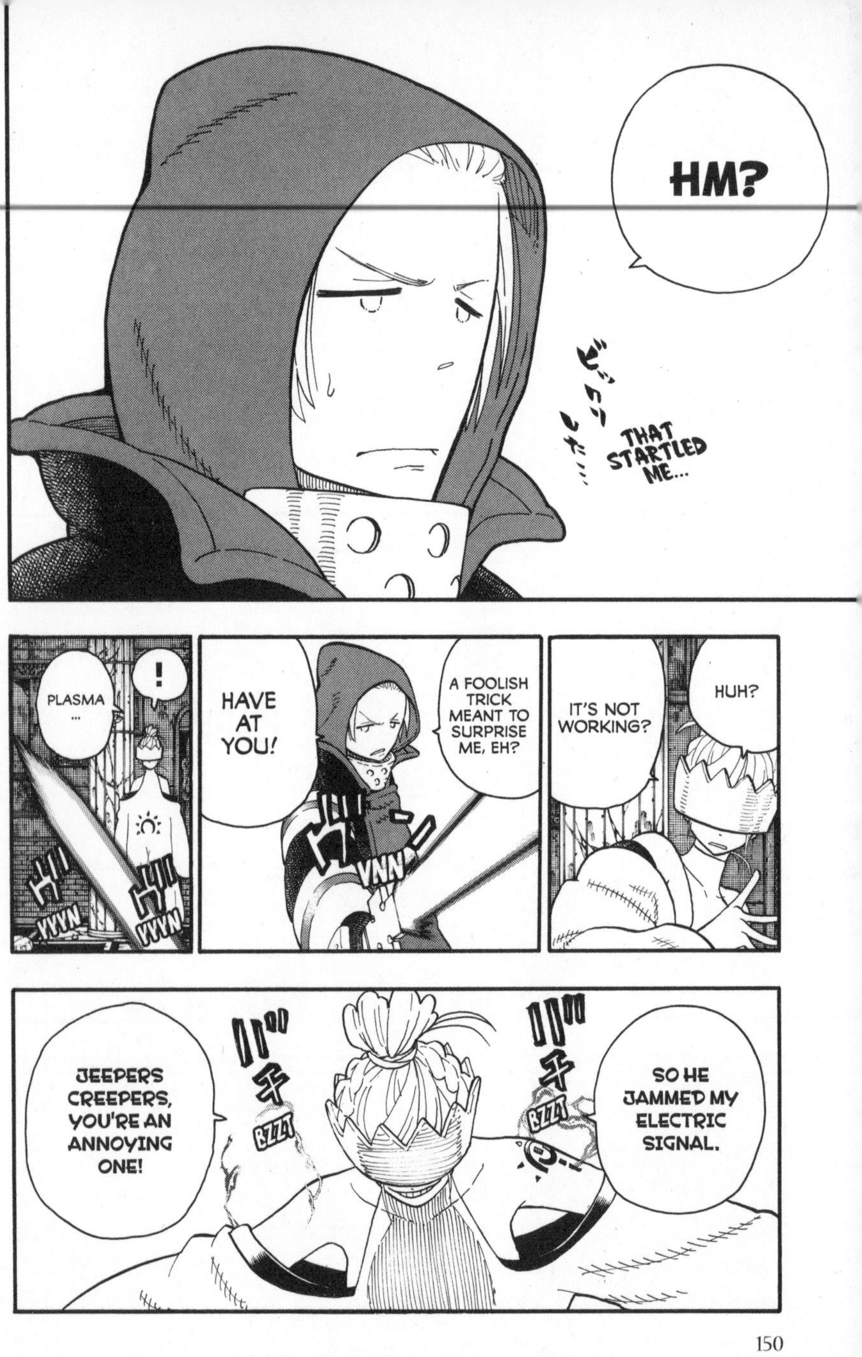
HM?
THAT STARTLED ME...
HUH?
IT'S NOT WORKING?
A FOOLISH TRICK MEANT TO SURPRISE ME, EH?
HAVE AT YOU!
VNN
!
PLASMA ...
VVVN
VVVN
SO HE JAMMED MY ELECTRIC SIGNAL.
BZZZT
BZZZT
JEEPERS CREEPERS, YOU'RE AN ANNOYING ONE!

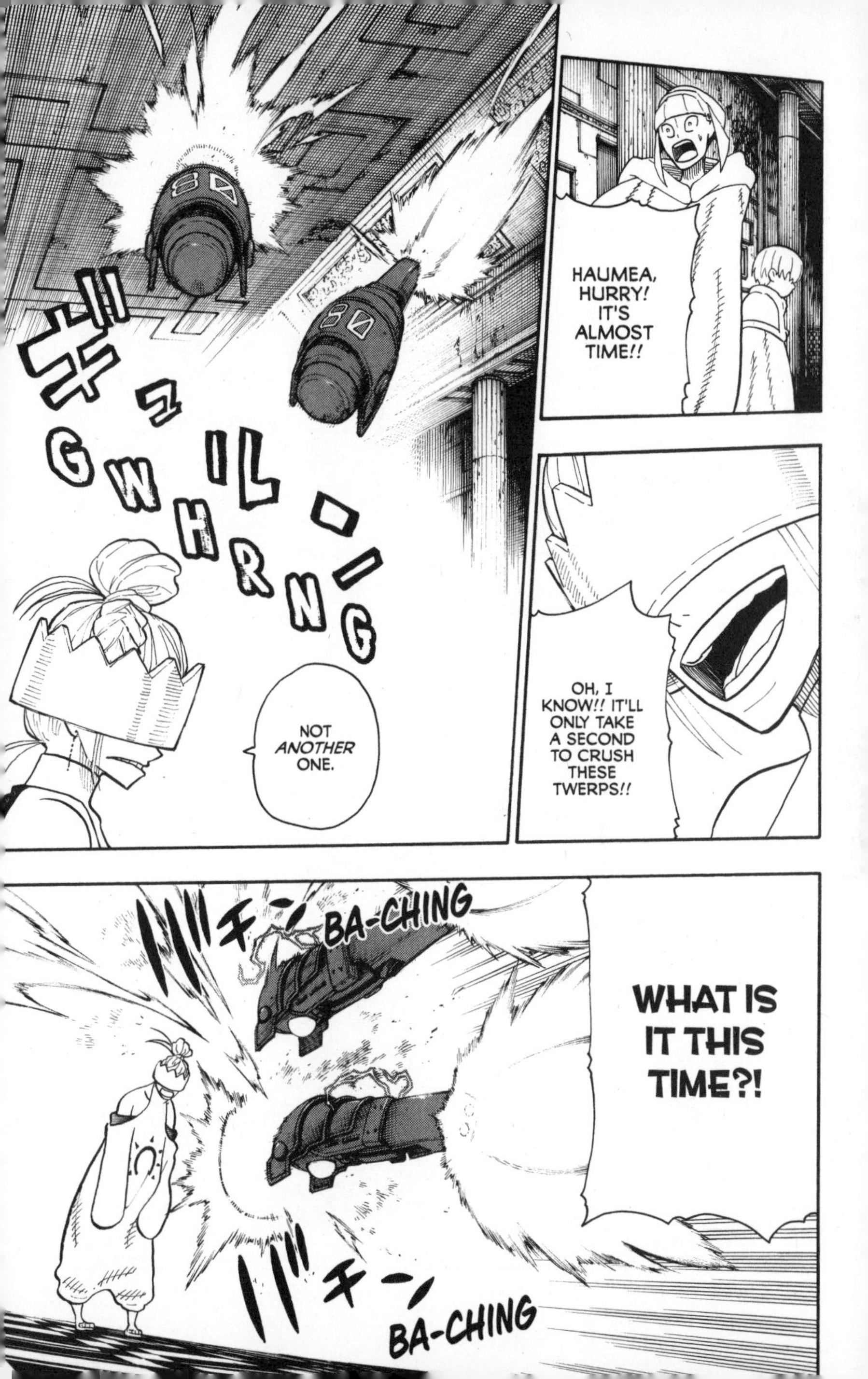
HAUMEA, HURRY! IT'S ALMOST TIME!!
OH, I KNOW!! IT'LL ONLY TAKE A SECOND TO CRUSH THESE TWERPS!!
GWHRNG
NOT *ANOTHER* ONE.
WHAT IS IT THIS TIME?!
BA-CHING
BA-CHING

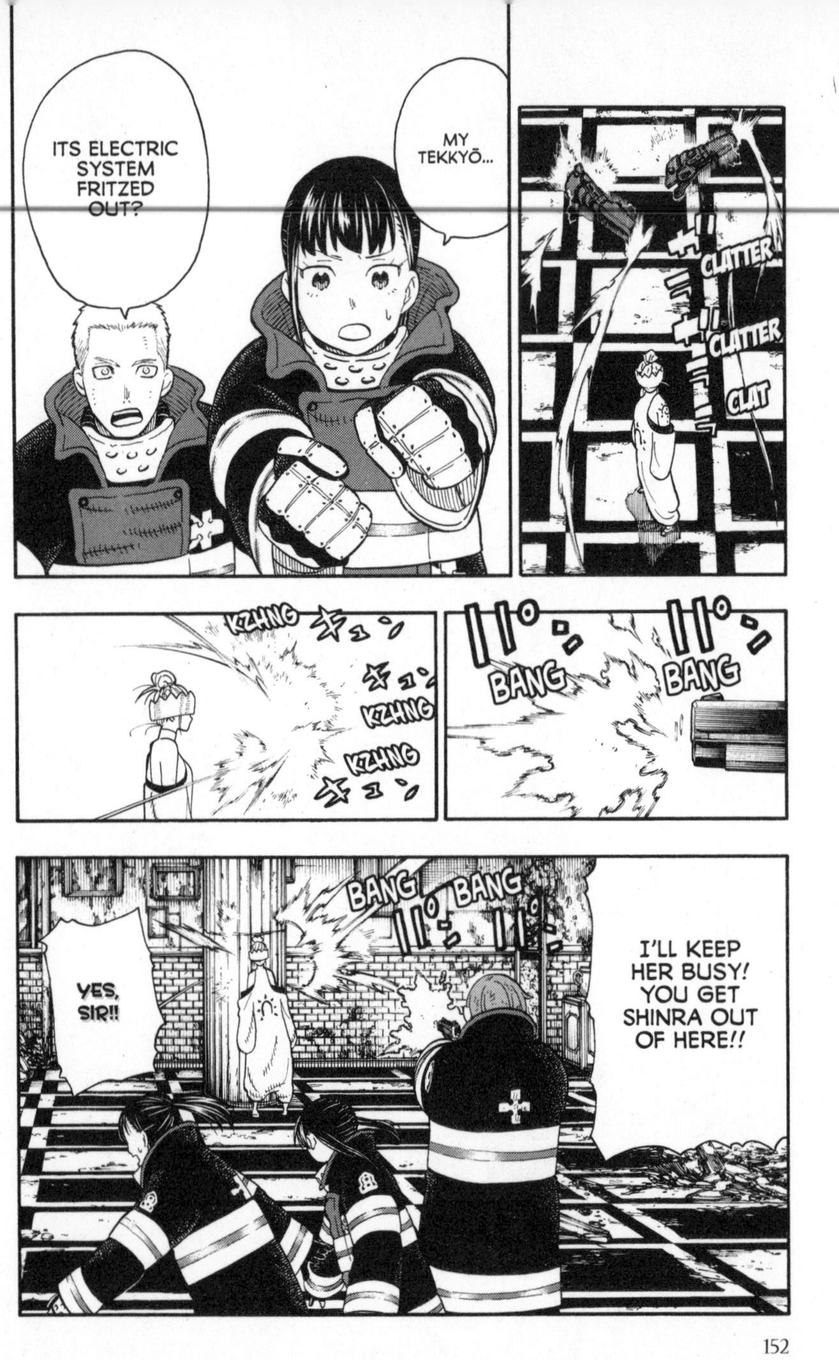
CLATTER
CLATTER
CLAT
MY TEKKYŌ...
ITS ELECTRIC SYSTEM FRITZED OUT?
BANG
BANG
KZHNG
KZHNG
KZHNG
BANG
BANG
I'LL KEEP HER BUSY! YOU GET SHINRA OUT OF HERE!!
YES, SIR!!

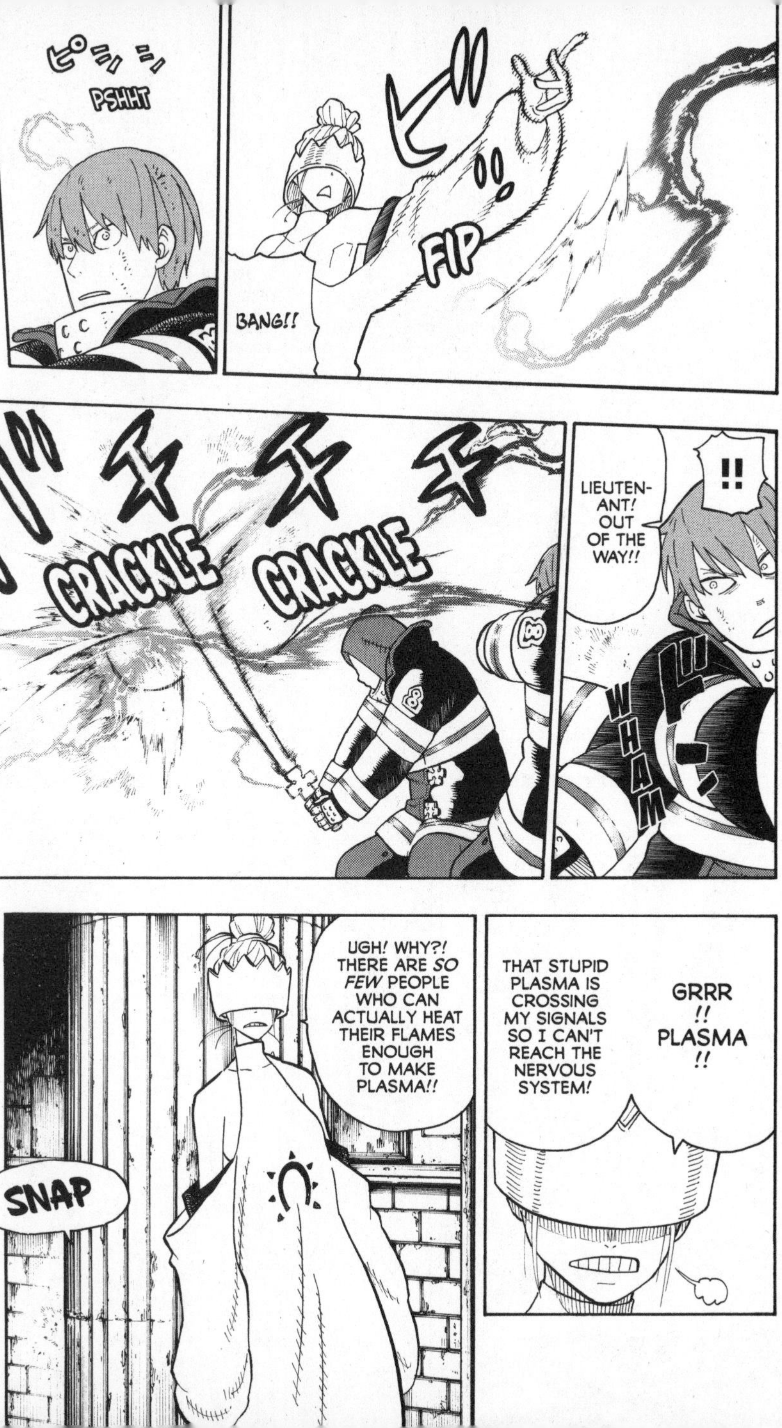
FIP
BANG!!
PSHHT
!!
LIEUTEN-ANT! OUT OF THE WAY!!
WHAM
CRACKLE
CRACKLE
GRRR!! PLASMA!!
THAT STUPID PLASMA IS CROSSING MY SIGNALS SO I CAN'T REACH THE NERVOUS SYSTEM!
UGH! WHY?! THERE ARE SO FEW PEOPLE WHO CAN ACTUALLY HEAT THEIR FLAMES ENOUGH TO MAKE PLASMA!!
SNAP

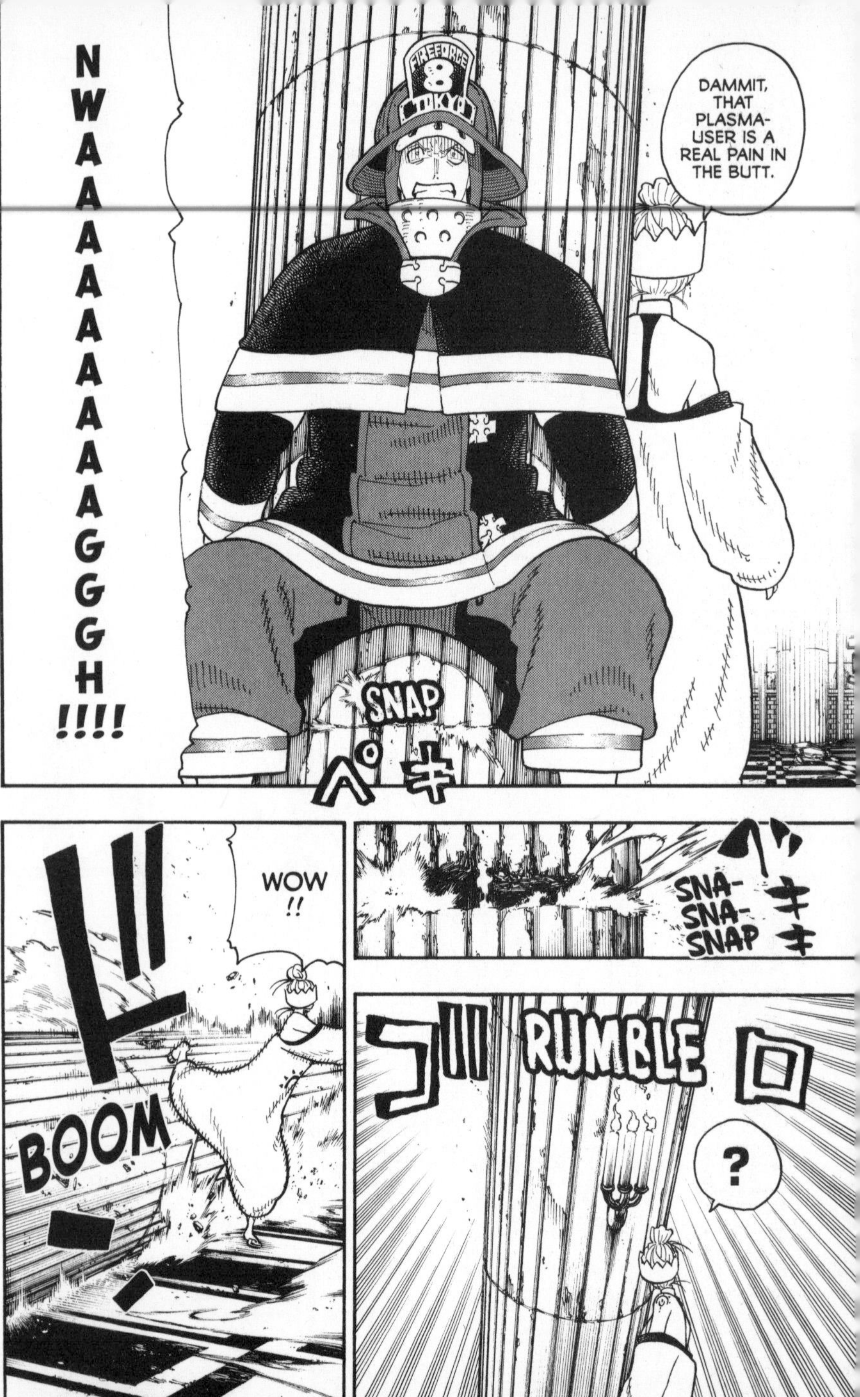
DAMMIT, THAT PLASMA-USER IS A REAL PAIN IN THE BUTT.
NWAAAAAAAAAGGGH!!!!
SNAP
ペキ
SNA-SNA-SNAP
ベキキ
RUMBLE
ゴロ
?
WOW!!
ドゴ
BOOM

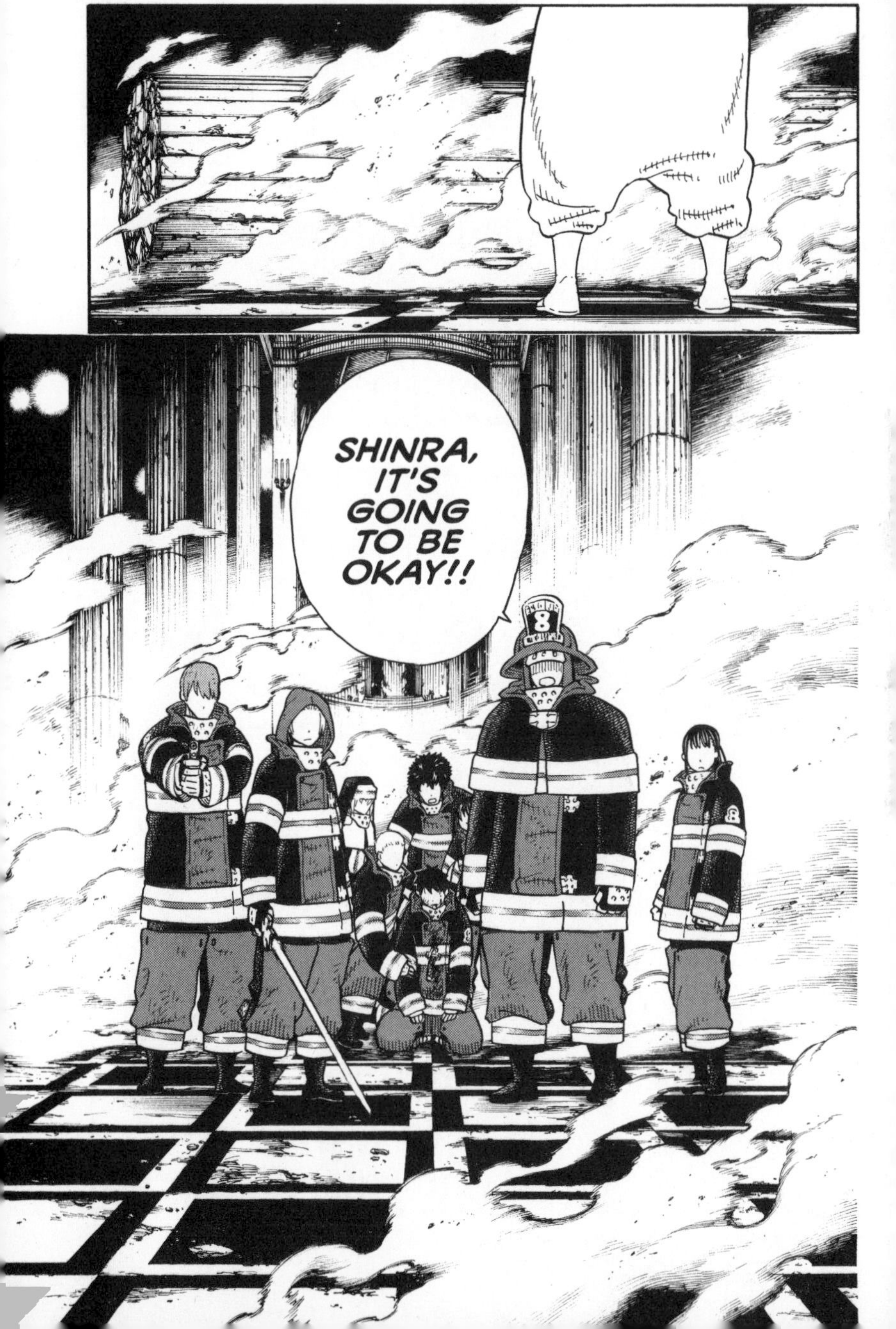
SHINRA, IT'S GOING TO BE OKAY!!

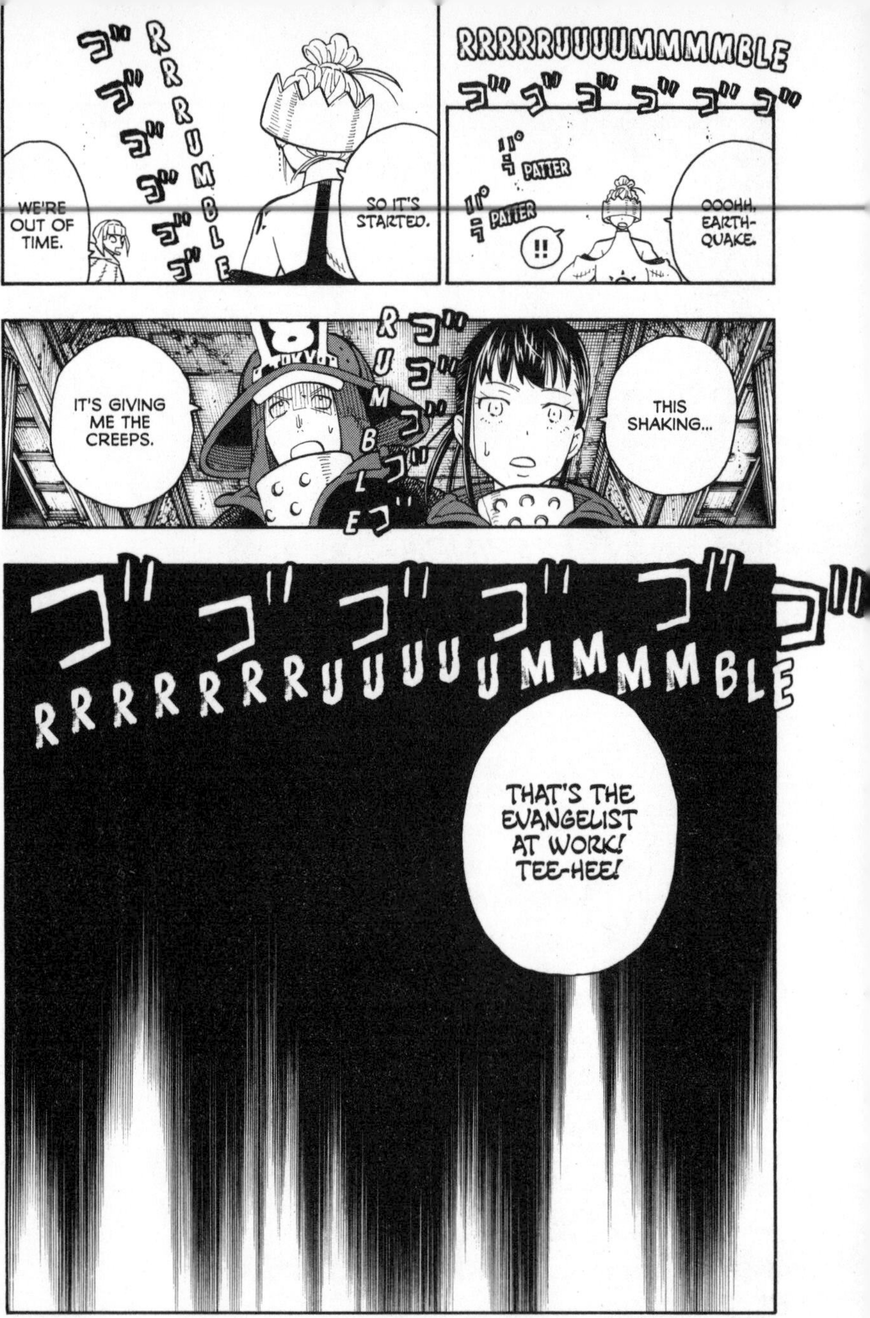
RRRRRUUUUMMMMMBLE
ゴゴゴゴゴゴ
OOOHH, EARTH-QUAKE.
PATTER
PATTER
!!
SO IT'S STARTED.
RRRUMBLE
WE'RE OUT OF TIME.
THIS SHAKING...
RUMBLE
IT'S GIVING ME THE CREEPS.
RRRRRRRUUUUUUMMMMMBLE
THAT'S THE EVANGELIST AT WORK! TEE-HEE!

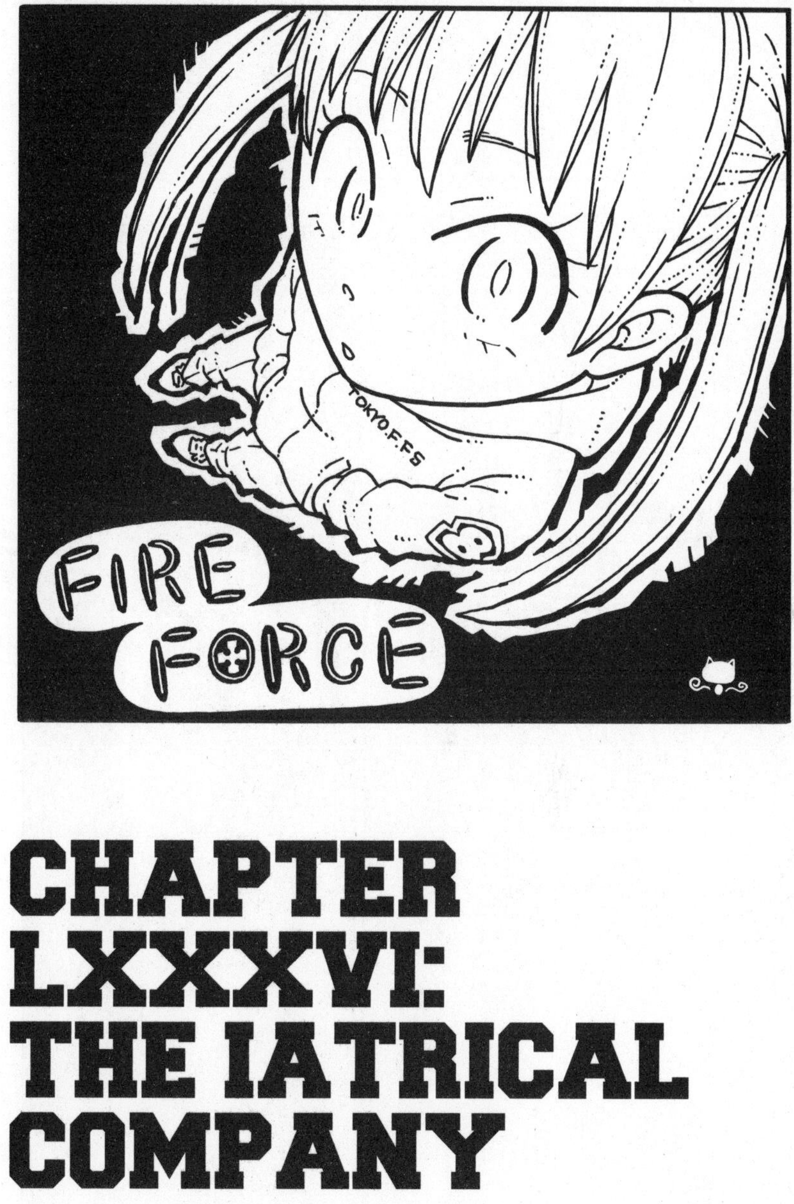
TOKYO.F.F.S
FIRE FORCE

CHAPTER LXXXVI: THE IATRICAL COMPANY

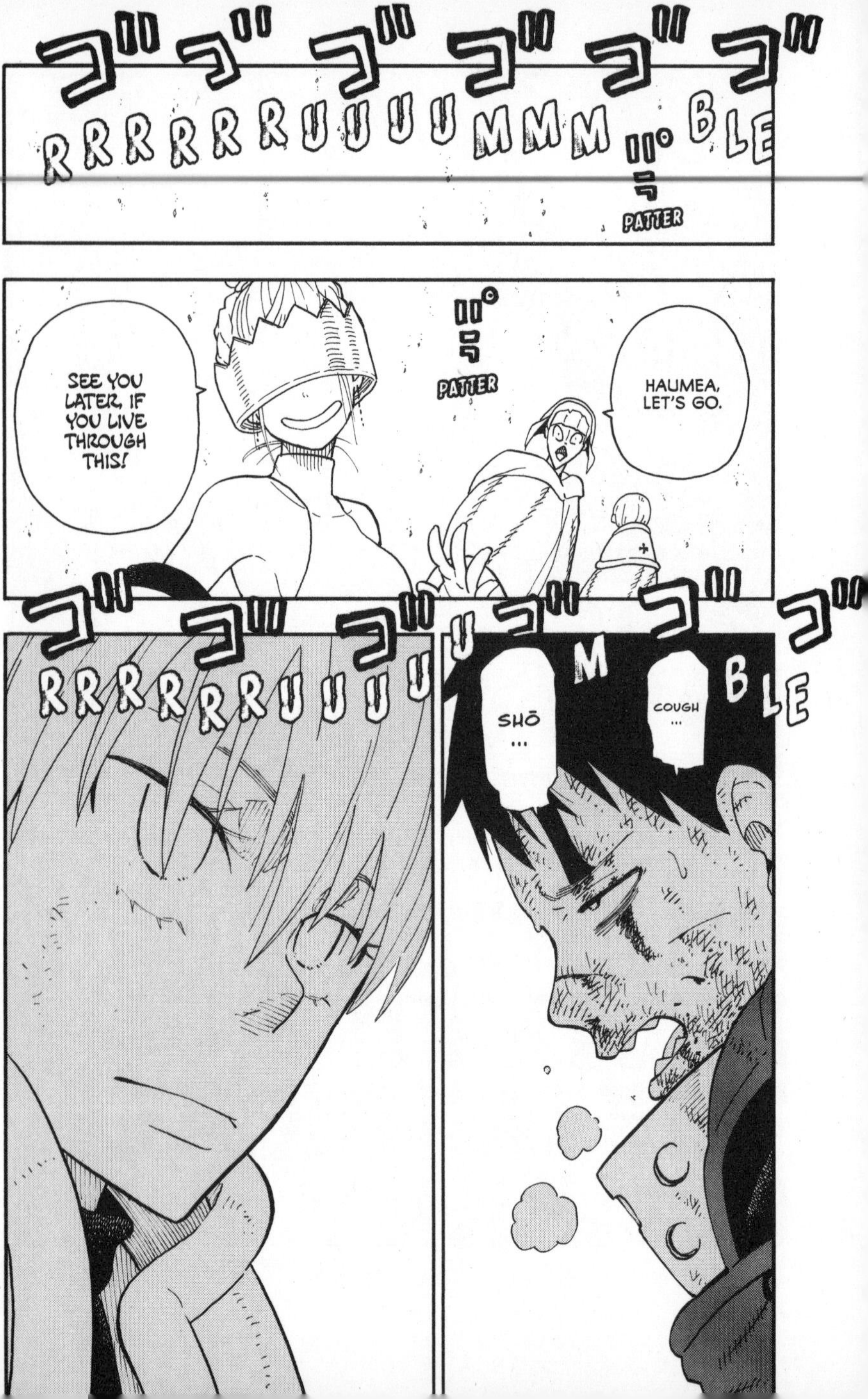
RRRRRRUUUUMMMBLE
PATTER
PATTER
HAUMEA, LET'S GO.
SEE YOU LATER, IF YOU LIVE THROUGH THIS!
RRRRRRRUUUUUMBLE
COUGH ...
SHŌ ...

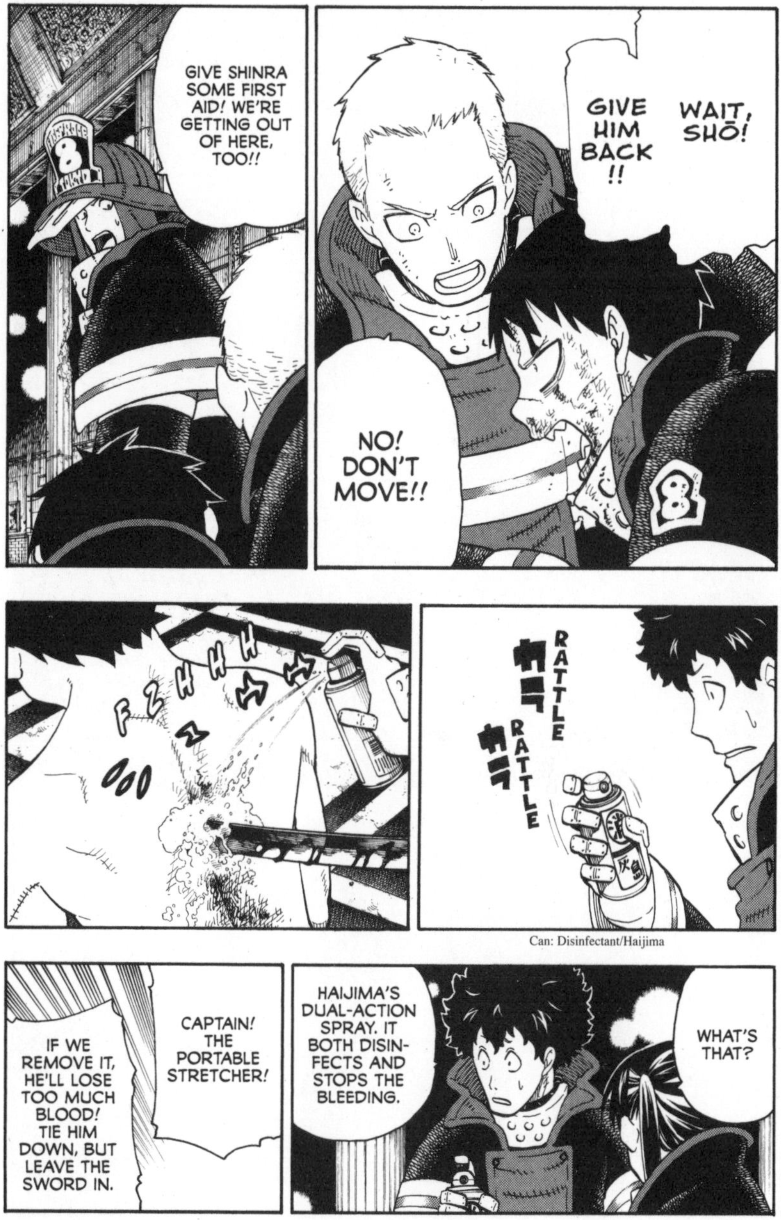
WAIT, SHŌ!
GIVE HIM BACK!!
NO! DON'T MOVE!!
GIVE SHINRA SOME FIRST AID! WE'RE GETTING OUT OF HERE, TOO!!
RATTLE
RATTLE
FZHHH
WHAT'S THAT?
HAIJIMA'S DUAL-ACTION SPRAY. IT BOTH DISIN-FECTS AND STOPS THE BLEEDING.
CAPTAIN! THE PORTABLE STRETCHER!
IF WE REMOVE IT, HE'LL LOSE TOO MUCH BLOOD! TIE HIM DOWN, BUT LEAVE THE SWORD IN.
Can: Disinfectant/Haijima

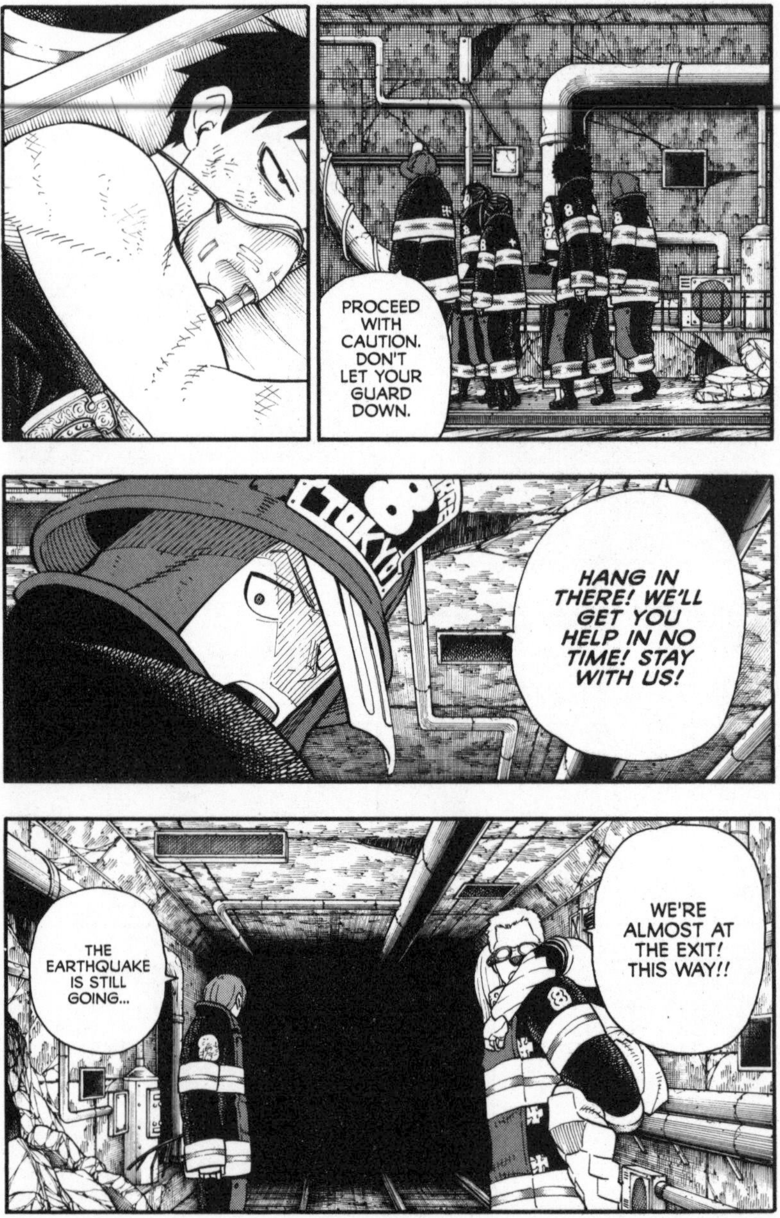
PROCEED WITH CAUTION. DON'T LET YOUR GUARD DOWN.
HANG IN THERE! WE'LL GET YOU HELP IN NO TIME! STAY WITH US!
WE'RE ALMOST AT THE EXIT! THIS WAY!!
THE EARTHQUAKE IS STILL GOING...

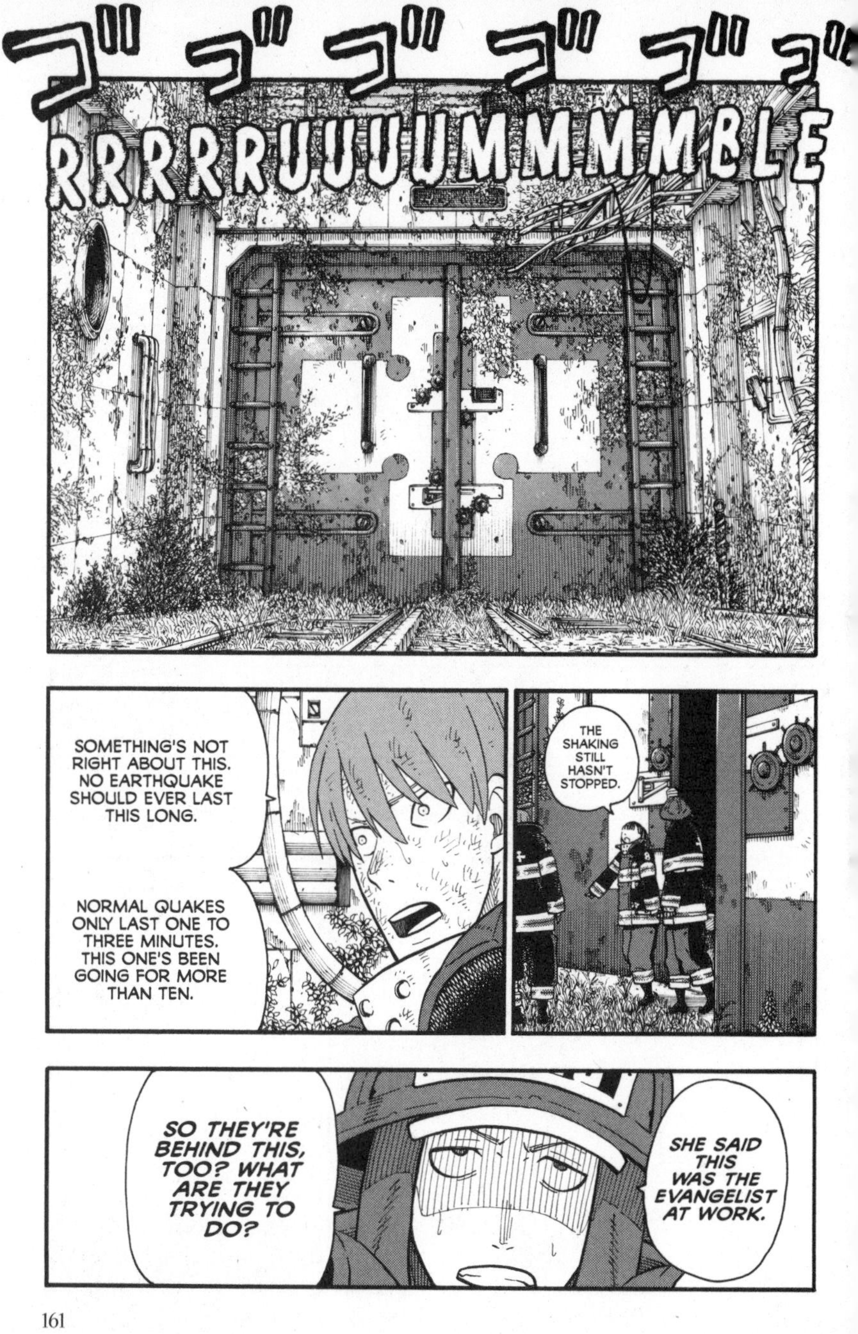
ゴゴゴゴゴゴ
RRRRRUUUUUMMMMMBLE
THE SHAKING STILL HASN'T STOPPED.
SOMETHING'S NOT RIGHT ABOUT THIS. NO EARTHQUAKE SHOULD EVER LAST THIS LONG.
NORMAL QUAKES ONLY LAST ONE TO THREE MINUTES. THIS ONE'S BEEN GOING FOR MORE THAN TEN.
SHE SAID THIS WAS THE EVANGELIST AT WORK.
SO THEY'RE BEHIND THIS, TOO? WHAT ARE THEY TRYING TO DO?

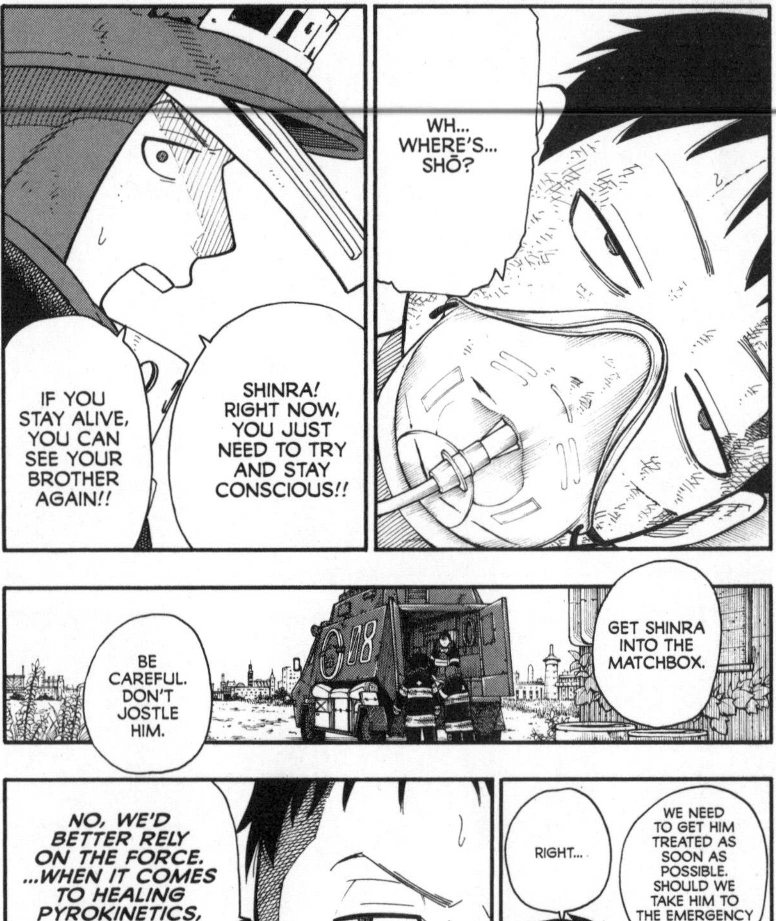
WH... WHERE'S... SHŌ?
SHINRA! RIGHT NOW, YOU JUST NEED TO TRY AND STAY CONSCIOUS!!
IF YOU STAY ALIVE, YOU CAN SEE YOUR BROTHER AGAIN!!
GET SHINRA INTO THE MATCHBOX.
BE CAREFUL. DON'T JOSTLE HIM.
WE NEED TO GET HIM TREATED AS SOON AS POSSIBLE. SHOULD WE TAKE HIM TO THE EMERGENCY ROOM?
RIGHT...
NO, WE'D BETTER RELY ON THE FORCE. ...WHEN IT COMES TO HEALING PYROKINETICS, NO ONE'S BETTER THAN HER.
I'LL CALL AHEAD! GET READY TO HEAD OUT!

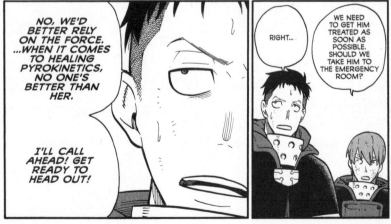

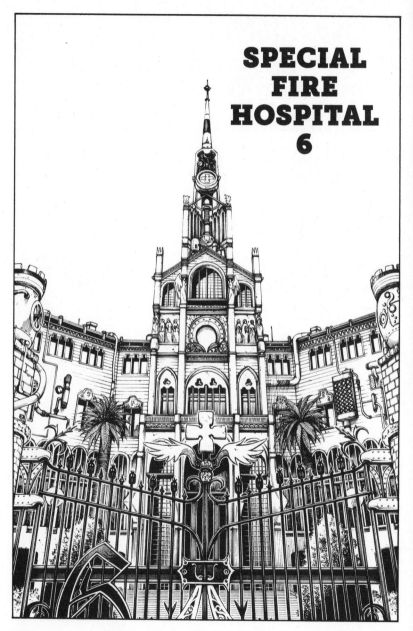

SPECIAL
FIRE
HOSPITAL
6

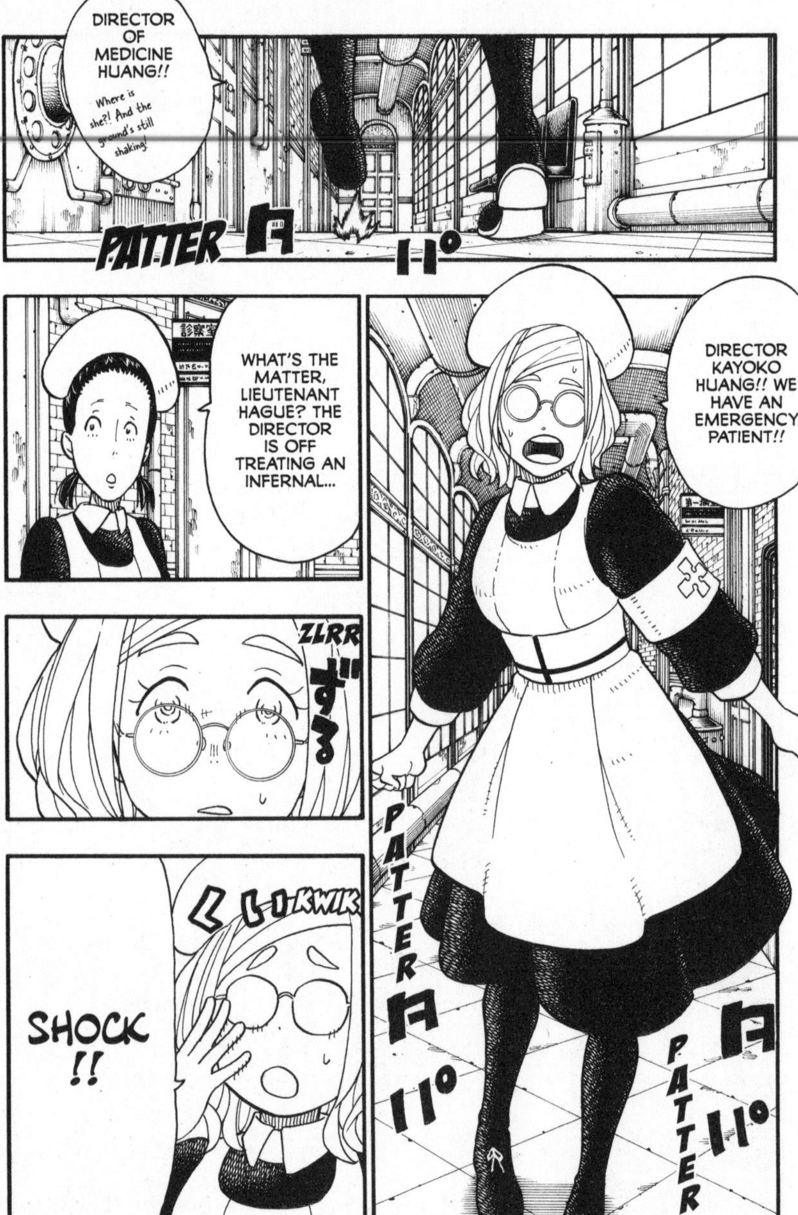
DIRECTOR OF MEDICINE HUANG!!
Where is she?! And the ground's still shaking!
PATTER
DIRECTOR KAYOKO HUANG!! WE HAVE AN EMERGENCY PATIENT!!
PATTER
PATTER
WHAT'S THE MATTER, LIEUTENANT HAGUE? THE DIRECTOR IS OFF TREATING AN INFERNAL...
ZLRR
KWIK
SHOCK!!

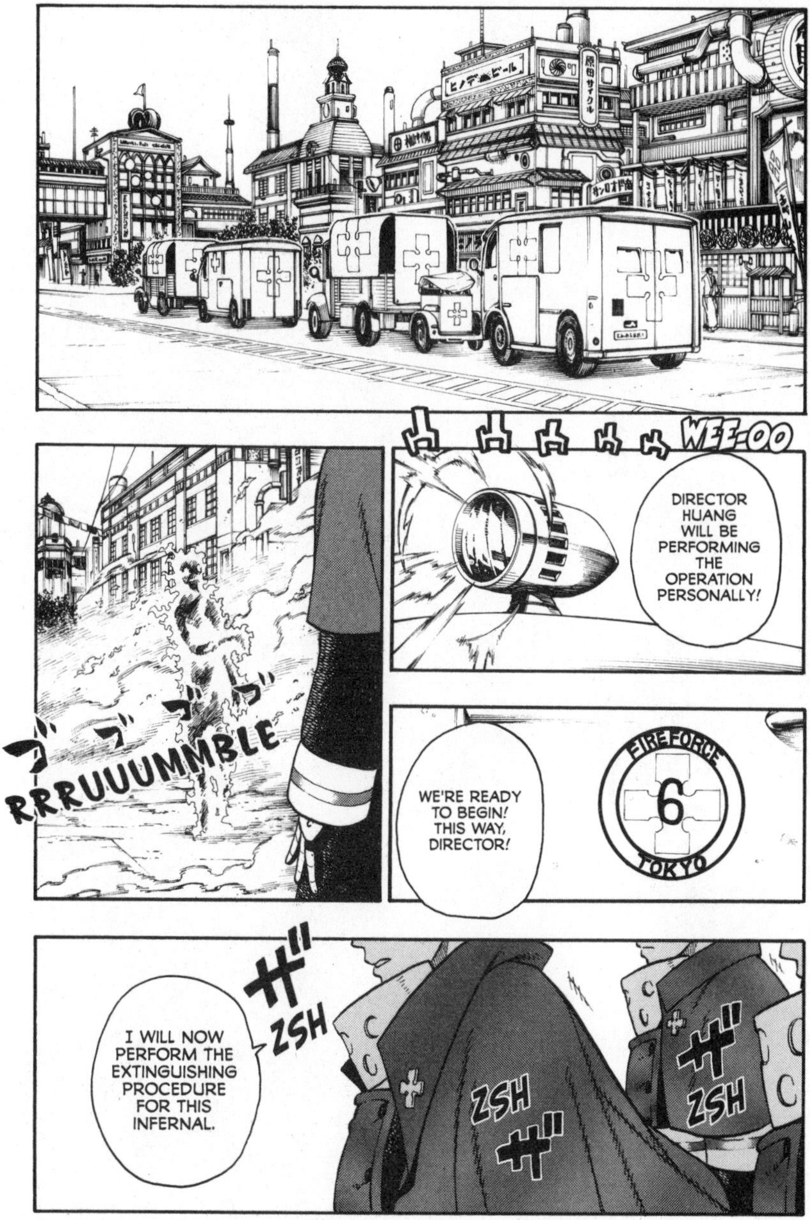
WEE-OO
DIRECTOR HUANG WILL BE PERFORMING THE OPERATION PERSONALLY!
FIREFORCE 6 TOKYO
WE'RE READY TO BEGIN! THIS WAY, DIRECTOR!
RRRUUUMMBLE
ZSH
I WILL NOW PERFORM THE EXTINGUISHING PROCEDURE FOR THIS INFERNAL.
ZSH
ZSH

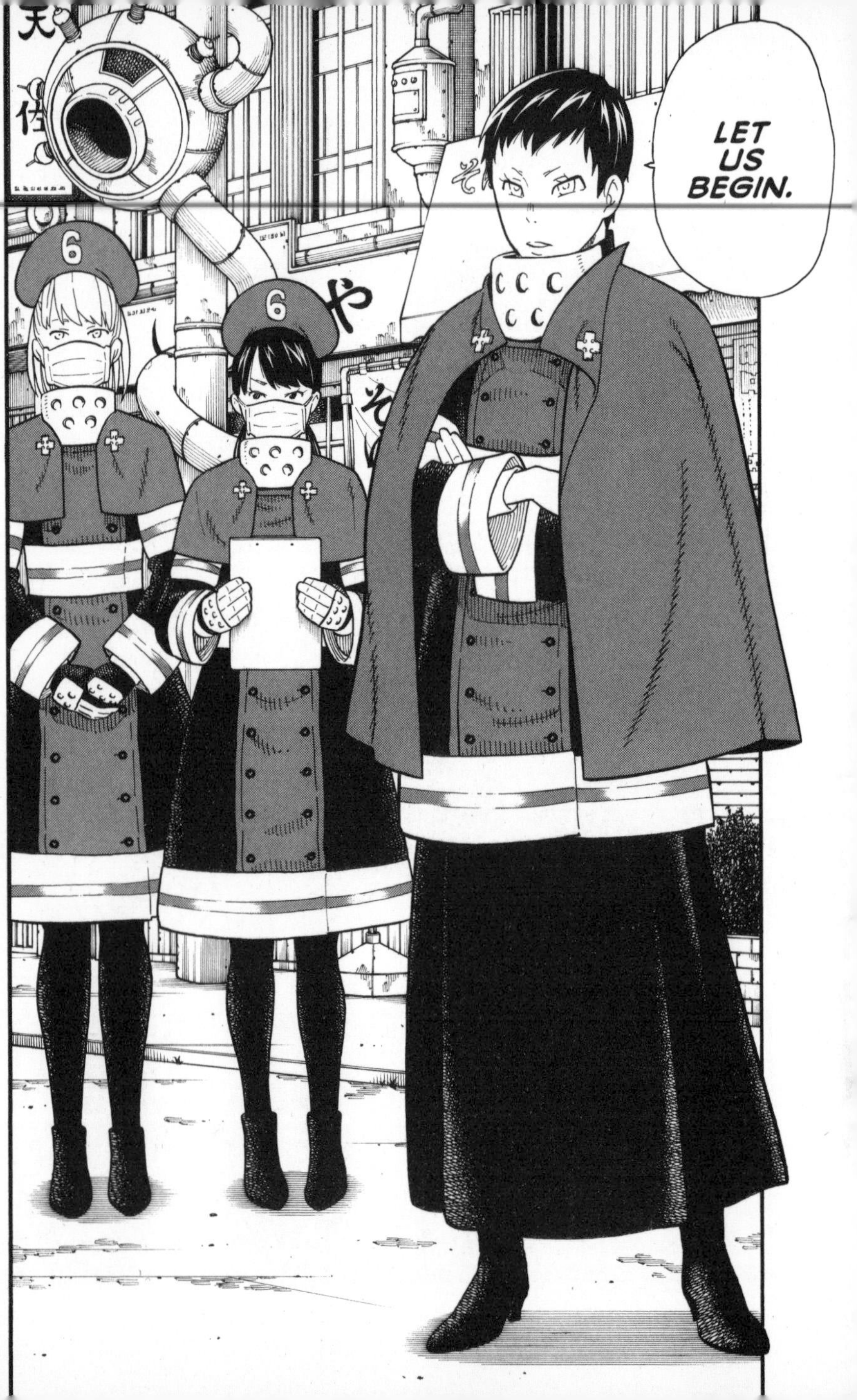
LET US BEGIN.

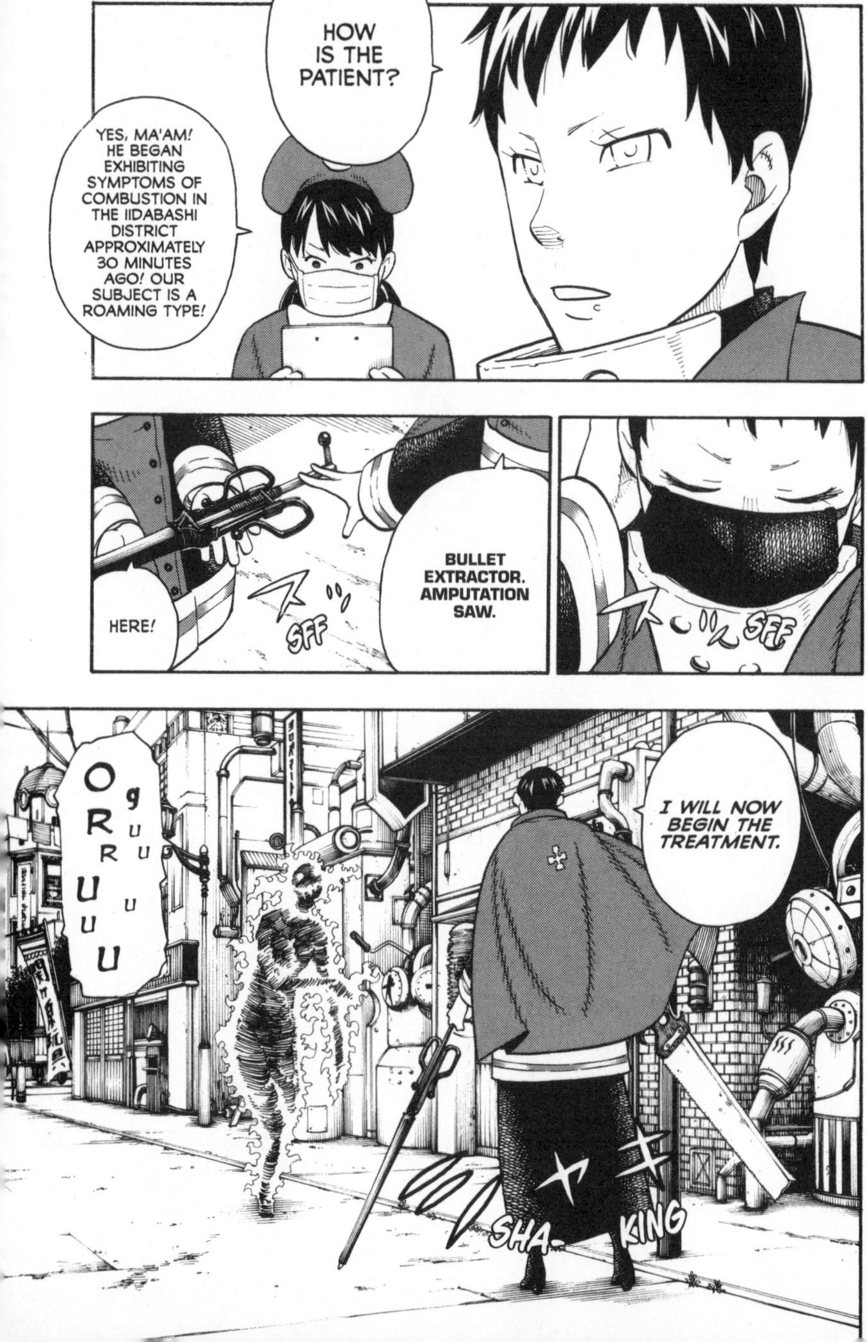
HOW IS THE PATIENT?
YES, MA'AM! HE BEGAN EXHIBITING SYMPTOMS OF COMBUSTION IN THE IIDABASHI DISTRICT APPROXIMATELY 30 MINUTES AGO! OUR SUBJECT IS A ROAMING TYPE!
SFF
BULLET EXTRACTOR. AMPUTATION SAW.
HERE!
SFF
I WILL NOW BEGIN THE TREATMENT.
ORRUUU
gUUU
SHA-KING

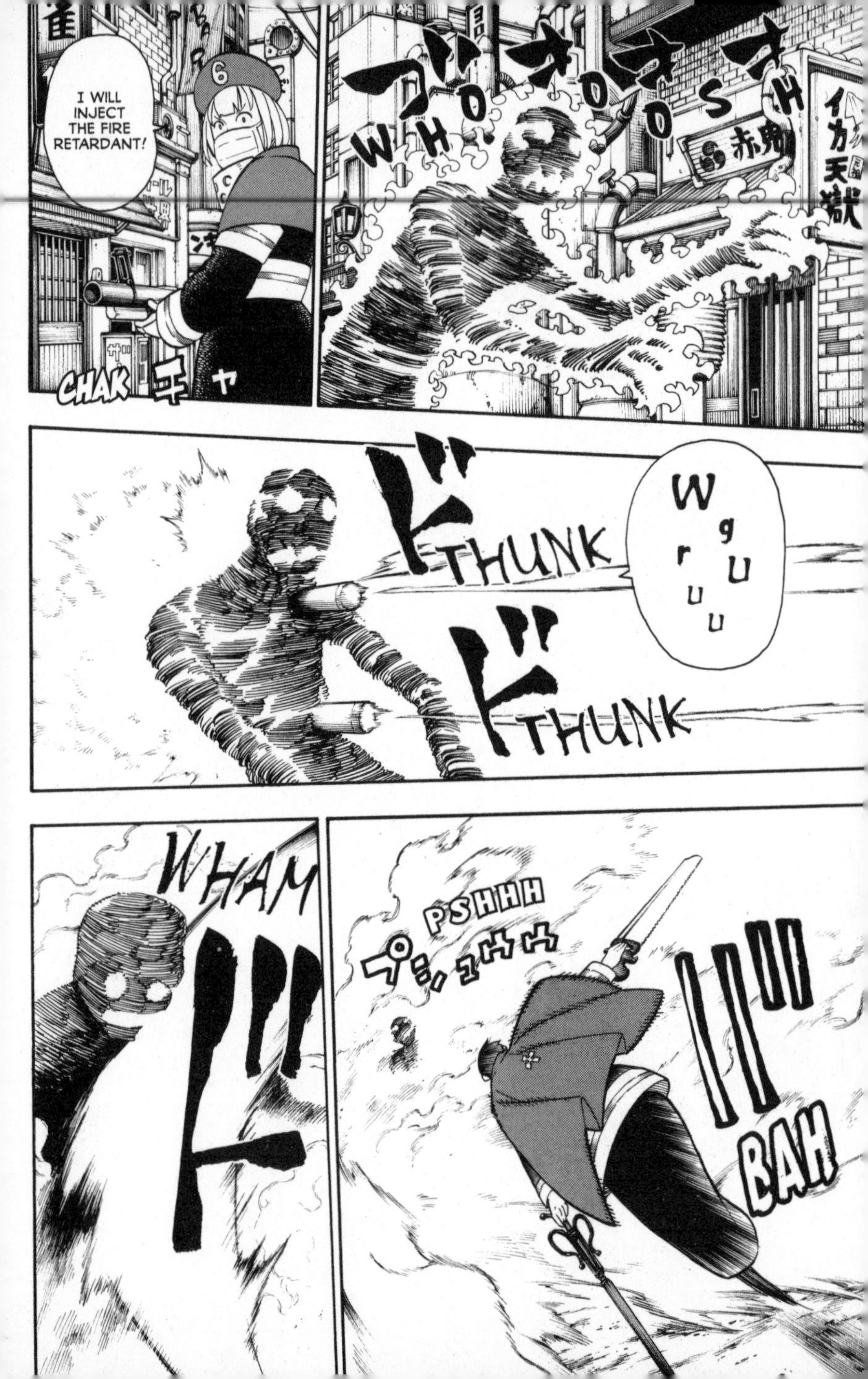
WHOOOSH
I WILL INJECT THE FIRE RETARDANT!
CHAK
THUNK
Wgruuu
THUNK
PSHHH
BAH
WHAM

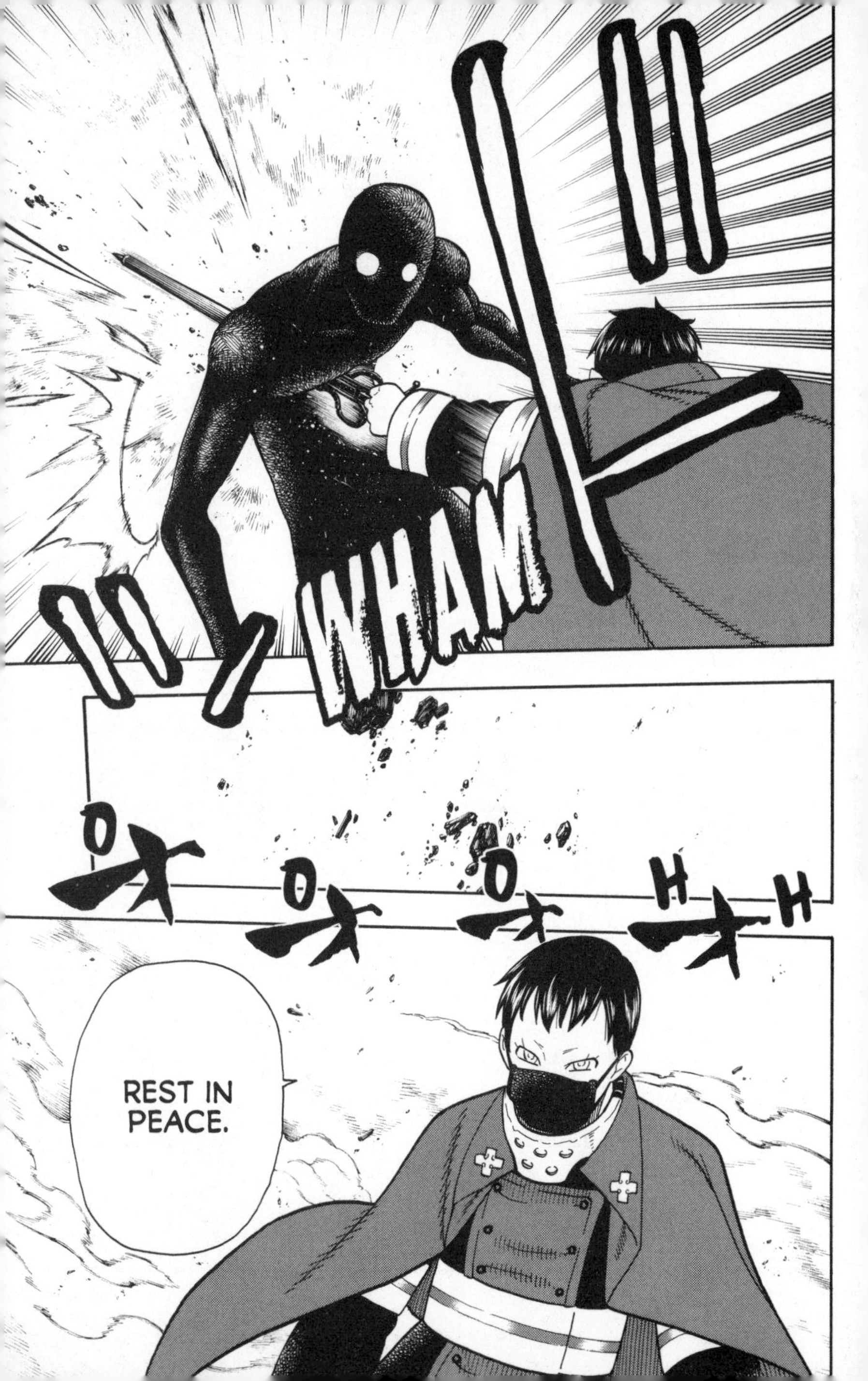
WHAM
OOOHH
REST IN PEACE.

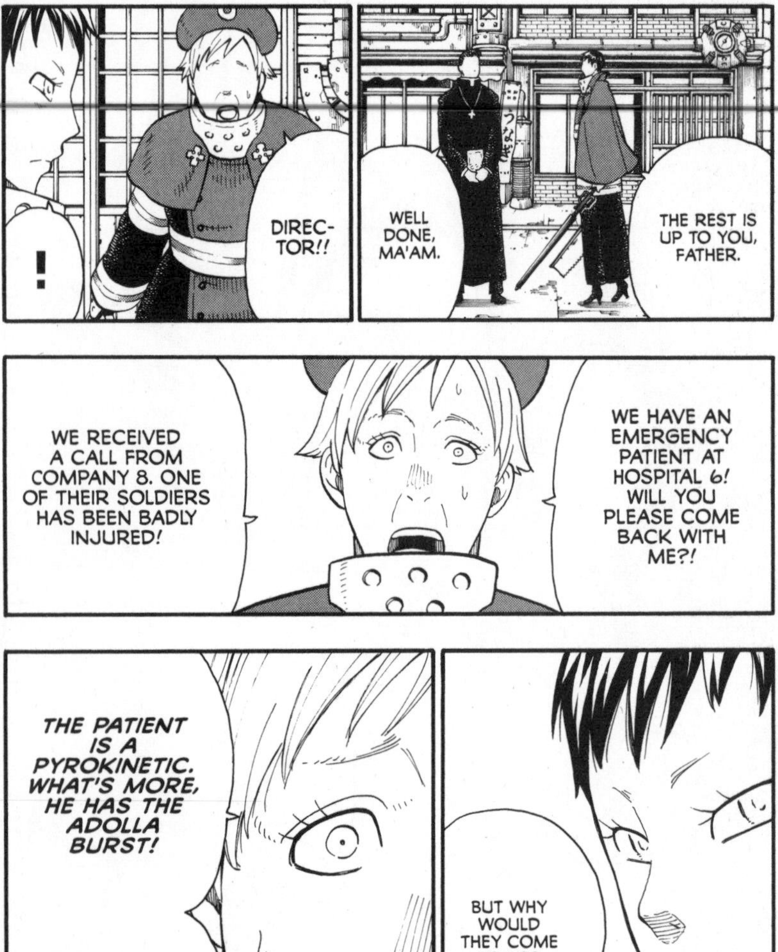

THE REST IS UP TO YOU, FATHER.
WELL DONE, MA'AM.
DIREC-TOR!!
!
WE HAVE AN EMERGENCY PATIENT AT HOSPITAL 6! WILL YOU PLEASE COME BACK WITH ME?!
WE RECEIVED A CALL FROM COMPANY 8. ONE OF THEIR SOLDIERS HAS BEEN BADLY INJURED!
BUT WHY WOULD THEY COME TO US?
IF A SOLDIER GETS INJURED ON A CALL, ANY HOSPITAL CAN TREAT THEM.
THE PATIENT IS A PYROKINETIC. WHAT'S MORE, HE HAS THE ADOLLA BURST!
HE IS IN EXTREMELY CRITICAL CONDITION! THEY NEED YOUR HELP!

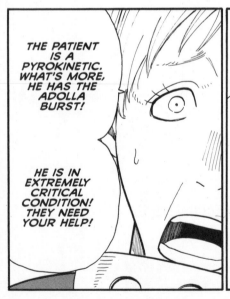

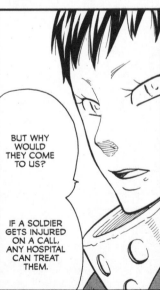

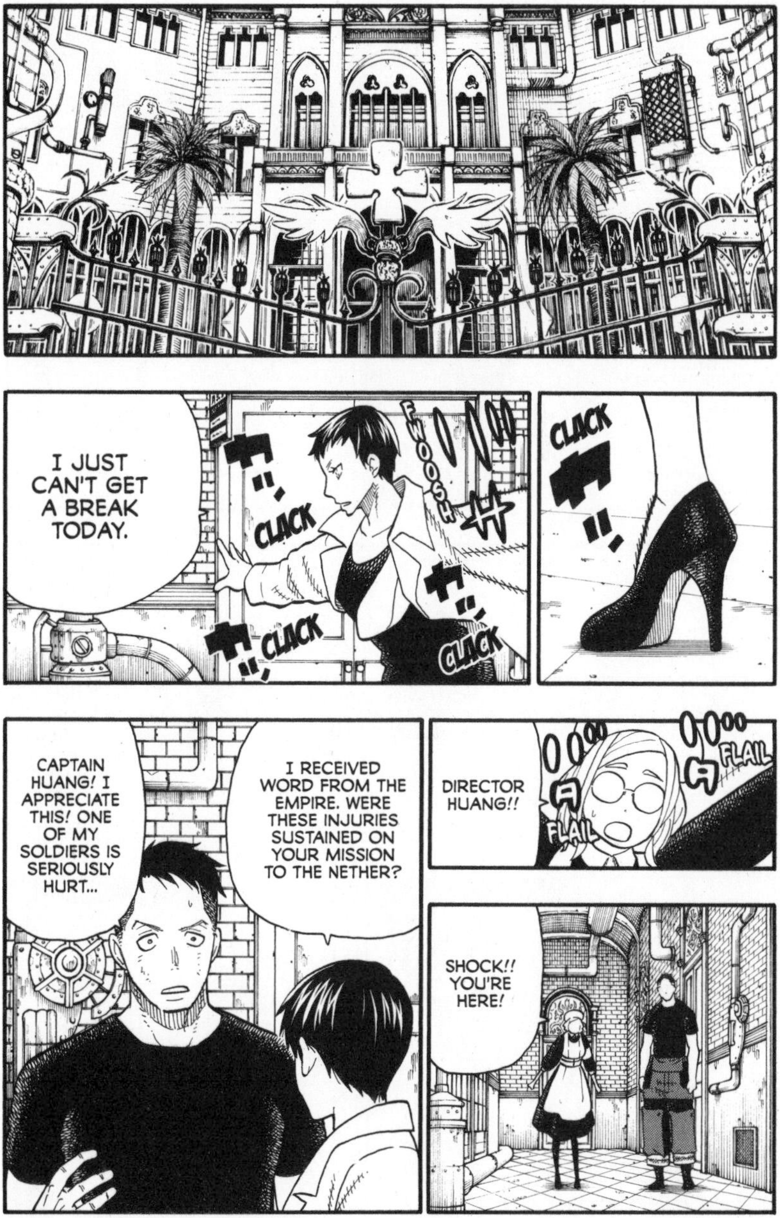
CLACK
FWOOSH
CLACK
CLACK
CLACK
I JUST CAN'T GET A BREAK TODAY.
DIRECTOR HUANG!!
FLAIL
FLAIL
SHOCK!! YOU'RE HERE!
I RECEIVED WORD FROM THE EMPIRE. WERE THESE INJURIES SUSTAINED ON YOUR MISSION TO THE NETHER?
CAPTAIN HUANG! I APPRECIATE THIS! ONE OF MY SOLDIERS IS SERIOUSLY HURT...

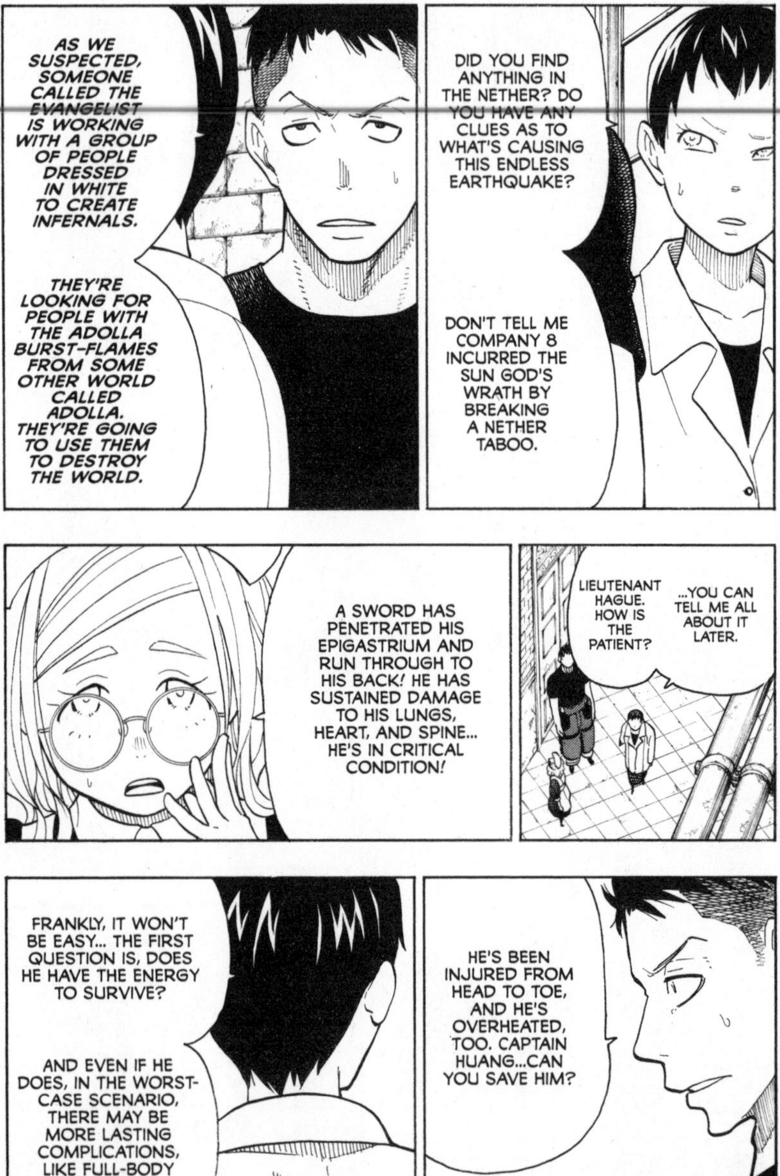
DID YOU FIND ANYTHING IN THE NETHER? DO YOU HAVE ANY CLUES AS TO WHAT'S CAUSING THIS ENDLESS EARTHQUAKE?
DON'T TELL ME COMPANY 8 INCURRED THE SUN GOD'S WRATH BY BREAKING A NETHER TABOO.
AS WE SUSPECTED, SOMEONE CALLED THE EVANGELIST IS WORKING WITH A GROUP OF PEOPLE DRESSED IN WHITE TO CREATE INFERNALS.
THEY'RE LOOKING FOR PEOPLE WITH THE ADOLLA BURST-FLAMES FROM SOME OTHER WORLD CALLED ADOLLA. THEY'RE GOING TO USE THEM TO DESTROY THE WORLD.
...YOU CAN TELL ME ALL ABOUT IT LATER.
LIEUTENANT HAGUE. HOW IS THE PATIENT?
A SWORD HAS PENETRATED HIS EPIGASTRIUM AND RUN THROUGH TO HIS BACK! HE HAS SUSTAINED DAMAGE TO HIS LUNGS, HEART, AND SPINE... HE'S IN CRITICAL CONDITION!
HE'S BEEN INJURED FROM HEAD TO TOE, AND HE'S OVERHEATED, TOO. CAPTAIN HUANG...CAN YOU SAVE HIM?
FRANKLY, IT WON'T BE EASY... THE FIRST QUESTION IS, DOES HE HAVE THE ENERGY TO SURVIVE?
AND EVEN IF HE DOES, IN THE WORST-CASE SCENARIO, THERE MAY BE MORE LASTING COMPLICATIONS, LIKE FULL-BODY PARALYSIS.

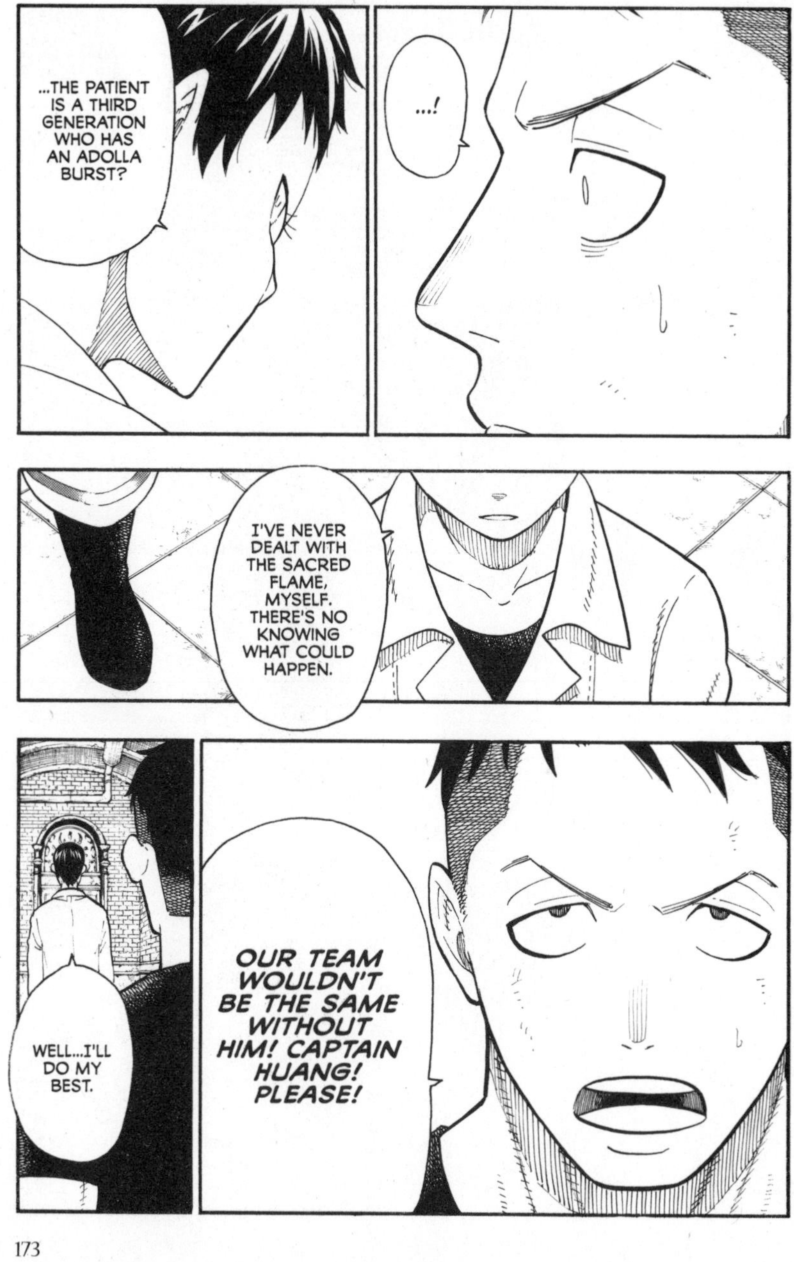
...!
...THE PATIENT IS A THIRD GENERATION WHO HAS AN ADOLLA BURST?
I'VE NEVER DEALT WITH THE SACRED FLAME, MYSELF. THERE'S NO KNOWING WHAT COULD HAPPEN.
OUR TEAM WOULDN'T BE THE SAME WITHOUT HIM! CAPTAIN HUANG! PLEASE!
WELL...I'LL DO MY BEST.

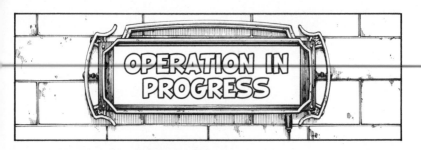

OPERATION IN PROGRESS

GREAT SUN GOD... PLEASE, KEEP SHINRA-SAN'S LIGHT BURNING.

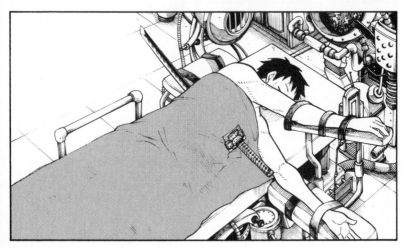

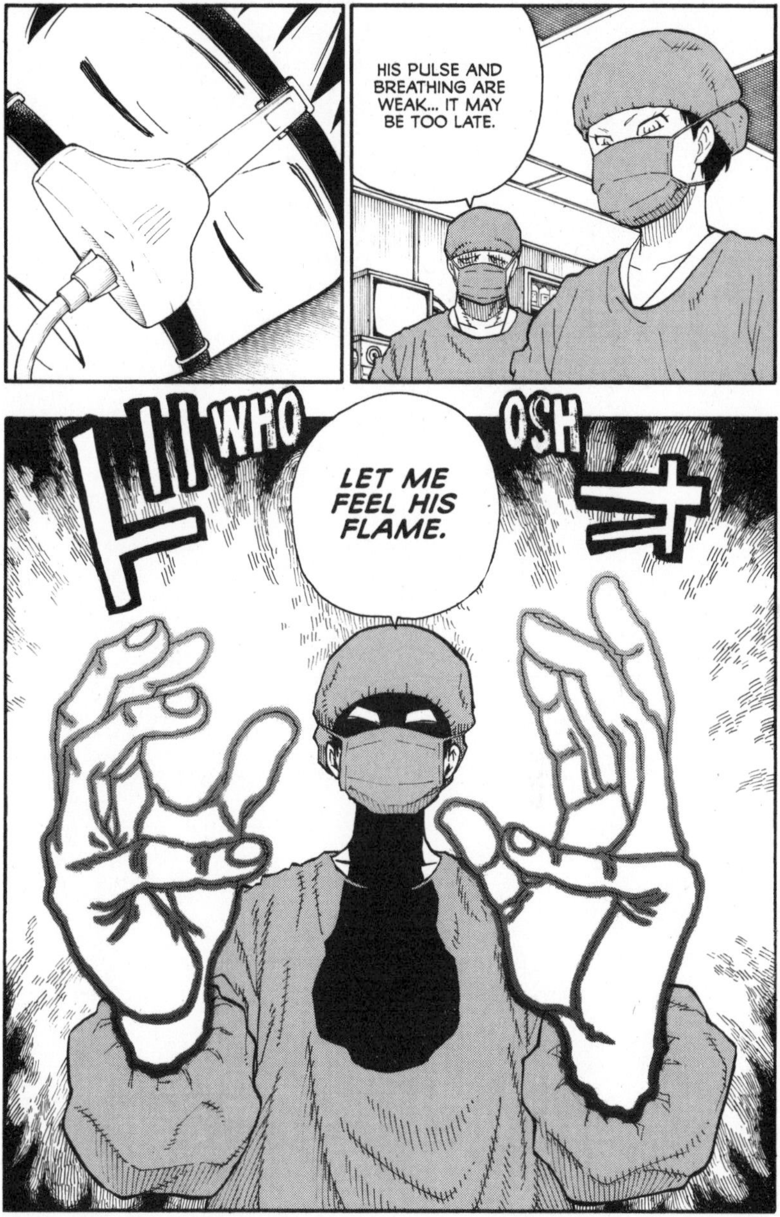
HIS PULSE AND BREATHING ARE WEAK... IT MAY BE TOO LATE.
WHO OSH
LET ME FEEL HIS FLAME.

FIRE FORCE

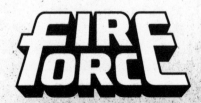

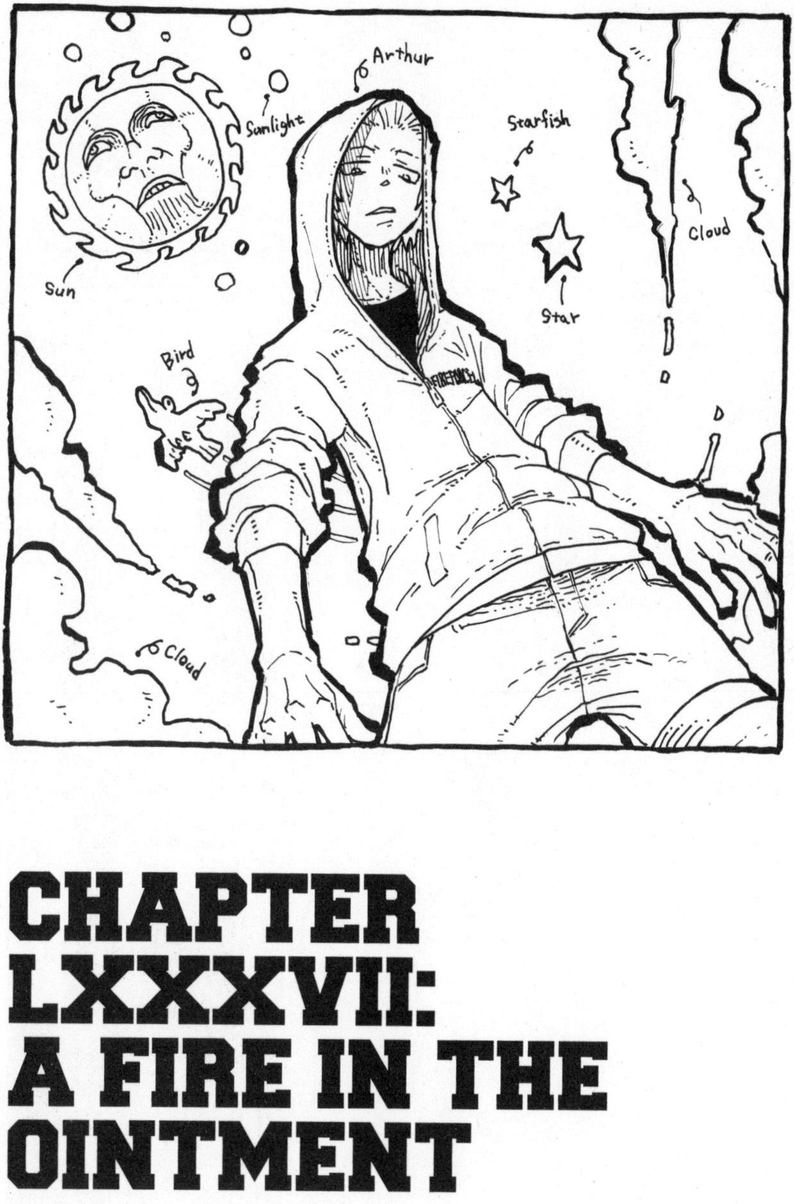
Arthur
Sunlight
Starfish
Cloud
Sun
Star
Bird
FIREFORCE
Cloud

CHAPTER LXXXVII: A FIRE IN THE OINTMENT

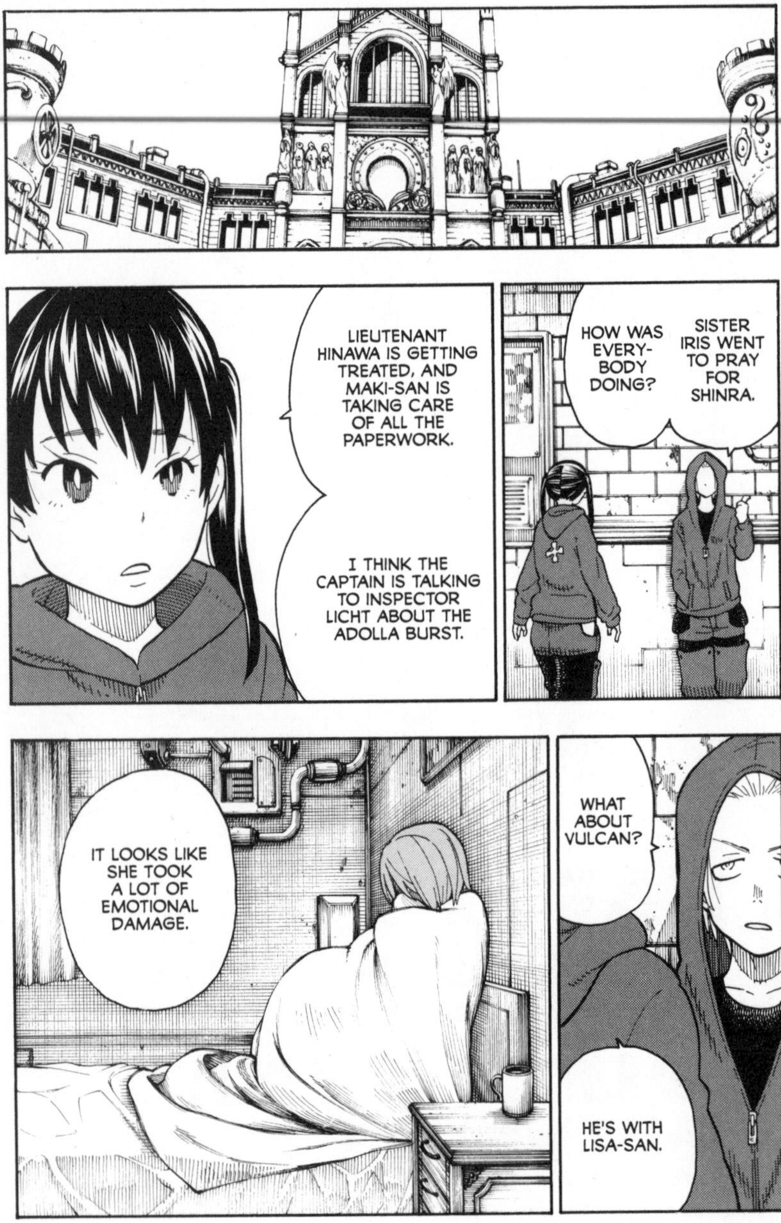
SISTER IRIS WENT TO PRAY FOR SHINRA.
HOW WAS EVERY-BODY DOING?
LIEUTENANT HINAWA IS GETTING TREATED, AND MAKI-SAN IS TAKING CARE OF ALL THE PAPERWORK.
I THINK THE CAPTAIN IS TALKING TO INSPECTOR LICHT ABOUT THE ADOLLA BURST.
WHAT ABOUT VULCAN?
HE'S WITH LISA-SAN.
IT LOOKS LIKE SHE TOOK A LOT OF EMOTIONAL DAMAGE.

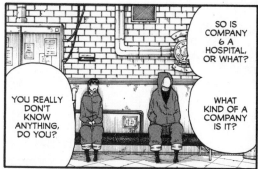

SO IS COMPANY 6 A HOSPITAL, OR WHAT?
WHAT KIND OF A COMPANY IS IT?
YOU REALLY DON'T KNOW ANYTHING, DO YOU?
FIRE FORCE
6
TOKYO
YOU KNOW THAT MEDICAL CARE IN THE EMPIRE CONSISTS OF RELIGIOUS RITES THAT CAN ONLY LEGALLY BE PERFORMED BY MEMBERS OF THE HOLY SOL TEMPLE, RIGHT?
SO LIKE COMPANY 1, MOST OF COMPANY 6'S SOLDIERS ARE MEMBERS OF THE CHURCH, BUT IT SPECIALIZES IN MEDICINE.
WHICH MEANS WE'RE EITHER IN A CHURCH OR A HOSPITAL.
IT'S A SPECIAL FIRE FORCE COMPANY!
ははーん
UH-HUH.
APPARENTLY NO ONE CAN COMPARE TO COMPANY 6'S CAPTAIN HUANG WHEN IT COMES TO HEALING PYROKINETICS.
I HEARD SHE USES HER SPECIAL ABILITY TO TREAT HER PATIENTS...

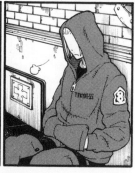

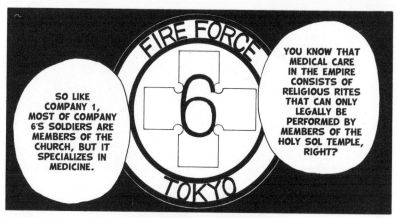

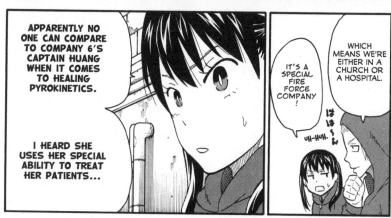

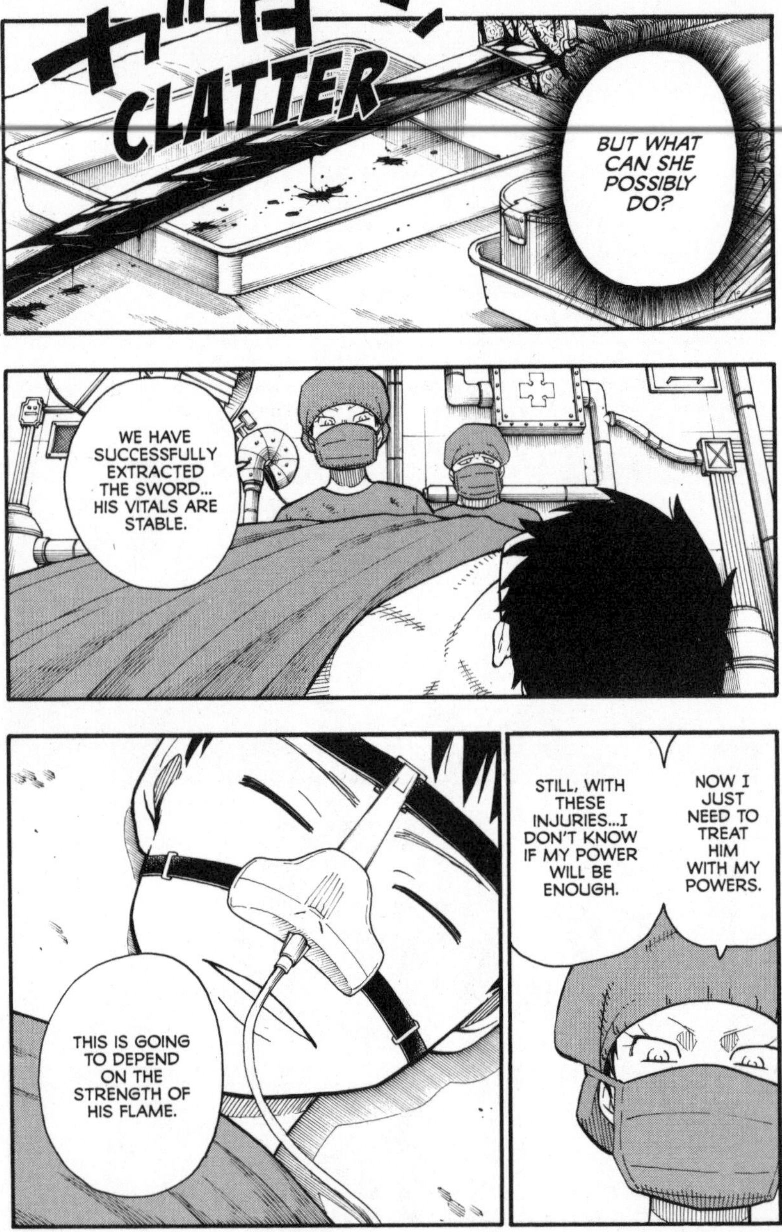
ガタン
CLATTER
BUT WHAT CAN SHE POSSIBLY DO?
WE HAVE SUCCESSFULLY EXTRACTED THE SWORD... HIS VITALS ARE STABLE.
NOW I JUST NEED TO TREAT HIM WITH MY POWERS.
STILL, WITH THESE INJURIES...I DON'T KNOW IF MY POWER WILL BE ENOUGH.
THIS IS GOING TO DEPEND ON THE STRENGTH OF HIS FLAME.

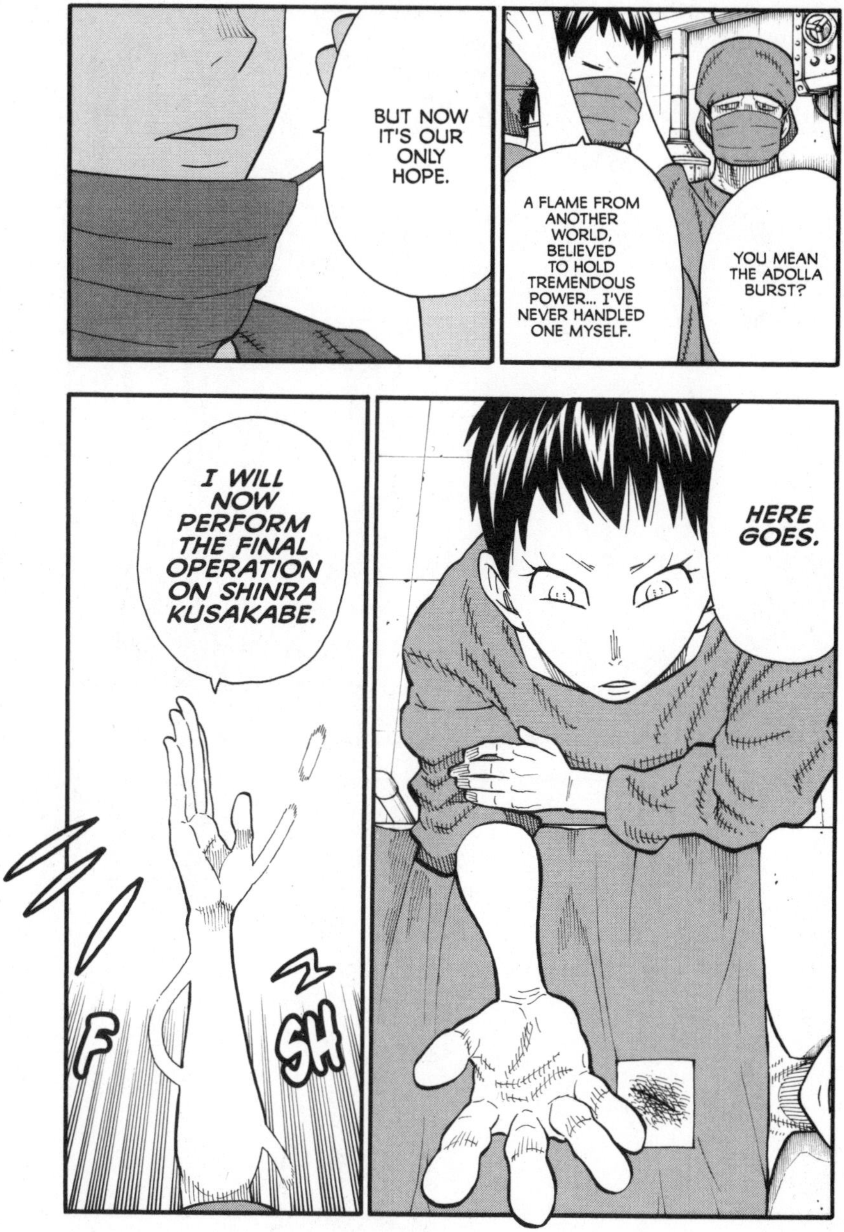
YOU MEAN THE ADOLLA BURST?
A FLAME FROM ANOTHER WORLD, BELIEVED TO HOLD TREMENDOUS POWER... I'VE NEVER HANDLED ONE MYSELF.
BUT NOW IT'S OUR ONLY HOPE.
HERE GOES.
I WILL NOW PERFORM THE FINAL OPERATION ON SHINRA KUSAKABE.
FSHZ

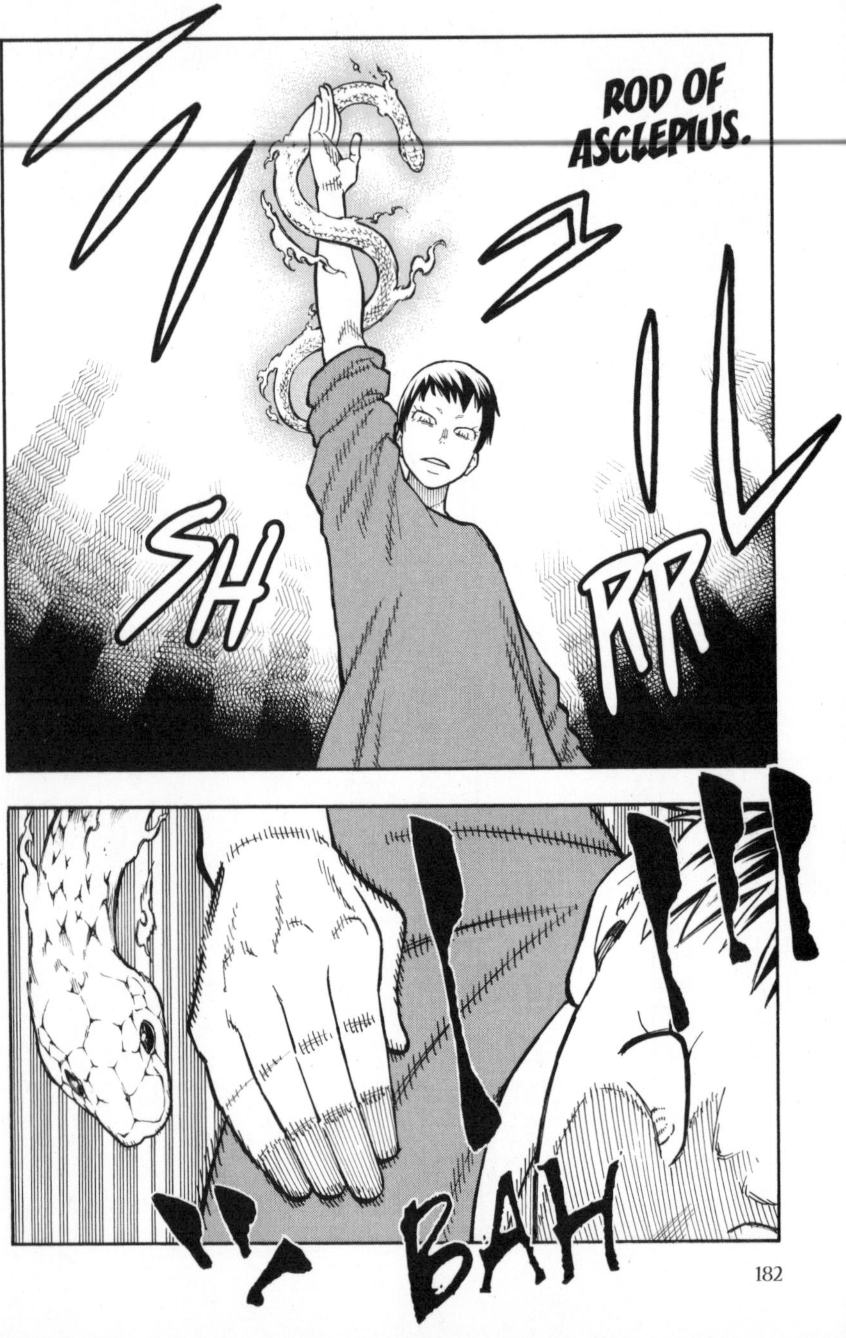
ROD OF ASCLEPIUS.
SHRR
BAH!!

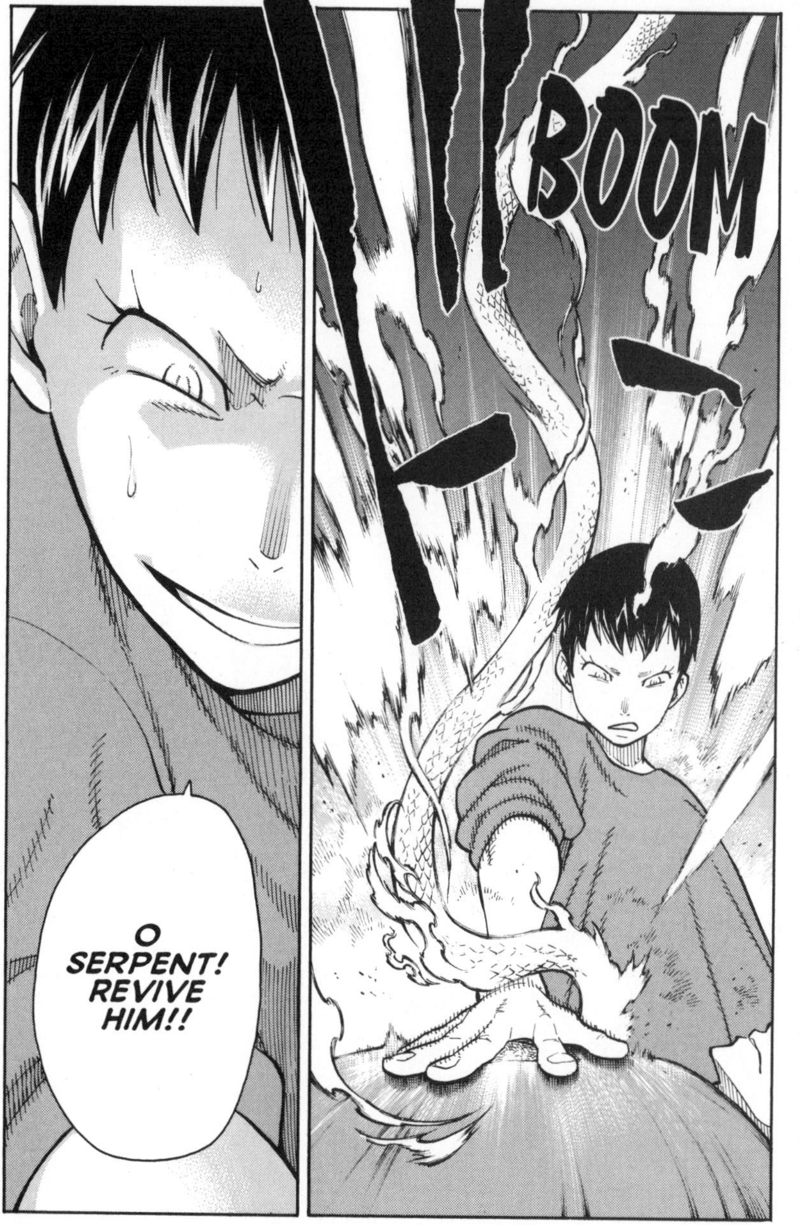
BOOM
O SERPENT! REVIVE HIM!!

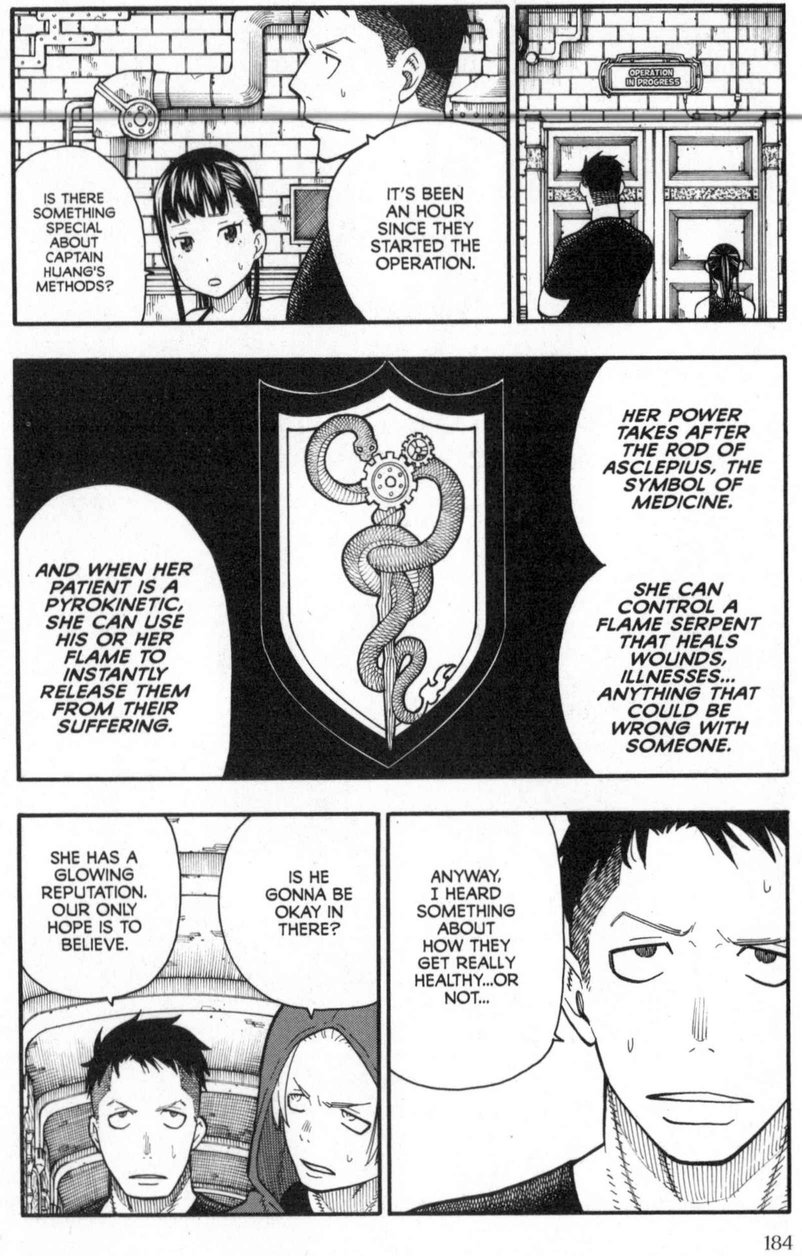
OPERATION IN PROGRESS
IT'S BEEN AN HOUR SINCE THEY STARTED THE OPERATION.
IS THERE SOMETHING SPECIAL ABOUT CAPTAIN HUANG'S METHODS?
HER POWER TAKES AFTER THE ROD OF ASCLEPIUS, THE SYMBOL OF MEDICINE.
SHE CAN CONTROL A FLAME SERPENT THAT HEALS WOUNDS, ILLNESSES... ANYTHING THAT COULD BE WRONG WITH SOMEONE.
AND WHEN HER PATIENT IS A PYROKINETIC, SHE CAN USE HIS OR HER FLAME TO INSTANTLY RELEASE THEM FROM THEIR SUFFERING.
ANYWAY, I HEARD SOMETHING ABOUT HOW THEY GET REALLY HEALTHY...OR NOT...
IS HE GONNA BE OKAY IN THERE?
SHE HAS A GLOWING REPUTATION. OUR ONLY HOPE IS TO BELIEVE.

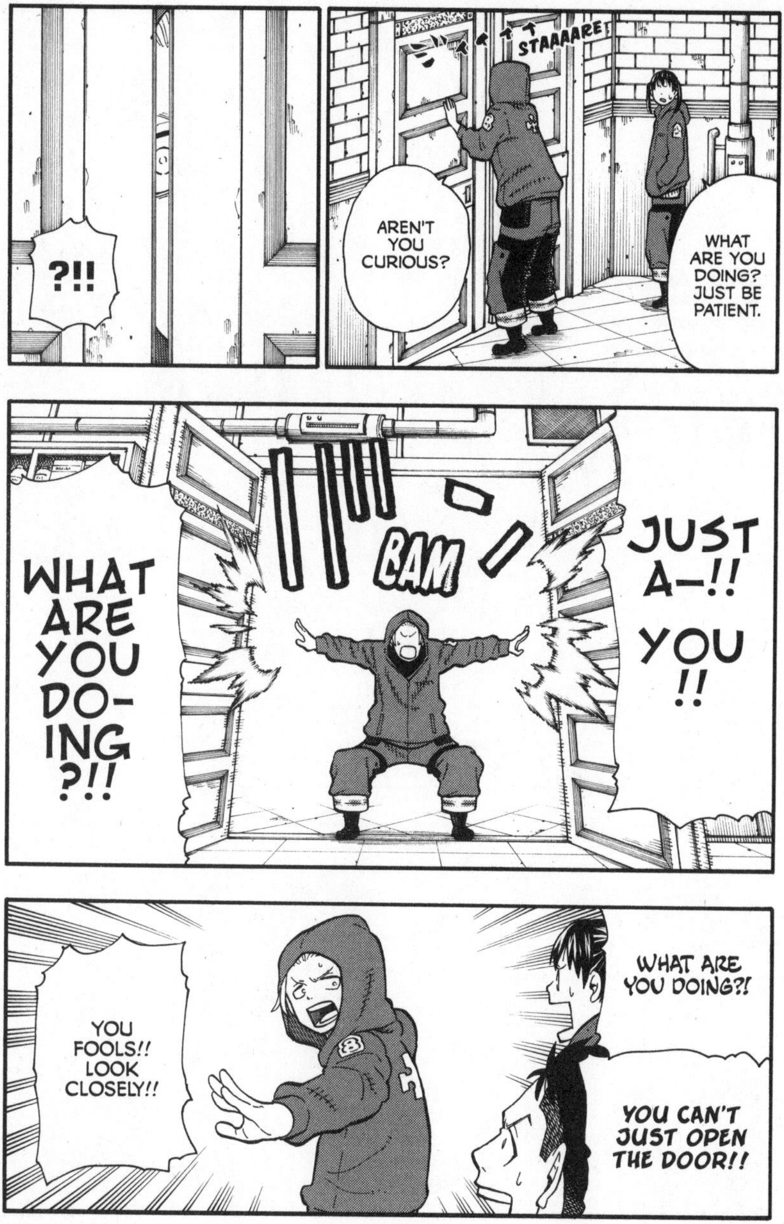
STAAAARE
WHAT ARE YOU DOING? JUST BE PATIENT.
AREN'T YOU CURIOUS?
?!!
JUST A—!! YOU!!
BAM
WHAT ARE YOU DO-ING?!!
WHAT ARE YOU DOING?!
YOU CAN'T JUST OPEN THE DOOR!!
YOU FOOLS!! LOOK CLOSELY!!

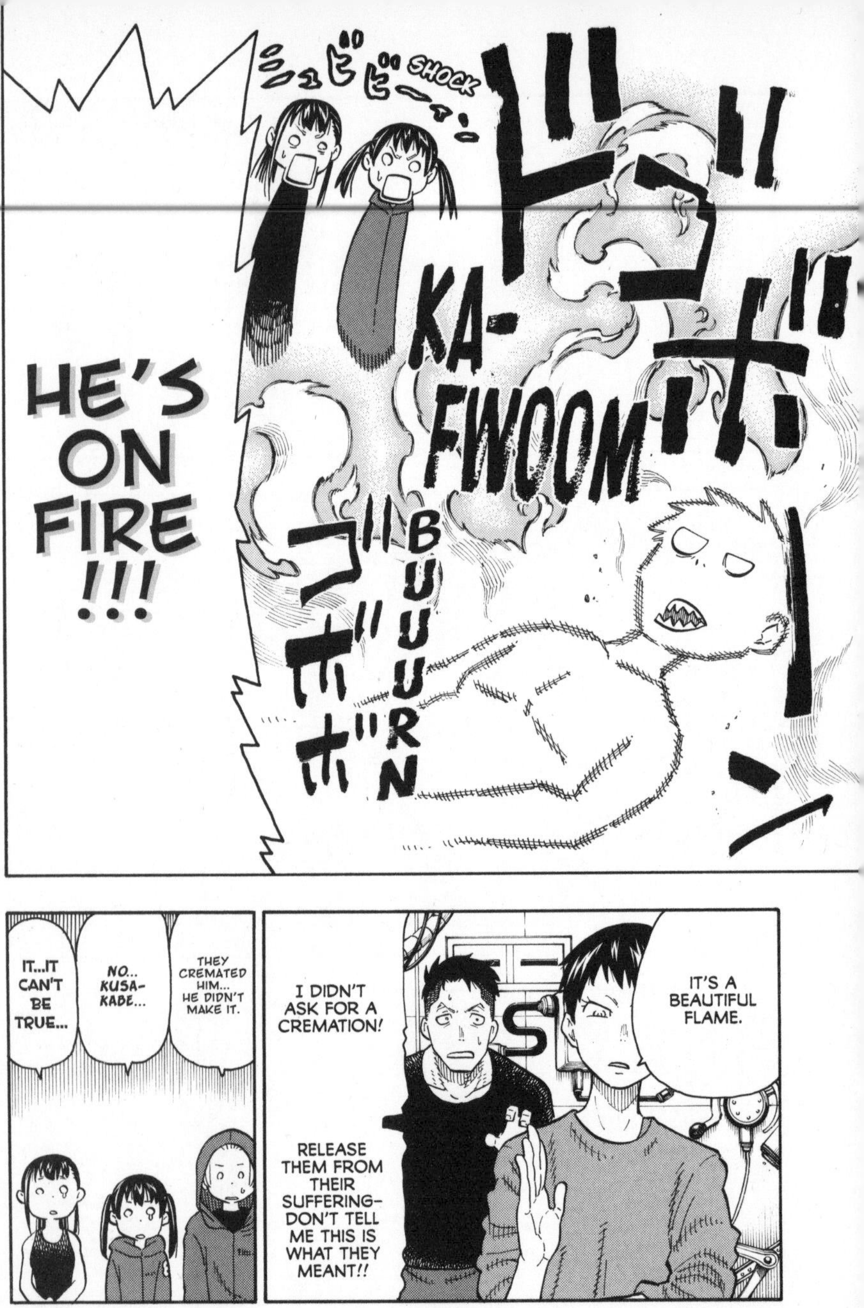
KA-FWOOM
SHOCK
BUUUURN
HE'S ON FIRE!!!
IT'S A BEAUTIFUL FLAME.
I DIDN'T ASK FOR A CREMATION!
RELEASE THEM FROM THEIR SUFFERING– DON'T TELL ME THIS IS WHAT THEY MEANT!!
THEY CREMATED HIM... HE DIDN'T MAKE IT.
NO... KUSA-KABE...
IT...IT CAN'T BE TRUE...

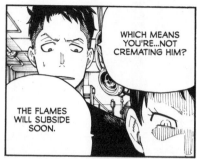

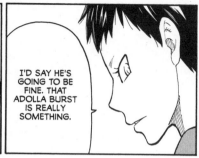

I'D SAY HE'S GOING TO BE FINE. THAT ADOLLA BURST IS REALLY SOMETHING.
WHICH MEANS YOU'RE...NOT CREMATING HIM?
THE FLAMES WILL SUBSIDE SOON.
MY FLAMES AMPLIFY THE BODY'S REGENERATIVE POWERS.
FOR EXAMPLE, FOR AN EXTERNAL INJURY, THE CELLS AROUND THE WOUND WILL DIVIDE AND MULTIPLY, EVENTUALLY CLOSING THE WOUND.
WHAT I DO IS ACCELERATE THE CELL DIVISION AND METABOLISM AROUND THE AFFECTED AREAS IN ORDER TO ENHANCE THE SELF-HEALING PROCESS.
MUSCLE TISSUE... DERMIS... EPIDERMIS...NERVE ENDINGS... ALL OF HIS SEVERED ORGANS ARE NOW IN THE PROCESS OF RECONNECTING.
IF THE PATIENT IS A PYROKINETIC, I CAN USE THEIR FLAMES TO HEAL THEM EVEN FASTER.
THE FLAMES YOU SEE NOW ARE BRINGING HIS BODY BACK TO LIFE.

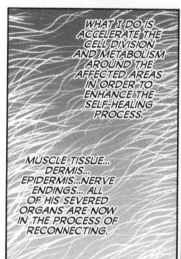

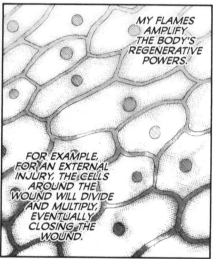

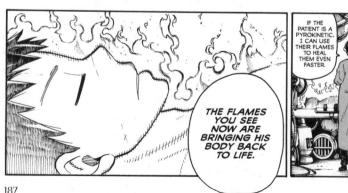

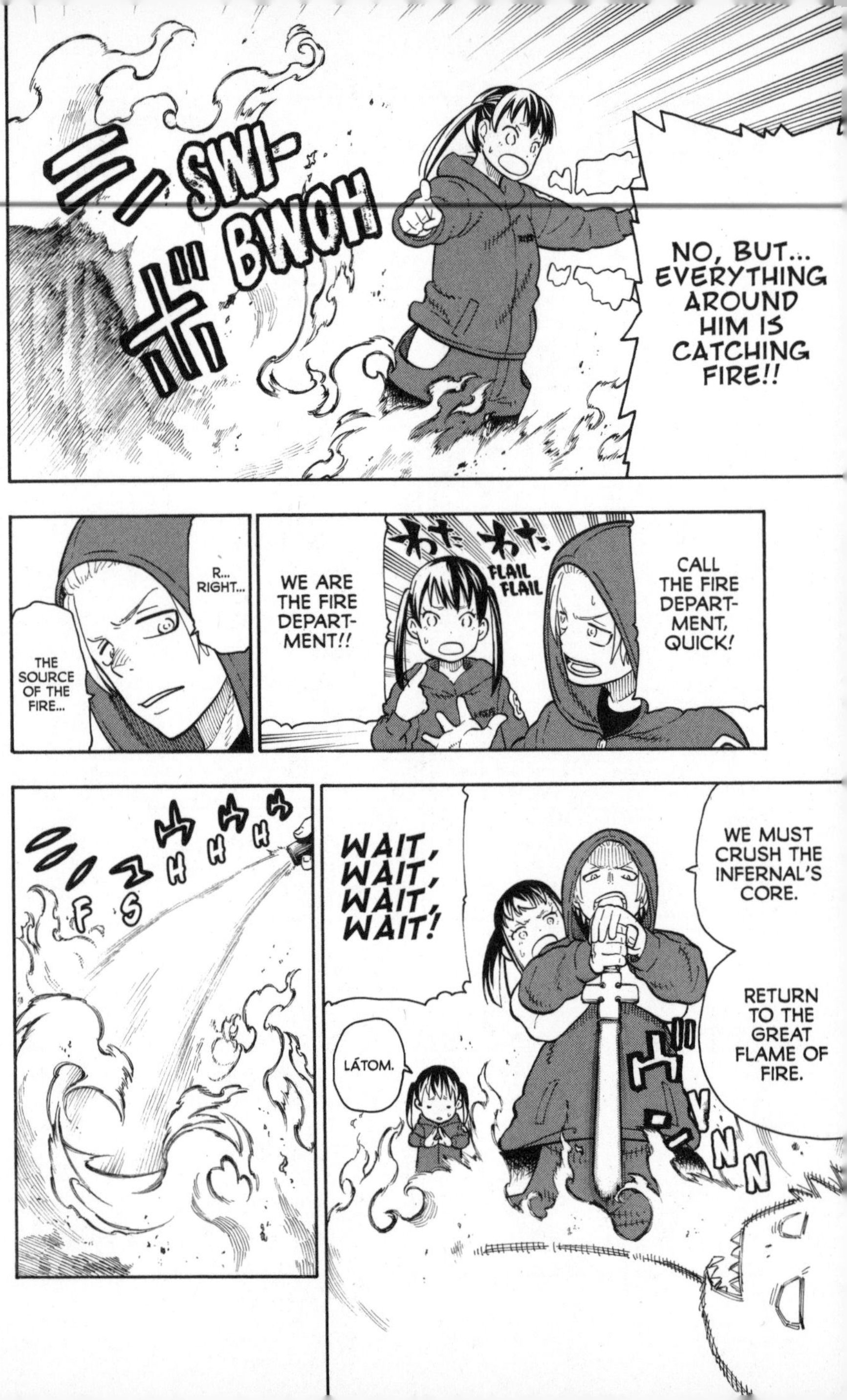
SWI-BWOH
NO, BUT... EVERYTHING AROUND HIM IS CATCHING FIRE!!
CALL THE FIRE DEPART-MENT, QUICK!
わた わた
FLAIL FLAIL
WE ARE THE FIRE DEPART-MENT!!
R... RIGHT...
THE SOURCE OF THE FIRE...
WE MUST CRUSH THE INFERNAL'S CORE.
RETURN TO THE GREAT FLAME OF FIRE.
WAIT, WAIT, WAIT, WAIT!
VNN
LÁTOM.
FSHHHH

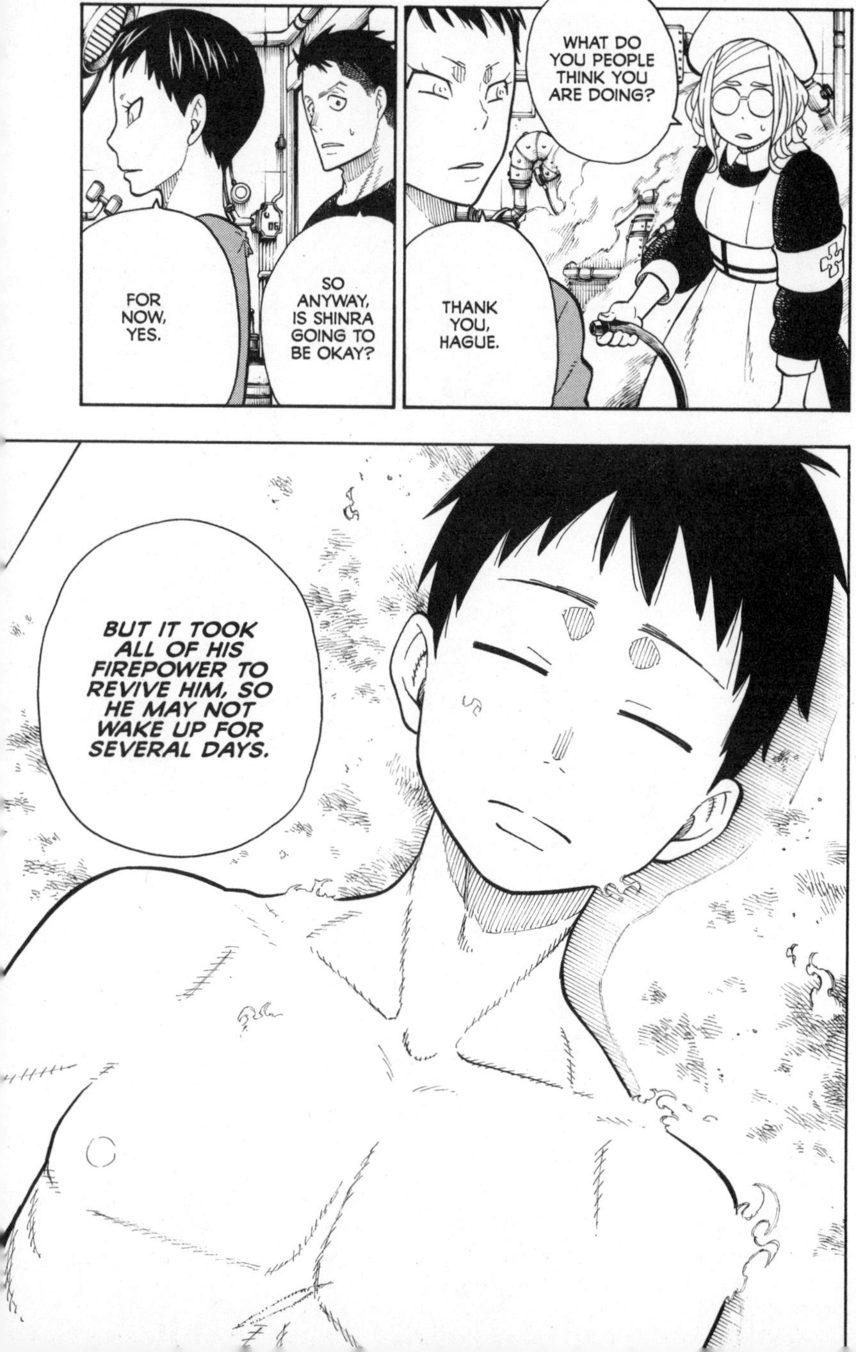
WHAT DO YOU PEOPLE THINK YOU ARE DOING?
THANK YOU, HAGUE.
SO ANYWAY, IS SHINRA GOING TO BE OKAY?
FOR NOW, YES.
BUT IT TOOK ALL OF HIS FIREPOWER TO REVIVE HIM, SO HE MAY NOT WAKE UP FOR SEVERAL DAYS.

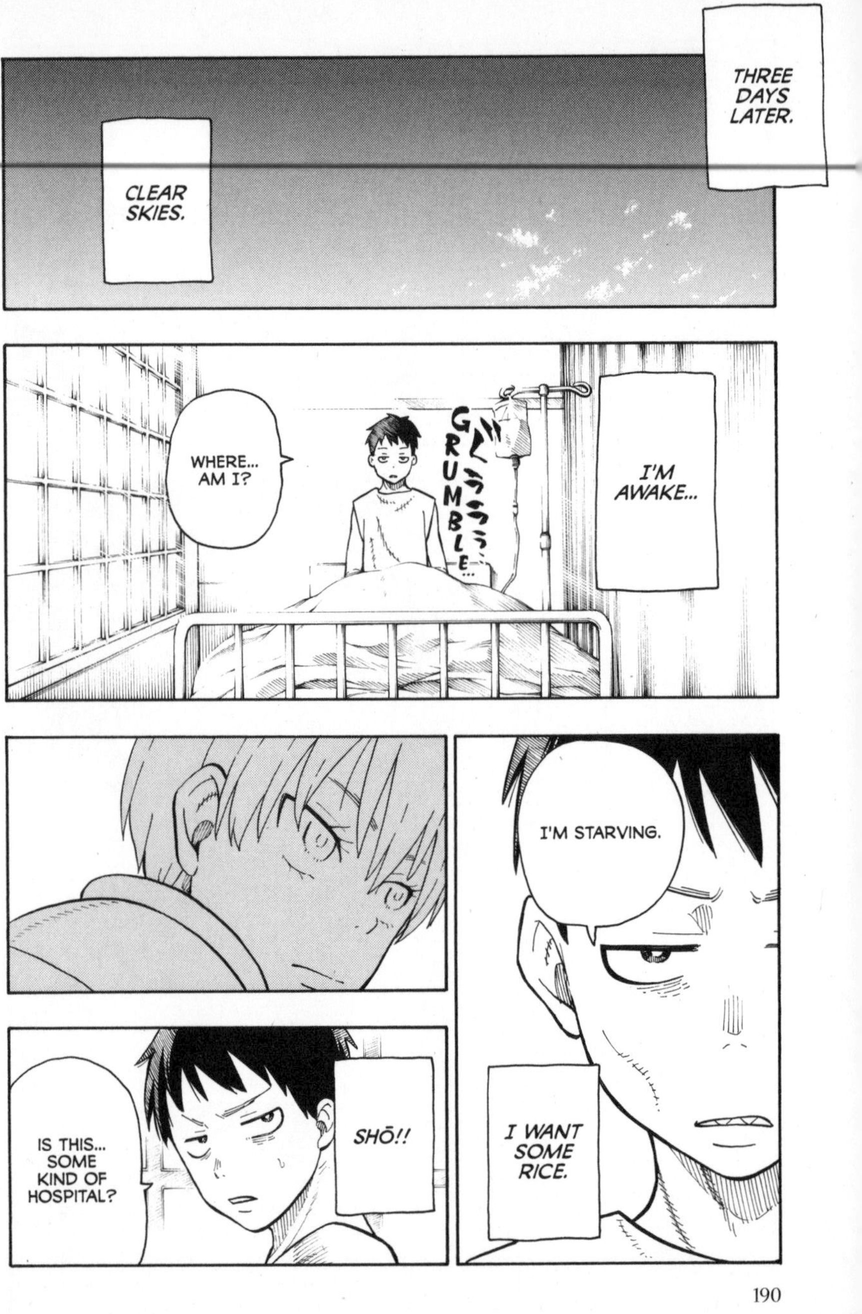
THREE DAYS LATER.
CLEAR SKIES.
I'M AWAKE...
GRUMBLE...
WHERE... AM I?
I'M STARVING.
I WANT SOME RICE.
SHŌ!!
IS THIS... SOME KIND OF HOSPITAL?

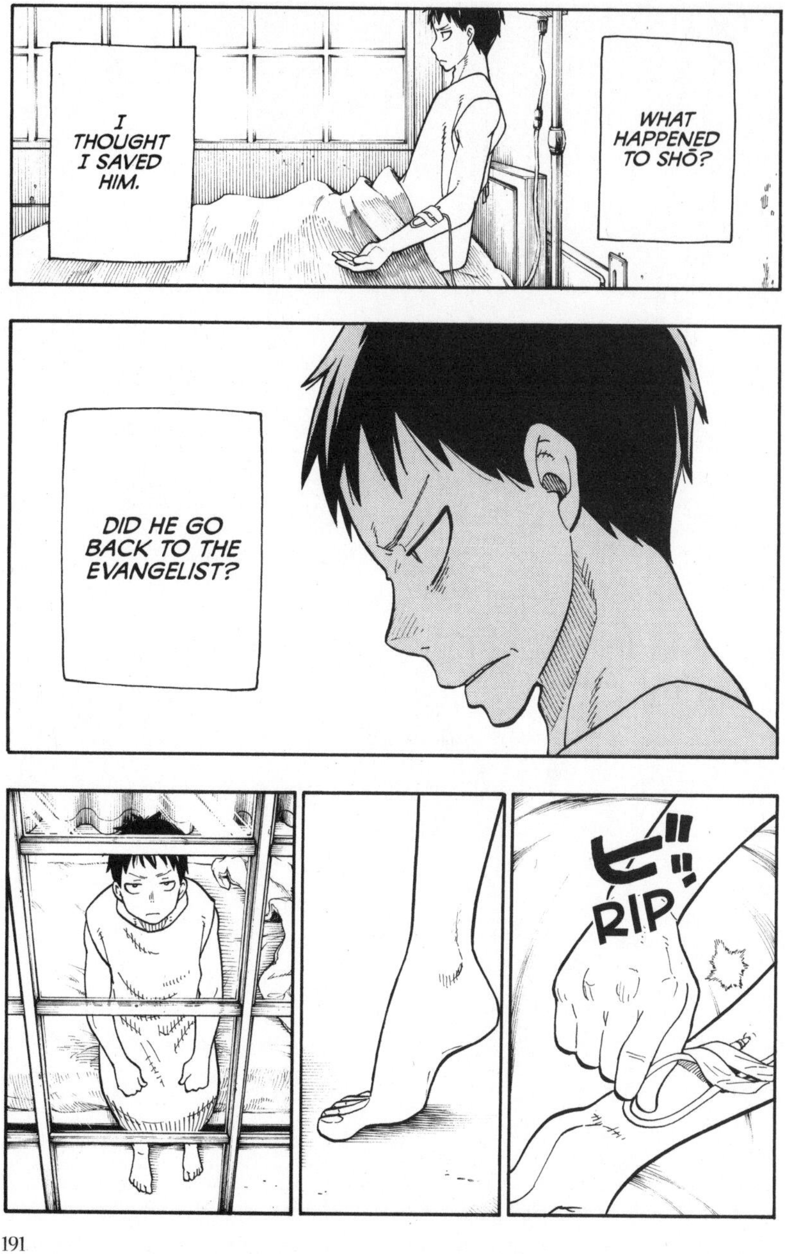
WHAT HAPPENED TO SHŌ?
I THOUGHT I SAVED HIM.
DID HE GO BACK TO THE EVANGELIST?
ビッ
RIP

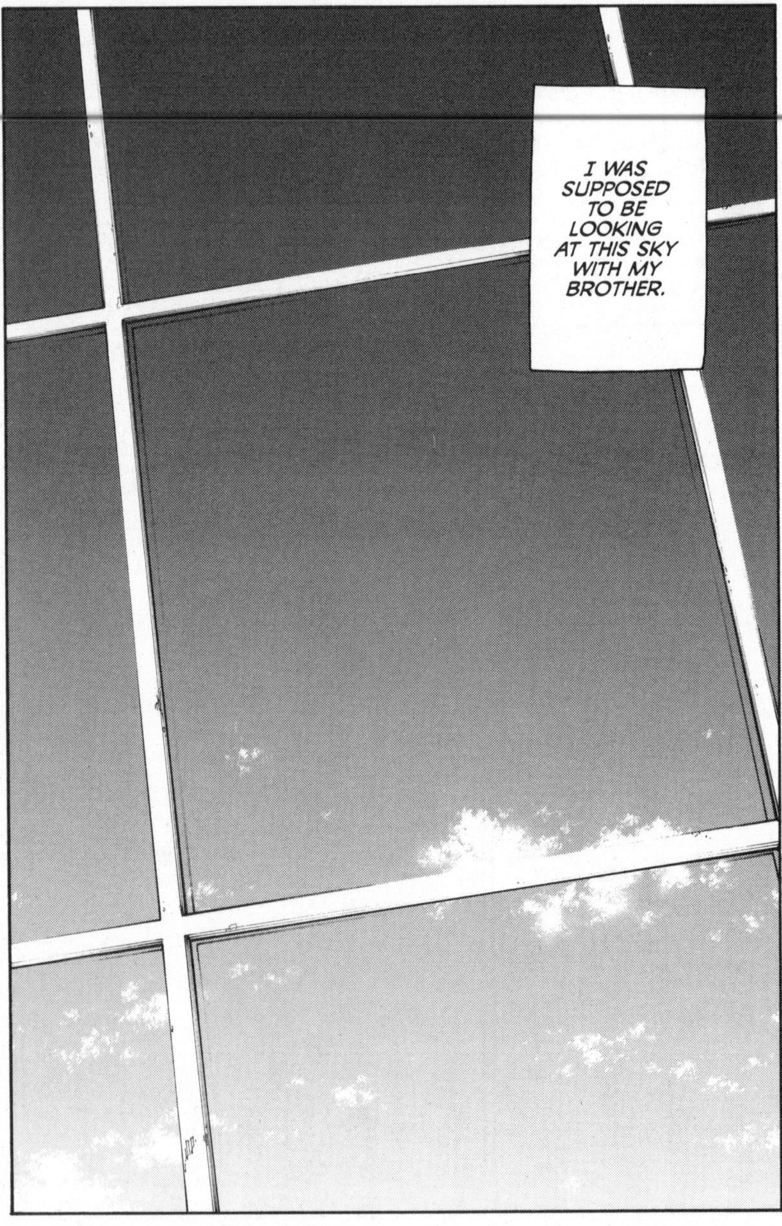
I WAS SUPPOSED TO BE LOOKING AT THIS SKY WITH MY BROTHER.

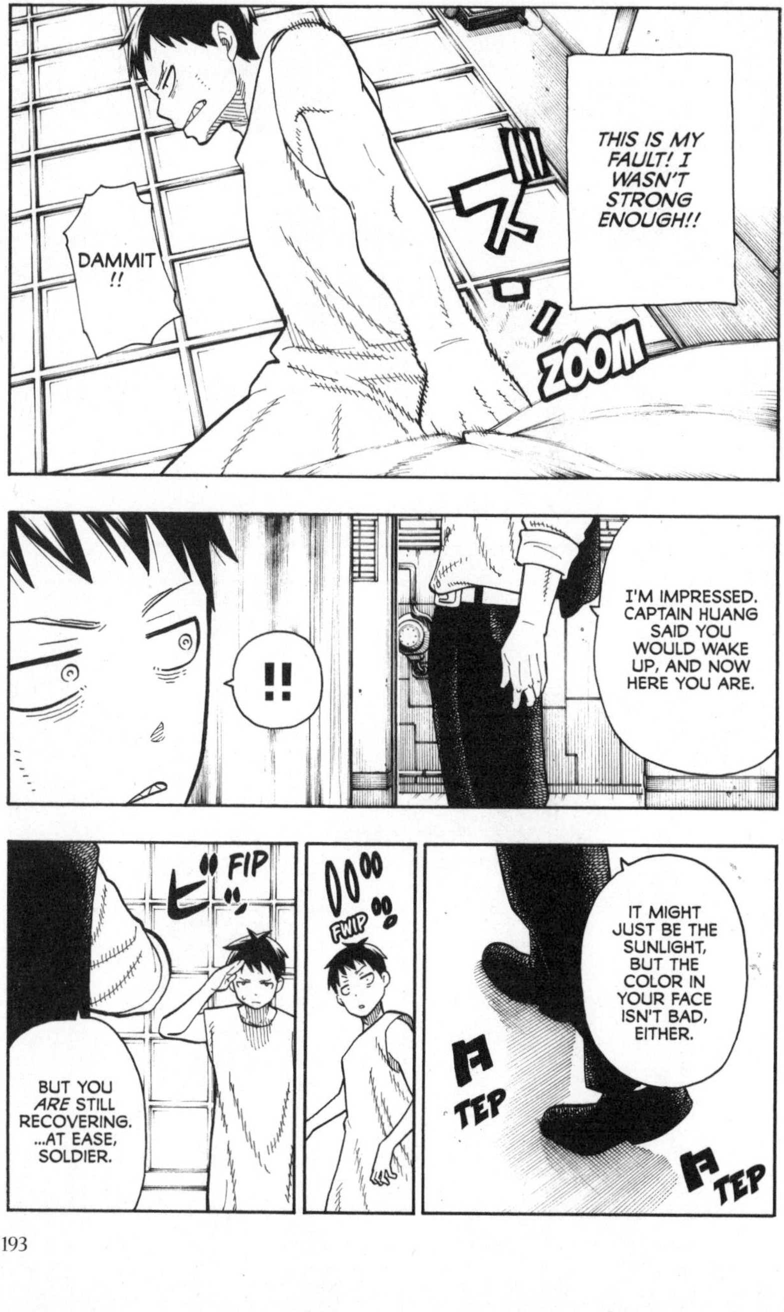
THIS IS MY FAULT! I WASN'T STRONG ENOUGH!!
ZOOM
DAMMIT!!
I'M IMPRESSED. CAPTAIN HUANG SAID YOU WOULD WAKE UP, AND NOW HERE YOU ARE.
!!
IT MIGHT JUST BE THE SUNLIGHT, BUT THE COLOR IN YOUR FACE ISN'T BAD, EITHER.
TEP
TEP
FWIP
FIP
BUT YOU ARE STILL RECOVERING. ...AT EASE, SOLDIER.

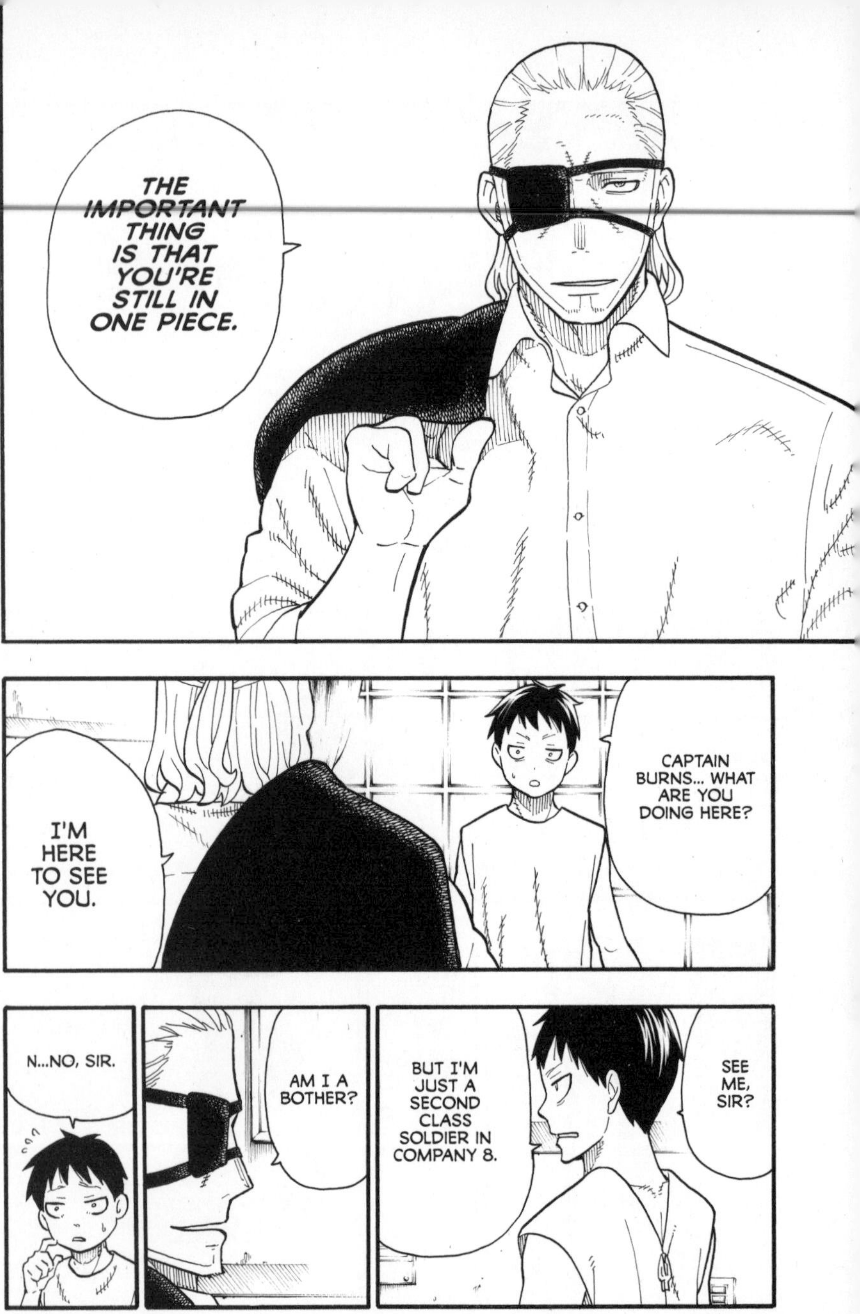
THE IMPORTANT THING IS THAT YOU'RE STILL IN ONE PIECE.
CAPTAIN BURNS... WHAT ARE YOU DOING HERE?
I'M HERE TO SEE YOU.
SEE ME, SIR?
BUT I'M JUST A SECOND CLASS SOLDIER IN COMPANY 8.
AM I A BOTHER?
N...NO, SIR.

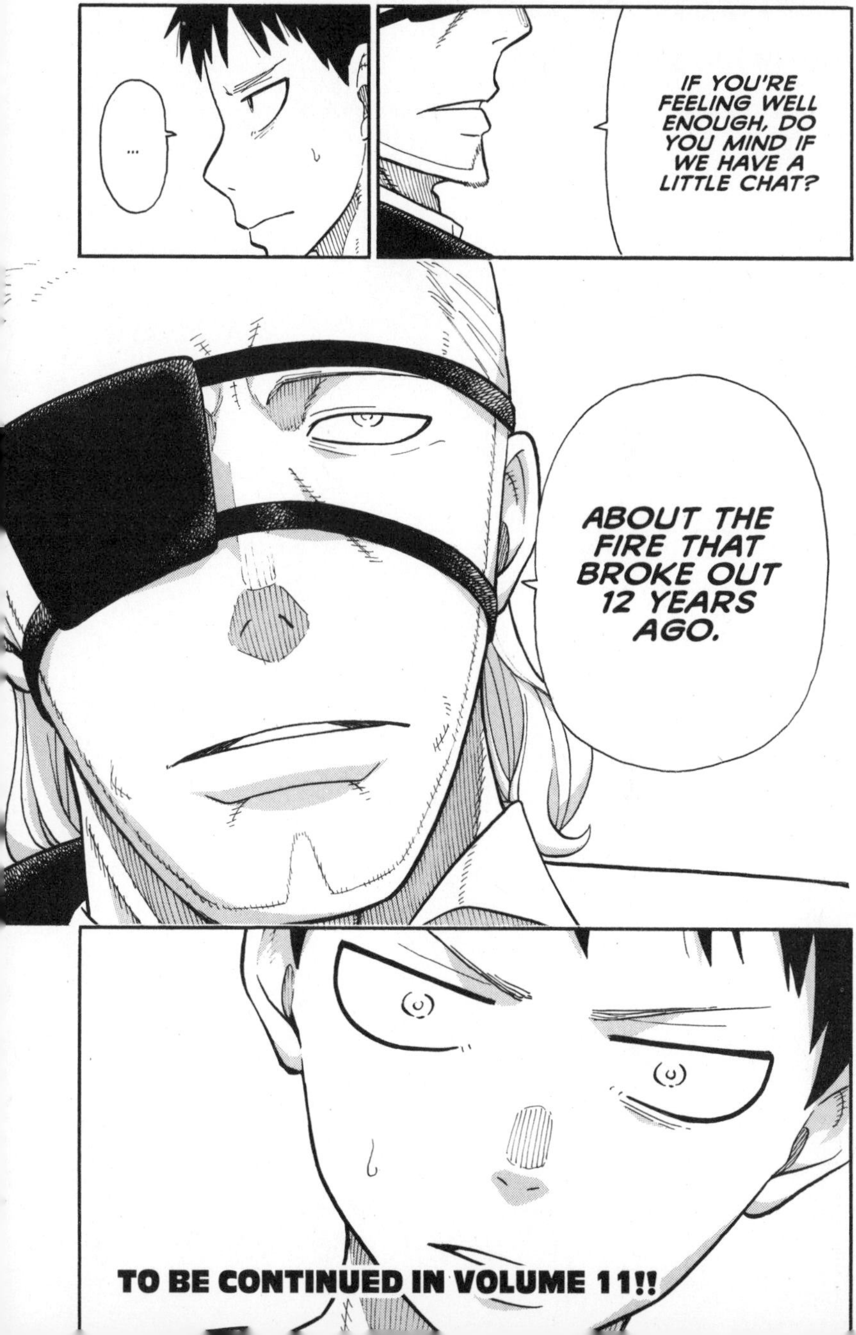
IF YOU'RE FEELING WELL ENOUGH, DO YOU MIND IF WE HAVE A LITTLE CHAT?
...
ABOUT THE FIRE THAT BROKE OUT 12 YEARS AGO.
TO BE CONTINUED IN VOLUME 11!!

Translation Notes:

Alo-hello, page 138

This is a combination of "aloha" and "hello." In the original Japanese, Haumea greets Shō with *oharō*, a combination of the Japanese *ohayō* and a Japanese pronunciation of the English *hello*. This term was made famous in Japan by Rinoa Heartilly of *Final Fantasy VIII* fame. To replicate the cute language mixing, for this version the translators combined Hawaiian and English, because of Haumea's Hawaiian name, and because they feel it sounds adorable.

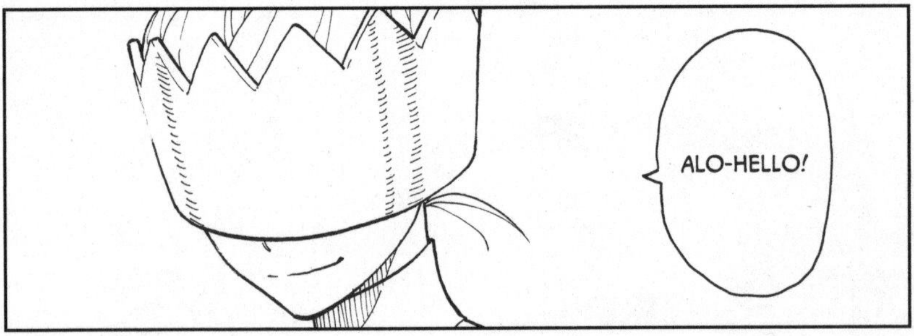
ALO-HELLO!

FIRE FORCE

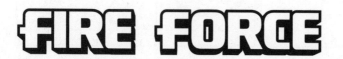

AFTERWORD MANGA: ATSUSHIYA

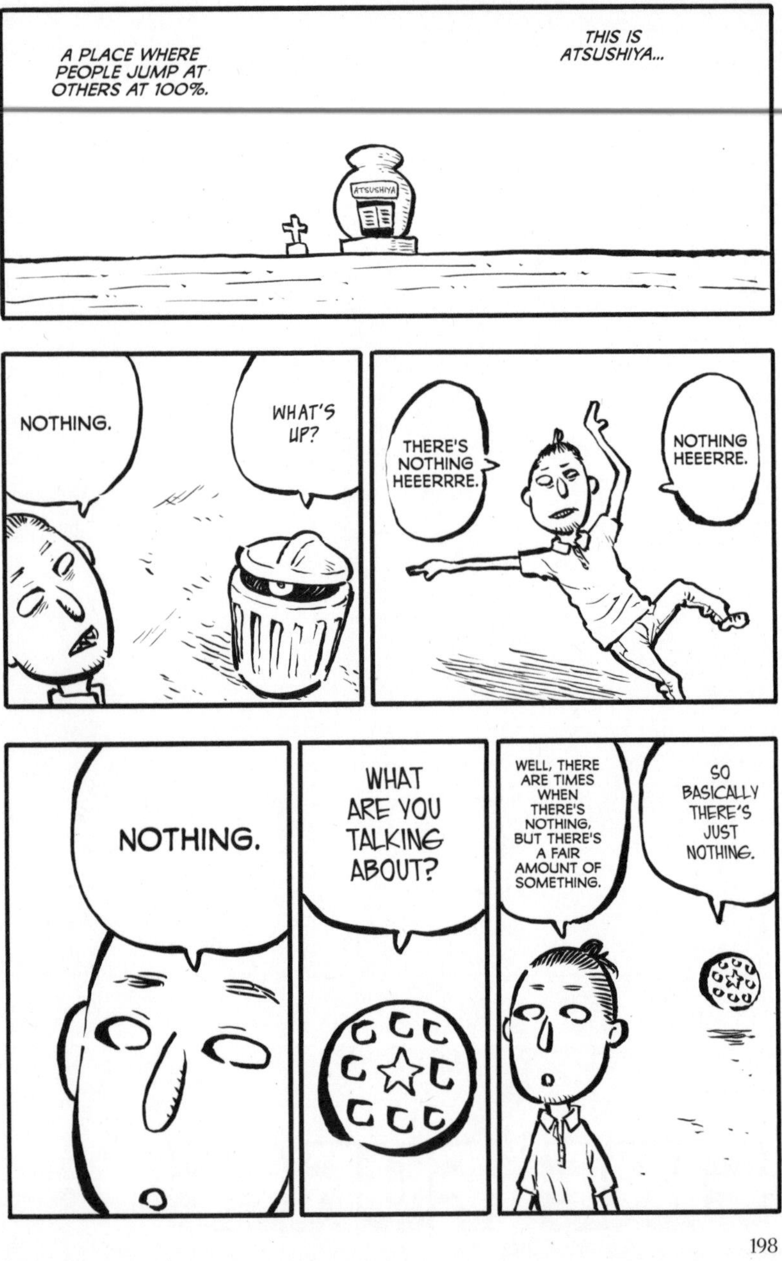
THIS IS ATSUSHIYA...
A PLACE WHERE PEOPLE JUMP AT OTHERS AT 100%.
ATSUSHIYA
NOTHING HEEERRE.
THERE'S NOTHING HEEERRRE.
WHAT'S UP?
NOTHING.
SO BASICALLY THERE'S JUST NOTHING.
WELL, THERE ARE TIMES WHEN THERE'S NOTHING, BUT THERE'S A FAIR AMOUNT OF SOMETHING.
WHAT ARE YOU TALKING ABOUT?
NOTHING.

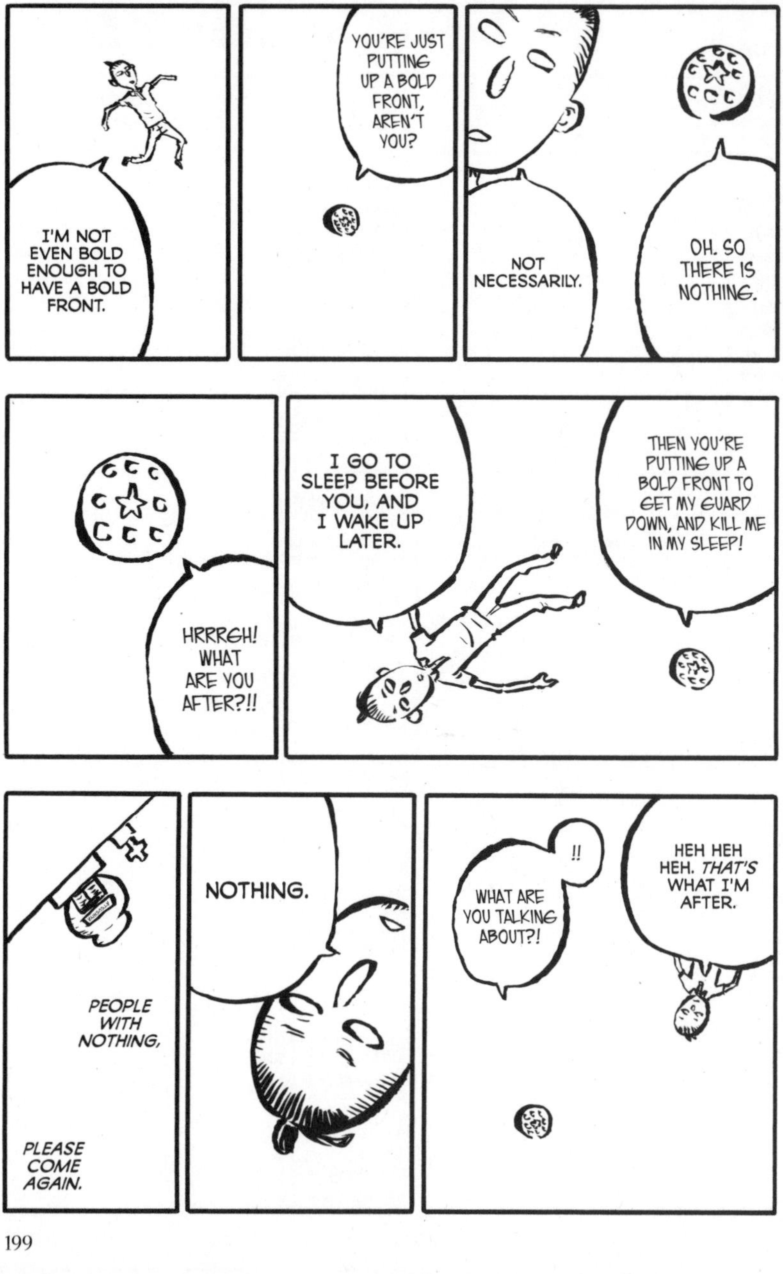

OH. SO THERE IS NOTHING.
NOT NECESSARILY.
YOU'RE JUST PUTTING UP A BOLD FRONT, AREN'T YOU?
I'M NOT EVEN BOLD ENOUGH TO HAVE A BOLD FRONT.
THEN YOU'RE PUTTING UP A BOLD FRONT TO GET MY GUARD DOWN, AND KILL ME IN MY SLEEP!
I GO TO SLEEP BEFORE YOU, AND I WAKE UP LATER.
HRRRGH! WHAT ARE YOU AFTER?!!
HEH HEH HEH. *THAT'S* WHAT I'M AFTER.
!!
WHAT ARE YOU TALKING ABOUT?!
NOTHING.
PEOPLE WITH NOTHING,
PLEASE COME AGAIN.

VULCAN JOSEPH

AFFILIATION:
SPECIAL FIRE FORCE
COMPANY 8

RANK:
ENGINEER

ABILITY:
NON-POWERED

FIRE FORCE

Height	178 cm [5'10'']
Weight	72 kg [159 lbs.]
Age	18
Birthday	April 18
Sign	Aries
Bloodtype	B
Nickname	Fire Soldier Loather, Haijima Hater
Self-Proclaimed	I dunno! Just call me turdface.
Favorite Foods	Lisa's cooking! Fries! Soda!!
Least Favorite Food	I wouldn't hate food!
Favorite Music	Punk! With a lot of distortion!!
Favorite Animal	All of them!
Favorite Color	Metallic!
His Type	A girl who plays along and eats a lot!
Who He Respects	Dad and Grandpa, my ancestors who made Amaterasu
Who He Has Trouble Around	Dr. Giovanni
Who He's Afraid Of	No one in particular
Hobbies	Drums!
Daily Routine	Animal watching! Mech maintenance Catch with Yū Remodeling Company 8 Cleaning up after Iris...
Dream	To revive the world!!!!
Shoe Size	28.5 cm [10.5]
Eyesight	1.5 [20/12.5]
Favorite Subject	Technology! Biology!
Least Favorite Subject	The annoying ones.

VIKTOR LICHT

AFFILIATION:
SPECIAL FIRE
FORCE COMPANY 8

RANK:
SCIENCE TEAM (FIRST CLASS FIRE SOLDIER)
HEAD OF RESEARCH (HAIJIMA)

ABILITY:
NON-POWERED

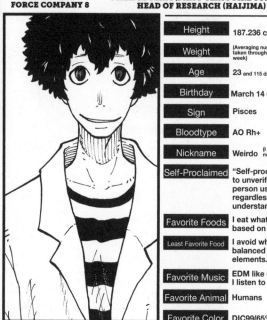

Height	187.236 cm [6'1.71496''] (measured exactly one hour after getting out of bed)
Weight	(Averaging numbers taken throughout the week) 72.358 kg [159.54939 lbs.]
Age	23 and 115 days (at time of recording)
Birthday	March 14 02:35 (@ Delivery Room 3, in Imperial Central Hospital West Wing)
Sign	Pisces
Bloodtype	AO Rh+
Nickname	Weirdo (I do understand common sense, whether or not I choose to use it.)
Self-Proclaimed	"Self-proclaimed" essentially refers to unverified information that a person uses to describe him or herself regardless of the truth behind it. Is this understanding correct?
Favorite Foods	I eat what will give me a balanced diet based on its nutritional elements.
Least Favorite Food	I avoid what will not give me a balanced diet based on its nutritional elements.
Favorite Music	EDM like dubstep and house. I listen to reggae and rap, too.
Favorite Animal	Humans
Favorite Color	DIC99(65%) + Y(11%)
His Type	Large-breasted.
Who He Respects	I respect aaall of you.
Who He Has Trouble Around	People who set research budgets.
Who He's Afraid Of	People who cut research funding.
Hobbies	DJing
Daily Routine	I eat and sleep.
Dream	Last night, it involved a countless number of fairies hanging onto the hair at the nape of my neck.
Shoe Size	29.224 cm [11.7224]
Eyesight	1.35 [20/14.815]
Favorite Subject	Independent study
Least Favorite Subject	I don't divide my study into categories.

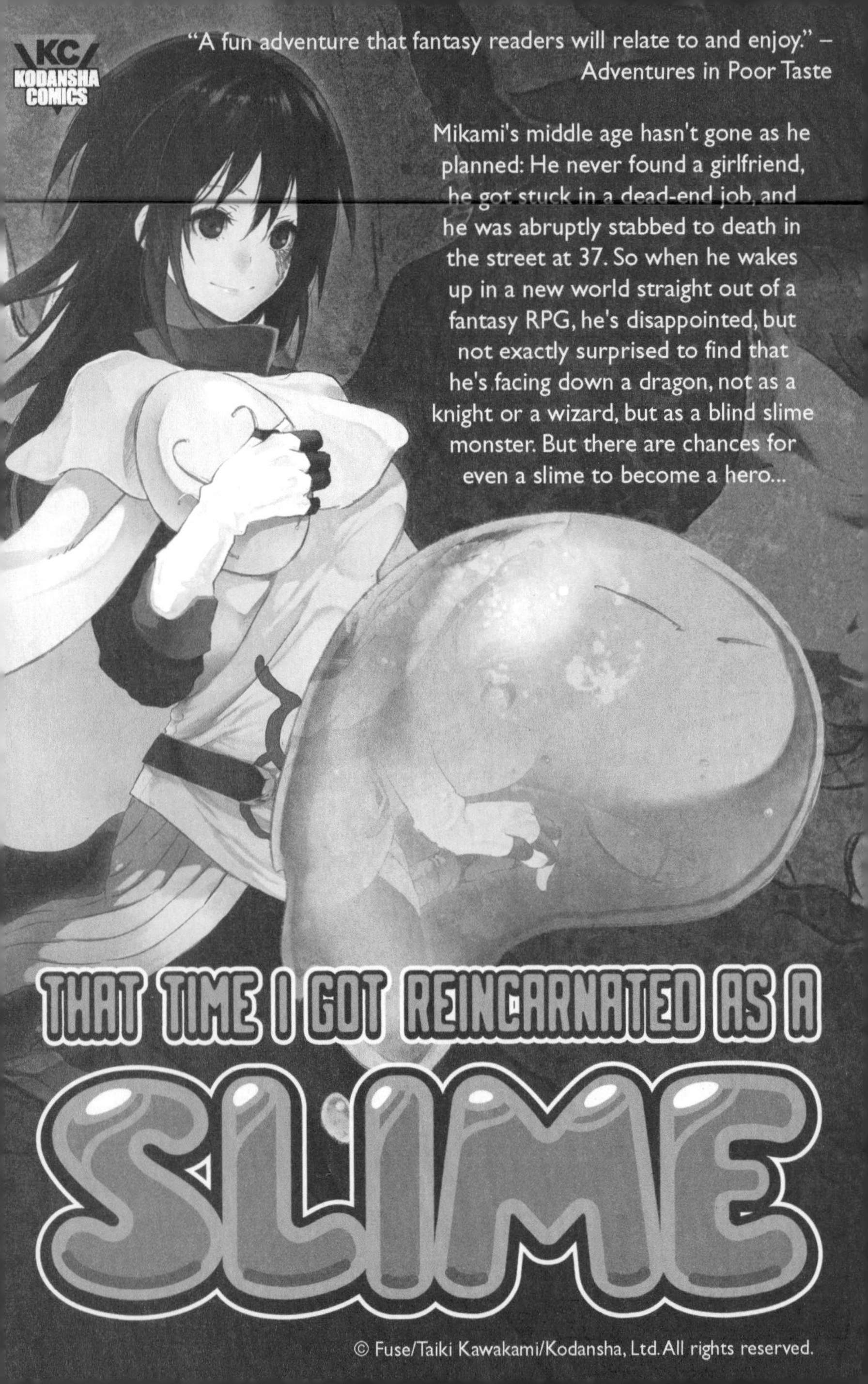
KC KODANSHA COMICS
"A fun adventure that fantasy readers will relate to and enjoy." – Adventures in Poor Taste
Mikami's middle age hasn't gone as he planned: He never found a girlfriend, he got stuck in a dead-end job, and he was abruptly stabbed to death in the street at 37. So when he wakes up in a new world straight out of a fantasy RPG, he's disappointed, but not exactly surprised to find that he's facing down a dragon, not as a knight or a wizard, but as a blind slime monster. But there are chances for even a slime to become a hero...
THAT TIME I GOT REINCARNATED AS A
SLIME
© Fuse/Taiki Kawakami/Kodansha, Ltd. All rights reserved.

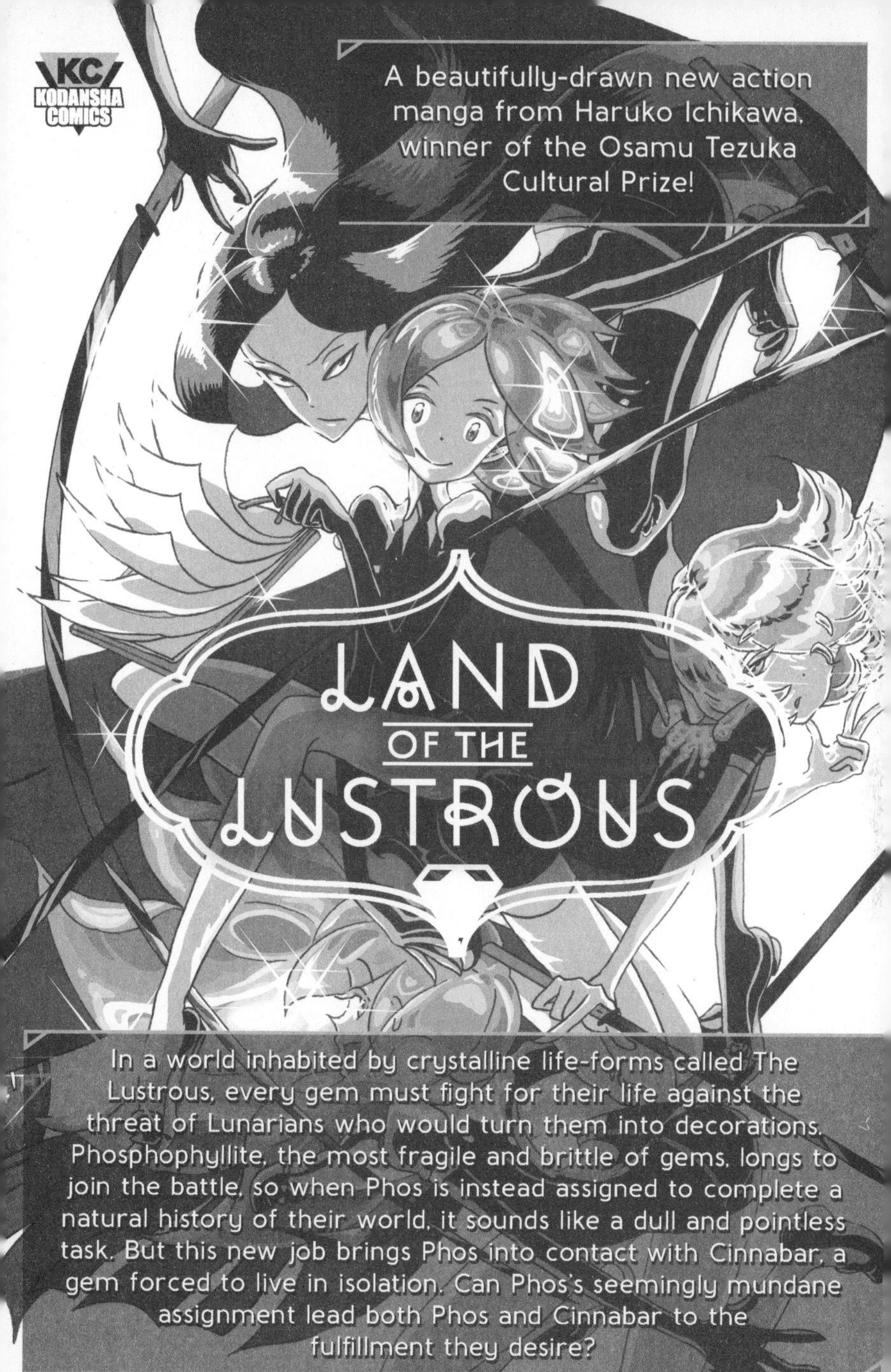
KC KODANSHA COMICS
A beautifully-drawn new action manga from Haruko Ichikawa, winner of the Osamu Tezuka Cultural Prize!
LAND OF THE LUSTROUS
In a world inhabited by crystalline life-forms called The Lustrous, every gem must fight for their life against the threat of Lunarians who would turn them into decorations. Phosphophyllite, the most fragile and brittle of gems, longs to join the battle, so when Phos is instead assigned to complete a natural history of their world, it sounds like a dull and pointless task. But this new job brings Phos into contact with Cinnabar, a gem forced to live in isolation. Can Phos's seemingly mundane assignment lead both Phos and Cinnabar to the fulfillment they desire?

FAIRY TAIL S

For the members of Fairy Tail, a guild member's work is never done. While they may not always be away on missions, that doesn't mean our magic-wielding heroes can rest easy at home. What happens when a copycat thief begins to soil the good name of Fairy Tail, or when a seemingly unstoppable virus threatens the citizens of Magnolia? And when a bet after the Grand Magic Games goes sour, can Natsu, Lucy, Gray, and Erza turn the tables in their favor? Come see what a "day in the life" of the strongest guild in Fiore is like in nine brand new short stories!

KC
KODANSHA COMICS

A collection of *Fairy Tail* short stories drawn by original creator Hiro Mashima!

Japan's most powerful spirit medium delves into the ghost world's greatest mysteries!

Story by Kyo Shirodaira, famed author of mystery fiction and creator of *Spiral*, *Blast of Tempest*, and *The Record of a Fallen Vampire*.

Both touched by spirits called yôkai, Kotoko and Kurô have gained unique superhuman powers. But to gain her powers Kotoko has given up an eye and a leg, and Kurô's personal life is in shambles. So when Kotoko suggests they team up to deal with renegades from the spirit world, Kurô doesn't have many other choices, but Kotoko might just have a few ulterior motives...

IN/SPECTRE

STORY BY KYO SHIRODAIRA
ART BY CHASHIBA KATASE

New action series from Hiroyuki Takei, creator of the classic shonen franchise Shaman King!

In medieval Japan, a bell hanging on the collar is a sign that a cat has a master. Norachiyo's bell hangs from his katana sheath, but he is nonetheless a stray — a ronin. This one-eyed cat samurai travels across a dishonest world, cutting through pretense and deception with his blade.

NEKOGAHARA

STRAY CAT SAMURAI

By

Hiroyuki Takei

HAPPINESS

ハピネス

By Shuzo Oshimi

From the creator of *The Flowers of Evil*

Nothing interesting is happening in Makoto Ozaki's first year of high school. HIs life is a series of quiet humiliations: low-grade bullies, unreliable friends, and the constant frustration of his adolescent lust. But one night, a pale, thin girl knocks him to the ground in an alley and offers him a choice.

Now everything is different. Daylight is searingly bright. Food tastes awful. And worse than anything is the terrible, consuming thirst...

Praise for Shuzo Oshimi's *The Flowers of Evil*

"A shockingly readable story that vividly—one might even say queasily—evokes the fear and confusion of discovering one's own sexuality. Recommended." —The Manga Critic

"A page-turning tale of sordid middle school blackmail." —Otaku USA Magazine

"A stunning new horror manga." —Third Eye Comics

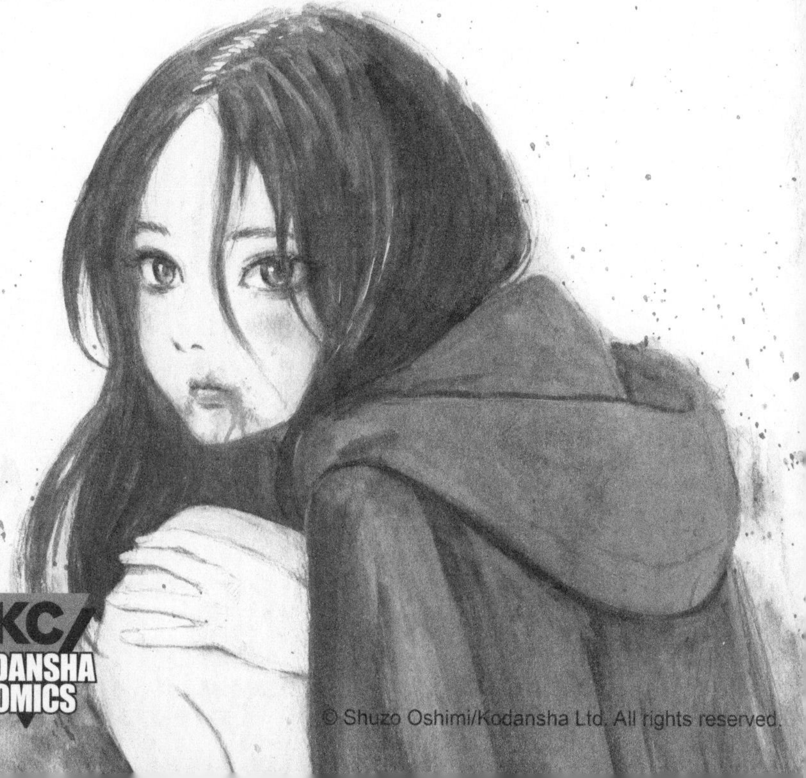

KC KODANSHA COMICS

EDENS ZERO
エデンズゼロ

HIRO MASHIMA IS BACK! JOIN THE CREATOR OF *FAIRY TAIL*
AS HE TAKES TO THE STARS FOR ANOTHER THRILLING SAGA!

A high-flying space adventure! All the steadfast friendship and
wild fighting you've been waiting for...IN SPACE!

At Granbell Kingdom, an abandoned amusement park, Shiki has lived his
entire life among machines. But one day, Rebecca and her cat companion
Happy appear at the park's front gates. Little do these newcomers know
that this is the first human contact Granbell has had in a hundred years! As
Shiki stumbles his way into making new friends, his former neighbors stir at
an opportunity for a robo-rebellion... And when his old homeland becomes
too dangerous, Shiki must join Rebecca and Happy on their spaceship and
escape into the boundless cosmos.

KC
KODANSHA
COMICS

CUTE ANIMALS AND LIFE LESSONS, PERFECT FOR ASPIRING PET VETS OF ALL AGES!

For an 11-year-old, Yuzu has a lot on her plate. When her mom gets sick and has to be hospitalized, Yuzu goes to live with her uncle who runs the local veterinary clinic. Yuzu's always been scared of animals, but she tries to help out. Through all the tough moments in her life, Yuzu realizes that she can help make things all right with a little help from her animal pals, peers, and kind grown-ups.

Every new patient is a furry friend in the making!

The adorable new odd-couple cat comedy manga from the creator of the beloved *Chi's Sweet Home*, in full color!

Sue & Tai-chan

Konami Kanata

Sue is an aging housecat who's looking forward to living out her life in peace... but her plans change when the mischievous black tomcat Tai-chan enters the picture! Hey! Sue never signed up to be a catsitter! *Sue & Tai-chan* is the latest from the reigning meow-narch of cute kitty comics, Konami Kanata.

THE SWEET SCENT OF LOVE IS IN THE AIR! FOR FANS OF OFFBEAT ROMANCES LIKE *WOTAKOI*

Sweat and Soap © Kintetsu Yamada / Kodansha Ltd.

In an office romance, there's a fine line between sexy and awkward... and that line is where Asako — a woman who sweats copiously — meets Koutarou — a perfume developer who can't get enough of Asako's, er, scent. Don't miss a romcom manga like no other!

◄ KAMOME ►
SHIRAHAMA

Witch Hat Atelier

**A magical manga
adventure for
fans of Disney
and Studio
Ghibli!**

The magical adventure that took Japan by storm is finally here, from acclaimed DC and Marvel cover artist Kamome Shirahama!

In a world where everyone takes wonders like magic spells
and dragons for granted, Coco is a girl with a simple dream:
She wants to be a witch. But everybody knows magicians
are born, not made, and Coco was not born with a gift for
magic. Resigned to her un-magical life, Coco is about to
give up on her dream to become a witch...until the day
she meets Qifrey, a mysterious, traveling magician. After
secretly seeing Qifrey perform magic in a way she's never
seen before, Coco soon learns what everybody "knows"
might not be the truth, and discovers that her magical
dream may not be as far away as it may seem...

The boys are back, in 400-page hardcovers that are as pretty and badass as they are!

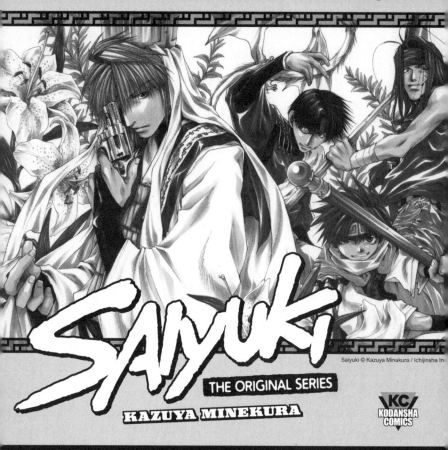

Saiyuki © Kazuya Minakura / Ichijinsha In

SAIYUKI

THE ORIGINAL SERIES

KAZUYA MINEKURA

"AN EDGY COMIC LOOK AT AN ANCIENT CHINESE TALE." —YALSA

Genjo Sanzo is a Buddhist priest in the city of Togenkyo, which is being ravaged by yokai spirits that have fallen out of balance with the natural order. His superiors send him on a journey far to the west to discover why this is happening and how to stop it. His companions are three yokai with human souls. But this is no day trip — the four will encounter many discoveries and horrors on the way.

FEATURES NEW TRANSLATION, COLOR PAGES, AND BEAUTIFUL WRAPAROUND COVER ART!

THE HIGH SCHOOL HAREM COMEDY WITH FIVE TIMES THE CUTE GIRLS!

"An entertaining romantic-comedy with a snarky edge to it." —Taykobon

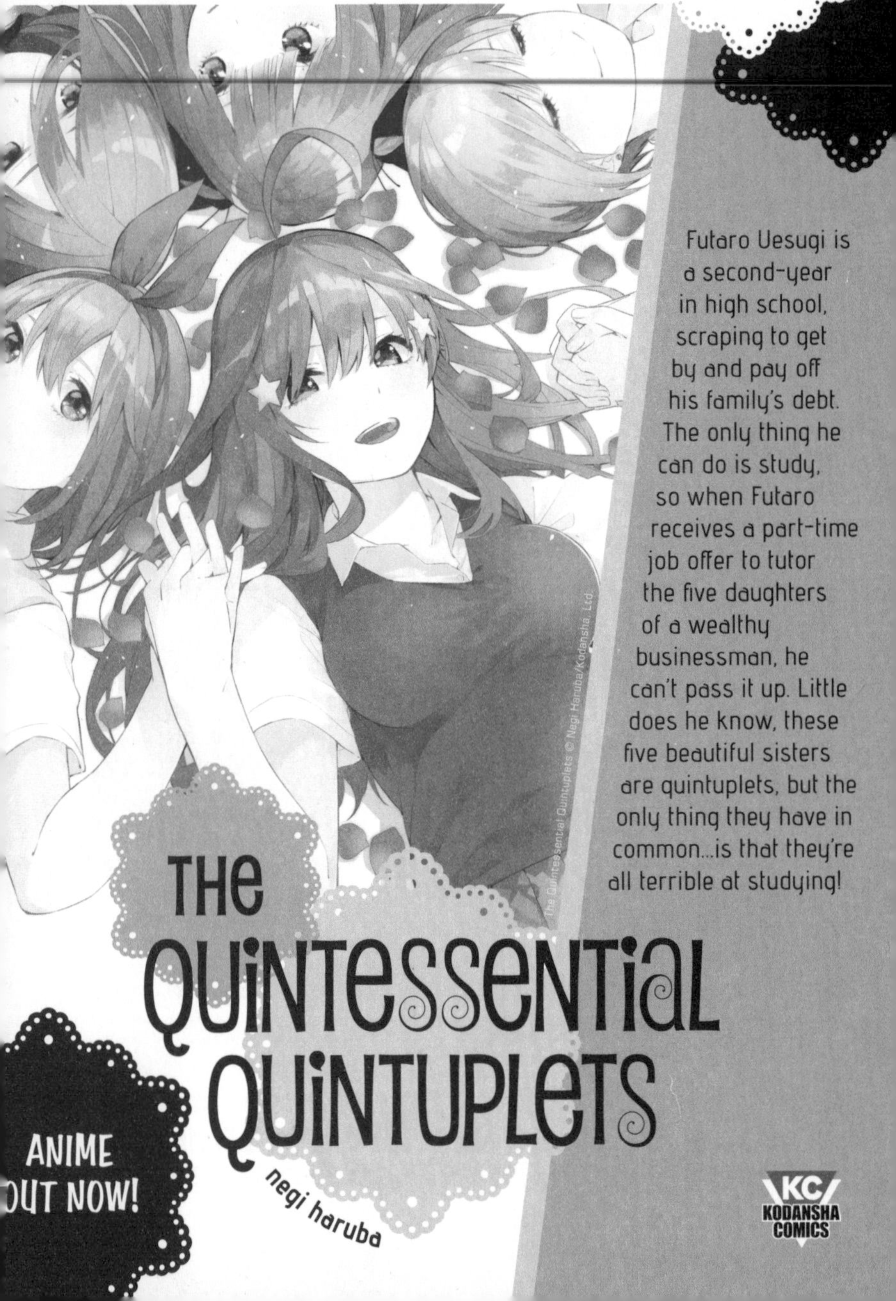

Futaro Uesugi is a second-year in high school, scraping to get by and pay off his family's debt. The only thing he can do is study, so when Futaro receives a part-time job offer to tutor the five daughters of a wealthy businessman, he can't pass it up. Little does he know, these five beautiful sisters are quintuplets, but the only thing they have in common...is that they're all terrible at studying!

THE QUINTESSENTIAL QUINTUPLETS

negi haruba

ANIME OUT NOW!

KC KODANSHA COMICS

A SMART, NEW ROMANTIC COMEDY FOR FANS OF *SHORTCAKE CAKE* AND *TERRACE HOUSE*!

LIVING-ROOM

MATSUNAGA-SAN

Keiko Iwashita

KC
KODANSHA
COMICS

A romance manga starring high school girl Meeko, who learns to live on her own in a boarding house whose living room is home to the odd (but handsome) Matsunaga-san. She begins to adjust to her new life away from her parents, but Meeko soon learns that no matter how far away from home she is, she's still a young girl at heart — especially when she finds herself falling for Matsunaga-san.

Magus of the Library

Mitsu Izumi

MITSU IZUMI'S STUNNING ARTWORK BRINGS A FANTASTICAL LITERARY ADVENTURE TO LUSH, THRILLING LIFE!

Young Theo adores books, but the prejudice and hatred of his village keeps them ever out of his reach. Then one day, he chances to meet Sedona, a traveling librarian who works for the great library of Aftzaak, City of Books, and his life changes forever...

PERFECT WORLD

Rie Aruga

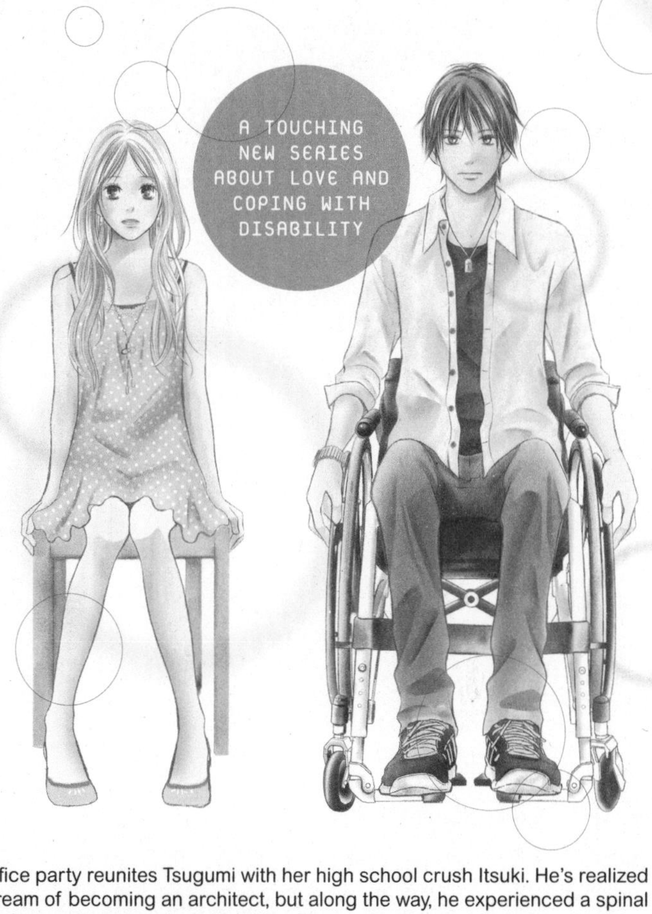
A TOUCHING NEW SERIES ABOUT LOVE AND COPING WITH DISABILITY

An office party reunites Tsugumi with her high school crush Itsuki. He's realized his dream of becoming an architect, but along the way, he experienced a spinal injury that put him in a wheelchair. Now Tsugumi's rekindled feelings will butt up against prejudices she never considered — and Itsuki will have to decide if he's ready to let someone into his heart...

"Depicts with great delicacy and courage the difficulties some with disabilities experience getting involved in romantic relationships... Rie Aruga refuses to romanticize, pushing her heroine to face the reality of disability. She invites her readers to the same tasks of empathy, knowledge and recognition."
—Slate.fr

"An important entry [in manga romance]... The emotional core of both plot and characters indicates thoughtfulness... [Aruga's] research is readily apparent in the text and artwork, making this feel like a real story."
—Anime News Network

KC KODANSHA COMICS

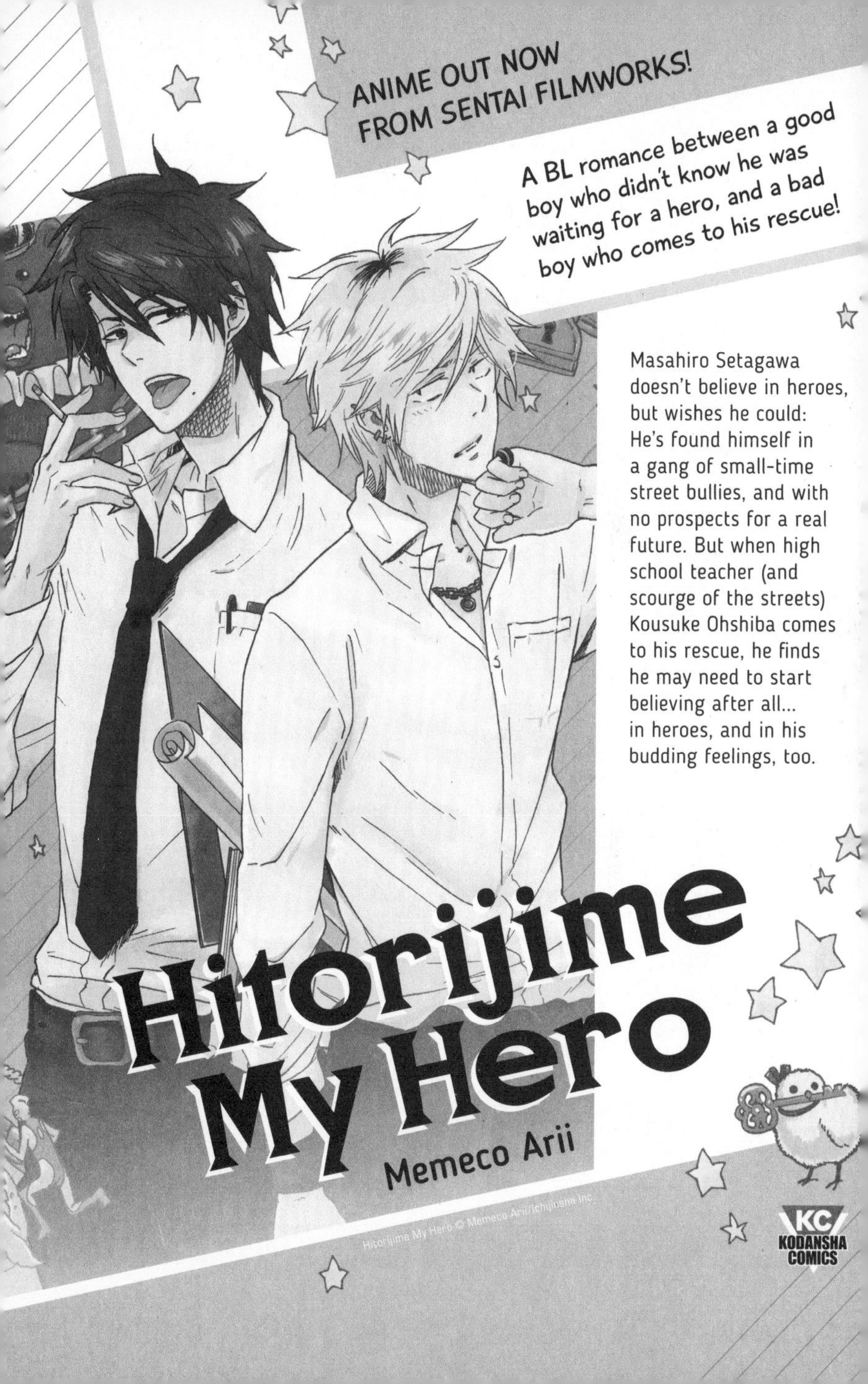
ANIME OUT NOW FROM SENTAI FILMWORKS!
A BL romance between a good boy who didn't know he was waiting for a hero, and a bad boy who comes to his rescue!
Masahiro Setagawa doesn't believe in heroes, but wishes he could: He's found himself in a gang of small-time street bullies, and with no prospects for a real future. But when high school teacher (and scourge of the streets) Kousuke Ohshiba comes to his rescue, he finds he may need to start believing after all... in heroes, and in his budding feelings, too.
Hitorijime My Hero
Memeco Arii
Hitorijime My Hero © Memeco Arii/Ichijinsha Inc.
KC KODANSHA COMICS

A dark and sexy body-horror action manga perfect for fans of *Prison School* and *High School of the Dead*!

Shuichi Kagaya is a smart kid, and most smart kids his age would be thinking about college. Shuichi is also a monster, and he's smart enough to know that monsters don't go to college. But after he uses his monstrous form to save his classmate Claire Aoki, it doesn't matter what his plans for the future were, because he's not the one making the decisions anymore. Now that the seductive, sadistic Claire knows Shuichi's secret, she's got her own ideas about what a monster is good for—because he's not the first monster she's met...

KC
KODANSHA COMICS

GLEIPNIR

"You and me together...we would be unstoppable."

Something's Wrong With Us

NATSUMI ANDO

The dark, psychological, sexy shojo series readers have been waiting for!

A spine-chilling and steamy romance between a Japanese sweets maker and the man who framed her mother for murder!

Following in her mother's footsteps, Nao became a traditional Japanese sweets maker, and with unparalleled artistry and a bright attitude, she gets an offer to work at a world-class confectionary company. But when she meets the young, handsome owner, she recognizes his cold stare...

KC
KODANSHA
COMICS

Young characters and steampunk setting, like *Howl's Moving Castle* and *Battle Angel Alita*

Beyond the Clouds © 2018 Nicke / Ki-oon

A boy with a talent for machines and a mysterious girl whose wings he's fixed will take you beyond the clouds! In the tradition of the high-flying, resonant adventure stories of Studio Ghibli comes a gorgeous tale about the longing of young hearts for adventure and friendship!